VELVET MEETS THE IRON CURTAIN

The Autobiography of a Czech Dancer

JIRI SEBASTIAN VOBORSKY

ISBN 978-1-0980-9848-3 (paperback)
ISBN 978-1-0980-9849-0 (digital)

Christian Faith Publishing, Inc.
832 Park Avenue
Meadville, PA 16335
www.christianfaithpublishing.com

Printed in the United States of America

The applause of the thousands lasts but a moment.
May the moment be not lived for the thousands,
But be poured out for the audience of One!
—Jiri Sebastian Voborsky

Dear
Anna Gardner.
the Lord is writing
your story!
Fuller - thin
. always!

Jiri
Isaiah 53

To the one who loves me most, my wife and my best friend,
Cassandra Teresa Voborsky

FOREWORD

I first met Jiri Voborsky in Zagreb, Croatia, in the spring of 2014. I had heard of him for a few years through his colleagues at Ballet Magnificat. The organization I lead, European Initiative, partnered often with Ballet Magnificat, so in those preceding years, I had heard enough to form a rather defined opinion about the Czech ballet dancer.

The prebilling of Jiri was quite impressive. He was presented as an uber-intense man who strove for excellence not only in dance but also in every area of life. I was told that he had the discipline of an Eastern European mingled with a boyish enthusiasm, rooted in his devotion to Christ. After a brief handshake with this dynamo, I stood mesmerized with hundreds of others as I watched Jiri and Ballet Magnificat's Omega Company perform in Zagreb's old town square.

And so our friendship began that day. Jiri was full throttle, all the time. I loved his zeal, his confidence, and most of all the sincerity of his faith. That spring day in Zagreb, our ministries partnered together to share the gospel through a contemporary and powerful rendition of the story of the Prodigal Son. Jiri showed me his leadership qualities—persevering through a sudden and fierce thunderstorm that nearly washed away anything not bolted to the ground. The rains made the stone surface of the square even slicker, a formidable challenge for him and the other dancers. Jiri was "full steam ahead," and the result was that many Croatians gave their lives to Christ that afternoon.

After the outreach, the European Initiative staff along with the Ballet Magnificat dancers gathered for a debrief. I led the meeting and began to share with Jiri and the seventeen dancers under his leadership, about the spiritual condition of Europe. It was a moment that left a distinct mark on my life.

I shared statistics that underscored the spiritual apostasy that had engulfed former Christian Europe: less than 3 percent of all Europeans are saved. Then I read a quote from the *International Herald Tribune*, a European publication of the *New York Times*. It stated, "Contemporary Europe has become the most godless civilization the world has ever known." As I shared that quote, the room became eerily quiet—the weight of a spiritually destitute Europe had just landed on all of our shoulders. The only movement in the room was Jiri lifting his hand to his face wiping away the tears streaming down his cheeks. All eyes were now on him. He paused and then spoke with such heartfelt emotion to all of us, sharing his deep grief over the spiritual depravity of his parents and other Czech family members. The statistics that I shared were numbers to all of us in the room, but to Jiri, those numbers were people—his family.

From those first days in Zagreb until now, Jiri and I have continued our friendship. Through his leadership, Ballet Magnificat and European Initiative have partnered together, utilizing the extraordinary artistry of dance to bring the gospel to thousands of Europeans in Germany, Serbia, Hungary, Romania, and Spain. I am honored to unite with Jiri to bring the life and love of Jesus to Europe.

As you read the pages of *Velvet Meets the Iron Curtain*, you will embark on a journey that begins with a Czech family, the Voborskys. You will experience a vivid picture of life under Soviet socialism, a life that will surprise you in some ways. You will feel like you are living in the Voborskys' third-floor spartan flat in Ústí, Czechoslovakia, staring at Jiri's father's aquarium. You can't help but smile visualizing the Voborsky family crowded around a minuscule black-and-white TV while watching one of the two state-controlled television stations. You will feel Jiri's pains, his fears, and his struggles; but you will also rejoice with him when he meets his Savior a few years later in the Czech city of Liberec.

This is one man's journey, distinctly his own, yet with a common thread known to all of us, it is a journey to understand "who I am" and to find the One who knows us best and loves us most. The cultural riches of Jiri's experiences both in Czechoslovakia and the new world God had waiting for him in America are woven together beautifully in *Velvet Meets the Iron Curtain*. Jiri's life is a fascinating read of how God can take a gift within a man and do far more than could ever be imagined.

Jiri's remarkable life is a reflection of this verse found in Ephesians 3:20, "Now to Him who is able to do exceeding abundantly beyond all that we ask or think, according to the power that works within us."

Enjoy your time with Jiri!

Jeff Serio
Director, European Initiative Berlin, Germany

OVERTURE

We all came to the high school's classroom on time prepared to face another arduous day of the Czechoslovak public high school education system. I was in my third month of living in a dorm and learning to juggle the twelve academic classes of the *gymnázium* (*gum-naaz-ium*) along with a full schedule at the state ballet school, both running almost simultaneously.

I had said goodbye to my parents knowing that I'd get to see them just once a month for the next four years. Plainly put, I was overwhelmed, but I loved the challenge. I felt invincible. I was running in high gear, fueled only by enthusiasm and the freshly baked pastries I purchased every morning across the street from the ballet academy.

However, this particular morning was different. Our algebra professor, Mr. Vondráček, walked into the classroom with a dismal expression on his otherwise handsome face. His bright-blue eyes signaled an unusual expression of sorrow. His long-sleeved shirt was spruced up with a thin black tie evincing sadness, I assumed. He gazed across the classroom toward the thirty-eight young freshmen. He took a long, deep breath, then slowly uttered, "The riot police surrounded and brutally beat a group of university students peacefully marching through Prague on Friday. This group was commemorating the fiftieth anniversary of a suppressed demonstration against the Nazi storming of Prague University in 1939." He paused and lifted his head, his blue eyes suddenly determined. "This madness needs to come to an end."

We sat there in complete silence. What happened three days ago was unknown to most, if not all of us, in the room. The Communist government did an exceptional job keeping the flow of information tight. Little did I know sitting there that day, that November 17, 1989, would change the course of history, the course of my beloved homeland, and the course of my life.

FIRST ACT

CHILDHOOD BEHIND THE IRON CURTAIN

1) Winter 1974

It was a cold autumn day, Friday November 1, 1974, to be exact. A light dusting of snow covered the ground of Ústí nad Labem, the regional capital of the North Bohemian sector of Czechoslovakia. Bohumila and Miroslav, two young soon-to-be parents, both in their early twenties, rushed to the hospital, arriving just in time to welcome their firstborn son. I was born healthy and without any complications. As it was the custom back then, my mom and I stayed in the hospital for a week of observations. Meanwhile, my dad gathered his family and close friends to celebrate my arrival with freshly brewed Czech beer, Bohemian champagne, Becherovka liqueur, and other alcoholic beverages. Loud singing and guitar playing carried all the way throughout the eight-story apartment building where forgiving neighbors understood the reason for such celebration. My life had begun.

For you created my inmost being; you knit me together in my mother's womb. I praise you because I am fearfully and wonderfully made; your works are wonderful, I know that full well. My frame was not hidden from you when I was made in the secret place, when I was woven together in the depths of the earth. Your eyes saw my unformed body; all the days ordained for me were written in your book before one of them came to be.

—Psalm 139:13–16

2) Life behind the Iron Curtain

As one does not choose where or into what family they are born, I am no different. What was divergent about my placing was the fact that my parents lived in a beautiful landlocked nation comprised of two groups of people, the Czechs and the Slovaks, living together in a picturesque, culturally rich, historically prominent and prosperous Central European nation of Czechoslovakia. The year was 1974, and by then, this small nation had been barred behind the Iron Curtain for the past twenty-six years since the Communist Party took control of the government, of the people, and of the proposed direction for the future. Czechoslovakia was veiled under the blanket of socialist oppression; and its people were stripped of any possible hope for freedom, democracy, and unstinted self-expression. I was born destined to serve my nation and its ideals. I was born to become sold out to blindly serve the needs of the political agenda. I was born to be submitted and to join in with the others in following the leading of the party without questioning its practices, its decisions, its leadership. I was to grow up believing that Communism served its people, provided for their needs, protected their well-being, and built their prosperous future even if the momentary struggles were painful, difficult, and seemingly unsurpassable. I reminisce of unique moments to paint a picture of life lived under a constant eye of this ideology, reflected in the comprehension and understanding of a young boy.

Where does one start? Not everything beyond the Iron Curtain was bad, that's for sure. I have the greatest memories of growing up in the small flat on the third floor of a large apartment building, sharing a bedroom with my brother and parents. There was a large wardrobe dividing the room into two sections, that we called the kids' room and our parent's bedroom. Our small kitchen accommodated my dad's elaborate cooking and my mom's amazing baking. The small table served as a great station for family games, homework, and wooden block castle building. My dad loved to fish, and often our only bathtub was occupied by freshly caught carp and eel that Dad would bring home from his fishing trips. The fish had to swim in the tub to clean themselves from the inside out before being cooked and served for all to enjoy, or so we were told. Bathing was difficult during these times when the fish were in the tub, as we only had one bathroom. The solution to our hygiene challenge was found in using my grandparents' apartment located on the first floor of the same apartment building. They always had candy and chocolates to give me and my brother, and so it was not a bad deal at all to do so.

Our living room was the hub of family life. A black-and-white television set played the two stations of the Czechoslovak state TV airing programs in both official languages, Czech and Slovak. Our record player and radio were proudly set up next to the television set. Oh, the memories of listening to the wide array of records playing adventures and fairy tales, classical and bluegrass music, Czech pop singers or ABBA, all while enjoying a game of chess with my dad. This was the norm. The corner of the room was dominated by a large aquarium, my dad's proud possession. It was filled with a huge assortment of fish of so many colors and sizes. A piece of modern wall furniture was filled with books and Mom's great collection of Czech crystal glass and wine glasses. A plain sofa and two large chairs completed the furnishing of the room. To the outside world, it was simple and adequate. For us, it was profoundly beautiful. This room was the heartbeat of our home.

There was always enough food to go around, hot water, the heating provided by the city; we even had a telephone—a big deal back in the day. I never knew hunger, nor was I ever cold or without appropriate clothing. Life was simple with very few choices that would make it complex, yet we lacked nothing. My parents devoted their energy and love to my brother, Míra, and me. We were cared and provided for, we laughed a lot, and we made memories together. What more could one ask for?

The only thing completely absent in my childhood was any kind of spiritual upbringing. Both my mom and dad were the products of the Communist society and its teaching, which taught us from a young age that what one can touch and feel is real and everything else is an unnecessary distraction in and of life. I'd never seen a printed version of the Holy Bible. Not until I was sixteen years old. I'd certainly never heard of Jesus and the rescuing work He accomplished through the cross and His resurrection from the dead. We never graced the doors of a church, not for Christmas, not for Easter. The glorious cathedrals in Ústí and around the country were empty structures purposed to stand as a resolute reminder of the weaknesses of those who came before us, who relied on the help of God to make it through life. We were modern people. We were smarter than them. We were dependent on socialist ideals to navigate the road called life. This road promised progress, happiness, and safety. In return, it demanded a complete devotion. Religion, where dependence on God was practiced, was a defiant enemy needing to be abolished. It was viewed to be a dangerous disease slowly eating away the competent focus in one's life. God was not real. God did not exist.

The fool says in his heart, "There is no God."
—Psalm 14:1

3) Early Years

The Communist government believed that family was a necessary foundation to a healthy and joyous society. Paid maternity leave of four years was a guaranteed benefit to every young mother who just brought a child into the world. A child was to be raised as a devoted member of the socialist society and, through their gifting, serve the needs of the people and their leading Communist Party.

Long strolls in the park were the norm. As a baby, I would be dressed in warm clothes, no matter what heights the mercury climbed on the thermometer mounted to the outer frame of our apartment window. A knitted hat was a part of just about every outfit. Legs would be covered in *punčocháče* (*pun-chou-kha-che*), a stretchy knitted pair of tights designed for both genders. Completely immobilized, I was then placed into a stroller apparently built to withstand any possible weapon that could be used against it. These were heavy and impractical for the limited storage space that each family had. Blankets were placed to insure that no wind could ever cause sickness or even the slightest cold. When my mom would decide to do the grocery shopping for the family, she would leave the stroller outside of the store and proceed in to gather the needed produce and items. Yes, I would be left outside in the stroller as well. Often there was a long line of strollers parked next to each other; and if a baby was distressed and crying, any stranger could and would step into the role of a comforter, pick the child out of the stroller, and rock it to bring it comfort. After the baby calmed down, it was then placed back into the stroller, and the unknown person went about their business. As times have changed, this practice, sadly, no longer takes place.

Potty training was intense, and great pressure was placed on the child to catch on quickly. The living conditions made it difficult to wash and dry cloth diapers to reuse them for the youngling, and disposable diapers were unavailable for purchase in the regular market. I was potty-trained by the time I reached my first birthday. I wish that everything else in life came as easily as potty training.

At the age of four, I was placed into a kindergarten, as my mom returned back to the workforce. Kindergartens were a free babysitting provision of the government for the working parents. We were taught to structure the day into individual sections and be diligent to understand what the purpose of each one was. A heavy focus was placed on creativity. The beginnings of political education started in these institutions of early learning. We sang songs celebrating the successes, promises, and provisions of socialism; and until this day,

I can recall lyrics and melodies of some of these tunes. We learned to ride tricycles and bicycles; eat in an organized and polite way, using both forks and knives; nap on demand; and respect the other children around us. The teachers, called comrades, were held in high esteem, and we were taught to respect them dutifully.

At the age of six, I started first grade. It was a big deal to cross the threshold into elementary school, and as every child, I could hardly wait to begin the process of learning and attending a regular school. Comrade Rytířová was my teacher from first to fourth grade, fully responsible for teaching me and my thirty-nine classmates to read, write, count, comprehend, and start to practice critical thinking. She was amazing, and I loved being in her class.

> *Train a child in the way he should go, and when*
> *he is old he will not turn from it.*
>
> —Proverbs 22:6

4) Politics Meet First Graders

In the first grade, I proudly joined the Sparks. The Sparks was the first level of indoctrination designed to systematically teach us and instill into us the beliefs and values of Communism and socialism. The Sparks would be invited and encouraged to join the Pioneer movement upon reaching the fifth grade. To be active members in these organizations was both expected and rewarded. A list of achievements accomplished by each child was kept in the records of the student, to be inspected when considering the student for admittance into a desired high school and university, upon reaching the age of fourteen and eighteen years, respectively. The pressure was on, discreetly and in an amusing manner, I must add.

> I promise before all,
> like a brightly shining Spark,
> that I will live for my homeland,
> to help its future to embark

This is a loose translation of the "Spark pledge" that I so proudly recited in front of my classmates, the teaching staff, and principal of the school. I was sold out, and with my eyes wide open, I believed and trusted without measure all those around me. Life was beautiful.

There is a way that seems right to a man,
but in the end it leads to death.
—Proverbs 16:25

5) East German Adventure

Memories of family camping vacations in Central Bohemia, as well as frequent summer holidays in East Germany come to mind. The cold Baltic Sea was a wonder for a boy from a landlocked country. There are several fine recollections of traveling to the "Deutsche Demokratische Republik" for our summer vacations. Our family was no different in that every family trip was a stressful undertaking, often accompanied by arguments and tense moments along the path of adventure. To travel to East Germany, all we needed were our passports and *doložka* (*dough-lozh-ka*), a government-issued document required to be filled out by all citizens departing from Czechoslovakia. In it, all items of value were to be declared. My mom would splendidly fill out all the information while mumbling complaints under her breath, listing all the jewelry and other valuables we were bringing with us. Money we were taking out of the country, and all the equipment we brought with us to use in the large family tent were also required to be written down. These were later compared upon our return while the car was carefully searched. The roughly eight-hour car ride to the north coast of Germany was always done through the night. Years later, I was reminded of the East German autobahn, designed and constructed by Adolf Hitler for the use by the German advancing army during WWII, when receiving an intense deep tissue Turkish massage in Istanbul. As the ride up the aging highway was rough and painful, so was the massage I received in Turkey.

During one particular trip to East Germany, my parents already spent all the permitted amount of money. Just two days prior to our return home, my mom spotted a pair of gorgeous curtains strikingly displayed in the shop window in the city of Stralsund. She had to have them. My dad kindly reminded her that we have reached the government permitted spending limit, only to be met with her look worth a million words clearly stating that she could care less. She wasn't leaving Germany without these curtains, and my dad had no choice but to submit. Being the good husband he was, he did just that. Two days later, shortly before reaching the border crossing between the two communist nations, my dad pulled our car off the highway onto a small side country road. The time to conceal the curtains had come. There, parked away from all traffic, I saw something that I will never forget. My mom stepped out of the car and removed her spring jacket. With my dad's assistance, she wrapped the must-have curtains around her body with an expression of determination and intentionality. "Tighter, tighter," she demanded. Then she placed the jacket back on and returned to the car. "Drive please," she said. As we neared the border, she looked at me and asked me to be silent and not say a word. "Yes, Mom," I replied as my mind raced with all the different scenarios of what could possibly take place if she were caught. "*Guten abend*," said the border officer as he greeted us upon arrival at the patrol station. "*Dobrý večer*" (Czech for "good evening"), was my dad's reply as he did not speak nor refused to speak German. "*Reisepass bitte*" followed, and my dad handed him his and my mom's passports. My brother and I were not required to have our own documents since we were minors. We were simply registered in our parents' passports. The officer carefully looked over the pages with my parents' photos and then proceeded to search the car. Mom sat still and pretended to be tired and sleepy, exhausted from the journey. This is where I get my acting skills, I suppose. The officer searched every little crevice in the trunk of the vehicle. He even requested for my parents to open the doors. There he saw two little boys, one of them soundly asleep, and so he just casually looked around. He carefully compared all items he found on the doložka we filled out prior to leaving Czechoslovakia. "*Alles ist gut*," he said and returned the passports to my dad. We pulled through the border post and drove toward the Czech side of the crossing. A sleepy border guard checked our passports and signaled to us to drive on. We did it! My mom had her curtains and a story to tell. I realized through that experience that when she decides to do something, there is very little that can stop her. Other trips to the northern neighbors of Czechoslovakia were a lot less dramatic or memorable.

Nothing in all creation is hidden from God's sight.
—Hebrews 4:13

6)   Communism Could Not Stop Christmas

Christmas holidays are another set of marvelous memories worth spending a little time and a little ink on. Tradition is a power-ful thing. Christmas has been celebrated in the Czech lands as long as anywhere else in the world. The holidays were an exciting time of being together, enjoying the family and, yes, opening presents found underneath the Christmas tree beautifully decorated for the occa-sion. The aroma of potpourri, baked cookies, and the small spruce tree filled our little apartment with the sweet smell of Christmas. My grandparents, living just three floors below us, were a big part of the annual festivities; and I loved seeing them cuddle together, sip eggnog, and open gifts carefully purchased and wrapped for each other. My grandfather and I were close. He was a special friend to me. My grandmother was a master baker and every year made a large assortment of authentic Czech Christmas cookies. My parents did a great job of convincing my brother, Míra, and I that "Little Jesus" was the one who brought us gifts and placed them under the tree. It's ironic to think that the sentiment of the Communist govern-ment was to erase Christ from the mind-set of its people. And largely, it succeeded. Of all the holidays, however, it was Christmas when "Little Jesus" remained to be a part of the narrative. We never heard the Christmas story so powerfully depicted in the gospel of Luke. We didn't believe that Jesus actually existed, and we never consid-ered the sinful nature of mankind hopelessly lost and condemned, waiting for the Messiah to ascend and save. Yet even in a small way, Jesus prevailed to be a part of the season. It was this time of each year when we were kinder to each other as if unconsciously recognizing the imprint of the gentle Creator God in one another. A candlelit dinner of homemade potato salad and Wiener schnitzel was served on my mom's fine china atop a stately decorated table covered with a crisp white tablecloth embellished with small green pine branches. The feast was a prequel to the ringing of the bell announcing that the gifts have arrived. Christmas Eve was always filled with Christmas carols played from the LP records that my parents collected over the years. In these, the true meaning of Christmas was boldly proclaimed, as if unnoticed by the censorship of the government, "We bring you the good news" or "Born is Christ the Lord. Let us rejoice." We played them every year but never truly heard their resounding message until years later after the Lord opened my eyes to believe and receive His love. And so I love Christmas, the carols, the fellowship, and the sweet family time. Even now, with my own family living here in America, I cook Wiener schnitzel and make a homemade potato salad, and together we honor the gift of Jesus Christ by exchanging presents on Christmas Eve.

I bring you good news of great joy that will be for all people. Today in the town of David a Savior has been born to you: he is Christ the Lord.
—Luke 2: 10–11

7)   My Beloved Grandparents

As we were growing up, occasional Saturdays were spent going to work with my grandfather who was a trusted mailman in Ústí's neighborhood of Vaňov. These are great memories to this day cherished in my heart. We would sort the mail together before facing the day and the weather outside. The route would start at eight o'clock and was done all on foot. Around ten o'clock, we would arrive at the local grocery store where we would buy hot bagels and freshly sliced ham. We would sit on a little wall surrounding the store and watch the Elbe River flow toward Hamburg before being emptied into the

Baltic Sea. These breaks never went without a captivating story or two. The massive ruins of the gothic medieval Střekov Castle, rising high on the other side of the river, gave these moments with my grandpa a unique, almost magical, atmosphere.

My grandmother, named Bohumila, which translates from the Czech language as "lover of God," had an interesting childhood. Her father, Jan Křiklava, my great-grandfather, served as the gardener for the aristocratic family of Von Aehrenthals, who owned and lived at a

sprawling chateaux complex in a small Czech town of Doksany, located northwest of Prague. My grandmother would spend countless hours sharing with me the fascinating details and memories of her life growing up on the estate, watching her dad serve Count Lexa von Aehrenthal and his family. My grandmother was the same age as Countess Marie Caroline Lexa of Aehrenthal, and growing up, they were close friends. The large chateaux was an ideal place to play, discover, meet numerous guests of noble roots, dress up, and sneak into lavish balls at the chateaux's ballroom that also served, on occasions, as a private movie theater for the family and guests. My grandmother would be invited to ride in a horse pulled carriage to the near and bit larger town of Roudnice, for Saturday jewelry shopping sprees. My great grandfather was responsible for taking care of the gardens surrounding the residential wing of the chateaux, and he enjoyed his job of serving such fine owners and employers. The Count Von Aehrenthal and his family were well respected and loved throughout the town of Doksany as so many were employed on the estate. At the end of World War II, the entire property was confiscated by the Czechoslovak state on the basis of President Beneš' decrees. The Aehrenthals were forced to leave everything behind as they had to return to Austria in the postwar era. My grandmother recalls standing in the portal of the ornate baroque entry gate to the complex, watching her friend, Marie Caroline, and her family drive away, under the watchful eye of the government officials, never to return—never to see their home, never to see each other again. Growing up, we would visit the complex many times, being the silent witnesses of the sad decay of the chateaux and its gardens. The Communist government had no finances or man power to take care of all the confiscated properties around the country, and so many of them fell to a state beyond repair. We would cross the barriers to walk through the park, closed to the public, and climb through what used to be a window into the house where my grand-mother grew up and where my mother spent countless summer holidays and Christmases while visiting her grandparents during her childhood. Every visit to Doksany was so special as I would experience a satisfying mixture of feeling the thrill of exploring forbidden land and getting to see my grandmother's story firsthand. She always became strangely perky as we would stroll through the complex, and her heart and mind were flooded with all the memories so deeply connected to this place.

It was during one of my frequent returns to the Czech Republic, this time in the summer of 2017, when I brought my own family to visit Doksany. This visit became remarkable in that I found an unlocked door leading to the interiors of the chateaux. Never before was I able to see with my own eyes the hidden places that were so deeply treasured in the memories of my grandmother. As I happened to check the doorknob this one visit, I could not believe that it was unlocked. With my phone in hand, I slowly opened the door and slipped into the entry hall of the mansion. I had no idea if anyone was inside, but I did not care. I was ready to ask for mercy should I get caught inside of the forbidden palace. I slowly walked up a wide staircase leading to the residential portion of the chateaux. It was just as amazing as I had imagined it. It felt as if time simply stopped inside of these gorgeous interiors. There was no furniture anywhere to be found, but each room had a different color theme, a beautiful and unique one from the other. Ornate and decorative Baroque-style heating stoves were situated in the corners, and elaborate paneling decorated the ceilings of each room. It was fascinating. Then I found a hallway leading, as if, around the corner of the building. I could not

24

help but follow its lead. The wooden floor squeaked with every step, and I worried I might run into whoever unlocked the door before I snuck in. I advanced on. Then, and suddenly, the hallway led to a large French double door. I had to open it, and as I did, I beheld the ballroom. The beautifully conserved and exquisite room decorated with well-preserved paintings encased in oval-shaped frames, systematically placed between the large windows of the two opposing walls. This was where the balls took place. This is where the aristocratic entertaining happened. At the end of the banquet hall was a large mural depicting the very moment of the founding of Doksany by Gertruda, the Duchess of Bohemia. I was beside myself. I had to get my wife, Cassandra, and the children to see this. I ran downstairs and brought them all inside. If we were to be discovered and caught, then we might as well have seen it—all of us. They loved what they saw. We all marveled at the fact that we were, after my forty-three years of hearing about these rooms and the life they once held, standing inside and seeing it with our own eyes. I will never forget this special and unique visit to Doksany. I felt transported in time to my grandmother's childhood and her experiences growing up here. It was emotional and deeply moving for me. I am thankful.

Every good and perfect gift is from above, coming down from the Father of the heavenly lights, who does not change like shifting shadows.
—James 1:17

8)   Precious Prague

The highlights of my early childhood, however, were frequent train trips to Prague. My grandfather, native of Prague, and I would lose all track of time when wandering the streets of the then gray but, nonetheless, beautiful capital city. They always excited me beyond words. Prague was filled with so many interesting people from places near and far. Foreign airline agencies were proudly lining Pařížská ("Paris Street" in English) displaying images of distant lands. Their shopping windows were decorated with models of large jets painted in their liveries and colors. As it was almost impossible for the

Czechoslovaks to travel to most of these destinations, the emotions of a young boy pressing his nose against the glass were, for sure, stirred and inspired. Pistachio ice cream, to my memory only available in the Wenceslas Square pastry shop, was bought for one Czechoslovak crown. The flavor of the lightly green delicacy sealed the experience deeply into my senses. The visit to the city wasn't complete without a jaw-dropping walk through Prague's Little Quarter, where the flags of foreign embassies and state government buildings flew high above our heads. These trips with my grandpa awakened in me a love for the city as well as an interest for what was perhaps hidden in the world beyond the Iron Curtain. I loved, and still love, the Golden Prague.

> *Put your hope in God, who richly provides us*
> *with everything for our enjoyment.*
>
> —1 Timothy 6:17b

9)   My First Experience of Fear

A not-so-good recollection from my childhood is one that is deeply embedded in my mind. My mother was a nurse. She had a desire to become a surgical nurse, which required further schooling in addition to her medical high school nursing diploma. She was diligent and determined to receive the necessary education while having a family. Many mothers do. The difference in her case was the ideological education that accompanied the medical degree. To this day, I remember hearing my mother shouting and clearly disapproving the teachings of Marx and Lenin while complaining and questioning as to why the socialist and Communist ideology had to be a part of the medical degree. The danger of her loud verbiage was the perspicuous echo of the apartment building where almost no conversation was ever deemed completely private. My dad would remind her to keep her voice down, to no avail. She was adamant. But what if someone reported or recorded what they heard her say? My dad worried, worried for our family's well-being. I remember lying in bed, with my little brother sound asleep in a bed next to mine, being filled with fears. What would happen to us if my mom got us in trouble? Who were Lenin and Marx? What was so bad about their views and teachings? Why was it wrong to voice her opinion? Who was right? Who was wrong?

My mom received the highest possible grades in all her medical exams. The political final examination, however, didn't go as planned, and she received a low B. One more exchange of heated opinions between my revered parents followed, and then it all ended. Nobody reported anything. Our family life returned to the normal tracks. But inside my mind, something changed.

I will destroy the wisdom of the wise; the intelligence
of the intelligent I will frustrate.
—1 Corinthians 1:19

10) Jiri the Builder/Folk Dancer

My passion from a young age was to build. Always and everywhere. Tall towers, fortresses, igloos in the winter, paper models of Czech castles and chateaux, and water dams on fishing trips with my dad. Everything around me, from blocks to my dad's tools, was a useful material to create larger or taller structures. I loved designing cities on large wrapping paper, involuntarily provided by the Czechoslovak postal service, courtesy of my grandpa. These were always accompanied by a detailed index corresponding to the numbers on the drawn buildings. I was on my way to becoming what I thought would be the greatest job known to mankind—an urban architect.

But then one day, while still in the first grade, a lady walked into our classroom and asked if anyone would be interested in joining a folk dance group. This group, Kvítko (*Kvee-tko*, Czech word for a "small blossom"), was organized by the Regional House of Pioneers and the Youth. Before I knew what had happened, my hand was raised, and I signed up. Little did I know then just how pivotal and significant this simple motion of my arm would be in the next four decades of my life. These were good memories.

For we are God's workmanship, created in Christ Jesus to do good works, which God prepared in advance for us to do.
—Ephesians 2:10

11) Ballet?

I did well in school. I became a Pioneer upon reaching middle school. I became a class president as well. I loved the visits of the Soviet Pioneers and was often selected to represent our school during these *Družba* (*Droo-zhbaa, friendship* in Russian) visits. I kept folk dancing, and slowly with time, my passion for dancing grew. I was naturally gifted with rhythm and musicality. Kvítko won several regional dance competitions and one year was selected to represent the North Bohemian region in the national folk art festival in Moravia. After our performance there, I was sought out by a professor from the dance conservatory in Prague. "Can you do a split?" she asked. Without a reply, I dropped to the ground with one leg in front and one behind my body. "You seem to have a natural movement ability," she continued. "Thank you," was my response. "Have you ever considered studying ballet?" I had not. I wasn't even sure if I had even seen a ballet performance prior to this exchange! "You should consider auditioning for the Conservatory of Music and Dance next year." She followed up with a quick conversation with the director of the dance ensemble and disappeared into the crowd. I quickly forgot the entire encounter and enjoyed the rest of the festival. Little did I know...

The director of the Kvítko ensemble, Ms. Fimbingerová, spoke to my parents about the conversation with the conservatory professor during the art festival and offered to assist us in submitting an application to the ballet conservatory in Prague. She also strongly encouraged them to pursue the opportunity as their son, in her opinion, did have a unique talent, indeed, and a career of a professional ballet dancer might be something I was destined for.

Before long, my mom and I were boarding the "Vindobona" train at the Ústí main train station. Our two-hour train ride to Prague was filled with so many interesting people traveling between Berlin (East Berlin to be exact) and Vienna. The little twelve-year-old boy, however, paid no attention to anyone or anything that was around him. He was going to audition for the best ballet school in the country.

My parents arranged for me to stay with our relatives in the city. We reached Prague on time and took a tram to our relatives' home, beautifully nestled above the Vltava River right above the Orion confectionery factory that, each morning, filled the air with the sweet smell of chocolate.

The ballet auditions had three rounds. The first round had very little to do with ballet and much more to do with the examination of my flexibility, ability to coordinate movement, rhythmic exercises, and such. I passed without problems. The second round was a bit more technical. A handful of us were given a ballet class. A small committee of the conservatory professors and the school director were observing. I was nervous. No parents were allowed in the room. I felt alone and all on my own. I did my best. The results were in. Once again, I passed the second round. The third round of the auditions had just two of us in the room. Little did I know then that only one could be chosen. The school had allotted only sixteen boys to join, and fifteen had already been selected a year before. If I were to be selected, I would join a class already one year in session. Growing up, I was taught by my parents, as well as all my elementary and middle school teachers, to always do my best. Never to try to stand out or draw attention to myself. Just do my best and leave the rest up to those in leadership. And so I did.

A few weeks later, we received a letter. The decision of the small committee was that Jiri Voborsky would be commencing his studies at the Conservatory of Music and Dance in the 1987–1988 school year. I couldn't believe it. I made it. I was chosen to join, chosen to belong. My head was spinning. There were sacrifices to be made. I was to leave my parents at the age of twelve and live with my relatives. I was to be responsible. I was to grow up a bit quicker than others my age. None of that mattered. I was ready and willing. I found my purpose. I was to become a professional ballet dancer and perhaps, one day, dance with the ballet company of the National Theater.

"For I know the plans I have for you," declares the Lord, "plans to prosper you and not to harm you, plans to give you hope and a future."
—Jeremiah 29:11

12) Rejected

I left Ústí right before the summer break was about to end. My mom came to Prague with me to help me learn how to navigate the big city's subway system, tramline network, and the hustle of the Czechoslovak capital. All of a sudden, the city had changed. It wasn't the same Prague that I so admired with my grandfather. Now it was a place where I needed to focus and do my best, to excel in my studies and reach my dream.

I met my classmates. They were young boys like myself. They had a year advantage, and I was determined to catch up and prove that I truly belonged. One interesting surprise was that both I and the other boy that auditioned with me were in the class. I didn't think twice about it.

The conservatory was hard and challenging in every sense of the word. On the academic side, I had to catch up in French. All the ballet students had to study French along with the mandatory Russian, and I was behind. In middle school, I had chosen English when I started sixth grade to add on to Russian. But French was not going to stop me from doing well. *"J'apprendrai le français!"* was my inner motto. The ballet technique classes were a pure Vaganova method, the ballet technique created and perfected by our nation's great role model, the Soviet Union. We danced all day, five days a week. The conservatory didn't have a building large enough for all the classes, so the frequent use of the mass transport system became a necessary part of each day. I recall studying late at night at my relatives' house.

These were exhausting but thrilling days. I was given a chance. I was living my dream. I was given an opportunity, and I was tenacious to follow it through to the end.

One September morning, a couple of weeks upon moving to Prague, my mom stepped into the ballet studios during the first ballet class of the morning. She disrupted the class. Her makeup was running down her face. My class professor met her at the door, and they stepped out of the studio. "What is going on?" I was desperately wondering. "Why is my mom here? Is something wrong?" Nobody knew. Then the teacher returned and slowly, with her eyes looking directly at me, walked across the ballet studio. "Come with me, Jiri, please," she said. "Yes, Comrade Professor," was my reply. We walked together with her arms around my shoulders. I didn't know that I was to never see my classmates again. As we exited the room, my mom embraced me and, with a resolve in her voice, said, "We are going home." The two women shook hands, and the professor gently stroked my head. Before long, we were on the train traveling back to the hills of Northern Bohemia, going home. My mom didn't say much. Tears were continually flowing down her face. All I knew then was that my days in Prague were over. When we arrived in Ústí, my dad and brother met us at the train station and drove us in our Soviet-made *Žiguli* (*Zhee-goo-lee*) car to our apartment. About a week later, we received a letter from the conservatory stating that "a mistake was made by the exam committee" and that "Jiri Voborsky had no potential to ever become a professional ballet dancer." I was confused. I was hurt. I was devastated. It wasn't until years later when my mother told me that the other boy in my class at the conservatory was a nephew of Jiří Bělohlávek, the chief conductor of the Prague Symphony Orchestra who demanded an enrollment of his nephew to the school. The brief conversation between my mom and the professor of the conservatory made that clear. One of us had to go. And who was I to remain? My dad was "just" an honest worker who had no post to use as a leverage to advance his son. One of the two boys had to be let go. Jiri was to be the one rejected. What I did not know then was the simple truth that the Creator God, Whom I didn't know nor believe in, was already moving pieces of His master plan for His glory and for His purposes.

> *What I have said, that will I bring about:*
> *what I have planned, that will I do.*
>
> —Isaiah 46:11b

13) Back in Ústí

I changed. I went through a season of declining grades, a lack of will to do anything. I stayed in my room. I was heartbroken. The only recollection from this time that I have is remembering my dad saying, "If you were meant to dance, you will dance." But in my mind, I was done with the world of ballet. Never again was I to put ballet shoes on. Never again was I to make myself vulnerable and open for another devastating blow. My dream to dance had died.

I returned to middle school and continued my education. I loved languages. Both Russian and English classes were my favorite. Geometry came easily, and I loved geography. There were so many interesting places all around the world to learn about. It was very difficult for Czechs to travel, as it was the case for all Eastern European nationals, but in this class, I could dream of distant places while seeing pictures and gathering fascinating information about them. I slowly returned to my normal rhythm of being an overachiever.

One day in the seventh grade, I was summoned to the principal's office. I was certain that I didn't do anything wrong, but one can never be sure. As I walked into his office, there was my class teacher seated on the right and the Pioneer Organization school director standing on the left side of the principal, who was seated behind a large desk. The window behind them made it difficult to see their facial expressions as the autumn sun was shining brightly into the office. I walked in and politely greeted them all. "We have a question for you," said the principal. Silence followed, and a slight awkwardness was tangibly hanging in the air. The Pioneer Organization director spoke next. "We have received a letter from Prague." *Oh no*, I thought. *Could this be a dramatic continuation to the conser-*

vatory fiasco? "The Politburo is looking for a group of talented and dedicated Pioneers to represent our country," she continued. "The comrades in Prague are looking for thirty young boys and girls to send them to three different nations around the world." The principal interrupted her, almost sounding as if he wanted to cut the meeting short. We both could agree on that. "We selected you and Dita to represent our school, city, and region." I was stunned. "What do you think?" I didn't have much to say, as I was caught completely off guard. My class teacher, who knew me the best, could see the hesitation in my face. "It would be an honor for you to go, Jiri." "Yes, Comrade Teacher," I replied politely. "It would be such an honor."

It took several more weeks of meetings between the school and my parents. Finally, the Central Committee of the Czechoslovak Communist Party sent a letter letting us know that Dita and I would join eight other Pioneers in representing the Czechoslovak Socialist Republic on a monthlong trip to Italy. We were to be the folk dancers in the group. All the team members had some unique talents and gifting, and all of us were to be shining representatives of the accomplishments of the Communist society. All I knew was the fact that I would be going beyond the Iron Curtain, to Western Europe. The government would provide everything necessary for the trip, including an airline ticket. I had never flown on an airplane before. We had taken several field trips to Prague Ruzyně International Airport with my class but only to watch the airport's bustling traffic from an observation deck. Nobody in my family had ever flown before either. I was so excited. This trip also made me return to Kvítko and continue folk dancing, purely as a hobby, not as a potential career vector in my life.

I remember going to a visa office in Ústí, a beautiful, impressive two-story building located in the center of the city. There were two large doors inside this former industrialist's villa, confiscated by the regime in 1948. One had a sign stating "Communist Bloc" and the other "Capitalist Bloc." As my mother and I walked in, we noticed a long line by the former and no one by the latter of the two doors. The looks of everyone were piercing and sharp as we walked to the "Western" door and knocked. "Come in," sounded from behind them. As we walked in, I turned my head to look at the people in the long line. They all seemed as if without joy, without purpose, without life. The doors closed, and my mother and I faced a police officer sitting behind a large desk looking intimidating and in charge. The interview was short. We had all the necessary documents. It was clear that he had received the pre-approved notice from the higher-up level of the government. We learned that prior to my departure I would have to spend a week at the Central Pioneer Camp in the charming locality of Seč (*Sech*) reservoir in the eastern part of Bohemia, where I would receive final instructions prior to leaving the country. This statement was followed by the issuing of the exit visa into my passport, permitting me to leave the country. My Italian visa was going to be issued subsequently by the Italian Embassy in Prague. My excitement about the trip grew.

> *No eye has seen, no ear has heard, no mind has conceived*
> *what God has prepared for those who love him.*
> —1 Corinthians 2:9

14) Crossing the Iron Curtain

That summer couldn't come fast enough. Finally, in July of 1988, my parents drove me to the camp and said their goodbyes. Three groups of Pioneers were all prepped to be sent out as representatives. One was going to North Korea, one to West Berlin, and one to the Tuscany region of Italy. Behavioral standards, rules, and expectations were the topics of the lectures. Getting to know each other on the team was also a must. The government was entrusting us with a unique responsibility, we were told, and we needed to fully understand and grasp the weight of the mission. Finally, the day to leave arrived, and we were driven to the Ruzyně airport. This time, we were not to look from the observation deck. This time, we were to be the ones walking on the tarmac boarding an airplane. "Czechoslovak Airlines" was painted on the side of the TU 134, a Soviet-made aircraft. It was a beauty, I thought. It seemed massive and much larger than I imagined. The flight was amazing in every sense of the word as I got to see, for the first time, my beloved Prague from up above. The meal served was delicious, and I tried to enjoy every fleeting moment of the two-hour trip to Milano. I was eager to dive into this feat of representing Czechoslovakia, representing my people, my government, and its ideals. I was ready. Upon arrival, we were met by the workers of the Czechoslovak Consulate General and escorted to the building proudly flying the Czech flag. The adventure had begun.

Italy was as fascinating as I had imagined. Milano left an impression of a busy metropolis, much different from Prague. The city was overwhelming to soak in for a group of young teenagers from the Eastern European Bloc. Overflowing with many large eye-catching and overstimulating billboards and flashing neon signs, there was so much to look at and absorb. The city seemed dirty and overcrowded. The streets were packed with noisy traffic. All drivers seemed passionate about letting others know through loud klaxons that they were there and in a hurry. One walk through the city was marked by seeing a young lady kneeling on the pavement of the street. A little baby lay beside her crying as if trying to catch our attention. The lady was bowing down, and a small paper cup was held in her shivering hands. "She has no home. She has no food," we were told. "She and the baby are destined to live on the streets." We had never experienced such a thing. My heart was filled with a desperate notion of hopelessness. How could this be? How could someone be homeless or without a job? Did the government not provide for their needs? We had an innumerable amount of questions directed to our chaperones. Our experiences of the city were always carefully examined by our counselors upon every return to the hotel. They did a good job of utilizing these conversations to point out the benefits of our socialist society, much happier and better than this capitalist pretense of utopia, we were told.

The performances were carefully planned. We never knew where we were being driven to perform. We were not allowed to be in contact with anyone in the crowd. Our job was to do what we did well—smile big and let our happiness shine brightly. And so we tried. The crowds quickly became admirers as we would finish our sets and conclude with a bow while gleaming with luster and youthful enthusiasm. The moment we finished each performance, we were whisked away to the consulate for dinner and then taken to the hotel for a quick debrief before lights out. If I remember correctly, we spent about ten days in Milano before we changed location. We performed in other cities of Tuscany. Florence, Pisa, and Sienna, all of which made an impact on me. I never thought that I would see the famous white-stoned leaning bell tower of Pisa with my very own eyes. These cities were much smaller than Milano and seemed to have more of the renowned Italian charm and beauty. Days turned into weeks, and before we knew it, we finished the tour with the last performance. A trip to the island of Elba was the finale of the trip. A few days of vacation and rest on the beautiful beaches of this spectacular 'Isola' were almost magical. The warm waves were splashing against our bodies as we swam in the turquoise water. I noted the significant difference between the warm Mediterranean and the cold Baltic Seas. The only other southern sea available to the Czechoslovak citizens to visit was the Adriatic Sea, off the coast of Yugoslavia, but only a very few were permitted to travel there for holidays. My family never did. Our group of young excited Pioneers was looked after by the chaperones; but, unlike the rest of the trip, we were not being watched by anyone from the consulate. The respite on Elba flew by with almost supersonic speed, and we knew that our time to return home was approaching rather quickly. Then a day before we were to board the Czechoslovak airliner, we were driven back to Milano to have the final debrief at the consulate. We all had to convey our impressions of Italy. The overarching notion of the consulate employees seemed to be worrisome that we would be returning home smitten by our empirical observation of the Western world. Their worry was legitimate as we were leaving changed by a broadened horizon of understanding and experience. The flight home was enjoyed to the very last moment as I did not know if I would ever get to fly again.

Landing in Prague was exciting. My family was waiting at the crowded arrival hall of the Ruzyně airport and welcomed me with almost embarrassing enthusiasm. I said goodbye to the other teammates knowing that I would most likely never see any of them again. That was also a part of the government plan. The larger the distance between us, the easier the silencing or political cleanup would be, should an unwanted occurrence of the politically inappropriate flow of information arise. I was proud to be chosen to represent my country, I was glad to return to it. But there was a small seed of knowledge planted within me. The knowledge that people beyond the Iron Curtain live in freedom that we, the Czechoslovaks, did not know.

The rest of the summer break was spent in enjoyment of life and everything it had to offer. I often wonder why it was so much easier to find the simple pleasures and blessings of life when we were young, while as adults we struggle so badly to do the same. My parents went

to work every day, and my brother and I were left home alone, which was just fine with us. My mom worked as a surgical nurse at the eye department of the North Bohemian State Hospital, and my dad was a bus driver for the Ústí public mass transit company. They both enjoyed their jobs and believed with heartfelt conviction that we all have a place in the process of building the country and contributing to society. An interesting note is that my parents married when my mom was still in high school. Her graduation diploma has her married name on it. I was born some two years after they said their "I dos." Bohunka was twenty years old. My parents enjoyed a wonderful marriage. Interestingly enough, divorce was a rare occurrence in a socialist state as the government understood that family is a key component to a healthy society, and divorce was, therefore, a difficult process to undergo. Both notions, sadly, seem to be vanishing rapidly today. Mom and Dad got married young, and yet their marriage was strong and thriving as they were devoted to each other and to my brother and me. Summer breaks were often filled with swimming at the public pool, visits to the zoo, fishing trips with my dad and grandpa, bike rides around the city park, and enjoyment of classical music played on our vinyls. Yes, I loved Beethoven and Mozart. As most siblings do, we spent the summer days going our separate ways and often only to spend time together when a plate of hot food was served before us. Neither one of us realized that this was to be the last summer enjoyed together, for the upcoming year was going to part and separate us, and we were never to live together again.

> *The plans of the Lord stand firm forever, the purposes of his heart through all generations.*
>
> —Psalm 33:11

15) The Dreaded Choosing

In September, I was to start the eighth grade, which was the final grade of middle school. In the Czechoslovak education, it is then when the students with a certain grade point average are permitted to choose a high school with a specific focus on a field of interest and future career. Once a school is determined, the student has to take an entry exam. Its results, in combination with the grades of middle school, placed the students into a lineup. Then the top thirty or so are enrolled to start studies at the particular school. I was certain as to what field I wanted to pursue. Architecture! As life would have it, it is much easier to have a dream than it is for this dream to come true. There were several architectural high schools and many fields of architecture to choose from. The lines of aspiring students to fill the classrooms of these schools were long. The competition was intimidating and inspiring all at the same time. Not only did I have to wisely select a specific field of architecture, but I also had to make the cut and be chosen to be admitted into the school. Ústí had several specialized high schools such as school of chemistry, economics, high school of engineering, and a medical high school. There were two grammar high schools, known as gymnáziums (*gum-naaz-ium*), for those students who couldn't make up their mind or devote themselves to a specific lifelong field of occupation. There was no high school of architecture in town. I, as well as thousands of other aspiring eighth graders, was eyeing schools in Prague. Would I be able to return back to the city and face my past? I wasn't sure but, at the same time, I had no choice. In order to become an architect, I had to overlook my fears at the mature age of fourteen years. The norm in the educational system was the fact that young high schoolers would leave their parents and move to a town that had a school of their interest, live in dorms with other students, and face the challenges of life at a younger age than is usual here in America. What I never considered was the price the parents were willing to pay in saying goodbye to their children knowing that they will, more likely than not, never share life under the same roof again. My parents were no different. They never wanted to stand in the way of either my brother or me to pursue our aspirations and dreams but desired to be our support, even if that meant some shed tears on their faces and the pain of broken hearts as we would part ways. Choosing and deciding was a difficult and stressful process for every student who desired to follow their dreams.

In him we were chosen, having been predestined
according to the plan of him who works out everything
in conformity with the purposes of his will.
—Ephesians 1:11

16) My Brother, Míra

My brother, Míra (*Mee-ra*), officially Miroslav, named after my father, was born four and a half years after me. He and I could not be more different. Our hobbies, interests, and personalities are as dis-

tinct as could be. While in first grade, he was chosen to try out for and was accepted to a state-run gymnastic center. Little did any of us know the immense dedication his inclusion in the center would require on the whole family. Every day, six days a week, Míra would spend countless hours in the gym under the watchful eye of the head coach, other coaches, and instructors of the center. Slowly but surely, his unique ability and talent became indisputable. I remember my parents saving money to purchase a video camera to film my brother's workouts, routines, and meets to assist him by providing the ability to review his performance, technique, and deficiencies. Over time, Míra would place in the regional competitions. The rings were his strength, where he excelled the most. The head coach, Petráček, believed in him and pushed Míra hard to be versatile, however, and not settle for just one discipline of the sport. He was preparing Míra for something big. He knew how to inspire and motivate, how to counsel when discouragement came, and how to be a friend, and how to be the engine that my brother and my parents needed. Before my brother ever reached middle school, he became the Czech national champion in the junior division on several occasions. He continued to work hard. His little frame was ideal for the sport. Many a time, my parents worried that gymnastics would stunt his growth. Míra didn't care.

There was a goal to be reached. He became the national champion in the senior division. Then, in 1993, the invitation and challenge arrived. Time had come to move to Brno, Czech's second-largest city, for Míra to train to earn a spot on the Czech Olympic Team that was heading to the 1996 Summer Olympiad in Atlanta. Míra would be representing his nation as a young athlete. The decision was difficult to make. Would the family move to Brno with him, would just one parent move, would he go alone? He was prepared for the challenge; he trained for many years and numerous hours just for this, to grace the largest stage of the sport world—the Olympic games. The decision was made that Míra would move to Brno as he was to start high school. My parents were to stay in Ústí and travel for his competitions and championships. After a spring training camp, in the spring of 1993, when Míra was still in eighth grade, he woke with a severe pain in his pelvis. At first everyone thought it was the body responding to the strenuous workout at the camp. The pain was increasing, and its intensity was beyond bearable. It was time to visit a doctor. With fear and hesitation, my parents, my brother, and his trusted head coach went for a consultation and initial testing at the state hospital. The results came back quickly. They were devastating. Míra was diagnosed with osteophytes, bone spurs in all joints of his lower extremities. Surgery was an option, but due to the vast spreading of the bone spurs, the prognosis was looking bleak. All of his joints were affected. The doctor recommended an immediate discontinuance of his training. For now and most likely for good. Míra resisted. This was his passion. This was his love. This was his dream. My mom and dad did not know what to say. Their hearts hurt for their son. It was the coach who brought the needed wisdom into the room. This was a hard moment for him to face; it was harder still to verbalize his thoughts carefully and passionately. But he knew that life after gymnastics was to come, and he wanted for my brother to be able to have a normal adulthood and run after his own kids one day. He looked Míra in the eye, and with a tender yet authoritative voice, he made the decision to do whatever was necessary for the healing to come, in this case, to stop all training and competing. Right away and with finality. Even if healing were to come with time, the interval missed in the gym would be too colossal to bridge at this level of training. Everyone in the room knew this was the right thing to do, that this was the right decision. Everyone in the room felt the pain of Míra's emotions facing the dying dream. Míra was to never put on his jersey, never to chalk his hands, to still his breath and focus his mind on the apparatus before him. Míra was not to go to Atlanta as a proud member of the Czech Olympic Team. His identity as a gymnast came abruptly to an end.

Míra went to study at the medical high school in Ústí and received his nursing degree. He passionately served as a nurse in the emergency room of the Ústí Hospital, worked for an intensive care unit there and later in Prague, and eventually moved to work in a clinic in the city of Dublin, Ireland. Today he is working for the Royal College of Surgeons; is happily married to Klára, a Czech girl he met in Ireland; and, without pain, runs after their firstborn son, Thaddeus. I am so proud of my little brother who grew up to be a man with a big heart for those who face tremendous challenges, difficulties, and crises in their lives. He lives to be an encourager for them—to find the will to fight an uphill battle, to face a seemingly impossible storm, to take a step even if a small one, a step toward a hope in the healing that might arrive tomorrow or in the days to come. I love my little brother!

We love because he first loved us.

—1 John 4:19

17) An Unexpected Detour

It was late March of 1989, and I was gearing up for my entry exam to the architectural high school. I was aiming to land a spot either in the class of urban architecture or the class specializing in transportation infrastructure. My grades were great, and if I did well on the entry exam, my chances were good. I was still dancing in the Kvítko ensemble, purely for the fellowship with longtime friends and the enjoyment of the craft. But then, once again, an unexpected turn on the road of life emerged. Without a warning, without a preconceived indication to brace for a sharp curve to the unexpected detour, I was tossed to travel down a path I was not prepared to explore.

It was a beautiful late afternoon in Ústí. As I was growing up, the city was often veiled in a heavy industrial smog. Two large chemical factories and the mining industry near the outskirts of the city had taken a toll on the regional environment. There were days when, through the school radio system, the principal announced to avoid any outdoor activity and, due to high levels of smog in the air, to stay at home. This day stood in stark contrast to these usual weather conditions. It was a perfect day. Ústí is situated in a hilly region of the Ore Mountain Range, dividing German Saxony from Bohemia. The Elbe River offers many unique areas for rest and relaxation along its banks, as it peacefully flows through the city. In combination with the river, the hills called Porta Bohemica, the *Gate of Bohemia* in Latin, warmly surround the city as if inviting the inhabitants to come and unplug from the hustle of life.

This particular day, I remember walking through the streets of the town from the bus stop to the Regional House of Pioneers and the Youth (RHPY). The RHPY was located in another former residence of a proud owner of the local chemical factory. Like most properties in the country, it, too, was confiscated during the turbulent time of the Communist takeover in February of 1948. The interior of the palace was decorated with dark-colored wooden panels and hand-carved embellishments created by artisans of the past. An enormous staircase stood facing the large entry hall, clearly designed to impress. Large tall mirrors were strategically dispersed throughout the halls and chambers of the villa to allure the beholder and elevate the prestige of the owner. Every piece of the interior was meticulously selected and strategically placed, from the floors to the furnishings, to the ceilings and their chandeliers, to outdo the other aristocratic members of the upper class and their residences. The socialist regime did not change the decorations of the palace but rather enjoyed the benefits of the free property expropriated from the wealthy industrialist. Over the years, the magnitude and the beauty of the building sadly faded into oblivion with my every return to it. The Kvítko ensemble practiced on the third floor in a large ballroom enhanced by a magnificent fireplace. This day, we were to practice our usual repertoire and perhaps learn a new choreography sequence. Upon arrival, the ensemble director, Ms. Fimbingerová, introduced us to Mr. Pokorný, the artistic director and choreographer in residence of the Šalda State Theater in the Czech city of Liberec (*Lee-be-retz*). He came to Ústí to work with the local professional ballet company and visited our practice to set choreography on the dancers of the ensemble. Without thinking twice about it, I changed my clothes and stretched in preparation for the rehearsal. The ninety minutes flew by, and to my astonishment, I had a really good time—and I mean a really good time. We finished the rehearsal, and as the dancers started to disperse from the hall, Ms. Fimbingerová and Mr. Pokorný cornered me by the previously mentioned fireplace. There was no way to slip away. I was trapped. "Mr. Pokorný," my director commenced, "please meet Jiri Voborsky." My face most likely resembled the "surprise emoji" to be invented some thirty years later in the century yet to come. "He is the one I spoke to you about." "How are you, Jiri?" he continued. "I hear that Prague Conservatory did not treat you well," he said. The following moments are, to this day, considered to be my most embarrassing ones in my entire life. I started to cry uncontrollably. I had no idea that the experience in Prague had left in me a deep wound filled with streams of tears ready to explode when least expected.

Both of them gave me a moment to gather myself. It was a long moment, but eventually I managed. "Yes, Prague was a disaster, sir," I replied. "Today, you did really well," Mr. Pokorný said. "There is a rare and raw talent hidden within you. I strongly believe that you need to give ballet another chance." I was floored. "No, no, no, I am signed up to take the entry exam to become an architect," I hesitantly replied. "I didn't think that I was cut out for the ballet world. The conservatory said so!" I said with conviction. "Well, I disagree," he said as he interrupted my mumbling. "The way you worked today implies the opposite. I see potential, and I would go as far as to refute the decision of the conservatory." He carried on. "Starting this September, I am opening a state ballet school in Liberec. Unlike the one in Prague, our curriculum will not be modeled after the Soviet schools. We want to have the first ballet school in the country that teaches all forms of dance. It will be a huge experiment, and the first class of students will be under close scrutiny of the government. But the green light has been granted. The State Theater is granting permission for the students to collaborate with its ballet company. The best of the best will be teaching ballet technique classes, Graham and Limon modern dance classes, tap, jazz, pantomime, character dance of many different styles, and even acting. The stage experience alone, working closely knit with the professional dancers, will make this school stand out among similar institutions in the nation." My head was spinning. An unexpected scale weighing between the two career options was almost too much to bear. "I have to think about this, sir," was the best reply I could think of at the moment. "No problem," he responded, "the auditions for the school are set for April, and Ms. Fimbingerová has all the necessary details. I hope to see you in Liberec." I was stunned. *What just happened?* As I awkwardly stumbled down the grandiose staircase, I caught a reflection of myself in the large mirrors adorning the walls of the former palace. I saw a young boy caught in an unpredicted entanglement of feelings and emotions. As I looked closer into my own eyes, I had to admit to myself about the colossal and overwhelming sense of a desire I thought was long dead. I couldn't explain it. It made no sense. But it was there, deep within. Alive and well. It was the desire to dance.

I had a good twenty-minute ride on the trolleybus line number 55 back to my neighborhood of Ústí. *Time to think. How would I explain this to my mom and dad? What would they think? What would they say?* By the time we arrived at the Mírová stop, the air had cooled down quite a bit. The sky displayed a still and pleasant spring dusk, but my mind was too preoccupied to pay attention to the weather. I walked to our apartment building and took a deep breath while riding the elevator up to the third floor. When I got home, I stepped into the usual atmosphere of the early evening of the family life. My mom was in the kitchen, and my dad sat in the living room waiting for the television programming to air the evening news. "*Ahoj*," the Czech word for both *hello* and *bye*, was all I could utter. As it is with all parents and their natural God-given instinct that accompanies parenthood, it didn't take but a microsecond for my mother to know that something was wrong. Then the usual, I would say universal and predictable question followed: "What's wrong?" The size of our small apartment prevented any private conversation without the other family members to overhear. My dad must have heard the question and joined my mother and me in the small kitchen. "I…hm… I have something to say… Hm, how should I put it?" My dad followed firmly, "What is it?" I leaned against the kitchen counter and started to share about the exchange with Mr. Pokorný that happened a mere hour ago. As I was talking, the emotions of confusion and excitement were rising within me all over again. I finished. They both understood clearly the huge dilemma inside of their fourteen-year-old. "I told you that if you are to dance, you will dance," my dad said. But the choice between the two completely different paths of my life was overwhelming. I expected to be deterred by my father to pursue dance after my fiasco in Prague. The opposite was the case. He was behind me no matter what choice I made. It meant the world. I had nothing to fear, for my father had my back—I had his support. My mom chimed in as if this was no big deal at all by saying, "Try out for both schools, and pick the one you like better." That was genius. A jaunty smile perked up on my face. "That is what I'll do. What a great idea! Thank you both so much!" What I learned that day was the simple truth that my parents loved me and I loved them.

> *How great is the love the Father has lavished on us,*
> *that we should be called the children of God.*
>
> —1 John 3:1

18) Preparing

I signed up to take ballet classes at the local performing arts school that offered afternoon classes for recreation and, well, fun. A former ballerina of the North Bohemian State Theater of Opera and Ballet, Radmila Salamanczuková, was the ballet teacher at the school, and her firm hand in the ballet studio was a bit too much for those who desired to do ballet simply for fun. I, on the other hand, loved the fact that every class gave me something new, something to take away, something to be challenged by. I was preparing for the auditions, and I needed to be pushed. As I kept returning to the ballet studio, I started to fall in love with the ballet art form all over again. There is something so stimulating about the athletic aspect of classical ballet that so uniquely meets the stern requirements of aesthetic beauty and elegance. Plainly said, I was hooked. With every passing class, the architect inside me was dying, and the dancer within was being born. The auditions were scheduled for mid-April. By the time they arrived, I felt ready—ready to give it, once again, my all.

> *Whatever you do, work at it with all your heart,*
> *as working for the Lord, not for men.*
>
> —Colossians 3:23

19) Onto Liberec

My grandfather and I boarded an intercity bus on a regularly scheduled route from Ústí nad Labem to Liberec. It left precisely at six in the morning scheduled to arrive in Liberec a little after eight. The auditions were held at the ballet studio of the local culture house. We knew that if all went well, we would arrive with plenty of time to find the building and prepare for a day of exhausting and stressful tryouts. I visited Liberec with my parents and brother as a young child. I do not remember the reason for the visit, but I do recall taking a cable car up the steep mountain of Ještěd, located in the periphery of Liberec, beautifully topped with a prizewinning tower that accommodated a restaurant, a hotel, and a TV antenna. Liberec was considered to be the seventh-largest city in Czechoslovakia. It was known for its unique layout, impressive and famed city hall designed after Vienna's own. I knew nothing else about the city or about the Šalda State Theater. I did not care to see the sights. Today, I was focused on the task at hand.

A remembrance of riding a train to Prague some two years prior was vivid in my mind. Same purpose. Same mission. Same nerves. I was two years younger then, but this time, something felt right. A sense from within made this time around feel different. Maybe it was just self-persuasion, a self-comforting attempt of sorts. I couldn't put my finger on the source of the emotion, but regardless of its origin, it brought me much-needed calm and peace, and I was thankful.

Upon arrival at the Liberec Central Bus Terminal, my grandfather and I walked down a short hill onto a large boulevard hustling with trams, buses, cars, and pedestrians. The city was alive and ready to face another day. Was I? We knew not where to turn, which way to go to find the culture house. My grandpa, being a mailman who easily befriended anyone and everyone, wasted no time before asking the first person we met. "*Tamhle*" (*Tum-hlah*) was a quick and short reply accompanied by an arm movement pointing to a large modern building across the street. Czechs are known to be closed off to outsiders, to be pessimists, wanting to be left alone. Only when a relationship is tested by time and common experience do they then open themselves up to others. This citizen fell perfectly into this description of a Czech national, and so his "there" was about as much as we could expect to receive, that is, if any assistance was offered at all. The close proximity of the bus terminal to the culture house surprised us, but we did not complain. The light rain falling onto the city made us retreat into a nearby café, Nisa, named after the river flowing through the city. We purchased some much-needed breakfast and let a little time pass by. Around 9:15, we both sensed the rising tension within me and decided to walk the short distance to the culture house and get myself prepared for the auditions. The time to shine had come.

> *Let your light shine before men, that they may see your*
> *good deeds and praise your Father in heaven.*
> —Matthew 5:16

20) Auditions—Take 2

The Liberec Culture House was an impressive structure built out of brick and glass stating the architect's intent to design a futuristic modern building that combined both purpose and style. Dark tinted glass walls carefully designed to sit at a forty-five-degree angle created both the sides and the top of the structure. It looked contemporary and sleek. Inside were a large conference room, smaller rooms serving as clubs for different groups of dedicated folks, a movie theater, and—of course—a ballet studio. "Your name?" said the lady at the counter in the entry foyer. "Jiri Voborsky," I replied. "Here you are, I see," she said as she pulled out a large envelope consisting of my application, letter of intent, and everything else requested by the conservatory for each applicant to submit. "Welcome and good luck" followed as she handed me a number to be pinned to my white T-shirt. My grandfather politely indicated that from this point on, I was on my own. He had a unique ability to indicate compassion and even love through his bluish-green eyes. I learned to decipher his signals when he would get in trouble at home. It was usually over something silly like spilling a touch of grandma's sauce on his white undershirt when we would eat lunch together at their apartment. He would not say a word, and yet through, his eyes he communicated a full paragraph of information. He also had a great sense of humor, always useful in de-escalating the situation on the home front. Here we were standing on the brim of potentially something huge in my life, and I knew that his certitude in me was strong. He could not go with me into the studio; I had to face that giant on my own. We both knew and understood that simple reality. This was my challenge to fight and my battle to win. And so I walked away as he took a seat to do what he did when he had a free moment—that is read the daily issue of *Lidové Noviny* (the *People's News*).

I found the dressing room area and stepped inside to change. I was surprised as to how many boys and girls of my age were all over the place mingling throughout the culture house. Some knew others, but most of us were strangers flying a solo flight. I changed and started to look for the studio. Just a few turns down the hall and I entered a large room. One whole side of the studio was the glass wall I admired from the outside. By now, the spring sun shone through the clouds as the soft morning rain ceased to fall. The sun's beams were illuminating the room. Mr. Pokorný was there and, with a smile on his face, came to me to welcome me and shake my hand. "I am glad you made it, Jiri," he said. "Thank you, sir!" I responded. I was encouraged and spurred on by his greeting. He then walked away, as there were pressing matters to figure out before the auditions started. There were so many of us all over the studio. Some were stretching, while some just stood and looked around eyeing their competition. There were some adults hovering near the piano. *Who were they?* I wondered. Right at ten o'clock, Mr. Pokorný clapped his hands to get our attention. "Good morning, everyone, and welcome to the official auditions for the Liberec State Ballet School. My name is František Pokorný, and I am the State Theater's choreographer in residence as well as the artistic director of the company. I will be serving as the initial principal of the conservatory. We are so glad you are here. Not everyone who is present today will be joining us in the fall, but the very fact that you are here, perhaps even facing your own fears, will help you in life to never fear but to always step forward to explore your abilities and talents. I would like to introduce to you Professor Eva Gabajová, formerly a ballerina with the National Ballet as well as a principal dancer with many companies throughout the nation. She received her diploma of pedagogy from the College of Dance of the

Prague University of Performing Arts. She will be conducting today's exams but also will be the ballet technique class professor starting in September." Professor Gabajová humbly curtsied, clearly indicating her discomfort as her accolades and accomplishments were listed. As I first saw this older woman, I took an immediate liking to her. Though in her late fifties, there was a flame of resolute dedication to the craft and everything necessary to keep classical ballet thriving in a changing world. "I also invited a handful of the company dancers from the theater to observe the auditions and see what level of talent will be joining the academy," Mr. Pokorný continued. "Don't worry. They are nice...usually," placing his arms around the shoulders of these young company artists. "They are here to encourage you throughout the day. Finally, here is my good friend, Ellen Nagyová, the pianist-in-chief of the company, who will be playing for us today." He finished the welcome speech while standing behind the gray-haired woman sitting with her straight, long back elegantly held behind the baby grand piano. "And now it's time to dance."

Professor Gabajová stepped into the middle of the room. Her gentle charming personality from a brief moment ago vanished as if into thin air. She was in charge, and there was no dispute about that. "Line up according to your numbers." It was then when I realized that the girls were numbered in lower numbers and the boys were numbered in higher numbers. There was no ballet class to start, at least not then. Just like in Prague, we started with a series of exercises exploring our flexibility combined with the exams of looseness and mobility of our joints. The company dancers and Mr. Pokorný were making notes in their files. The silence in the room was deafening. Breathing and occasional noises of pain and discomfort were the only sounds heard. A small relief echoed through the room every time someone made such a noise since the attention of the staff went to them and away from the rest. This went on for a long while. Finally, the "torture" came to an end. One can only pretend greater flexibility than others or fake the feign comfort in awkward positions for so long. Then we took a short break before lining up at a ballet barre to start the actual dance class. The combinations were surprisingly simple, but the progression of the class seemed overwhelmingly fast.

Little did we know that once we advanced to the center, we would be divided up into small groups of only six aspiring dancers. I felt so exposed and vulnerable in such a setup. A quick thought of hesitation flashed through my mind. *What was I doing?* I remembered Prague's auditions. "Focus" was my motto. *You can do this, Jiri,* I encouraged myself. I went in the last group of boys as our numbers corresponded with the alphabetical order of our last names. Never before was I so thankful to be a Voborsky rather than an Adams, as I had more opportunity to review the given combinations. Again, the simplicity was surprising. It appeared more and more clear throughout the duration of the class that it wasn't the accomplished dancer the staff around us was looking for. Rather, the raw talent and natural ability to move gracefully combined with a spark or something that set us apart; riding on the wave of technical potential was the hidden key to successful completion of the audition. And before we knew it, the class was over. "Take a break as we want to speak to you individually," was announced. The looks on all of our faces were comically similar. Sheer horror and panic masterfully appeared in our expressions. "Did he say 'one-on-one conversation'?" asked the girl standing next to me. I could not utter a word, so a simple nodding of my head followed. "My name is Petra," she continued. "I am Jiri," I said. Little did we know then of the great friendship that was yet to come starting with this brief and, frankly, awkward conversation. The individual consultations were quite simple in nature and consisted of questions aiming to uncover the reason for which we were auditioning for the school. Easy!

The last part of the audition was a choreography sequence. Once again, the steps were demonstrated with fast progression. That seemed to be the common theme throughout the day. Mr. Pokorný was undoubtedly in his element, and the company dancers enjoyed displaying their talent in the given spotlight of opportunity when showcasing his choreography. We tried to keep up. Frustration was setting in throughout the room. Here, more than in other parts of the audition process, the gap between the applicants' abilities was palpable. *Just keep moving,* was my thought. *Don't stop. Just don't stop,* was running through my head. I didn't. After we finished dancing, we were given a few moments to change our clothes and freshen up. We gathered in the studio for the concluding remarks. "Great job, everyone," Mr. Pokorný started. "We will send you a letter with the results soon. Now, because the conservatory is brand-new, the government wants to see some results before granting it the status of a fully certified secondary-level school. This means the graduates will receive a conservatory diploma, but the official high school graduation diploma must be earned in a regular high school. There are many different ones here in Liberec. You will need to take an entry exam and be accepted into one before you will be permitted to study at the conservatory. It will mean that you will attend two high schools at the same time. You will need to qualify for and maintain an ISP, individual study plan, so that you can attend dance classes running simultaneously with your academics. This has never been done before. Some government officials are convinced that this is simply too much to handle for students your age. But we believe that passion, dedication, sacrifice, and loads of hard work can make the impossible a possibility." The rest of his remarks fell on deaf ears. My mind was flooded with thoughts, worries, and doubts of how one can study two separate schools at once. I decided to cross that bridge once I knew the results of today's efforts. And so with that final thought, I politely thanked all the staff of the academy and walked to meet my grandfather. He and I grabbed a quick dinner and at five o'clock caught a bus back to Ústí. I felt good about the day. I did my best. Time would tell. As we were leaving Liberec, I looked toward the Ještěd Mountain and had a sense that this wasn't my last glimpse of it. I couldn't wait to receive the letter from the conservatory. With heavy eyelids, I rested my head on my grandad's shoulder and let my body slip into a light but, nonetheless, restful sleep.

Trust in him at all times, O people; pour out your
hearts to him, for God is our refuge.

—Psalm 62:8

21) The Decision

The apartment building that my family and I lived in had all the mailboxes in the entry area located on the bottom floor. Each metal box had a slit at its top and a row of finger-size holes at its bottom, allowing the owners to see whether or not they received any mail. It was easy to peek in and clearly know if anything was in the box. As I would come home from school each day, I would stop by the mailbox to pick up the mail. Normally, getting the mail was not all that exciting. Ever since the auditions, however, I could not wait to see and find an envelope addressed to my name that was sent from the state ballet school. Meanwhile, I connected with the middle school counselor who assisted all the eighth graders to know how, where, and when to apply for the entry exams into high schools around the country. One must remember that all this was before the Internet and the omniscient Google search engine. Together, she and I decided that if I were accepted into the Liberec Conservatory, the best high school to attend would be the gymnázium with the focus on the liberal arts. The entry exams were right around the corner, and from what we knew, the amount of students applying was enormous. I had the disadvantage of being from out of town. Gymnáziums, typically speaking, almost always accepted local students first and then, room permitting, filled the few remaining open spots with those from out of town. I had to make a decision to send in a letter of intent to this school or do the same for the school of architecture in Prague. I could not do both; I had to choose. Time was running out, and there was no letter from Liberec in the mailbox. I was frustrated and anxious. My parents did not know how to help me. The choice rested on my shoulders. Again, I was fourteen years old. This was a tough call to make.

I lived in a neighborhood of Ústí known as Northern Terrace, which in Czech is Severní Terasa. It housed roughly thirty thousand people. We all lived in large apartment buildings built out of pre-manufactured panels. These complexes had between eight and thirteen stories each. Most apartments were identical to ours. From the window of our flat, I could see three elementary and middle schools.

There were three large shopping centers within walking distance from our apartment building, also a small single screen movie theater, a post office, dental clinic, and a police station. To walk to and from school, I had to pass a large park sprawling through the middle of this section of the city. The Družba, or Friendship, Park was beautiful. There were fountains and playgrounds and benches tucked among flower beds overflowing with gorgeous flowers of countless colors and fragrances. There were statues and other works of art, and trees creating many shaded places where young mothers found rest when strolling their babies. The park was truly breathtaking and so inviting, even if for just a moment, enticing one to sit and forget about the problems and stresses of life. My middle school best friend, Vítek, and I would often sit on a bench before parting ways to go home and conversed with enthusiasm about everything that was heavy on our minds and hearts. There were days when I would lose track of time and let my mind go to places and thoughts no one knew anything about. It was here, in the Družba Park where I sensed that Liberec was the right choice for me. Whether I was accepted to the ballet school or not, the liberal arts gymnázium in Liberec was the school for me to apply to. The next day, the counselor sent in the necessary paperwork, and I submitted my official application. A few days later, as I entered the foyer of our apartment building, I noticed an envelope in our mailbox. I unlocked the box and saw the sender in the upper-left corner as "State Ballet Conservatory, Vítězná St. 7, Liberec." To my own surprise, I did not open it right there. I rode the elevator up to the third floor, calmly unlocked the door, took my shoes and my backpack off, and then sat with the closed envelope at the kitchen table pondering what to do. *What if I did not make it? What if I did?* I knew that I had to open it and see for myself what the decision was. The notice was brief and to the point. It was similar to the letter I received from Prague two years ago in that it stated plain facts without any extra fluff around them.

> Based on the results of the recent auditions, Jiri Voborsky is selected to enroll in the state ballet school in Liberec and is to commence his studies

in September of 1989. This decision, however, is pending upon his acceptance into a certified high school of his choice for the 1989–1990 academic school year.

I finished reading the letter and found myself gazing through the kitchen window. In my body, I was sitting in our kitchen, but in my mind, I imagined Jiri the ballet student in a professional ballet school. I was excited. The only remaining obstacle was the entry exam and its much-needed excellent result. I had to study hard and do my best to prepare for it. My grades have recovered since their decline after Prague. Now I just had to nail this most important exam of my life and do superbly well on it.

For it is God who works in you to will and
act according to his good purpose.
—Philippians 2:13

22) Entry Exam

It was an early morning. Both my mom and dad decided to drive with me to Liberec for the 1989 Official Federal Government High School entry exam. We had to be there by eight, and so we left Ústí around five thirty. My brother, Míra, was asleep as we were leaving, and his face was marked with peace and carelessness. The opposite was true for me. I was nervous. The entry exam consisted of two parts: a Czech language test and a mathematics test. Each one was then divided into sections pertaining to different areas of its field such as grammar, spelling, comprehension of the given text, creative writing, algebra, precalculus, geometry, and so on. There were no multiple choices. The student either knew or simply did not know the answer; they could or couldn't reckon the correct solution to the given problem. With every incorrect answer, the grade of the test declined. It was as simple as that. The total score was then combined with the student's seventh- and eighth-grade point average to calculate the final score of the exam.

We arrived at the school earlier than planned. My parents accompanied me all the way to the stairs of the building before my mom unexpectedly embraced me and whispered, "*To zvládneš*" (*zvlaa-dnesh*), loosely translated as "you can do it." My dad placed his hands on my shoulders and just looked intently into my eyes. He did not say a word. Then they returned to the parked car and drove away to enjoy the day in Liberec and relish being alone. We were to meet again after it was all over, around twelve thirty that afternoon. I walked up the steps. A large Czechoslovak flag was flying suspended above the entry door. A panoramic red banner stating "With the Soviet Union We Stand United Forever" was affixed to the facade of the school. Upon entry, a large picture of the Czechoslovak president, Gustav Husák, welcomed everyone walking in. The current students of the school glanced at the nervous eighth graders, signaling their pity as well as superiority, knowing that they had to undergo the same pressure of this test not too long ago themselves. This was real, and I started to perspire. *Too early for that*, I thought.

Clear signs pointed us to the classrooms set aside for the exams. The setup was simple: a pencil, a ruler, a protractor, and an eraser carefully placed at each desk. At eight o'clock sharp, the school bell rang, and the principal of the school welcomed us through the school radio. A professor walked into the classroom and checked the roll of the registered students. Everyone was present. We started with the Czech language portion of the test. Reading and comprehension was no problem; grammar, however, was difficult. The Czech language is known for its complex grammar and its rules. Spelling and dictation was stressful. I slowly and meticulously plowed through every question. I had two hours to complete all parts of the Czech portion of the exam. I didn't think it was possible for a 120 minutes to go by so fast. Well, they did. A thirty-minute break followed. Everyone engaged in a conversation with those around them comparing the answers they submitted with each other. I felt good about the answers I wrote down. The language was not the problem; math was. And that was yet to come. The thirty-minute break was over before we knew it. Another professor walked in, greeted us, and passed the papers with the mathematical problems on it. Another two-hour segment of sweating, and agony began. This time, it was strenuous. My strategy was to solve what I knew first and then return to the more problematic areas. Geometry was easy, algebra was okay, but calculus was hard. I did not come up with all the answers. Some problems were unsolved before time ran out. That was not good. This could potentially change everything. Discouragement moved in as quickly as the pencil hit the desk, and the papers were collected. The only small comfort in the moment was that many others also did not complete all the problems. There was hope, hanging on a thin hair of others' incompetence, that my overall combined grade of both parts of the test would place me high enough in the lineup. I had to be patient; I had to wait and see. This wait was going to be excruciating.

I walked out of the gymnázium to see my parents leaning against our car, both of them smoking a cigarette. My dad smoked a lot all my life. My mom smoked occasionally when life served her an agitating situation or threw an unexpected surprise her way. This day might not have been surprising, but it was for sure extremely stressful for them both.

"How was it?" they asked in almost perfect unison. *What kind of question is that?* I thought. Then again, we humans have the incongruous ability to ask obtuse questions when we don't know what else to say, how to console or comfort someone, or how to convey our support and understanding of their strenuous situations. I guess my soaked shirt and my pale face signaled the answer clearly. Not knowing what else to say, my dad, the optimist in the family, broke the awkward silence with "Lunch?" My mom threw the remainder of her unsmoked cigarette to the ground, followed by the universal twist of one's foot to extinguish the smoke, and opened the door of the car to get in. "Good idea," she said as she settled in our white Škoda (*Sh-code-ah*), a recently purchased upgrade from the Soviet-made Žiguli we owned since I was a little kid. I followed her lead and got in while taking a brief look at the imposing building of the gymnázium, wondering if my incomplete test would forever close the doors to this school and inevitably to my pursuit of the dance education at the conservatory. We drove away to find a place to eat. I was famished. We all knew that food would not solve the tension prevailing in the atmosphere inside of the car, but it would hopefully lighten up the mood some. We were right.

Trust in the Lord with all your heart and lean not on
your own understanding; in all your ways acknowledge
him, and he will make your paths straight.

—Proverbs 3:5–6

23) Hopelessness Meets Reversal

The results came in. They were discouraging. The letter was simply a disclosure of the conclusion of the exam and whether or not the applicant was admitted to the school. My test grade was a high average, but because I was not a local applicant, I was disqualified from being accepted due to the volume of students desiring to study in this particular high school. I was devastated. Not only was I now unable to study in Liberec in either the gymnázium or the conservatory; I also missed the opportunity to claim a spot in the architectural high school in Prague. I was overwhelmed with a deep feeling of loss and despair. As a young fourteen-year-old, I felt as if I missed my chance—as if I boarded a train that was not connected to a locomotive, thus going nowhere. Why did I make such a foolish decision and cave to the desire of pursuing dance again? Did I not learn my lesson in Prague? Was I really that naïve? It did not matter. It was too late. I would have to wait a year to try to take an entry exam in hopes that I wouldn't be too old to do so. It would also be difficult to take that kind of test while not being in school where the necessary skills are being reviewed every day. There was no other option. Discouragement moved in quickly like water that pours out of a reservoir when the floodgates are open after a heavy rain. It moved in, and I was unwilling to fight it, uninspired to face the reality of my situation. I was hopeless.

Often, when we find ourselves in a desperate moment in life, in a place where everything seems to be closing in on us, there is that special someone who comes to our rescue. As I found myself fretting and feeling sorry for myself, my parents contacted the middle school counselor for her advice and direction. "You can always file an appeal and explain the reason for which Jiri has applied to that particular school in Liberec. I can also add a letter of recommendation stating his academic achievements, his work ethic, and even Jiri's extracurricular activities. It is imperative to include the positive results of his audition for the conservatory with the appeal. I think there is a good chance for them to reverse the decision." She was right. The reversal arrived fairly quickly. I could not believe it. The dead-end street presented an unexpected and unforeseen outlet. What was a hopeless "no" a few weeks ago was now a clear "yes." I was officially going to start studying at two separate schools that September, move to a dorm, and, wait, the dorm! We needed to apply for and secure a place for me in the government-run dormitory in Liberec. With the help of the school counselor, we did just that. Everything was lined up, and I was set to move.

> *He determined the times set for them and the*
> *exact places where they should live.*
>
> —Acts 17:26b

SECOND ACT

TIME TO SAY GOODBYE

24) Moving Away

The rest of the eighth-grade school year, as well as the summer, is a blur. My mind was preoccupied with exciting thoughts of my life in Liberec. It's interesting to me how our imagination often highlights all the positives of what we look forward to, as it completely omits the difficulties of what is yet to come.

The day arrived when my parents and I drove to the Central High School Dormitory on Zeyerova Street in Liberec. We did not need to bring anything but my clothes. We were informed that the rooms were fully furnished and that I needed to bring solely my personal belongings and whatever was required for my school. And so we hit the road, this time without the stressful almost panicky feeling in my gut, with the destination—Liberec. My mom wanted to help me settle in the dorm, though I believe that deep down she and my dad wanted to see the place their firstborn was going to call home away from home, in the hope that the visual connection would bring them much-needed peace of mind. Upon our arrival on Zeyerova Street, found with the assistance of a folded city map, rather than a Google map phone application, we were all surprised to find the dorms housed in a refurbished monastery. A beautiful high iron fence, decorated lavishly and affixed onto a knee-high stonewall, was separating the dormitory complex from the street. Behind it were two massive buildings adorned with steeples, large neo-gothic windows, and a belvedere. One structure housed the female and the other the male student body. Between the two structures lay a large esplanade decorated with trees that, through massive crowns, proudly featured their age. One knew that they have been silent witnesses of so many pages of history.

We stepped into the building designated for the male students. The busyness within reminded me of an anthill that's freshly stirred with a stick held by a naughty child. Everyone was going in a million different directions, hustling to get situated before locating a former chapel now serving as a conference room. There was a scheduled mandatory meeting for all the freshmen and their families. Prior to that, I had to find my room and the in-residence counselor. A broad staircase led to the second-story hallway. One larger-than-life window flooded the stairs with the warm late-summer sunlight, bringing much-needed life into the cold interior of the nineteenth-century dormitory. Once on the second floor, we walked down a long corridor toward a section assigned to the freshmen of the 1989–1990 school year. A counselor welcomed me and my parents and in a very proper way shook all of our hands. "What is your name?" she asked while holding a large folder in her hand. "Voborsky," I said. "My name is Mrs. Hegerová, and I'll be your counselor. This way, please follow me," she continued as she started to walk with quite a defined rhythm in her step into another section of the building. I noticed large bulletin boards hanging on the walls perfectly situated between the Gothic broken arch windows on the right side of the hallway. On them were politically inclined and presumably encouraging materials serving to remind us of the power of the Communist party and its desire to provide for the well-being of the youth and our society as a whole. *Whoever decorated these went all out*, I thought as I tried to keep up with Mrs. Hegerová. "Here you go," she said as she opened a door to what was going to be my room for the next four years. "The bathroom is across the hall, and the showers are in the basement," she said. My parents and I walked in as she remained outside to meet the other arriving students. The room was narrow. Perhaps it was the tall ceiling that caused the room to feel that way, but, nonetheless, it was going to be a challenge to fit myself and my roommates into the small space. The furbishing of the room, promised to be provided in the materials mailed to us prior to our arrival, consisted of three single-size beds accompanied by small nightstands, one square middle-size table with three chairs, and a large wardrobe with three compartments on its left side and a space to hang a few things on its right. A large light fixture was hanging from the ceiling in the middle of the room. Right above each of the beds were small lamps attached to the wall. The room had no power outlets. It was basic but very clean, and for that I was thankful. As we stood inside the room, another young student walked in. "Hello, my name is Michael," he said as he stretched his hand to shake mine and to signal that he desired to be a friend from the very beginning.

"Jiri," I replied as I was less eager to mirror his initial enthusiasm. But he was right—we were going to live together for the next four years, and so we might as well be on good terms. "Is it going to be just the two of us here?" I asked as I noticed that Michael already claimed one of the three beds with his coat thrown on it.

"No, there is one more student living here, I was told," was his reply. "He should be here soon." My parents decided to go wait outside before we walked together to the meeting with the director that afternoon. Michael was thin, and his curly long blond hair indicated the possession of a personality with huge character. "What type of high school are you coming to study?" he asked as he jumped on his bed as if testing its ability to withstand the impact.

"Well, I am a gymnázium student but also a conservatory student," I responded as I purposely withheld the fact that it was a ballet school and not a music school to which I was coming to study. That little nugget was to be shared a little later on, I thought.

"Cool," said Michael. "I am also studying at a gymnázium here in town. I am from Štětí (*Sh-te-tee*). Have you ever heard of it?"

"Hm, sort of," was my hesitation-filled response.

"I have come to Liberec to study at a gymnázium with the emphasis on mathematics and physics," was his follow-up.

"You have got to be kidding me," came out of my mouth without even the smallest ambiguity. "I am not a big fan of math," I continued. "But I'll have to manage to do well in it to receive an ISP and keep it through the four-year process of my studies. I'll have to find a cadence in doing two schools at once."

"If you ever need help, just let me know as I will need help with languages," said Michael. "Do you do well in linguistic studies?" he asked as his face displayed a small hint of hope in my positive answer to his question. Part of the educational system in Czechoslovakia was to start studying Russian as the first foreign mandatory language in fifth grade. In sixth grade, students had to choose another foreign language, usually English or German. Even though growing up close to the German border, I selected English, not having the slightest idea that one day I would live in an English-speaking country and call it my home. It was the loud careless noise of the East German tourists visiting Ústí that forever affected my view of the German language. In the gymnázium-type of high school, students often selected a third language to study, typically French or Latin; but I would categorize those as overachievers. As it is an absolute must for the Czech people to learn foreign languages, the system's design generates a significant strain on the students who might struggle to learn them. Michael seemed to be one of those.

"Yes, languages come quite naturally to me, and I feel that we will be a great help to each other," I said as I tried to convey with my facial expression that the proposed partnership in tutoring is a great idea. "By the way, I am from Ústí nad Labem, just down the river from Štětí."

"Cool," said Michael. "So what type of instrument are you coming to study at the conservatory?" he continued.

Panic flooded my mind as I was trying to desperately find the most diplomatic answer that would not scare my roommate of four years. The word *ballet*, all of a sudden, seemed to be the most difficult word to utter. "Well, it's not a music conservatory but a dance conservatory," was my confession.

"You mean like a ballet school?" Michael gouged deeper into my misery with a straightforward-asked question.

"Yes, a ballet conservatory that is in partnership with the State Theater here in the city," I said as my eyes fell onto, and for the first time noticed, the gray linoleum that covered the floor.

"I look forward to seeing you dance one day, Maestro!" I was shocked to hear him say that without even a hint of sarcasm.

Before I could say anything to respond, our third roommate walked in followed by Mrs. Hegerová. "Fellows, this is Michael, an incoming student at the high school of mechanical engineering," she said as she gazed over the room as if inspecting its status of cleanliness and order.

"Ahoj," said Michael as he extended his hand to meet and greet us. "Ahoj," Czech for *hello*, was our reply.

"My name is Jiri, and this is Michael, Michael," I said while shaking his hand. I started to laugh. "Too bad I wasn't named Michael, as it would be all three of us sharing the same name," I added. They both chuckled, and we all perceived that we would be great roommates during our tenure here in Liberec.

Before we knew it, it was time to hustle into the former chapel for the mandatory meeting with the director. Little did we know then that the gathering was going to be more or less a lecture suited for a course of analytical institutionalism at a college of political science somewhere, rather than the presumed "welcome" that all of us and our parents anticipated. As we trotted into the room, I was struck by the detailed attention that must have gone into transforming this former place of worship into a contemporary space while completely erasing any and all evidence of its original purpose. The only indication to the intended design of the chapel were tall narrow gothic-styled windows that, no doubt, used to be bedecked with stained glass religious-themed images and the floor plan shaping the space in a typical gothic cruciform layout. All original interior decorations and furnishings had been replaced with politically motivated slogans, Communist imagery, and simple, uncomfortable wooden chairs.

The director stepped behind a small podium and lightly tapped the microphone. "Good afternoon, everyone, and welcome to Liberec. We are excited that you are here, and we, as staff, look forward to getting to know your children during their stay here with us." It was clear that the focus of his opening monologue was on the gathered parents rather than the students in the room. "The students are expected to be the foreshadow of the bright future for our beloved homeland. They are to inspire one another to study diligently and to display dedication to the ideals of the Czechoslovak people. Their new home here will be a place of assistance in the pursuit of their degrees, as well as an encouragement to find joy in the political involvement in the Socialist Union of Youth in preparation to one day proudly join the Communist Party of Czechoslovakia. They will be required to work the grounds, clean their rooms, decorate the bulletin boards in correlation with each current holiday, follow the rules, and overall demonstrate their maturity that goes beyond their age. This is their home away from home, and they are to become a family. The expectation of their cooperation goes without saying." His tone and his facial expressions were of a comrade who views himself a bit above his actual political rank, position, or influence. We had to admit that his dedication, though, was unwavering; and he believed every word he said that day. I caught myself drifting in my mind to tomorrow, when, for the first time, I would step into this new exciting chapter of my life and into the pursuit of the future here in Liberec and hopefully even beyond. *I will work hard, I will be focused, I will strive for a place on the stage here at the State Theater only to use it as a stepping-stone to the National Theater. The price to pay will be high, but I am willing. I am ready to pay it and to win the prize called "success."* The director spoke for a long time challenging all of us present, the students and parents alike, to understand what was at stake and to do whatever was necessary to prevail and accomplish what we set out to do while there in the next four years.

After the welcome lecture concluded, everyone slowly exited the room. All of us realized, as if surprisingly and unexpectedly, that we had to part ourselves from the parents and start standing on our own. Goodbyes were heard all across the crowded hallway leading from the former chapel. Some were crying, mostly the parents, as they walked out and left us behind. It was now up to us to prove to them and the world that our upbringing was adequate and thorough for the task at hand. Time would tell. I saw my mom and dad get into their car, and all of a sudden, I came to understand that this next month until I would get to go home again was going to be hard and long. Little did I know just how much and, above all, how lonely.

Do not fear, for I am with you; do not be dismayed, for
I am your God. I will strengthen you and help you; I
will uphold you with my righteous right hand.

—Isaiah 41:10

25) The Commencement of the School/s

I woke up early. Adrenaline, I assumed. Michael the math whiz was already up, whereas Michael the engineer was happily snoozing on. I had to get dressed, eat breakfast, and find my way to the gymnázium. I wasn't sure exactly how to get there, but I knew that I had to take a bus and transfer to a tramline at the Šalda square stop. I was hoping that other high schoolers would be going to the gymnázium as well, and I could simply follow them.

I was surprised how crowded the washroom was. The sinks lining one side of the bathroom were overwhelmed with the number of eager freshmen that were all on the same page of facing the "big day," as well as struggling, like I was, with the uncertainty of knowing how to find their school before 8:00 a.m. I squeezed in to brush my teeth. This was not the time to meet any of them—to try to get their names, to make acquaintances. I had to stay focused on getting out of the washroom in record time. I managed. I got dressed in my room while keeping an eye on the alarm clock sitting on my tiny nightstand. It was showing 6:50. Both Michael and I were bewildered by the calm slumber of our third roommate who had his alarm set for 7:15. We made our beds, as that was one of the requirements of the dorm directorate, and hustled to the cafeteria inconveniently located in the girls' building. Once we arrived, the line for food was enormous, and Michael and I both felt the increase in our doubts of the first day being marked with success. As long as the line was, it was also moving quickly. The group of kitchen ladies dressed in white standing behind a metal-framed window was used to the morning rush of hungry high schoolers and dished out breakfast items with speed and efficiency. By 7:10 or so, we were on our way to the bus stop. Both of us rode together to the Šalda square where our paths parted. Neither Michael nor I had purchased bus tickets in advance, and so we rode the transit system without paying. That was stressful. The bus stop by our dormitory was not equipped with a ticket machine, and that left us with no choice. On my to-do list for this first day was to purchase a long-term public transportation pass, but this morning, I had to ride without a ticket hoping that I would not get caught. The bus ride was only two stops. Who knew? The Šalda square stop was a busy transfer place. The trams were running in two directions, and I had no clue which way was the right way or which number was the correct tramline that would take me to my school. *How many times in life do we feel that we have no idea which way is the right way?* I thought. I was correct in anticipating many students crowding around the stops. I had to ask for help, no matter how uncomfortable it might have been. I was pointed to the right stop and tramline number just in time to catch the approaching double-car tram. What I did not anticipate was just how immensely crowded these transportation vehicles would be. The positive was that no one was validating the commuters' tickets, and that was, at least for today, a huge relief. The streetcars had three sets of doors each. Before each door had an opportunity to fully open, by folding like an accordion to both of its sides, the morning rush straphangers were jumping out of the cars to continue their commute. Those of us on the outside gave them a moment to exit before we would, in the same stress-filled manner, enter the trams. Once inside, I was shoved into a gentleman who was clearly annoyed with life and its inconveniences. As I was squeezed in between the many bodies crowding the tram, I found myself barely standing on one foot that was not even my own while attempting to hold on to any part of the streetcar for balance. Due to its crowding, that was an unnecessary worry. All of us were forced to quickly become extremely intimate with complete strangers. What blew me away was the ability of some around me to read the daily newspapers, or even books, while performing this challenging act of balancing in the moving vehicle while invaded by these sojourners pressing deeply into one's personal space. Little did I know then that I myself would soon become an expert of doing just that while trying to catch up on my studies during the daily commutes.

The tram ride was much longer than the bus connection to it. I noticed when we passed the conservatory building, which was a useful location to know, that the transit hub was located near the school. There I would be able to purchase tickets and the pass later. I was paying a detailed attention to the route and the surrounding buildings and even landmarks to assist me in becoming familiar with the city of Liberec.

We arrived at our stop, Vápenka, where all the students got off the tram. The stop prior to Vápenka was dominated by a delightful smell of freshly baked bread. The scent was flooding the streets from a huge government-run bakery factory which provided bread to all the smaller bakeries as well as the supermarkets around town. From now on, the fresh-out-of-the-oven aroma would be a helpful reminder that my terminating stop was coming up. After I crossed the street, I followed the crowd of students up a steep hill through several blocks of the city until we emerged by the imposing structure of the liberal arts gymnázium. I did not realize at that moment that this building would become a continual source of stress, sleepless nights, worry, and an overwhelming sense of anxiety for the next four years.

Once inside the school, it was easy to locate my classroom on the third floor. Thirty-eight freshmen were gathering in and slowly finding unclaimed and available seats. The setup was typical for a Czech school. The desks were arranged in three rows of seven. Each desk was shared by two students. I chose to sit in the first row on the opposite side from the professor's desk. In the front of the room was a large blackboard, a sink with a bar of soap, and a hand towel hanging on a hook. The wall behind the professor's desk had a framed photograph of the Czechoslovak president, Husák, with the national coat of arms hanging below. The best feature of the classroom was the three large windows sprawling across the wall opposite the door, allowing a large amount of daylight to flood the room and bring the much-needed encouragement to the minds of the students. The rear wall of the classroom had a bulletin board with Communist slogans and images. The bulletin boards were a popular and inexpensive tool to continually display political propaganda to the students and the staff of these institutions of higher education. "Is this chair taken?" interrupted my intake of the class and the people. "No, it's not taken," I said. "My name is Radek. Can I sit here? I can't see that well, and so I need to sit up front," he continued. "Please," I said as I gestured hand motion toward the chair on my left-hand side. "My name is Jiri, and it's nice to meet you, Radek." We shook hands, and he took the seat.

The bell rang precisely at eight. A man in his early thirties walked in to a sigh of the female segment of the class. "Hello and good morning, everyone. My name is Josef Vondráček, and I will be your class professor." His deep-blue eyes reflected warmth and positive encouragement. The September sunlight pouring in through the large windows greatly highlighted his curly hair. He wore a dress shirt with the top two buttons unbuttoned. A belt around his waist nicely sculpted his physique. That for sure was going to be a distraction to the ladies attending his classes. There was something calming about him, I thought. That notion changed the moment he continued to speak. "I will be teaching you math these next four years. I would like to start by stating that there are thirty-eight of you. Please, look around, for there will most likely not be thirty-eight of you graduating. This institution requires a lot from each student. You will need to work hard while here, and you will need to work hard while at home. You cannot progress or keep up if you don't put in the necessary work of studying. There are twelve academic subjects that are a part of the curriculum: Czech language and literature, two foreign languages of your choice, math, physics, chemistry, biology, philosophy, history, geography, music and visual art class, and a computer science class. The schedule is pretty straightforward with each day being divided into eight individual forty-five-minute periods. We start at eight, and you will be glad to leave here at three forty. There is a forty-five-minute lunch period starting at one o'clock. Czech language, math, history, geography, philosophy, will be taught here, every other subject has its own special classroom located around the building. Major final tests are announced in advance. Oral exams, as well as quizzes, are to be expected at the beginning of every class without prior notice. Your grade simply will be the average of all your grades collected throughout the semester. In order to move to sophomore year, you will need to have passed every subject." As he hurled this information out at us in a brisk and overwhelming manner, he would walk through the two aisles between the three rows of desks and give each of us the class schedule. It seemed that no one breathed. Then he walked to the front of the classroom and sat on the corner of his desk. "The school does require a lot, but we are here for you. Not all of you will do well in all the subjects. We have different strengths and expertise, even academically. The purpose of the school is to pre- pare you for university studies in the future. To be accepted into the college of your choice, you need to have excellent graduation grades. We will do our best to prepare you for the graduation exam, but you need to put in the required work. We all know that gymnázium is also called the 'grammar school'"—his fingers signaled the universal sign for quotation marks—"because the courses here are packed with so much material to learn and comprehend. When you start to feel overwhelmed, and you will, remind yourself that you have qualified to be here and that you possess the wits to successfully graduate from this institution prepared for whatever will be required of you when attending college." He smiled a little to ease the tension in the room. "Now I will give you your textbooks. Please take care of them in order to pass them along to those after you, unless you yourself will need them should you have to repeat a grade," he said as he laughed at his own joke. "To do that, I will need some men to come with me and assist me in bringing the books here. Volunteers?" All of us guys in the room raised our hands. He selected six men from the row by the windows to follow him. The amount of textbooks they returned with was alarming. Every subject had its own large encyclopedia-like course book, and we needed to never come to school without the correct book corresponding to the schedule. He passed them all to us. "Now let's get to know each other a little." One by one, each student would state their name and where they were from. Professor Vondráček also asked us to share which subject was our strength and if we knew what type of major we would like to study at a university following the gymnázium studies. There were only three of us from out of town. I was the only student living in a dorm, as the other two commuted daily to Liberec from towns nearby. A lot of the students present desired to study law, there were some aspiring journalists, one actress-want-to-be, several desired to study political science, and some wanted to become teachers. Radek, sitting next to me, wanted to study oboe at a music conservatory after his graduation from the school and today, indeed, plays in the orchestra of the National Theater in Prague. Some classmates achieved their goals and received law degrees, two are chairs of University Departments, many publish books, several of them are high school professors today, and at least one, to my knowledge, has become a lifelong diplomat. There, indeed, was one student who was dismissed from the gymnázium in the junior year due to her inability to keep up with the required work. I was the only student who desired to become a dancer. I felt comfortable in the gathered and versatile endeavoring student body where every student dreamed to reach high goals.

After we were dismissed, as this was a short day, I had to meet with Professor Vondráček and the head principal of the school regarding the necessary individual study plan approval I needed in order to be able to study at both schools simultaneously. It took me a while to locate his office. As I did, a quick thought of a gangster movie clip flashed through my head. I knew that with my potential struggles in mathematics I would be knocking on these doors quite often and should things not go well, I would most likely be proverbially banished by the "godfather" with the curly hair and deep blue eyes who dwelt behind them.

I knocked with determination to demonstrate my resolve in establishing a good partnership with my class professor, as I would most likely need his tutoring and support during the course of the school year. "Come in," came from behind the door. And so I entered. "Hello, Comrade Professor," was the expected greeting to the faculty members of the gymnázium, as well as any other high school in the country. "I am here to talk with you about my ISP. I understand that I need to meet with the head principal as well, but I felt that I needed to start here with you." "Sit down please," was not what I expected to hear first, but it brought me a huge sense of peace to be invited to do just that. This meeting was crucial, and I guess my nerves were clearly demonstrating their drama skills accompanied by glittering sweat appearing on my forehead and my brow. "Mr. Voborsky, right?" he went on. "Yes, Comrade Professor." He looked through the files of the thirty-eight students in his class, piled up on his desk. To my astonishment, they were perfectly alphabetized. My life records highlighting all its successes and all its failures fit into a narrow folder placed toward the bottom of the pile. "Here we go," he continued as he delicately pulled my file out of the lineup while not wanting to besmirch the rest of the stack. "I see that your middle school grades are great and that you were able to juggle a lot prior to finishing middle school. I do see here that you were not accepted into the gymnázium until after you filed your appeal. Let's see why you weren't accepted right away…" His voice intensity decreased as if he was more or less talking to himself rather than to me. He carried on reading through my records and then said, "I see, you did not do that well on your entry math exam, right?" With that, he looked at me as if expecting me to say something profound. My mind went blank. "Right," was all I could come up with. I felt as if I just spoke a death sentence over myself. *Think! Think!* was going through my head, but nothing was coming out to assist in my defense. "Math is a bit of a struggle for me," I continued as if enjoying the self-humiliation and belittling of myself in front of the one who was most likely born with a natural inclination to delight himself in algorithms, derivatives, and integrals of functions. "Well, to be honest with you, Mr. Voborsky," he said, continually looking into my eyes making me feel intimidated, "many struggle with different aspects of math. The bottom line is that the school reversed its original decision and, after looking over all your grades and your reasoning for applying to study with us, decided to enroll you to do just that. You will need to work hard, and now you know where my office is should you ever need help or extra tutoring. In order to keep your ISP, you will need to remain on the A and B honor roll, and that will be extremely difficult as you might miss many lectures. Do you know the conservatory schedule yet?" "I do not. I have my first meeting there at two o'clock this afternoon," I replied while focusing to keep looking into his deep blue eyes and not show my demureness by looking away. I had to win this staring contest if this was the last thing I ever did, I persuaded myself. "Let's go up to the head principal's office for the official interview," he said. I couldn't have agreed more than to leave this awkward conversation with a man who most likely felt as sorry for me as I felt for him.

The head principal's office was located on the second floor of the main building. Professor Vondráček knocked on the door and, with a wink directed at me, opened it boldly once we heard the command to enter. The office was the same size as the classrooms of the school as it was located directly beneath one of those, thus sharing its identical floor plan. Three large windows were decorated with curtains; and besides the photograph of the president and the coat of arms of Czechoslovakia, there were no other Communist or political elements present. A long diagonally situated table was leading toward a perpendicular desk of the principal. There were five chairs on either side of the long table as this room must have been used for the faculty conferences. The wall behind the desk was graced with large bookcases filled with volumes of important-looking books and decorated with Bohemian crystal dishes, a coffee mug set, and several glass vases of different sizes. The rest of the furnishing of the office was a brown-colored loveseat and two matching sofa chairs surrounding a small coffee table. A brief moment after we closed the door behind us, a lady seated behind the desk, fervently working over documents sprawled across its surface, slowly lifted her head to look at whoever just walked in. Her eyes were looking through a pair of reading glasses and yet displayed a feeling of care and an ardent character of a leader who cared for the well-being of those who followed. I could tell right away of the deep admiration Professor Vondráček had for his superior. "Dr. Kutínová (*Koo-tee-no-vah*), this is Jiri Voborsky, and he is coming here today to be officially interviewed for your approval for the requested ISP he needs to study here at the liberal arts gymnázium in order to be able to concurrently attend the state ballet school." I was encouraged by the tone of his voice as if signaling his suggested approval of my request. Dr. Kutínová walked across her office slowly extending her arm to meet me and to shake my hand. "I have read your request," she started, "and I am curious to hear more about your aspirations to become a ballet dancer. We do not meet people like you every day. Both Professor Vondráček and I stand amazed by the commitment you are making to follow your dream. Tell us about that please." As we stood there in her office, I was able to convey not only verbal information but, more importantly, my heart's desire to make the dream of becoming a dancer come true. They understood that I was ready to do whatever life and its demands requested of me and determined to run the race over these next four years. As I was speaking, I sensed a rise of unique boldness granting me the furtherance of my case and ultimately gaining the approval of the principal to be granted the needed ISP. As long as I maintained a high grade average, I was permitted to study at the school on my own terms. I could attend and or miss lectures, and I could schedule individual test times with professors. But most importantly, I was able to attend and fully devote myself to the studies at the conservatory. This battle was won, and I felt such relief.

I walked down the streets from the school in rapid agility. I needed to catch a tram toward the center of the city. I remembered passing the conservatory earlier that day, but I was not quite sure which stop would be the closest one to the ballet school. My excitement was increasing as I rode through the streets of Liberec. Today was the day I was going to meet the other students that I saw during the auditions. I had no idea who made it in and who was eliminated. I remembered the girl I met that rainy day, Petra, and I wondered whether or not she was invited to attend the school as well. The tram stopped at the imposing 1859 brick building of the Czechoslovak Railways directly situated across the Peace Avenue from the Glass Export Corporation. This company was directly responsible for the sale of Czechoslovak-made crystal glass to the world. I knew that the next stop would be mine to exit the tram.

As we rode down Peace Avenue, my heart rate increased in frequency. The next stop was it, and I jumped out of the tram the moment the doors opened. I waited for the double streetcar to leave the station before I crossed the street. As I was walking across, my eyes caught a glimpse of the large building of the state ballet school proudly standing on a corner of two streets. Its large curved façade was topped with a green-colored domed tower overlooking the two intersecting roads. The ballet academy was a part of a large performing arts school, daily packed with students coming in to perfect the art of playing a musical instrument, to be coached in voice training, or to learn the craft of visual art and its forms. As I approached the building, I heard music as well as classical voice lessons flow beautifully out of the open windows. I reached the main entrance shortly before one thirty in the afternoon with a good half an hour to spare until the beginning of the first class. Upon entry, the gentleman sitting behind a window in the entry hall pointed me to the third floor of the building. "Take the elevator, and on the third floor, turn to the right," he said. The arts school building had two large sections. The historic building was a four-winged structure surrounding a large courtyard. Each wing had classrooms on one side and a wide corridor overlooking the center of the building on the other. The modern section of the school held the ballet studios. As I walked in, it was apparent that the final finishing touches were yet to be done to complete the new structure. As I located the elevator, other dancers caught up with me. These were going to be my friends for the next four year. The elevator was small and crowded. Nobody said a word. Once we reached the third floor, we saw a sign directing us to the right hallway leading toward the ballet studios. It was then when we all knew that we were to be classmates. Exchanges of names took place accompanied by kisses on the cheeks. It was interesting to me, as that was not a custom among the general population of Czechoslovakia to do so. In the dance world, one artist would not meet another without the symbolic cheek-to-cheek kiss. I followed suit. We all walked into the ballet studio where others were already present. Petra was among them. "Ahoj, Jiri," she said, "do you remember me?" "Ahoj," I replied, and we greeted each other in the new artsy way of a cheek-to-cheek peck. Petra went ahead and introduced me to some other dancers she met moments prior to my arrival. Everyone was so young and so eager to start this new exciting adventure of following our dreams of reaching the stage and receive the applause and the recognition that was to come, should we apply ourselves to the rigid requirements of the academy.

Professor Gabajová entered the studio exactly at 1400 hours. If one can imagine an older lady who once was a ballerina, Mrs.

Gabajová would most likely fit perfectly into that image. She walked and stood in a perfect turned-out manner while her upper body reflected a regal buoyancy and cheerful optimism. A shawl—worn loosely over her shoulders, allowing her thin long neck and pressed down shoulders to highlight her dancer posture—was always a part of her attire. She would accompany her poised arm gestures with a dramatic movement of her upper body and head beautifully graced by shortly cut silver gray hair. Professor Gabajová was often recognized on the streets of Liberec by the general public while also being remembered by the theatergoers for her artistry shining powerfully from the stage when delivering her moving performances of the classical repertoire. Her ability to draw the audience into whatever role or tale she was dancing set her apart as one of the greatest principal dancers of Czechoslovakia. Now she walked into the ballet studio facing a generation a few years younger than her own children. She knew that the very first impression she was going to make was crucial for her ability to have the full, undivided attention of the students in order to shape them into those who would follow in her footsteps in the art of classical ballet.

"Good afternoon, everyone, and congratulations," was her opening headline. "You are the first class of the Liberec State Ballet School. We have so much to prove, so much to accomplish, so much to learn. Everyone's eyes are on you. There are many in Prague waiting to see if this experiment of ours will bear the fruit we believe is possible. There are some doubters but also so many supporters. The best dance experts our country has to offer will be commuting here from Prague, as well as Bratislava, to give you the opportunity to glean from their expertise and learn everything they have to offer. In just a moment, Mr. Pokorný will come in with the principal of the academy to welcome you and share with you the basic structure of the curriculum of the school. While we are waiting for their arrival, I would like for you all to introduce yourselves to each other." It turned out that there were thirty-two of us selected for the first grade of the conservatory, sixteen ladies and sixteen gentlemen. We all also shared what type of regular high school we were attending alongside the dance studies. Many of us were gymnázium students, to my surprise, but there were students of the economic high school, medical high school, architectural high school, and others. Everyone shared the same anxiety over the schedule received in these schools earlier today. We realized the suspenseful anticipation of receiving our schedule here to see how we can blend them together. Professor Gabajová followed our introductions with assigning our places at the ballet barre. We started to realize the attention to detail that was going to be a part of the learning process here. The large ballet studio sprawled across the entire width of the building. Four large windows were evenly placed across the wall opposite the entry door. The busy street below was hustling with early afternoon crowds of traffic and pedestrians. Being on the third floor, however, made the noise of life beneath vanish and be beyond perceptible. In the hours and years yet to come, to be spent in this room, many times I would find myself interrupted by gazing into the streets underneath, desiring often to be out there rather than in here. There were mirrors attached to two perpendicular walls of the ballet hall. Two permanently attached ballet barres, one slightly above the other, were affixed to the mirror walls. Free standing barres were also located in the room. An upright piano was placed diagonally in the corner of the studio. Behind it was a sound system box, always to be locked and unlocked by a key received from the man sitting in the entry foyer of the school. Next to the sound system cabinet was a door leading to a small closet. The last items in the studio were two large acrobatic mats rolled up against the wall. I had never taken a ballet class with thirty-one other dancers. I understood the competitive force coming from all these around me, as we would challenge each other to be stronger, to be better, and to leave the studio every day noticed by the faculty.

Mr. Pokorný entered the studio with the director of the performing arts school. Both of them welcomed us to the academy and challenged us to recognize the unique opportunity at hand to do what had not been done before—to learn everything the conservatory had to offer, to rise above our age, and to set our gaze on the goals cherished deeply in our hearts. We all stood there as we listened to them sharing their inspirational remarks and their passions with us. It was apparent that they truly believed in the uniqueness of this school. It was not until several years later when we learned about the deep efforts Mr. Pokorný had to put into making the Liberec Ballet School possible. The greatest obstacle he faced was the Communist regime fearing to veer from the purely Soviet model of ballet education, not knowing what consequences there could be should this school succeed and produce graduates that could outshine those of the Prague, Bratislava, and Košice conservatories, that purely followed the structure and curriculum of the prestigious Vaganova Academy in Leningrad. His ongoing trips and meetings at the Department of Education in Prague, as well as the Politburo, were not disclosed to us or the faculty of the academy. His perseverance and courage made the opening and continuation of the school possible—securing all the necessary approval notices, finances, and certificates required by the socialist government. All this was taking place while Mr. Pokorný continued to lead the ballet company of the state theatre, serving as its resident choreographer, all the while being responsible for the academic direction of the conservatory. Mr. Pokorný also taught the *pas de deux* class, stage course, choreography, and acrobatic classes.

This day, however, Mr. Pokorný focused on the work at hand. "The curriculum that we structured and put together here is designed to excavate the greatest amount of the potential hidden in each and every one of you. We saw something special in you all during the auditions. Now we will do our best to bring it forth. There will be two ballet technique classes every day. There will be pointe classes for the ladies and allegro technique classes for the men. We hired professors from Prague to come and on a regular basis teach you Martha Graham modern technique class and Limón technique class. We will study different styles of character dance, pantomime, tap dance, jazz, and partnering also known as pas de deux. There is a stage presence class on the roster which will include acting, story conveying, stage makeup and basics of costuming. You will have a history of dance class, choreography lectures, theory of music, and all of you will have to study a musical instrument. After we dismiss you today, you can find the office in the historic section of the building and sign up for the instrument of your choice. Here is the schedule for this first semester. As you look over it, we want you to know that in order to move to the sophomore, or the second level of the academy, you will need to perform and pass a ballet technique class exam in front of a committee of dance experts and the general public. This exam, as well as all the other exams between each grade, will be held at the historic building of the Liberec F. X. Šalda State Theater. Your parents are welcome to attend these public exams as they are not permitted to view any of the classes here. Every student of the conservatory has received an allotment of ballet shoes and pointe shoes, for the ladies only, of course. These are to be received at the costume assembly facilities of the theater located nearby. As students of the school, you will receive a student card allowing you to attend any performance of the ballet, opera, or drama companies free of charge. At the commencement of the second semester, you will begin to participate in the ballet company's productions, starting as a supporting cast member. Some of you might be offered contracts as corps de ballet members with the company, if we feel that your work ethic, your grades, and your dedication, as well as your technique, meet the requirements. Questions?" I was overwhelmed. I realized that my expectations of what the study would look like did not meet the actual presented load just quantified upon us. The schedule that was passed to us included a ballet technique class that started at six thirty in the morning. This class concluded at eight fifteen, giving us the opportunity to attend the academics in the regular high school, only to return for the afternoon ballet class starting at one forty five. The dance schedule ended each day at five thirty. On Thursdays, we had to attend theory classes commencing at six o'clock, inconveniently held at the directorate building of the State Theater located some twenty-five minutes away from the ballet school. Tuesdays were reserved for our instrument private lesson, also following our last dance class. The first three Saturdays of each month had classes taught by the guest faculty members and would alternate between pantomime, tap class, and the two modern technique classes. I must admit that I had never heard of either of the previously mentioned names, Graham and Limón, but I was determined to walk to the city library and do my research. The last Saturday of every month was free allowing me to leave Liberec and go home for the weekend. The reality started to settle in and hit me pretty hard. How was I going to manage to combine the two schedules? When did the cafeteria at the dorm close, and would I make it there for dinner? Breakfast was not an option for two reasons: one, the cafeteria wasn't open at the time I needed to leave the dorm to be here on time, and two, I did not want to eat anything before dancing at such an ungodly hour of six thirty in the morning. *I have to make sure to eat a quick lunch at the gymnázium before I come here,* I encouraged myself. Then I panicked. "When was my lunch break starting there?" I did not remember that minor detail at the moment and had to locate and look at my high school schedule. I could not believe it. The lunch started at one o'clock. That meant that I had forty-five minutes to eat, to run to catch my twenty-minute tram ride, walk to the conservatory, and be at the ballet barre at one forty-five dressed in my white shirt and black ballet tights ready to exhale and start my demi pliés. The dorm cafeteria closed at six o'clock; and so on Mondays, Wednesdays, Fridays, and the weekends, I was able to eat two hot meals in one day if I rushed out of the academy the minute our mandatory acknowledgment of the professor at the end of each class concluded. The challenge would be arriving at the dorm in time to put my foot into the doors moments before the cafeteria staff would shut them closed. The rest of the week was going to be tough when it came to food. There was a little time carved into the weekly hullabaloo, to be able to study and keep up my academic grades. It was going to be a challenge, to say the least. Could all this be sustainable? Would I break, or would I rise to the occasion? I was not sure. Fear and insecurity started to show their ugly heads in my mind and heart. Only time would tell.

We concluded around four o'clock. My next must-to-do objective was to receive a pass to be able to use the public transit network unrestrictedly. Petra offered to show me where the pass could be purchased. I gladly utilized her offer as I had a very limited understanding of the general layout of the city. I was glad to have been born with a natural sense of direction and ability to navigate through unknown territory, but it would take some time to gain my bearings of this town. As we walked out of the academy building, the September afternoon started to cool down as the sun began to disappear behind the horizon, and the buildings of the city started to cast shadows onto the pavement of the streets beneath. It was a beautiful day, a busy day, a successful day; and I was thankful. After I received my transit pass, Petra and I parted ways, and I went to the dorm to eat my dinner and to get organized for the rest of this first week of my new life in Liberec. I knew one thing—I was going to sleep well tonight!

> *Do you not know that in a race all the runners run, but only one gets the prize. Run in such a way as to get the prize.*
> —1 Corinthians 9:24

26) Cheater

Days turned into weeks, and I started to slowly catch and find the rhythm of this new life while finding a balance between living on my own far away from the family I loved and missed so much and the undivided focus the studies required. Both schools demanded an enormous amount of attention, strength, zeal, and resolve. I would get up faithfully at five thirty while quietly sneaking out of my room in an attempt not to wake up my roommates, wash up, and be ready to leave the dormitory campus no later than ten minutes before six in the morning. I discovered a shortcut from the dorms to the ballet school, and with a swift vigor in my walk, I could reach the academy in eighteen minutes. That would give me enough time to get dressed, warm up, and stretch before the morning ballet technique class began. After its conclusion, I would run across the street from the conservatory and buy two freshly baked pastries only to catch the 8:33 tram number 3 taking me to the gymnázium in hopes to get there just after the second period had started.

It did not take very long for me to realize that the academics would require an enormous amount of studying done outside of the classroom. I increased my efficiency in speed reading as well as improved my ability to study in crowded public transportation vehicles while completely ignoring the noise, as well as the often ridiculous closeness, of other passengers. As I had anticipated, some courses would be an easy glide through the mandated curriculum, and I would do well. In contrast to these, there were classes that I found to be strenuously difficult from the beginning. It became apparent to me that to continually miss certain lectures would eventually become unbearable. I would fall too far behind, and the hopes of making even a B would vanish into thin air. One of those was chemistry. In the Czechoslovak education system, students entered the world of chemical science in the seventh grade. This nightmare of chemical bonds, electronic structure, thermochemistry, to name a few, would continue through the junior year of high school. As I did all right in middle school, once I reached the high school level of this particular subject, I started to struggle. I was unable to attend most of the oral lectures due to the schedule of the dance classes. The professor of chemistry, Mrs. Havlíková, was firm and disinterested in extending a helpful hand to those of us who desperately needed additional assistance in grasping the principles of the invisible world of chemical formulas. I was on my own. My roommate, Michael, was a great help in explaining what I did not understand from simply reading the textbook and instrumental in cohering for me the disconnected elements of my comprehension. While in my sophomore year of the gymnázium, I had scheduled a time to take a written test in Mrs. Havlíková's office. My nerves and fear to possibly fail this major exam forced me to do what I would never consider doing or risking before. I had explored the questions and problems present in the test from the classmates who had already taken the exam. I was smart enough not to receive 100 percent on it; but I used their answers to do, well, let's just say, very well. I had never cheated on a test before. I recall the deep struggle within my conscience between right and wrong, between honesty and dishonesty, between the present and the future of what I would turn into, should this habit of cheating become the new normal. No matter how badly I struggled with the cognitive battle, my determination to proceed with dishonesty prevailed. Other professors were also present in the office, and their occasional chatting gave me the opening to glimpse into my notes and to copy the answers. I finished the test as Professor Havlíková worked on unrelated things in her office. I submitted my test to her, expressed my gratitude for allowing me to be examined on my desired time, and without delay withdrew from her presence. The following week, I was attending a lecture of polymer chemistry when, upon the entry of Professor Havlíková, I was summoned to the front of the class. The chemistry lab was set up in a descending manner. Students were seated in rows of large long desks a step above from one another. As I got up to walk down to the front of the class, my heart was racing. "What was about to happen?" If guilt were a visible entity, I would most likely resemble a large neon billboard lit up and placed on a high hill for all to see. As I was approaching the blackboard, Professor Havlíková extended her arm with a piece of white chalk in her hand. This simply innocent movement was accompanied by a statement that has been permanently cemented into my memory: "Mr. Voborsky, you did exceptionally well on the written exam last week. I wanted to ask you to please demonstrate to the class the expertise of your knowledge in inorganic chemistry. It has become apparent that your appreciation of the organometallic compounds has grown exponentially. Would you solve the following double displacement please?" I reached for the white chalk and a piece of paper in her hand that stated the given problem. As I lifted my eyes to the large blackboard before me, a sudden panic mode triggered my emotions. I never wanted to vanish from existence, except for this very moment, that is. Professor Havlíková took three steps back toward her desk as she folded her arms across her chest. I did not dare to look her way, but I felt the burning laser-like stare coming in my direction. Double displacement is basically a process of bonds exchanged between two nonreacting chemicals, resulting in a creation of a new bond with similar qualities. A formula for this equation is simple, and once the given elements are plugged in, the results are fairly easily realized. The fact that I knew the answer in the moment shocked me more than I can convey. The present despair also caused me to remember the needed formula. And so I proceeded and with chalk dust flying from the blackboard, a motion picture—like moment unfolded in front of the rest of the class. All we needed was a climactic soundtrack of sorts to complete the drama of it all. After the dust settled, I stepped away from the blackboard to unveil my answer. I slowly turned my head to face Professor Havlíková, who did not seem to care to see the answer. She approached me with her arms still folded across her chest. Once but a breath away, she stated in a very condescending tone, "Impressive! I see that you have, indeed, become the expert. Please sit down." As I was walking away up those steps to my seat on the third level of the student section of the laboratory, I was certain without a doubt that Professor Havlíková perceived that I cheated. Deep down, I hoped that she would simply ask me. The guilt was so heavy to bear. The fact that I was able to solve the problem this day was short of a miracle, and we both knew that. I sat in my chair. My face was bright red, and I was sweating profusely. Some might say that I got away with cheating, but all I knew was the fact that I was now a cheater. And that bothered me terribly. If I could retake and redo this experience, I would not make the same mistake again. But in life, redos do not happen. We can only move forward and learn from our previous mistakes. I never cheated on another test again.

The Lord hates dishonest scales, but accurate weights are his delight.
—Proverbs 11:1

27) Bulletin Boards

Before I knew it, September yielded to October, and the streets began to be decorated with leaves of breathtaking, gorgeous fall colors. The sun no longer shone with the same warm intensity and chilly wind would force the citizens of Liberec to veil themselves in rain jackets and walk with the accompaniment of large umbrellas. One thing that happened every October was the nationwide preparation for the annual remembrance and celebration of the Soviet October Revolution of 1917. In all actuality, the preparations were purely done by the Communist Party and the governmental institutions, not by the Czechoslovak people themselves. Before I dive into the meaning of this mandated holiday, I want to take a moment to share the apprehensive dilemma I experienced in the dorm with the leadership there. Shortly after I somewhat succeeded in finding the path through the rhythm of balancing the schedule of two schools in the first couple of weeks of the semester, all of the freshmen were called to the hallway of the dorm. Our counselor, Mrs. Hegerová, summoned us to attention and then presented us with the following: "As you all have been told during the initial meeting with the director of the dormitory, every student here is responsible to contribute in taking care of the vast grounds of the campus. As the fall season is upon us, the falling leaves will require all students to find time to meet the required hours to complete their assigned yard work. I have brought a diagram that shows how the grounds have been parceled between each grade of the students here. Everyone must participate. Everyone has an assigned portion to care for and maintain. It will require about ninety minutes a week for each of you to dedicate to the yard work and such. I will post the assignment chart on the bulletin board to allow you to familiarize yourself with your new responsibility. You are dismissed!" With that, Mrs. Hegerová pinned the large piece of paper to the board and walked away. We were shocked to learn that, on top of everything school related, we also had to work here at the dormitory and keep a log of all our completed hours. My initial worry was not the calluses on my hands or the sore back as a by-product of the ninety minutes of weekly "yard exercise," but it was the difficulty of finding the ninety minutes to do this every week. Daylight was getting shorter, and soon it would be pitch-black upon my return to the dorm, too dark to work the grounds. I decided to voice my concern to the counselor and seek her advice. As I went into a detailed and deep, dramatically conveyed, description of everything that was already on my plate, I was hoping that Mrs. Hegerová would not see me as someone who was trying to get off the hook, so to speak. As I finished my unprepared and unrehearsed speech, I was doubtful that any leniency from her side would be gained. Mrs. Hegerová stood in the doorway to her office with puzzled facial expression, as if trying to solve an extremely challenging legal case suited only for the wisdom of the Supreme Court. Then she spoke: "I have no jurisdiction to decide whether or not you can be the only student excused from the required work, but I will bring your situation before the director of the dormitory to see what he wants to do."

"Thank you," I replied, and I walked out of her office and headed to my room. Both Michaels, my roommates, were already there, and as one can imagine, we had nothing good to say about this newly proposed manual yard work scenario. As it turned out, none of us had any spare time to dedicate to this task of ground beautification while balancing schoolwork and studies required by our schools. But we all concluded that there is no sense of complaining about this irreversible decision of the directorate and settled on simply waiting for the instructions and directions that were to follow. Two days later, I was sought out by Mrs. Hegerová to be informed of the decision of the leadership. "Due to the unique predicament you find yourself in, of studying two schools at the same time, the director has graciously pardoned you from the responsibility of working the grounds," I was told. Before I could do a little celebration dance, internally speaking of course, Mrs. Hegerová continued her notification with the following nugget: "We feel that all students who live in the dormitories here, and thus share the grounds of the complex, need to be equally responsible in sharing the load of the allotted work. Due to *your* unique situation, we have decided to exchange your responsibility for indoor work with the privilege of being responsible for the decoration and upkeep of the bulletin boards in the dorm. How does that sound?" My mind managed to do what it perfected itself in doing best, and that is to go blank. *Did I just hear Mrs. Hegerová correctly? I could have been raking leaves and possibly shoveling some snow, but instead, I am now the mastermind of designing politically stimulating bulletin boards that will most likely be completely ignored at best or at worst ridiculed by my peers at my expense!* And so I nodded and walked away in disbelief. I reached the corner of the two intersecting hallways when I heard Mrs. Hegerová call, "And we would like you to decorate them for the October Revolution we will celebrate this month, please. We have some materials that you can reuse as well as supply your own to make them as inspiring as possible." *Did she just say 'inspiring'?* I thought. Growing up, I would see the October decorations appear in my elementary and middle schools, as well as see them cloak the façades of prominent public buildings of Ústí, with images and slogans of this great political victory of the working class in Russia. But if honest with myself, my knowledge and understanding of the "Great October's" significance was at best textbook level amassed for a test only to be forgotten immediately thereafter. And so in order to do somewhat well on the bulletin boards, I needed to do some research. One must keep in mind that research of any kind back in the 1980s required a trip to the public library, and that was going to be a challenge due to the short and fleeting time available between all the necessary events of each day and the closing hours of the library. I attained making a trip to the Liberec City Library to start reading up on the 1917 events that later received the title of "The Great October Socialist Revolution." I knew the mere basics; that the October Revolution was a second phase of the February revolt of the Bolsheviks against the Russian Empire. What I saw, as I read the pages of the encyclopedia, was the strong and compelling push of the writers to convey the overwhelming victory of the people over the imperialistic influences of their day. I saw a picture of such strength basking in the desire to silence the voice of one leader and replace it with the voices of the people and their Communist Party. It was a well-packaged article that included a few historical events but was heavily tipping toward the side of ideals rather than the side of authentic facts. Over the years, I have gained a greater understanding of the true meaning of the October Revolution, as I grasped a greater cognizance of the dangerous propelling force the Communist influence had in Russia, which succeeded not only in overthrowing the tzar and his family but also accomplished to set a course for a surge of a radical regime now known as Communism. This insurgence gained momentum on the false promises of better lives for the lower working class while achieving a fairer and balanced distribution of power between all the classes of the society. What started as a hopeful road to a dreamlike life of those living in poverty ended up in slavery of millions of citizens, both in the Soviet Union and later in other Communist nations around the world, who were forced to bow their knee to the ideals and the teachings of socialism, no matter what their own personal convictions might have been. If any were to demonstrate their loyalty to anyone or anything else outside these doctrines, they needed to be silenced by indoctrination, reeducation, or, if necessary, elimination. The architects of the social reforms in Russia capitalized on the post-World War I dissatisfaction of the population with the current living conditions. They masterfully instigated and organized a general strike that ousted the emperor Nicholas II from power and replaced him with the interim government. Under its leadership, small revolutionary committees started to form. These were called "Soviets" and consisted of factory workers, farmers, and military representatives. The Petersburg Soviet of Workers and Military Delegates was the largest Soviet committee in the nation that successfully captured the power and the trust of the government as well as the parliament. The October Revolution, led by Vladimir Ilyich Lenin, was a continuation of the political reform that commenced in February of 1917, overthrowing the interim government and replacing it with a radical left-wing fragment comprised of the Bolsheviks. The Bolsheviks officially called themselves the Socialist Democratic Workers' Party of Russia and were the direct predecessors of the Communist Party of the Soviet Union. In a short amount of time, the Bolsheviks and their powerful Soviets were able to decimate all opposition and win the civil war. Upon the securing of their victory, the Bolsheviks founded the Union of the Soviet Socialist Republics, led by their entrusted leader, Vladimir Lenin. This is a brief description of just how Communism came to be such a strong and dominating power over millions of lives in the Soviet Union and the Eastern European nations, before growing like an infectious disease over many more countries around the globe. All throughout the Communist era of Czechoslovakia and therefore throughout my childhood as well, "The Great October Socialist Revolution" was celebrated every year to serve as a reminder of the sacrifice and the accomplishments of the Soviet comrades who had gone before us and who had our best interests in mind. We were to be motivated by their example, their endurance, and their dedication. This library-gained discovery was supposed to be my inspiration for the bulletin board. I was not sure how to highlight the qualities of these Soviet heroes, but I had no choice than to utilize my artistic gifting and my creativity to influence the boys of the dorm who were to pass the bulletins every day until another holiday called for new decorations.

It is very interesting to consider how so many times in life we prepare and ready ourselves for something that either never happens or something that turns out to be so different from what we expected it to be, usually a disappointment of sorts. My bulletin board for the October Revolution turned out to be so much less impressive than what I aimed for. To be honest, through the process of decorating an informational display with slogans that I did not believe in and images of happy Pioneers running through wheat fields while holding hammers and sickles in their hands, that seemed disconnected from the reality of our lives as high school students, I learned that if I am not motivated to do something or if I don't believe in its mission, my performance or my determination to really lay it all out there simply never materializes. And so I did what was asked of me, but I did not deliver what was expected. I struggled with that feeling of guilt, but life was too busy to dwell on something so insignificant as a bulletin board in a hallway of a dorm filled with busy students too preoccupied with their own troubles—too beset to pause and notice what was placed on the wall.

> *But the foolishness of God is wiser than man's wisdom, and the weakness of God is stronger than man's strength.*
> —1 Corinthians 1:27

28) Snippets of My Student Life

Life seemed to be set in the track of regularity. Gymnázium studies were going alright. Ballet school was going great as well. Since the separation from my parents and after the slightly awkward conference with the dorm director at the beginning of the first semester, I got to know Liberec a bit, and I felt more comfortable navigating the different aspects of a young student's life. Once in a while, I was able to call home from a phone booth positioned on the street between the two dorm buildings. There was always a long line of students clutching their coins and waiting for their turn to speak to their families. The cold autumn weather kept everyone's conversation brief and to the point, which made the turnover between callers short and swift. Our phone conversations centered around grades and my folks wanting to know that I was well and not too overloaded. I learned quickly that less information conveyed to them was overall a better thing, and so a bit of an innocent lie always managed to sneak into the conversation in an attempt to cover up any stress I was experiencing. But I loved the connection with them no matter how brief, and to this day, I try to call and speak with my mom every Sunday, this time without the little fibs.

I was getting used to the rhythm of morning ballet class, followed by a rushed dash over for some academic classes, with a daily stopover in the bakery, and then grabbing a quick lunch only to hustle back to the ballet school for the afternoon classes. Long hours dancing every day left me feeling exhausted but with a deep sense of satisfaction from the progress made in the ballet studio. Late returns to the dorm, correlating with often missing cafeteria dinners there, became the new normal; and my roommates became a great source of friendships and encouragement. As many young dancers do, I would spend the last couple of minutes before lights out stretching. Initially, as one can imagine, lying on a bed with my leg propped up by my head between my body and the wall, with an open textbook in hand, caused a great bewilderment by my nondancing buddies; but with time, even that became the norm to them both.

What I did not prepare myself for were the long intervals between seeing my parents only once a month. I was excited to catch the last train from Liberec heading to Ústí nad Labem around 6:40 p.m., to arrive home around 9:00 p.m., every last Friday of the month. I missed them tremendously, and I looked forward to seeing them again. It was so great to have my mom's cooking, have her do my laundry, and enjoy Saturday and half of Sunday with my parents and Míra, only to catch the 4:00 p.m. train to Liberec. My mom would always pack me a dinner to go as well as snacks to have for life in the fast lane. It was always so very difficult to say goodbye. The weekends when I was unable to go home, due to Saturday dance classes, were the hardest when I would sit in the dorm often completely alone. The dorms were usually almost entirely empty, and as a matter of fact, on most Saturdays, I was the only student residing there over the weekend. The dormitory operation was minimal consisting of prepackaged breakfasts and no hot meals. Those were lonely days. I would try to catch up on my studies and homework and get ahead knowing that the weekdays were merciless in offering me no time to study.

Turn to me and be gracious to me, for I am lonely and afflicted.
—Psalm 25:16

29) The Power of Art

Weekends also became my time to attend performances at the State Theater. Being a student on a limited budget, free visits to the theater were a great option in comparison to costly movie tickets and such. Most times, I would use the side stage entrance, designated for the performers, to sneak in after the performance had begun. I would walk past the guards by the stage doors, who quickly got to know me, allowing me to enter without showing the entry pass. Narrow backstage hallways of the historic theater building acquired a unique charm, and one immediately sensed the power of the long lineage of the many talented, exceptional artists that have graced these interiors since the opening in September of 1883. A narrow staircase led to the second story of the opera building. There, a network of corridors advanced to the enormous and—for a fifteen-year-old—magical backstage area while passing the dressing rooms for the soloists, a makeup studio, a wig shop, and the stage manager's headquarters. I would find a small space in the side wings of the stage and breathed in whatever was unfolding on it. One of these visits had a profound impact on me as a young artist in the making. "Magic Flute" by Wolfgang Amadeus Mozart was on a playbill that night. I was running a little late this particular evening, and the performance was well underway when I arrived. I walked through the large metal doors leading to the backstage just as the applause of the audience faded following what must have been an impressive presentation. The hush that followed was only broken by a bright follow spotlight shining from the third gallery of the theater. Into it, a large cylindrical balcony was lowered from the rafters while swaying calmly right and left. In it, high above the surface of the stage itself, an opera soloist held her stern and uncanny expression. Dressed in a larger-than-life pompous robe, bold and impressive wig, and a crown, she waited for the first note of the orchestra; and then the breathtaking singing commenced. The "Queen of the Night" is considered to be one of the most challenging soprano arias ever written. When performed well, the experience for the listener is beyond extraordinary. The opera singer has to beautifully glide and land on high F notes throughout the aria. As it's usually the case, this is sung in the original German; and though the lyrics convey a very dramatic message of vengeance, death, and despair, the force of the voice balanced with beautiful and gentle crystal-like sounds is simply mesmerizing. The deep breaths and the veins on the side of the singer's neck demonstrate the strenuous and challenging effort this one song requires. While she creates both the sounds of champagne glasses gently hitting one another in joyful delight and the deep strong resounding vibratos that pierce the silent air of the auditorium, her artistry holds the viewers in breathless suspense. I stood below, and without a single slightest move, I watched as this spellbinding performance brought me to tears. Long streams were flowing down my face while flooding the floor I was standing on. Until that very moment, I had no idea that art could so deeply and profoundly reach into one's senses and, with a piercing effect, so beautifully and capriciously move one's heart and soul.

Without me having the slightest idea, the Lord used this unexpected moment as a preparation, to one day, use me as His artist to do just that. At this point in my life, however, I was not looking to find faith. I did not know that I was spiritually dead, that I was a sinner in a desperate need of a Savior. I was a by-product of a society that taught and strongly advanced the principles of the dependence of an individual on the government and its teachings, a society that taught us not to query the questions of faith and of God, a society that punished any attempt of one exchanging the blinded devotion to Marxism and Leninism for the surrender of their heart to the Lordship of Jesus Christ. I never heard His name. I did not know the truth. I was blind, but the Lord had started to move without me knowing so that one day my eyes would see.

Do you not know? Have you not heard? The Lord is the everlasting God, the Creator of the ends of the earth.
—Isaiah 40: 28a

30) The Velvet Revolution

As I was continuing running between the schedules of the two schools and everything else life placed on my plate, little did I notice the political climate around me changing. These next few pages are a memory of my experience of the Velvet Revolution, seen through the eyes of a fifteen-year-old student who was swept up by the excitement of being a small part of a larger-than-life moment in history. When the oppressive Communist regime was forced to surrender to the desire of the Czechoslovak people and abdicate its power to their longing for liberty, democracy, and freedom, the geopolitical climate of Europe in the late 1980s was noticing the winds of change starting to blow across the continent. Seated on the throne of power, the Czechoslovak Communist Party led the nation since February of 1948. After forty years, the momentous overthrow of this long-lasting period of oppression here and in the Eastern European block was, like an avalanche, coming unexpectedly, swiftly, and with force.

As these events unfolded all throughout the Communist portion of Europe, the Czechoslovak state-run media was directed to produce predetermined and erroneous broadcasts painting a picture that would serve as the perfect propaganda in the hands of the Politburo, and the Communist Party's leadership, to hide the truth. Despite the efforts of the government, the news of the liberation movement sweeping across Europe reached our land and, with great vigor, spurred the Czechs and Slovaks to join the electrifying effort to end the enslaving socialist oppression in the country. And then the fateful march of the Prague university students took place. This pivotal moment is considered to be the spark that ignited the revolt that is known and remembered as the Velvet Revolution in my cherished motherland.

It was November 17, 1989. As it is true for almost every single day of my life, and I am sure that I am not alone in this matter, I did not know the date that was showing on the calendar. I did know that it was Friday, as all Fridays do hold a special place in our minds as the last day of the week, serving as gateways into all the enjoyment and fun of the weekend. I got up, as I would every workday of the school year, ready to face the challenges relating to the requirements of my school life. The city of Liberec is located some two hours of driving time northeast of Prague, the capital of then Czechoslovakia. I did not know that just two hours away, a group of university students was gathering together to peacefully march through the cobblestone streets of the cold and wet city. These 110 kilometers separated me from the biggest moment in the modern history of Czechoslovakia, and I had no idea just how significant this particular Friday would be. As I worried about making it to school on time, landing my pirouettes, about passing a physics quiz, and making it to lunch, a short drive away, students just a few years my senior were risking their lives in the peace march commemorating the killing of a Czech student, Jan Opletal (*O-plah-taal*), by the Nazi regime in 1939. The International Students' Day was instituted to remember the Nazi and Gestapo forces' storming into the Czechoslovak universities at the beginning of World War II. Sadly, that day in 1939 was known for the killing, the arrests, and the concentration camps' imprisonments of the innocent Czech students and professors. It is painful to think that exactly fifty years later, that same day would also be marked with bloodshed and jailing of the young members of the future generation of Czechoslovakia—students desiring freedom to live lives as they dream them to be lived.

The political climate of the country provided no protection for those who would resist the regime. The Communist Party had used its iron fist to destroy and eliminate every resistance, understanding that a swift and harsh response to the imminent danger to its establishment was the best protection and the best warning to deter those who might have entertained the idea of a revolt. Political trials were televised. Brave heroes who believed that democracy was better than a dictatorship were mocked and publicly silenced in trials, where the outcome was predetermined before the court would ever first convene. Justice had no place in the courtroom. Truth was not to be heard. Construction of a narrative that would silence the hunger for freedom was the top priority, yet so many people would lay down their lives because they simply believed that liberty and democracy were worth that price. Leaders like Milada Horáková were mocked and ridiculed, and their message was twisted and smeared. Executions were celebrated as eradications of poisonous evil from the society. So much widespread deception. The government did an exceptional job of holding the nation in check. Fear was a powerful and an effective tool. Nobody fully trusted anybody around them. Reports of political misbehavior to the state police were common. Distrust and uncertainty reigned with force. Communism and its cousin socialism were proven to work only when the government suppressed and eliminated freedom from its people. They did not then, and do not now, deliver what they promise; and yet, even today, these ideologies are compelling forces thriving and gaining popularity all around the world, despite their horrific records. They masquerade themselves under a veil promising better welfare, provision, and peaceful globalism. They claim to be the answers to climate change, to poverty, to hunger, and even to sickness. They are promoted in subtle ways, and they are patient. Patient to wait and allow time to be their advocate, their ally, with slow but steady drips of deceit mixed with little truths they deliver, they convince, and they win. Communism and socialism are rarely publicly introduced for what they are; but no matter what they hide behind their backs, their dogma is clear, dangerous, and deadly.

Under these circumstances, the desire for true freedom was a propelling compulsion to keep fighting. In Czechoslovakia, a powerful movement of a small band of resistance intelligentsia was gaining popularity. With frequent imprisonments, beatings, confiscations of property, and heavy punishments, these heroes and dissidents were unable to be eliminated or silenced. They became an inspiration to the nation. One of these was a writer, Václav Havel.

That fateful Friday, the weather, though cold, was unable to stop or deter the will and resolve of the youth. As a group of fifteen thousand students marched through Prague, their voices started to cry against the regime. As their numbers grew, their boldness was empowered. Their zeal was bolstered. The government knew that a strong, clear, and loud message had to be sent. As the daylight vanished behind the horizon and darkness embraced the city, the march slowly and peacefully arrived on Národní Avenue, a boulevard leading from the National Theater toward the heart of the city, to Wenceslas Square. Candles in the cold hands of the students were illuminating the path onward almost as a symbol of the future, though fragile at the moment, yet alive and promising that change, indeed, was attainable. And then, out of nowhere, a large cordon of riot police with heavy shields and helmets, with stern and hate-filled faces, blocked and surrounded the students. There was no escape. These policemen had a mission to silence their voices. They were given orders to protect the unstable and crumbling regime from its certain collapse—no matter the price, no matter the force, no matter the inflicted pain. They were instructed to rip the desire for democracy out of the students' hearts and ensure that it would never return back. And so they tried. The cobblestones of the avenue were marked and flooded with blood, pouring from the faces and the bodies of these young men and women. They knew the risk. They were prepared to join the long line of those who paid the ultimate price. When reality meets the imagined expectancy, we often find ourselves weak or not fully equipped for the moment. But these students locked their elbows one with another, and with blows landing on their brows, they supported and held one another while looking into the eyes of their attackers. Banners in their hands stated, "We don't want violence. We want freedom," while they shouted, "*Máme holé ruce*," translated as "We hold no weapons," which clearly signaled their peaceful intent. The police did not care. The mission was clear—to silence these voices using any means necessary. They tried but did not prevail. After the attack and the beating, they were able to disperse the crowd and take some captive. What they did not know, however, was the fact that their mission had failed. Failed terribly. This cold Friday in November was the beginning of the end. The *revolution* had begun.

> *Therefore, you kings, be wise; be warned, you rulers of the earth. Serve the Lord with fear and rejoice with trembling.*
> —Psalm 2:10–11

31) I Joined the Revolution

The following Monday, I went to school. I had no idea that events of historic proportions took place on the previous Friday and over the weekend. Our class professor, Mr. Vondráček, stepped into the classroom, and right away, we all knew that something was wrong. He seemed distracted, as if battling between how he should behave and what his conscience was telling him to do. Then time froze. Professor stopped in his tracks and looked across the classroom. I will never forget the attention everyone paid. There was no need to require it or demand it. We all respectfully, almost joyfully, surrendered all our freshmen energy and breathlessly waited for what he was going to say. "The riot police surrounded and brutally beat a group of university students peacefully marching through Prague on Friday. This group was commemorating the fiftieth anniversary of a suppressed demonstration against the Nazi storming of Prague University in 1939. This madness needs to come to an end." He went on to sit on his desk, at the front of the class, with his legs straddling its corner. He knew that there was no turning back. He betrayed the government. He betrayed the Party. He spoke against it by acknowledging that the riot police were out of line, and its force was too radical. He looked at us, took a deep breath, and then continued. "I am wearing my black tie in support of those who were beaten, who were incarcerated, and who were punished for walking through Prague daring to dream of a future lived in freedom and democracy. For the past forty years, we were quiet, we were submissive, and we were willing to accept the regulations handed out to us by the party and the government. This time, they went too far. This time, they will lose. Over the last two days, the student body of the Academy of the Performing Arts in Prague initiated a refusal to attend classes this week. That decision was hugely supported by some theaters in the capital. Instead of performing, the artists are reading a manifesto of the university students, supported by the artists themselves, calling for a general strike on November 27. Yesterday, theaters in Brno and Ostrava also refused to carry out to stage the scheduled performances. The government is trying hard, and trying well, to keep the flow of information from transpiring. Things are unfolding quickly, though. Nobody knows how this will end. Nobody knows the next step needed to be taken. But nobody is afraid. The students are leading this revolt, and I state here that you all have my support. Every high school and every college in the country needs to stand united. The victory depends on the strength of our accord. The senior students met this morning, as some of them have heard from the local University of Engineering and Textiles of its pupils' refusal to go to classes. The leadership of the gymnázium is panicking. Their loyalty to the local council of the Communist Party and the fear to stand up to its demands is crippling. But remember your strength lies in your ability to stand together." As Professor Vondráček took a breath to continue, the speaker hanging on the wall of the classroom above the sink announced an all-school meeting in the gym. He did not complain. His facial expression clearly signaled his permission for us to go. As we opened our classroom doors, we met the other students walking through the high-vaulted hallways toward the staircase leading to the bottom floor, where another hallway led to the school's gymnasium. Everyone was talking as we walked to the meeting. The sense of excitement was palpable. This was beyond the desire of wanting to skip class. This was past the short-lived thrill of a roller coaster ride. This was a once-in-a-lifetime opportunity to change the world, and that was clear. As we entered the room, the commotion in the gymnasium was astounding. The size of the hall was not designed to fit all the students of the gymnázium at one time. Nobody cared. Everyone wanted to be inside and hear for himself what was spoken from the small stage. There was already a seemingly established student leadership core that welcomed everyone in. They had to repeatedly ask us to quiet down so they could speak. After a good ten to fifteen minutes, we all did just that. A senior, I had never met, looked across the gymnasium and, with a gleam in his eye, explained the situation in the nation. He slowly and methodically reiterated the unfolding of events from Friday evening to today. It was very trying and difficult to keep silent as the crowd grew excited and filled with a desire to participate—to do something, to be a part of the movement. We were told that a meeting was being organized to assemble the public in one place and call on the citizens of Liberec to join the general strike. We learned that the State Theater was approached by the Artists' Union to join the other theaters in the nation and open its doors for the gatherings. The historic theater was one of the largest halls in the city and would be ideal to become the headquarters of the resistance.

Meanwhile, we were encouraged to divide into smaller groups that would be tasked with specific responsibilities. There was a need for information gathering and processing, organizing of events, newsletter publishing, samizdat literature reproduction and circulation, and poster design and printing, as there was a need for flyer and pamphlet distribution runners. These were students who would connect our school with other schools and committees around Liberec. We were told that none of this was legal, and all of this was punishable under the current law. If anybody wanted to step out, there were no hurt feelings. To my knowledge, nobody did. There was such a powerful unity among us. It was unforgettable. The irony in all of this was the fact that the Pioneer Organization taught us from a very young age to work together, to be as if one united player, one united voice and force. Now we were mobilizing ourselves and utilizing those acquired skills to overthrow the regime that established the Pioneer Organization. I joined the group that was to distribute posters and pamphlets around the city. We were to divide Liberec into sections and then go in groups of two students posting these flyers on the walls. The leading person in the group had a bucket with glue, and the following student would attach the poster to the adhesive. These were applied to the surface of a building, post, bench, bus stop, or simply anywhere and everywhere to let the public know of the scheduled events as well as of the development of the general situation. Instead of sitting in classrooms, we would gather in school every day to receive specific instructions and then go our separate ways to complete the given mission. I remember walking swiftly through Liberec streets with flyers over my left forearm and, with a precision of a biathlon shooter, attaching them to the applied glue-soaked spots. It was exhilarating to do this, and through this small part, I played a role in bringing the establishment of the socialist society to its knees. In these uncertain times, my parents worried about me, but deep down, they were just as excited to hope and see the horrors of Communism come to a victorious defeat.

The State Theater opened its doors and, indeed, became the center of the resistance, and because of its relentlessness, the old regime eventually collapsed. The nation was filled with such incredible solidarity and unanimity. Dynamic demonstrations filled the city squares in towns all across the nation. The most incredible element of the revolution was its peaceful and violence-free manner. As the events continually developed, Václav Havel became the face and the leader of the resistance. Václav Havel was a playwright who used the ink as a weapon to fight the clutching power of socialism by writing plays that directly confronted, challenged, and criticized Communism. He personally experienced the calamitous punishment of the regime, during his frequent imprisonments. In 1977, he and other dissidents in Czechoslovakia started an informal civic initiative, Charter 77, which publicly criticized the government for falling short of several key elements, mainly its failure to respect and implement human and civil rights of the Czechoslovak citizens guaranteed in the nation's constitution adopted in 1960. He faced frequent and painful retributions, but in his heart, he believed that his and others' efforts would one day bring freedom and democracy to the Czech people. The end of the 1980s was that moment in time.

There is a time for everything, and a season
for every activity under the heavens.

—Ecclesiastes 3:1

32) The General Strike

It was a chilly and wet Monday. The whole nation seemed as if it was wading through the muddy current of slow but steady moving events leading to this day, November 27, 1989. This was the date when the government's opposition, the Civic Forum, called on all the workers, the intelligentsia, the students, the artists, the young and the old, the mothers and fathers, and all willing members of the society to join in a clear and loud two-hour general strike signaling to the Politburo of the Communist Party of Czechoslovakia, that its trust and power to lead the nation had been revoked. The party tried to, one more time to no avail, warn and discourage the citizens from participating in the strike, using tactics of "certain destruction and total collapse of the thriving economy of the republic due to such revolt." Despite the warnings, almost all the able members of the working force, agglutinated by the massive numbers of high school and university students, gathered in the squares of towns all across the nation. At noon, while the church bells rang the twelfth hour, the general strike commenced, and for two hours, the citizens continued to demonstrate the solidarity of the nation. The ringing of key chains, singing of the national anthem, the powerful speeches, the compelling yet peaceful comradery of often total strangers, underlined by the previously unseen unity of the people, thrust the Forum's demands powerfully to the attention of the leadership of the Communist Party and of the federal government.

I was a part of the large crowd gathering on the square in front of the Liberec city hall. The energy in the mass was galvanizing, astounding, and invigorating. The powerful singing of the national anthem while standing under large Czechoslovak flags waving above our heads made me so proud to belong to this small nation in the heart of Europe, a nation loudly and clearly demonstrating to the world that change can be brought about without the use of weapons, power, and force. Everyone was excited but very civil. We knew that we were standing unified, and that made us stronger than any weapon could possibly do. As I was singing the words of our beautiful national anthem titled "Where Is My Homeland," I paused to listen to the power of the crowd around me, and at that moment, I realized the privilege I was granted to be a part of such a pivotal moment in history. The following day, November 28, 1989, exactly three weeks after the collapse of the Berlin Wall, the Czechoslovak Communist Party stepped down from being the leading governing organ of the nation. Articles of the Constitution declaring socialism and Communism as the prospective way to the future, and the means to gain such hopeful prosperity and well-being of the people, were removed. After forty years of Soviet-backed oppression of millions of Europeans, including the Czechs and the Slovaks, the hideous reign of brutal and dictatorial ideology that stripped freedom, faith, democracy, prosperity, and even happiness from these lives was triumphantly abolished. Czechoslovakia and its people began a new exciting walk toward democracy, knowing that we had a long way ahead of us, learning how to live free, free without fear, without restrictions, without the constant censorship of every aspect of our daily lives. It was guaranteed to be a slow road, but we were ready to venture out on this exciting adventure. None of us could even imagine what the future would hold, but we believed with all our hearts that it was bright and full of hope.

Praise be to the name of God for ever and ever; wisdom and power are his. He changes times and seasons; he sets up kings and deposes them.
—Daniel 2:20–21a

33) A Fungi Barrage

Slowly but surely, life returned to the normal routine of tests, sleepless nights spent with my head falling into the open textbooks, and running between two impossible school loads. The country was going through a massive makeover as the young, and at the moment, a fragile democratic process started to find its way to the world stage. The free Czechoslovakia looked to be recognized as a valid player and a potential partner in trade and commerce. I had to focus on my schooling as many days of classes were missed during the Velvet Revolution. I knew that Christmas break was coming up soon, and

I had to press on to do well in my finals. Demanding tests in mathematics, physics, Czech language, Russian language, and English language; oral exams in history and geography; and the dreaded biology and chemistry quizzes seemed to be unsurpassable mountains that I had to climb to reach their summits in order to keep my grades satisfactory to the ISP requirements. And so I tried. And so I succeeded. The stress was equal amongst all the dance students as we all shared similar experiences of emotions in these final weeks of the first semester.

I have a great memory of Petra coming into the ballet studio in early December, moments before our afternoon ballet technique class started. "He is impossible," came out of her mouth as her schoolbag soared through the air in a beautiful arched trajectory, being tossed with obvious discouragement and almost anger. "What's wrong?" I asked watching the bag fly to its hard landing followed by a significant distance of a solid, almost-bowling-like, glide toward the wall of the studio. "He is impossible," she repeated, as if I did not understand such a simple statement the first time around. "Our biology professor gave us a mushroom test today. He walked into the class and commanded us all to pull out a blank piece of paper. He announced to us that he would show us a picture of several mushrooms. We had to identify them and write the abbreviated and shortened names of the pictured fleshy fungi. What he omitted to say was that these were to be shown at a rapid speed, making them difficult to be identified and even more challenging to be written down, thus the need for the abbreviations. And then he proceeded to sit behind his desk and, with a smirk on his face, said, 'Ready?' Our eyes resembled a cartoon character squinting its eyelids prepared to face an archenemy of sorts, ready to put up a fight to save his or her life. My hand trembled as I watched him slowly place his hand on the tall pile of eight-by-ten-inch photographs of mushrooms, stacked in front of him. And then the barrage of rapid and lightning-speed movements of short displays of mushrooms, one after the other, commenced. All I could do was to write the first letter for each of the two Latin names describing the toadstool and fungus. I did not know that it was possible to display anything in such rapid progression, and I was unprepared. Out of the fifty mushrooms, I managed to name about forty percent at best. He is impossible! Biology was followed by the German class, and once again, it is simply astonishing to realize how little one knows when push comes to shove and there is absolutely no information being transmitted from the head to the white paper in front of you! German grammar is absurd! I got two Fs in one day, and it's going to be a struggle—no, it's going to be a fight—to keep my grades up. Anyway, how was your day?" I had nothing to say, as my mouth was still hanging wide open while I tried to process all that Petra was saying in such a dramatic and convivial manner. "I nailed my English exam," I replied with an almost regretful tone as I did my best to be cordial and understanding of Petra's frustration. "Well, that's great," she said with clear sarcasm in her voice. I did not mind, because I clearly understood the enormous pressure everyone felt in balancing all the expectations and not dropping any proverbial spinning plates in our hands. Eventually, Petra was able to pull both of her grades up, and for years, we would laugh at her melodramatic conveying of that day.

> *He makes grass grow for the cattle, and plants for man*
> *to cultivate—bringing forth food from the earth.*
> —Psalm 104:14

34) Virtuoso? No, No, No

Another fine memory of the first semester was attending my piano lessons. As a mandatory prerequisite, all the students of the ballet academy had to learn to play an instrument. Though some chose unusual ones such as trumpet, tuba, French horn, and others, most of us selected piano, as the most practical choice for the future dancers. Every Tuesday, I had to hustle to arrive at a music school located about twenty minutes away, traveling via the public transportation system, where a piano and Mrs. Bednářová (*Bed-naa-ro-va*) waited to give me a lesson in a small music room. My piano professor was an elderly lady, in her late seventies, was my guess, who always had her gray hair pulled into a large loose bun. I remember her beautiful darker-toned skin marked with deep wrinkles and reflecting the many years of life. She would spend the first ten or so minutes of the lesson questioning me about my plans and aspirations for my future, about the progress I was making in my ballet studies, as she put it, and about life away from my family. I did not mind sharing my dreams with her, as I sensed her genuinely believing in all of them being attainable. After these initial conversations, Mrs. Bednářová turned into a professor whose goal was to turn me into an apparent piano virtuoso. "Here, play this," would be a mandate accompanying the opening of a piano book. Her handheld pencil circled the page with notes that reminded me of Chinese alphabet characters. I was an extremely slow music reader, and so I would always respond with a request, asking if she would play the song first, for me to be inspired by her unquestionable talent in piano playing. As she played the song, I would exude my hardest effort into memorizing as much of the music as possible. When it was my turn to play, I would pretend to be reading the notation as I would play. One of these Tuesdays, Mrs. Bednářová asked me to show her where I was in the music as I was playing. I had no idea, and so I did what she would do, and that is to circle most of the page of the book with a shy hand gesture, trusting that I would encompass the portion of the song I was trying to play. "You have no idea where you are, am I right?" she asked. "No, Professor Bednářová," I answered as I looked at the white and black keys of the piano. "Well, are you going to be a dancer or a professional piano musician?" she continued. "Dancer... Professor Bednářová," I mumbled. "Very well, then! I will teach you what you need to know to be able to play by ear, as long as you don't tell anyone that we are not following the curriculum," said Professor Bednářová. I could not believe that I was offered a secret deal by an old woman who recognized what was important and what would be most beneficial to her student, even if that meant to rebel and disobey the system. We made a pact, and for four years, I was taught to play by ear, which has been an enormous blessing in years to come, and until this day, I love sitting behind a piano being able to play just about anything, even though my technique might not be of a classically trained pianist. Later on, when dancing in America, I even wrote songs used in my own ballets. What a gift. Thank you, Mrs. Bednářová. You are the best!

Sing and make music in your heart to the Lord.
—Ephesians 5:19b

35) Ba-*no*-na

Christmas of 1989 was like every other prior to it when it comes to the warm family atmosphere. The authentic love filled our small apartment. Most of the conversations amongst ourselves as well as all the guests we hosted and friends we visited were largely about the recent changes in our nation. Everyone was thinking out loud, and everyone knew the best direction our nation should take. Or so they thought. One fine memory of the Christmas holidays was the abundance of fruit. I know it sounds silly; but under the recently eradicated Communist regime, frequent restrictions imposed on all sorts of goods were normal. But around Christmas, my parents always found a way to have plenty. Oranges imported from Cuba that were extremely difficult to peel but of great flavor, pineapples, kiwis, large juicy apples, nut mixes, and more were the custom for the large fruit bowl always gracing the living room table during the holidays. What was not always guaranteed were bananas. Bananas were a hot commodity, rationed per family, if at all available. My mother would find different ways to find a merchant that would, often for a bribe, keep a kilo of bananas for her at least once during each Christmas. Except for the Christmas of 1978. This was the one year our family had all the other fruits in the basket, but the slightly curved yellow-colored fruit was simply not there. I assumed that this year we simply did not receive the ration. It was not a big deal. That particular Christmas was exciting in a completely different way. My mom was pregnant, and in the upcoming spring, we were to receive an addition to our family. As a young four-year-old, I was hoping for a brother and not a sister, of course. And so not having bananas was not going to stop me from enjoying the most wonderful time of the year. It was not until many decades later when I was told the truth about the lack of bananas that year. It wasn't that the government did not supply them. It was not that the rations were limited. It wasn't even that my parents ran out of bribes to give to the lady behind the counter of the Fruit and Vegetables Store. The true cause of the lack, the true source of being forced to go without, was my yet-to-be-born brother. According to the confession of my mom, that winter, she was craving bananas during the pregnancy, and craving them badly. She paid the bribe, she bought all the rations permitted for our family, and then she sat on a bench in the park, and while the snow was falling, she ate them—she ate them all. My mom knew that once she would bring them home and saw the excitement in my eyes, she would not be able to enjoy eating them. She opted for the option more suitable for the given predicament: to sit in the park and eat them all. She said it was the most satisfying bench time she ever had. Until this day when I see bananas—and, yes, they are available all year round now in the Czech Republic—I remember this funny story of a pregnant woman craving this delicious fruit in the middle of winter in the nation behind the Iron Curtain. I picture my mom sitting there on the bench, swaying her legs while enjoying one banana after the other as the snowflakes gently land on her pooch. I love bananas to this day.

*Go, eat your food with gladness, and drink
your wine with a joyful heart.*
—Ecclesiastes 9:7

36) Me, Me, Me

I returned to the rhythm of the school year after the Christmas holidays concluded; the old year said its goodbye, and the new year loudly shouted its hello. It was always so difficult to board the Liberec-bound train knowing that the separation from my parents and brother was going to be long and hard. As the countryside passed outside the window of the train, my mind ventured on the trail of contemplating the immediate and the distant futures. I did not know what this new year of 1990 had in store, yet I was hoping to rise to the challenge of continuing to fight the battle I had chosen for myself. Sitting there on the train while watching the snow-covered landscape of my beloved homeland passing by, the landscape bruised by the abuse inflicted by the regime and its carelessness for it, I was breathing in the wintery feel of melancholy wondering if I had what it took to keep fighting this lonely battle. As the workdays kicked in and the demands of life knocked on my doors, I would slowly forget about how much I missed my family and how badly I wanted to be with them.

Shortly after resuming the studies after the holidays, Mr. Pokorný gathered all the conservatory students to the ballet studio to make an announcement. None of us knew what this was going to be about. "I know that we have been through a lot as a nation these past couple of months, and I am proud of you all for being willing to fight for what really matters. Now we have to focus on the work at hand and shift our focal point back to the tremendously hard work that ballet, as an art form, requested of us. Remember the upcoming exam at the theater in front of the public and the dance experts in June. That same evening, you will also perform a one-act ballet by Sergei Prokofiev, *Peter and the Wolf.* Your class professor, Mrs. Gabajová, will be the choreographer for the project. We will be watching you closely the next couple of weeks to see who will dance what role. Also, and this is exciting I believe, you all will appear in the State Theater's production of *Špalíček* (*Shpa-lee-check*), a ballet by Bohuslav Martinů, which will be premiering this year. We are looking to see what parts each of you will be cast in. Remember that this will be your very first step onto the stage of the theater as you join the artists of the company. Based on your performance in *Špalíček* as well as your exam in June, some of you might be offered a contract with the company while you continue to work hard here at the academy and hard in keeping your grades up." I could not believe this. We had attended the school for merely five months, and the first opportunity to be a part of a professional production was already on the horizon. *Wow,* I thought. This short little announcement brought a great amount of new zeal and enthusiasm into my inspiration to work hard, to get noticed, to make an impression. Something inside of me had shifted. Something had changed. There were sixteen male students in my class, and I had to be the best. That was not going to be easy, for so many had a great amount of talent. I knew that I needed to use my classmates to be my motivation, to be my inspiration, to be my drive. I did not want to make enemies while in the studio, but I resolved to leave friendships outside, and while in the ballet studio, I had to give my all to be the best. And so the new year of 1990 had begun to be the year when I would see if I had what it took to make it: to land a contract with the company. I was fifteen years old, and I was determined to succeed.

The casting for *Peter and the Wolf* was announced first. We all crowded around the small glassed casing in the hallway of the ballet school to see what role we were assigned. To be honest, I had no idea what characters there were in the ballet. I assumed that Peter would be one and Wolf would be another. Smart, I know! But beside these, what other parts were there to be filled? I did not know the plot that Prokofiev used as a compass for his musical composition. I did not know the story of the adventure Peter and the Wolf experienced. But regardless, no matter what role I was assigned to dance, it was guaranteed to be fun and challenge-filled. And so I looked to find my name on the list. Used to being listed at the bottom of any list, due to my last name starting with a *V*, I automatically started to read from the bottom. What I did not consider, as I have never done casting list reading before, roles are assigned by characters and not by the last names of the performers. I read as I continued to move up the list only to find my name next to the word *Peter*. I could not believe it. I did not know whether to be excited for being chosen to dance a lead character role or whether to be scared that if I did not meet the expectations of Mr. Pokorný and the panel of experts sitting in the audience during the public exam, this could be my first and my last role ever to be offered. Petra, who quickly became one of my close friends, landed the role of a bird. Little did we know then that a large portion of her choreography would require dancing in the tree. Petra and another dancer, Martina, also a bird, were to dance some ten feet above the stage in the tree built by the carpenters of the State Theater. What was quite amusing about the process of learning the choreography a few weeks later was the fact that Martina was deadly afraid of heights. Most of the time, when rehearsing, Petra was playing the role of a counselor, convincing Martina that she will not die and not fall from the tree, as much as she was focusing on the dancing itself. I loved the process of learning the choreography and enjoyed the progress when being coached by both Mr. Pokorný as well as Professor Gabajová. It became apparent that the performance needed to feature the potential of the conservatory students. Mr. Pokorný was proving to those who would travel here from Prague to examine us in June that his curriculum was strong and prepared the students to be versatile and well progressing. He was our "stage presence class" professor, and it was here when the coaching took place. Professor Gabajová would teach us the choreography, set the spacing and such; but it was Mr. Pokorný who would be pulling the acting out of us to "convey the story beyond the steps," as he put it. What surprised us all the most was the harsh atmosphere in the studio during his classes. He expected absolute focus from all of us the entire time. The lack of sleep, the must-do studying yet to be done, the unfinished homework, and the growling stomachs were often huge distractions to do just that. But he was used to working long hours with theaters all around Europe; and we all knew that no matter how hard, even harsh, he might be, he would deliver the best production possible and the artists would be the best they can be. And that was enough of an inspiration to keep pressing on.

God opposes the proud but gives grace to the humble.
—James 4:6

37) Silent Dancing

Along with Mr. Pokorný's class, we also had a pantomime class. This was taught by professor and mime, Mr. Jiří Kaftan. He was an accomplished artist featured on stages as a dancer and a mime, as well as in movies and television programs. Though extremely gifted in the craft of pantomime, Professor Kaftan struggled to establish the order and respect he deserved in the ballet studio. Many of us did not see value in what his classes were giving us as future dancers. How sad and unfortunate that is, now looking back. Many years later, when I started to do choreography myself, I realized that I had learned so much more in his classes than I gave him credit for.

We would do so many interesting exercises and concepts in these pantomime lessons. He thrived on a fast progression of improvisational exercises. On these we would get graded. We would stand around the studio and cover our faces with newspapers. Professor Kaftan would start clapping a rhythm for us to catch. While our faces were covered, he would call out different emotions like sadness, joy, surprise, fear, anger, and such; and we would uncover our face with the displayed emotion. To make the class challenging, Professor Kaftan then progressed to more challenging ones like sore stomach, longing for someone, and solving a mathematical equation, and then concluded with extremely abstract scenarios like tomatoes exposed to direct sunlight, a wet rag on a heating unit, and others. We would be taught how to exaggerate simple movements and make them visible from the third balcony of the theater. I do recall a lesson on receiving a plate of food in a restaurant, adding salt and pepper to it, and then enjoying the meal while finding out that the bottom side of the steak was burnt. A huge amount of time was spent on slow motion and how to depict action and reaction with attention to the smallest detail while moving in a laggard manner. We would pull animals by their horns across the studio and push heavy furniture sets across the room without ever having a single prop. These were great treasures to be gained, and I am grateful. As I recall all these experiences, I am wondering why I thought that the Professor Kafka's classes were boring. Presumably, the answer comes in that other classmates who might not have liked him and his methods easily swayed me and my opinion to view him in the same light. It is sad to admit, but peer pressure was a big deal, and the desire to fit in and not stand out was dominating a large portion of my attitude and my mind. I wonder how much of this same element affects me today as I go through life as an adult.

Do not conform any longer to the pattern of this world,
but be transformed by the renewing of your mind.
—Romans 12:2

38) Anxiety Takes Root

The premiere of the *Špalíček* ballet was approaching fast. Rehearsals shifted from learning our parts at the academy to rehearsing with the company of the State Theater. This was a brand-new experience, and my nerves were stretched to their limits. We were invited to attend the very first combined rehearsal. I had never seen the studio of the State Theater and had never met the dancers of the company except for those who were mingling around at the auditions to the conservatory some ten months ago. All of us students walked into the studio in close proximity to one another. There was comfort in the numbers and safety in the company of familiar faces. Mr. Pokorný introduced us as the students of Professor Gabajová's class and then proceeded to introduce the principal dancers by name. He then motioned to the corps de ballet dancers saying, "And this is the company." I found it strange that he would single out some by name and others as a group, but who was I to question him or think it being rude? I was a nobody, and my place was to listen and follow directions and follow them closely. The rehearsals at the theater's studio became a regular event, and attendance at the gymnázium and all the other high schools where we studied had to move to the back burner. I started to wonder how this was going to work once the performances started; and I was forced to mesh the two schools, the rehearsals, homework, studying, and the dorm schedules together. I kept saying to myself, "One bridge at a time, Jiri. One bridge at a time," but deep down, there was a foundation of anxiety being laid and firmed up in my heart and in my mind.

Do not be anxious about anything, but in every situation, by prayer
and petition, with thanksgiving, present your requests to God.
—Philippians 4:6

39) Navigating the New Norm

The winter snow and cold air slowly started to yield to the warmth of the spring. Colors began to show their beauty in the flowers and trees that responded with glee to the invitation of nature to burst with the newness of life. This was our first spring to be free. Communism was gone, but its footprints were still visible everywhere. The façades of the buildings were void of beauty, the air was polluted from the industry heavily focused on production, and the retail world was slowly waking up to the opportunities available from vendors and merchants near and far. The slowest change to come would occur in the mind-sets of the people who were chained, for over four decades, to lives void of liberty, choice, and self-esteem. One thing that was extremely visible all around us was the almost instantaneous flooding of the newsstands and bookstores with pornographic materials, formerly not available for purchase at these outlets. This was the unfortunate price to be paid for being free. The nature of mankind was showing its darker side, to the astonishment of the regular public who, generally speaking, did not care to see such inappropriateness all around them. I realized that it would take us, as a society, some time to find the balance between being free and yet not giving into everything available that used to be censored or forbidden.

At the ballet school, we were in full swing of preparing for the public exam, consisting of rehearsed barre and center ballet work, as well as Graham and Limón technique presentations, and the *Peter and the Wolf* premiere in the second portion of the evening. And the premiere of the *Špalíček* ballet was just around the corner as well.

> *But do not use your freedom to indulge the flesh;*
> *rather, serve one another humbly in love.*
> —Galatians 5:13

40) The First Taste

The day came when we were scheduled to rehearse for *Špalíček* on the stage of the State Theater. The rehearsal was to commence at ten o'clock, but all of the students arrived well in advance to get situated and find our way around the theater. Our dressing rooms were

on the third level of the historic building. One side of the theater was for the men and the other for the women. And so we divided and conquered, so to speak. Then came the moment when we were summoned to the stage. I will never forget the very juncture when I stepped from the wings to the stage and saw the breathtaking elaborate architectural jewel of the opera house, beautifully lit and intricately ornate. The very first impression of the interior was the elegance and affluence of the space. The red velvet of the seats blended beautifully with the golden colors of the paneling of the three balconies. On either side of the theater were elegant loges, and the walls all around the theater had exquisite rich red-colored velvet affixed to them. Sculptures of golden seraphim and cherubim adhered to the balconies and the detail of both, the architectural as well as the decorative elements, were extraordinary. Perhaps the most impressive feature of it all was the ceiling of the theater. There were four large mural compositions clasped in oval-shaped golden frames, and together they surrounded a large crystal chandelier that, in its design, matched all the other lighting fixtures of the interior. I could not fathom that I was going to be dancing in this beautiful place and maybe even one day receive a contract from the theater as a dancer. I was excited beyond words.

We, as the academy students, were to appear in several scenes of the ballet. *Špalíček* is a three-act production based on fairy tales of a

Czech writer, Karel Jaromír Erben. The first act follows the journey of Puss in Boots, the second then tells the story of a Cobbler who meets Death, and the third act depicts the tale of Cinderella. As the youngest members of the cast, we were privileged to dance quite a bit as the plot called for many different characters throughout the evening.

An exciting element about this first rehearsal was the State Theater's orchestra that played masterfully under the direction of the head conductor, Maestro Miloš Krejčí. What was played on a piano at the ballet studio sounded incredible when played by the full orchestra. The sets were not all in place for this first stage rehearsal, and the technical aspects were still in the making. The stage was covered with a unique painted cloth-like flooring that matched the color theme of the set designer for the production. A large number of professionals responsible for different aspects of the show were sitting around Mr. Pokorný, who was the head choreographer and producer of the performance and, throughout the rehearsal, were taking notes regarding their fields of responsibility. The principal dancers were wearing their costumes as the rest of the cast were still to be dressed. We were to locate a roster in the entry hall of the service entrance to the theater where information about the costume fittings was assigned to every performer, including the conservatory students. We were encouraged not to miss the assigned time windows for the fitting, and we well noted that exhortation. This was one long day for all of us, filled with the excitement of experiencing the process of seeing the creative vision of a man be fleshed out on the stage while being a part of the proceedings. I was inspired.

> *No eye has seen, no ear has heard, no mind has conceived*
> *what God has prepared for those who love him.*
> —1 Corinthians 2:9

41) My First Premiere

When I first moved to Liberec, dreaming of pursuing a career as a professional dancer, my dad's brother was a strong voice of opposition to the idea. Uncle Standa's concern for me as a ballet dancer was the potential difficulty in finding a place in a small number of openings in the professional companies, combined with the low pay scale of the profession. All these sounded like a legitimate reason to "return to architecture and forget this nonsense," as he put it. My dad would always respond to Standa's remarks with a simple response of "We are behind Jiri, and if he chooses to dance, then that is where our support will lie." As the premiere of *Špalíček* approached, my parents prepared to come to Liberec to be there for the moment I would perform for the very first time in a State Theater's production. What I did not know was that my uncle and aunt were also planning to come and attend the opening night.

The day of the premiere arrived, and we all felt prepared. The excitement was running high. It was a humbling thought to be a part of such a large-scale production. The orchestra, the ballet company, the technical personnel—all these elements came together for this one night at the theater. The costume mistresses and ladies responsible for our makeup and wigs took their time in making us feel special and valued as they did what they were experts in doing. Even though the nerves were running on a high voltage, as I would say, I was trying to breathe it all in and savor the whole experience. I knew that whether I would dance for a long time or whether I would end up professionally doing something completely different after the graduation from the academy, there would never again be this first time, the first time of dancing in a professional production. I loved and enjoyed every second of the opening night and every performance of *Špalíček* that would follow for the next couple of seasons. My parents were beaming with pride as we met after the show. I was thankful that they were there, that they drove from Ústí to support me. My aunt and uncle were moved as well. It would be the next September when my cousin would start training as a ballroom dancer. He later competed nationally and internationally, winning prizes in European ballroom competitions, and eventually became a sought-after performer in galas all over the continent.

It was a great night, and I was like a little child, riding a high wave of feeling a deep sense of satisfaction. The following Monday,

Mr. Pokorný gathered the whole class into the ballet studio to pour his accolades upon us as well. To see him satisfied and pleased was what we all longed for. None of us realized it at the time, but deep within, we all desired to make him proud, to make his premiere be the best it could be. He went on to say that the theater was going to compensate us for each performance. The money was not going to be much, but it was a policy, he said, that every performer was to be compensated. I was in disbelief and completely overjoyed with that announcement. I could not wait to get to the phone booth and call my parents to share this with them. This first year of living in Liberec was packed with unbelievable events, and as a young teenager, I was trying very hard to take it all in and keep my emotions at bay. As each experience arrived, whether the exhausting schedule of the two schools, the Velvet Revolution, the ballet premiere, and more, I realized every time, and deeper with each one, that the inability to share these experiences with my family was so extremely difficult. Often I found myself sitting in an empty dormitory on a Sunday, completely overwhelmed with loneliness and even sadness, missing my mom and dad, my beloved grandparents, and my brother. This was a tough field that I found myself in. I needed something to fulfil me. I needed someone to be my close companion, to be my friend. Where would I find such a person? When would I have time for such a relationship? Time would tell, I thought. Surely with time, I would find a way to combat these moments of loneliness and sadness. I had to be patient; I had to wait. This was the price I had to pay, and I was convinced that it was worth it.

*You will seek me and find me when you seek me with all
your heart. I will be found by you, declares the Lord.*
—Jeremiah 29:13b–14a

42) Jiri, the Perfectionist

The only obstacles standing between me and the end of the school year were the Czech, Russian, English, and mathematics finals at the gymnázium and the state public ballet exam, that I needed to pass in order to progress to the next level of the conservatory. I was well aware of the fact that the upbringing in Communism had marked me with a deep sense of desire to please everyone who was in authority over me and to always make a good impression, no matter how difficult it might have been in a given situation. As the end of the school year was approaching, this "inheritance" of the regime had placed me into a deep state of anxiety and stress. I also had to maintain a minimum of 3.5 grade point average in all twelve subjects, to keep the individual study plan awarded by the gymnázium, as to be able to attend both schools. Often I envied my dorm roommates, Michael and Michael, as I watched them enjoy other hobbies and pursue other interests to fill the free time they had in their schedules. Michael the math whiz became a member of the Liberec Aviation Club and was progressing to receive a small single-engine-plane pilot license, whereas Michael the engineer was passionate about paper modeling. As a young boy, I would often watch my father model incredible lures for his fishing trips, as well as construct paper models of different Czech castles and chateaux. While sitting across the table from him, watching him closely and enjoying the times spent together, I admired my dad's creativity, patience, and fine motor skills. Watching Michael model these intricate creations in our dorm room reminded me of my dad and of our times together. Math whiz Michael and I would help each other in preparations for the final exams in math and Russian, respectively, and these tutoring times would build a stronger friendship between us. I admired his ability to display patience with me when attempting to explain calculus formulas that came naturally to him and, to my admiration, made perfect sense. That was not so with me. Michael was a great help, and I am thankful for friends like him in my life. I wonder if I was as helpful to him as he was to me when it came to explaining the rules of Russian grammar. I wonder! The perfectionist in me was both an engine as well as a huge distraction.

It is God who arms me with strength and makes my way perfect.
—Psalm 18:32

43) Ballet Exam

The day of the State Public Ballet Exam was here. I was surprised as to how nervous I found myself to be. Many of my classmates also arrived at the theater not feeling their best. Just a few short days prior to the exam, Mr. Pokorný announced the committee that was to assemble and sit in the audience during the exam to grade us and evaluate our progress as students of the conservatory. The National Ballet's artistic director was to be the head examiner surrounded by six other experts in the field of dance.

It was a beautiful spring evening in Liberec. Due to its northern latitude, the days were already bright and daylight hours long. The crowds started to enter the theater and settle in their assigned seats. My parents were among the crowd as they would not miss this unique performance to see their firstborn sweat and struggle to win the battle with his own self and the nerves that were ready to put up a great offense. The evening commenced with a welcome to everyone by Mr. Pokorný, who then introduced the members of the committee. The National Ballet artistic director was a household name at the time, and his entrance into the auditorium caused a wave of "wow" and a round of applause to rise from the crowd. His presence also gave the exam a unique stamp of importance and value. The lights dimmed, and the red velvet curtain of the historic opera house lifted. There was a baby grand piano placed strategically in the corner of the proscenium. Ballet barres were placed in three directions around the perimeter of the stage. We walked to the rhythm of the entry music to arrive at our designated posts at the barre. A swift progression of ballet combinations followed as our bodies executed the rehearsed sequence. It was such a unique experience to be performing these exercises while being watched by professionals and amateurs alike. I found myself wondering, as the audience responded with acclamation to a particular portion of the performance, what were the examiners thinking at that very moment. The barre section came to an end, and we walked in a rehearsed manner to the center of the stage to continue the exam with exercise *au milieu* (French for *center*). We would orderly change from one group to the next to demonstrate our skills acquired in the first year of our studies at the academy, this time unable to rely on the support and comfort of the ballet barre. The pianist continued to play, almost as if this was her own recital, and we danced. The ballet portion of the exam concluded with a sequence of allegro displaying the youthful, and often admired, aplomb of a ballet dancer, defying gravity with leaps reaching great heights, often accompanied by rotations and tricks. The sophisticated and culturally well-trained audience recognized the efforts of the young dancers with sincere applause as the velvet curtain closed. Professor Schneiderová, an expert in the Limón technique, introduced the next segment of the exam preceding the intermission. Her speech conveyed the purpose of modern dance, largely unknown to a former Eastern European public who most often spectated ballet performances of the classical genre. She went into great detail explaining the academy's curriculum, teaching the students to master the integration of grounded technique met with a deep expression of a message communicated differently from a framework of a ballet performance. The exam was to be performed in the dance attire, mandated by the academy and typical for students of any professional ballet school worldwide. There was nothing to hide any mistakes made during the course of the exam. The nerves were slowly calming down as the evening continued. The Limón and Graham portion was much less stressful than the classical portion of the examination. The audience seemed to enjoy viewing this new and fresh style of movement and often interrupted the flow with exuberant applause. We reached the finale of the first act of the evening and during the intermission the stage was set up for the premiere of "Peter and the Wolf." The stage crew moved in the sets and decorations for the ballet, as we prepared ourselves with a quick review of the choreography sequences. The second act was to be performed in costumes supplied by the wardrobe department of the theater, and it had a feel of a production rather than an exam. The committee was looking for artistry and the ability of the students to dance and tell a story with feelings and conviction. I was excited about the ballet, for I had discovered that storytelling was my stronger gifting when compared to the ballet technique still being strengthened and built.

The velvet curtain lifted for the last time that evening. The music was prerecorded, and the orchestra pit was covered, adding more stage surface and giving us more space to dance. We enjoyed telling the tale of Peter and the Wolf. An interesting fact about the ballet is that Prokofiev, loyal to the Communist regime, recorded the ballet with the political motivation of Peter being a young Soviet Pioneer. The premiere of the ballet was performed for a gathering of the Soviet Union Youth in 1936. Our class was to be the last class to perform this ballet at the end of the freshmen year of the conservatory, as new titles were being reviewed for selection. We, the students, as well as the audience enjoyed the production, nonetheless, and the panel of the examiners also seemed to be pleased with what was presented. Mr. Pokorný concluded the evening by expressing his gratitude and thankfulness for the audience's support of the academy and its vision to cultivate the next generation of young yet well-rounded artists. He, again, acknowledged the visiting dance professionals and sincerely thanked them for their support of the school and for the recognition of its freshmen-level accomplishments. We took a bow and enjoyed the applause rising from the audience filling the orchestra level as well as all three balconies of the theater. The night was a success, and we hoped that the results of the panel would concur with that sentiment. We had to wait to receive our grades as well as any notes and recommendations yet to be submitted. The results were to come soon, but the wait was going to be long. No doubt about that.

Let them praise His name with dancing.
—Psalm 149:3

44) Grateful

After two long weeks, Professor Gabajová walked into the studio to read the praise of the panel that the academy received and announced that all of us were recommended by the examiners to be promoted to the sophomore level of the conservatory. She and the other professors were to grade us based on the exam as well as the recommendations received. I was so relieved as it appeared that my dance career might have been given a green light to take flight. The first year of high school was behind me, the grades in both schools were satisfactory to the requirements of the leaderships of both institutions, and my parents and I were proud of everything that I was able to accomplish in this first year of living and studying in Liberec. The last week of the school year was also marked with the offer of a contract for a corps de ballet position with the State Theater for the following, 1990–1991, season. I was thrilled beyond words. When all was said and done, I could honestly conclude that this was a very hard, very operose, but a very fulfilling first year. I was leaving Liberec, returning to Ústí for the summer, looking out the train window excited about getting some rest, making a paper castle model with my dad, and enjoying the summer break to its fullest. I had a deep sense of accomplishment and was filled with a great joy of being united with my family for longer than just two nights. The summer was going to be great. I was convinced of that. And I was thankful.

"Give thanks to the Lord, for He is good; his love endures forever" (Psalm 107:1).

THE (UNEXPECTED) INTERMISSION

45) Value

The value of something is defined only by what one is willing to pay for it. Growing up in a Communist regime, I never heard anyone talk about nor say to me directly that we as humans have value. The emphasis was always placed on the society as a whole, on the socialist ideals of Marx and Lenin's teachings, on the success of corporate achievements of us as a nation, and on the progress of growth yet to be made. The individual citizens were simply the instruments used to reach these goals of a progressive and happy socialist republic. When these were achieved, then and only then would the individual citizens benefit in their personal joy and happiness. I never saw that come to fruition in Czechoslovakia or in any other Communist or socialist nation anywhere in the world. One must wonder why that is.

As a young teenager, I had no time to think of such deep issues. I had a path laid out before me leading to the career of a professional ballet dancer and the value of who I would become was directly connected to how well I would succeed in that field and how much I would be able to contribute to the society and its people. In the eyes of the government, I was not significant as a person. What mattered was my work ethic, my devotion to socialism, and my ability to contribute to the needs of the nation and its leading body, the Czechoslovak Communist Party. That changed when the Velvet Revolution occurred and socialism was ousted. The value of the individual citizens, however, was never considered or embraced into the equation of the social changes of the new Czechoslovakia. The amount of wealth one had, the entrepreneurship displayed by others, the success stories of those returning from exile, and the heavy focus on material success—these were the driving forces of the new era. Becoming someone who mattered or someone who meant something in the eyes of the public, these were the successful ones—the models to be followed or envied. It's interesting to think that we, the Czechoslovak people, were politically free and yet chained and held back from pursuing true joy and fulfillment. Did these even exist?

> *How precious to me are your thoughts,*
> *O God! How vast is the sum of them.*
> —Psalm 139:17

46) Chosen

Little did I know that my sophomore year would bring another revolution into the trajectory of my life. This revolution would forever alter my destiny and destination. This was a miraculous rescue work done on my behalf—done out of a deep love for me, done because a value that I didn't know about nor realized that I had was seen in me. I am very humbled to know that I have been singled out, that I have been handpicked out of the crowd, that I have been chosen; for I am a beneficiary of a great work completed for me and on my behalf—a work that has granted me the privilege to belong to something far greater than mere success of one's life lived in the world. Until this very day, I wonder about and ponder the motive behind this selection. Why was I a chosen one? Why, out of the ten million Czechs, was I to be the one rescued, valued, loved, and saved? Only God in His sovereign wisdom understands the reason. I am not to question His decision, I am to be grateful. As the Lord is my witness, I do just that.

> *For he chose us in him before the creation of the world to be holy and*
> *blameless in his sight. In love he predestined us for adoption to sonship*
> *through Jesus Christ, in accordance with his pleasure and will.*
> —Ephesians 1:4–5

47) Professor Rucký

We assembled back in Liberec after the summer break's conclusion. There was energy and excitement in the air. Both my classmates at the gymnázium and ballet school were filled with a new zeal to dive into the sophomore year of school. The nerves of the first year were at ease as we knew the routine and the requirements that were placed on us by the school, our parents, and ourselves. The only unknown element was the load of the contract with the theater. I was not quite sure what to expect, but under no circumstance was I to miss out on the opportunity to step into the sphere of professional experience the contract offered. I was ready for this new year of school, a new year of challenge, a new year of life.

During the first week of the academy, Mr. Pokorný introduced us to a new professor, Mr. Evald Rucký, a former principal dancer of the National Ballet, dance partner of the Prix de Lausanne laureate, accomplished artist, and a recipient of a master's degree from the famous College of Music and Dance in Prague. "He will be your morning technique class professor, as Professor Gabajová will focus on the afternoon technique class. What you will learn and gain from having both a male and a female professor for your ballet technique education is invaluable and will benefit you greatly. Please help me welcome Professor Rucký, and give him the respect and honor he deserves by working hard in his classes." And we did.

The school year was underway, and I was focusing on starting the race, really a marathon, of the next ten months. The volume of the gymnázium's expectations was poured out upon us on the first day. It was astonishing to me how each professor viewed their subject as the ultimate and most important field to be discovered, explored, and most importantly attained. There was very little, if any, understanding and care that eleven other academics were also being grasped by our young sophomore student minds and that each day did, indeed, have only twenty-four fleeting hours, to fit in all the studying and homework. The advantage of this second year was solely anchored in knowing the demands and expectations of each individual professor, the rhythm in which pop quizzes and oral examinations would occur, the ability to determine what was crucial to know and what could be omitted, and in the continually perfected competency to study anywhere and at any time. The public transportation vehicles, in all their forms, were a great place to wedge in what was not achieved in home studies. My focus had to remain on trigonometric functions, polynomials, logarithms, and other daunting areas of the world of mathematics. The greatest challenge remained in chemistry. This was going to be my fifth year of wandering in the desert of elements, atoms, chemical equilibriums, and chemical analysis. This course might as well have been in Chinese simplified Mandarin, for it made no sense to my mind whatsoever, and this year was, once again, going to be defined by my struggle to comprehend the incomprehensible. I was reminding myself of the famous statement saying "That which does not break us makes us stronger," and until this day, I wonder if, in this case, that was not at all the case.

In the ballet school, the year started in a swift and intense manner as well. There was a large group of freshmen that joined the academy, and I was reminded of myself just a year ago when I saw their faces clearly signaling a total overload on every level. I was looking forward to classes with Professor Rucký. He seemed different from the rest of the faculty and staff. His slightly heavy figure clearly indicated that the discipline required by professional ballet dancers was long gone and done away with. His legs were dominated by strong calves that still possessed the ability to propel his body into great heights when he would demonstrate brisk petite jumps and almost suspend himself in the air during the leaps of grand allegro. But he was strangely different. His classes were tough. There was almost a split personality disorder displayed by Professor Rucký. He changed the moment the arm of the clock struck six thirty in the morning. His warm face changed as if veiled with a mask. It took no time to earn our respect and full attention in his classes. There was no tolerance for misconduct and misbehavior and no room for fun. His classes were intense and painful. He believed and taught with conviction that progress of the young ballet students was only attained with hard work and hard work only. He explained to us that each student would only gather from his classes what we would be willing to invest into them. Then at eight fifteen, the moment class would come to an end, he became, once again, a warm and friendly fatherlike character that was welcoming and even charming. Every one of his classes always concluded with a sequence of sixty-four *changement de pieds* (*shahnzh-mahn duh pyay*)—jumps where the feet of the dancer are switched in the air from one position into another. This jump is typically done at the beginning of the allegro segment of the class, which was also the case in Professor Rucký's lessons, but he added them again at the end of his classes to build strength, as he put it. They were done in a painfully slow tempo, and once finished, we all waited for the permission to collapse to the floor in complete exhaustion. Professor Rucký seemed to enjoy seeing pain displayed on our faces and in our bodies. He would sit in the chair and wait for the pain to diminish. Then he would invite us to come closer to him. While we stretched, he spoke with us about life and things that were on our minds. No other faculty member would do that. He was different, and we did not know why. I looked forward to his direct challenge in the studio. His classes were my favorite, even at the ungodly hour of six thirty in the morning.

Every day, Professor Rucký's class was accompanied by an extremely gifted and talented pianist, Mr. Pavel Holoušek (*Ho-low-sheck*). I don't know much about him, and sad to say, I never cared to find out more about him and his past. Often, he would arrive at the ballet studio only to stumble behind the piano in the corner of the room. He was intoxicated as he often came to the ballet school directly from an overnight bar in the city somewhere. He was unable to carry a conversation, yet he played masterfully. All we knew was the fact that he was the pianist virtuoso of the famous Czech circus Humberto that was a state-owned and state-operated circus, founded in 1951 but closed in 1982. I do remember Professor Rucký speaking with Mr. Holoušek as if trying to convey to him his deep care. These exchanges would occur after the ballet class's conclusion before either one of them was to leave the ballet studio. I thought that this was a unique gesture for Professor Rucký to display affection to a man who was drowning his sorrow in alcohol abuse as if trying to silence deep pain and misery. I had never seen anything like this. Professor Rucký was unique and so very different.

One morning, class was coming to an end, and the dreaded changement combination was approaching slowly but surely. We all braced to embrace the pain that was to come. Professor clapped the tempo, and Mr. Holoušek started to play in accord. Five, six, seven, eight…we jumped. "Higher, higher," was the encouragement from the seated Professor Rucký, who clapped to make sure that the music would not speed up as the pain and exhaustion started to show their ugly faces. "Almost there, just thirty-two more, weight forward, push through, push through…," was his command. Survival was the only thing on my mind as I counted each jump to reach the magical number—sixty-four. Then the burning pain of standing in a tight fifth position had to be endured until permission to relax was given. With that, all of us around the studio collapsed to the ground. As usual, Professor Rucký would pull his chair to the front of the studio while looking around the room enjoying the painful grimaces on our faces. This particular morning, he said something different. He softly invited us to gather around him as he called us "his little sheep." I had no idea what that was supposed to mean. Was this another way to let us know that he was superior to us and that we were his subordinates? The pain in our legs was slowly easing up, and some of us slued slightly closer to the chair not knowing what was about to be said. Professor Rucký looked at us, trying to make quick eye contact with each person present. His face beamed with a calm and warm expression of care and love, usually only expressed toward Mr. Holoušek, whose glossy eyes reflected a complete loss and embarrassment for being in such an atrocious clutch of life and addiction. *What was this about?* I wondered. Then he continued… "It has been such a privilege teaching you these past couple of months. I must admit that it is extremely hard to get up so early every morning to come here and teach you. I want to say to you that I am not doing this for my love of ballet. That love faded a long time ago. I am not doing this to earn extra income either. I am not sure what you know about me. I feel compelled, and strongly compelled, to share with you who I am and why I am here." Even those who did not care to be near his chair paid close attention, as we all knew that this was going to be interesting information to be communicated. "I have spent many decades devoted to ballet—to train hard, to secure a spot at the National Ballet, to be someone, to mean something. I worked hard every day, as you do, pouring my efforts into becoming a professional. I trained diligently to qualify and compete at the Prix de Lausanne ballet competition in Switzerland and earn the trust of the Czechoslovak government to send me as a representative. Slowly and surely, my efforts started to pay off. Recognition by the Ministry of Culture and by the National Theater was no longer a mere dream. The day came when the invitation to join the first ballet company in the nation became a reality. Everything I dreamed of and desired to achieve was mine. But it left me void. I know that all of you, or most of you here, desire to make it to that level, to become a dancer or a ballerina that people recognize and purchase tickets to watch. That might or might not happen. The dance world is a very competitive field. Even if you make it and you reach your dreams, you do not know whether or not that dream is as valuable as you are imagining it to be. It was not for me. I desired to matter, and ballet left me wanting more. I desired to walk into a restaurant and be noticed, perhaps even applauded because I was the principal dancer of the National Ballet. The post, when reached, was nothing that I expected. I was very frustrated. When I was competing in Switzerland, I was introduced to a person that changed my life. His name is Jesus Christ. He has completely eradicated my desires for the glimmer and gleam of the theater world. He fulfilled me differently from how I was expecting to be fulfilled. The consequence of my faith was a denial to teach ballet under the former regime, as I was deemed an enemy of the state. Now that the country has politically changed, I joined the academy not to teach ballet but to share the hope that I have found in the relationship with the living Jesus Christ. I know this might be a completely foreign concept, something you have never considered or even heard of, but God is real, and He loves you, each one of you so personally and so deeply." That was about all we could handle. *What is going on? Who is this? Is he crazy? This makes no sense! This is ludicrous. On one hand, Professor Rucký is so different from every-*

body else on the staff. But a religious fanatic? Is that who they send here to teach us? We were shocked. We were in absolute consternation. Nobody knew what to do or what to say. And so we walked away. Slowly, respectfully walked away. This was an unexpected encounter, and none of us were ready to respond to it or to receive it. We left Professor Rucký sitting there on that chair. Was he to come back the next day? Was he to be totally embarrassed and humiliated? Would he be willing to be the point of the ridicule and humiliation, surely to come? Religion, faith as he called it, of all things? That was the craziest most radical view of anyone I had ever met. This is the twentieth century, when science, space exploration, and other successful progresses were achieved. Humanity did this. All on its own. We did not need God. We were just fine all on our own. God was not real. How could anyone believe in something so absurd? I left the conservatory, walking to the tram stop. That day, I skipped my bakery visit. I had no appetite. I was pondering what would happen to my favorite professor. Why did he have to ruin his chances to continue teaching us by admitting that he was a deeply devoted religious person? I got on the tram number 3 and stared out the window without noticing anyone or anything that we passed. I was in a complete state of utter shock.

The next day turned out quite ordinary. Professor Rucký came to teach his class, as usual. We were there to take his class, as usual, and Mr. Holoušek came in intoxicated to accompany the class, as usual. And we danced. It was a normal technique class as if nothing unusual was said the previous day. At the conclusion of the class, Professor Rucký pulled his chair into the front of the studio and sat on it, watching us breathe heavily as the pain slowly started to ease up in our bodies. I was surprised to see him being completely himself. There was not even a hint of embarrassment displayed in his behavior nor even the slightest sign of feeling rejected or sorry about the awkward exchange the day before. He sat there with his warm and caring face. I was captivated by his resolve to believe in something so strongly, to have convictions anchored in such a manner that no matter what others might think of him, he was unmoved. Then I realized that he was a religious man even under Communism. He said it himself that he was considered to be an enemy of the state; and yet he did not back down from his beliefs, he did not recant, and he did not change his story. I was intrigued. "May I ask you something, Professor Rucký?" I said as others continued to either trickle out of the studio or continued to stretch before following suit. "Sure, anything," he said. "I was wondering…well, yesterday you mentioned… I am not sure how to put this." I stumbled through my words. Was I really prepared and ready to engage in a conversation about something that made no sense to me whatsoever? Did I care to know more about him and his faith? What really piqued my interest was to know how one could be a believer when religion was not permitted in a society that was overthrown a year ago or so. How was that possible? And so I continued… "I was wondering when you announced that you became religious, were there any consequences for such a statement…? I mean how could you do that under the Communist regime?" I felt awkward as I did not know any proper terms, and I did not want to call him something that could offend him, something that was not appropriate. My friend Petra was one of the few who stayed in the studio to listen and possibly join in a conversation with Professor Rucký. I was glad that I was not the only one who was thinking a lot about him. There were others who pondered what he said yesterday and how, if at all, it would change our view of him and of how we would relate to him from this point on. We gathered around the chair to listen and to debate religion should it come down to it. I knew nothing about the subject, and until this point in my life, I never considered the existence of God whatsoever. I was only interested to hear about him being an enemy of the state, as he put it. Professor Rucký looked at us intently. "I am glad that we can talk about this some more," he started. "I knew that what I said yesterday was revolutionary to you all, that it was a radical thought to hear, and even more radical thought to embrace. I am not naïve to think that you would welcome the notion that God exists without asking more questions. He created us to think, He created us to communicate, but He also created us to believe in Him and have a life-changing relationship with Him. You might not believe in God, per say, but everyone believes in something. There is that foundation on which your worldview stands. It might be your own talent or ability. It could be your dedication, your discipline, your hard work that you count on. It could be believing that there is a higher power. You just never titled it 'God.' You might be placing your stakes into the field of justice and fairness, believing that if you follow all the rules and regulations or the convictions of your own heart, you will receive whatever you are longing for. I am not here to convince you. I am not here to debate with you. I am here to share about what, better yet Who, changed my life. When I heard about the Lord in Switzerland, I was just as hesitant as you were yesterday. But the person who shared his faith with me had something I did not have. That I was certain of. Slowly but surely, the Lord started to change me, and over a long period of time, He opened my eyes to see that He, indeed, is real and that I so desperately needed Him to be my Savior. I am not a religious person, meaning I do not do some religious rituals required by some religious system of beliefs. I met the living God, and He altered me completely. When I realized that, I needed to…no, I wanted to serve Him. I started to talk about my faith, and I was called out on it. It was made clear to me by both the National Theater's leadership as well as the Ministry of Culture that if I continued to hold such views and talk about them with others, I would no longer be able to dance at the National Theater, an institution built to bring healthy encouragement to the people of our nation. My views were not aligned with the beliefs of the government, and I had a choice to make. In my heart, however, the choice was already determined. I found a source of life that no career, no post, no role, no fame, no recognition, no stature, no status could ever come close to. My friends and colleagues at the theater were telling me to keep my faith to myself and publicly continue as I was prior to Switzerland, but I could not do that. My desire was to learn more about Christ and to serve Him with my life. And so I had to leave the National Ballet." Professor Rucký spoke with such enthusiasm, such conviction sitting on the chair in a ballet studio. This was not a rehearsed speech. He spoke plainly not trying to sway our mood. There was nothing fancy about this moment—just a man speaking from his heart about something he believed in wholeheartedly. It was captivating and convincing. How profound his belief must have been to give up the career of the principal dancer at the National Theater. Was Professor Rucký crazy, or did he have something that was truly life changing? I did not know. I did not care. I knew that I had so much to learn from him as my ballet professor, and so what if he was a believer? It did not matter; it was secondary. I had school to focus on, a contract with the theater to enjoy, and a career and goals to achieve and reach. Professor Rucký was a help along the way, and I would be a fool to toss that opportunity aside because I did not see eye to eye on his religious convictions. The more I thought about it over the weeks and months to come, the more I enjoyed the inkling that I knew someone who believed in God, someone who openly professed that Jesus Christ was the Savior of the world—the Messiah who loved us, the God who saw value in us, and the Father who deeply cared for us. Life went on as Professor Rucký would keep pulling up his chair every morning to talk with us, to ask us about life, to answer any and every question we might have brought up to challenge his faith and find out more. But one thing I was certain of was the undeniable fact that he was gaining respect and value in our eyes simply because he was willing to take time, willing to invest in our lives. It made a powerful impact on many of our hearts.

Rejoice with me; I have found my lost sheep. I tell you that in the same way there will be more rejoicing in heaven over one sinner who repents than over ninety-nine righteous persons who do not need to repent.
—Luke 15: 6b–7

48) Two Sides of the Velvet Curtain

The busyness of life increased from the load of the corps de ballet contract. The academy students were selected for other productions at the State Theater. We would be included in other ballets the company was performing as well as opera productions and operettas, which were my favorite. Being a part of regularly scheduled programming was a high privilege, and initially it was everything I was hoping for it to be. Keeping up with school and studies, on the other hand, was a challenge. Every night after a performance, I would arrive in the dorm to two snoring roommates way after the ten o'clock lights out. I would take a textbook to the bathroom and try to finish homework or study in preparation for the next day. Often the textbook would wake me up hitting the floor, after slipping out of my hand as I slumbered off. I learned that these late nights would produce a very small harvest of wisdom and learning. The body was simply too tired to comprehend any more or gain any new knowledge. I was not sure how I would be able to manage keeping my grades up and keep all my plates in the air, so to speak.

Every opening night would take place on a Friday. The ballet students, if we were in the cast of the show, were invited to the theater club for a celebration of the successful premiere. This is where I started to learn an interesting thing about myself. I was an introvert. It did not bother me one bit to be on the stage in front of the crowd, but I was an absolute disaster when it came to socializing with the other performers during these parties. I was torn as I wanted to belong, and yet there was nothing I enjoyed more than going to the dorm and getting some much-needed rest after a long week of running around like a chicken without its head. Petra was experiencing a similar feeling. She was a bit more extroverted than me, but these parties had very little to offer to make her excited about them. We both went out of obligation and out of the desire to want to belong. We simply did not.

It started to be apparent to me that the theater world had two faces. There was life in front of the curtain, and then there was life behind it after the curtain closed. Short-lived relationships between different cast members were the norm. The pain of broken hearts and emptiness of life seemed to mark most of the artists who, under the bright lights of the stage, seemed to be on a mountaintop of their careers and of their lives just a few brief moments ago. Why was it like this? Why were these people hurting so badly? I did not know, but I was afraid that I might end up like them. The State Theater was not the National Theater, and perhaps things were different there, I would hope. Then I remembered what Professor Rucký said about his experienced hollowness on the "first stage" of the nation. I was puzzled and confused. I did not know why life was like this, but I saw it all around me behind the beautiful velvet curtain of the theater.

Do not be misled: Bad company corrupts good character.
— 1 Corinthians 15:33

49) As Small as a Seed

The year went on, and the routine became just that, a routine. Less and less time spent in a classroom of the gymnázium, more and more morning hours spent in rehearsals for the next upcoming production dance classes six days a week, and a painful heartache of missing my family were the constant elements of my life. I was struggling. I was working hard, and I wanted to enjoy everything life was offering me, yet I simply could not. I was experiencing a profound sense of overload. My gravitation toward perfectionism was killing the joy in my life. My grades were harder to maintain, the competition in the ballet studio was intensifying, and lack of steady and proper intake of food was reflecting in my weight loss. These in combination with an absence of proper and replenishing sleep produced a perfect storm of a life lived in constant overdrive. More and more, I was realizing that the dream of dancing professionally might not be all I had imagined. I was struggling to stay afloat and to keep my life intact.

Professor Rucký was daily and faithfully encouraging, scrupulously sharing his faith with the students after every class, and persistently modeling that life was, somehow, meant to be lived differently, with a deeper sense of fulfillment, meaning, and peace. But how?

Petra and I would often elaborate on Professor Rucký's remarks. When time would permit, we would find and spend a few moments sitting in a café enjoying an ice cream sundae to talk about the struggles of life as well as the novelty of what Professor Rucký was sharing with us. Little did we realize that there was a growing interest in our hearts to know more, to explore deeper the things he was talking about. Neither one of us was ready to admit it out loud, and definitely not publicly, but the curiosity in me was like a spring flower growing out of a tiny seed planted in the fertile soil.

During one of my visits at home, I mentioned to my parents in a very low-key manner some of the things I heard from Professor Rucký at school. The amazement and utter shock were clearly obvious on both of their faces. They dismissed it with a statement clearly indicating that there was nothing to be discussed, as such religious ideals were purely nonsense and completely fabricated lies, serving as a crutch in the lives of those who could not handle life on their own and in their own strength. Little did they know that their firstborn son belonged in that category. I was not ready to admit that God might exist, but I did need help in handling my life as it was apparently starting to unravel at the seams. I did not want to bother my folks with my burdens, and so I left Ústí with a smile on my face, perfecting the ability to mask my feelings and put on the act of being the one in control and thriving.

> *No one can come to me (Jesus) unless the*
> *Father who sent me draws him.*
>
> —John 6:44

50) All This Time God Was at Work

In the early spring of 1991, the morning ballet technique class was nearing its end, and the brutally slow series of the changement jumps was heading our way. Clap, clap, clap... "Five, six, seven, eight...one," was the clear command of Professor Rucký as we faced ourselves in the mirrors on the wall and started the last exercise. The burning pain faithfully showed up again. One would think that after all this time, the body would be accustomed to such "abuse," but the opposite was the sad reality. The aching muscles clearly indicated the reality that, no matter how long we tried to strengthen them, this last portion of the class was always to be taking its fateful toll. Then we stood there waiting for the permission to relax and to fall to the ground to ease the pain. Once again, Professor Rucký would drag his chair to the front of the studio to sit on it and watch us squirm in painful agony. He really seemed to enjoy that. Then he called us to gather, and we did. It was clear that most of us deeply valued him and appreciated his care for us, no matter what his personal beliefs might have been, for he genuinely loved us. This particular morning, he told us about a youth gathering at his church. People of our age were coming together, he stated, to fellowship, play games, worship God, and enjoy one another's company. Our blank facial expressions must have clearly indicated that we had no idea what any of that meant. Again, none of us grew up in any kind of religious upbringing. There was no understanding, whatsoever, to be able to relate and comprehend what he was talking about. In my own mind, when one spoke of church, I pictured a gothic structure of a cathedral with its impressive ribbed, vaulted ceilings. I imagined a sand-colored-smooth-stone-walled building decorated with statues of saints and stained-glass windows and filled with incense. I saw an ornate altar reaching imposing heights as the object of focus with wooden pews lining the two sides of the sanctuary forming a wide aisle leading toward a table bedecked with artifacts necessary for the ceremonies required to appease God and make the gathered feel better about themselves. A loudly played organ would create an atmosphere of reverence and even awe for the few assembled. This was my preconception of a church service. In my convictions and understanding, all these were completely useless and empty attempts of humanity to find and acquire stability in their otherwise broken lives. These so-called services accomplished nothing as God Himself, the very focal point of it all, did not exist. I had never witnessed a church gathering, so it was difficult to imagine and make sense of what Professor Rucký was talking about. What was a youth group, and how would that fit into what I was envisioning? He extended an invitation to all of us to come on a Wednesday when our schedule would allow it, and see firsthand for ourselves, what he was describing to us. Petra, myself, and another student, Marika, were the only ones who would accept his invitation and venture out to visit a youth group gathering.

The given note had an address of the Jednota Bratrská Church. In the English-speaking world, the church is known as the Moravian

Church, a Protestant movement that began in 1457 and is directly linked to the reformation work of John Hus. I didn't know or understand any of this at the time. We followed the written instructions and ended up on a narrow uphill street named after a Czech writer, Božena Němcová. At the very end of the street—standing on a hill overlooking the city below and on two sides surrounded by Communist-built apartment blocks—stood a two-story building. No steeple, no stained-glass gothic broken arch windows. We were perplexed. The street number on the building corresponded to the address on the note. The door was opened, and we cautiously walked in. A narrow hallway led to a staircase with a beautiful iron railing on its side. There were doors on the right and left sides of us. Again, one of those was wide open. We walked in to find a medium-sized room with plain white walls. No icons, no incense. There were no pews, just simple chairs facing the opposite wall. A straight upright piano was in a corner, but no one was playing it. A young man was playing a guitar instead while singing on top of his lungs. There were no microphones, and so he needed to project loudly to be heard and to be followed by those gathered. I was confused as to why they were already singing. We arrived on time, stepping into the building exactly at seven o'clock. There were a handful of high school—age men and women peppered throughout the room. With their arms raised and eyes closed, they sang with the leader. They appeared to sing to someone not present among them, as their focus was clearly in another place, in another sphere. What struck me was the overwhelming captivating peace in the room. It was tangible and strikingly different from anything I had ever experienced before. This peace stood in stark contrast to the chaos and busyness of my life that was so overwhelming at this time. We did not know the songs they sang, and so we sat down and listened and simply observed this unique experience unfolding all around us. After about fifteen minutes, to our surprise, our professor walked into the front of the room and welcomed us all to the student gathering.

He introduced himself as Evald Rucký, the pastor of the Liberec branch of the Moravian Church. *"Pastor" what!* I thought. *Our ballet professor is the pastor of this church, no way!* We were shocked. He never mentioned that before. Were we deceived and tricked into coming here? Did it matter that he was a pastor? My mind was racing. I looked at Petra and Marika. The level of their surprise of this utterance was clearly visible in their facial expressions as well. It was almost comical to watch them try to still themselves and remain calm and collected. Professor, or should I say Pastor Rucký, went on, "I would like to welcome three newcomers, who bravely decided to join us this evening. Please help me welcome my ballet students Marika, Petra, and Jiri. Can you guys stand up please?" We slowly and awkwardly stood up to the cheering and clapping of those around us. My face was slowly changing from its natural coloring to deep-red splotches indicating the embarrassment that I was experiencing at the moment. We sat back down. Professor Rucký welcomed everyone and started the meeting with a similar set of questions he would ask us at the end of a ballet class: questions concerning life and its struggles. Different people around us replied, and I observed a very comfortable and extremely natural conversation to evolve in the room. Another unique element was the fact that everyone called Professor Rucký "Brother Evald" as they responded to his questions. I understood that he was not their biological brother and quickly realized that this had something to do with the church setting we were in. It was strange, but I liked it. Professor Rucký was held in high esteem by everyone there, as it was the case in his academy class. They talked about their struggles at school, at home, in their relationships. Nothing seemed to be off-limits. Apparently, nothing was too awkward to be said. This lasted a good thirty minutes or so. The atmosphere in the room was inviting and very much family-like.

Professor Rucký proceeded to pick up a large book that was lying on one of the chairs. The book seemed to have seen better days, as it appeared worn out and used quite a bit. As he opened it, there were markings of many colors highlighting words and phrases of the text. He searched for a particular passage, I assumed, and once he found it, he closed his eyes. Then he started to speak. "Dear Lord, I thank You for this evening. I praise You, Lord Jesus, for who You are. I worship You, and I thank You that You are here in this room tonight, working in our hearts and souls. Have your way. Teach us as we read Your Word. Open our eyes to see You. I pray in Jesus's mighty name, amen." I realized that, for the very first time in my sixteen years of life, I witnessed a man praying. I was baffled by its simplicity and authenticity. He prayed from his heart, and as far as I could tell, it was not a memorized prayer that he recited. He spoke to someone he clearly believed was listening. I perceived it as somewhat sweet and powerful.

Professor Rucký proceeded to invite everyone in the room to open their Bibles to the given text. My memory does not recall the text he pointed out for everyone to find, but they all seemed to have no struggle in doing just that. A young lady brought a copy of a Bible to us already opened to the given text and placed it into my hands. I had never seen, moreover held, a Bible before. There was no one I knew, absolutely nobody I knew, who had a Bible in their living room gracing a shelf of their home library or anyone who would keep it on a nightstand to be read in the morning for a daily inspiration. We never learned about it at school, and until this moment, I never pondered what the Bible was and whether or not it possessed any value in its content. Now, at the age of sixteen, I was holding one. *What would my parents think if they knew?* flashed through my mind. Petra and Marika leaned in to follow along as Professor Rucký commenced to read. It became obvious and apparent that we were the only ones present who did not understand the perused text. "Amens" echoed across the room as different statements were read and articulated by "Brother Evald." After the reading concluded, a brief message and discussion about its meaning emerged. Everyone was involved in the conversation and seemed to love this exchange of thoughts and ideas. Professor Rucký was beaming with pleasure and joy as he watched these students discuss the scriptures and derive from them an application to and for their lives.

My soul faints with longing for your salvation,
but I have put my hope in your word.

—Psalm 119:81

51) For the First Time

Over an hour had passed. The ending time was approaching, and Professor/Pastor Evald stood up in front of the room. "This has been a life-giving evening. The Lord was here among us, and I praise Him for that truth. He unveiled His word to us, and I believe that He changed us tonight. I would like to conclude the evening with an invitation for anyone who does not personally know the Lord to come up front. We will pray with them and for them to invite the living God into their lives. This is a step of faith. This is a big step that requires boldness. Please, anyone, come up front if you do not personally know the Lord Jesus Christ." I caught myself gripping the seat of the chair. My knuckles were turning pale white. There was no way that I was going to go upfront and do any of what Professor Rucký was inviting us to do. Petra and Marika both were also glued to their chairs. We were trapped; there was no escape. To walk out would seem rude, and possibly devastating to Professor Rucký; but we could not, we would not, go to receive prayer. There was no way out! "The Lord has time, and so do we," Professor Rucký continued. He invited the young man to play his guitar and lead the gathered in worship songs while we waited. "I know there are some here who do not know the love the Lord Jesus has for them." I knew that he was looking at the three of us. I was looking down, staring into the carpet below, determined not to look at the professor. I knew that he was a stern man. I knew that any kind of argument would be won by him and lost by me.

Maybe he would quit; perhaps he would give up. I had to wait and let this moment of discomfiture pass. "Thank You, Lord, for Your faithful work for us and in us. I praise You for your patience, God," he continued. Everyone was standing and singing with their eyes closed. Could we sneak out? We could not. We were absolutely unable to leave the room even though the discomfort was palpable. "I know there are some here that do not know You, Lord. Draw them tonight, Father!" Evald prayed. I started to panic as I knew that I was losing this battle. Professor Rucký was determined to win, and unless we went up front for a prayer, we would be sitting there forevermore.

I looked at Petra and Marika. They were as confused and as alarmed as I was. "What should we do?" I whispered. "We will sit here endlessly unless we go up for a prayer," I continued. "Thank You, Lord, for Your victory," sounded from the front. I was getting upset and frustrated. It was clear to all of us that there was only one way onward and a prayer with the pastor was inevitable. Slowly, almost in shame, we rose from our chairs and slowly walked up front. I saw Professor Rucký smiling. He was not making fun of us, nor was he thinking that we were weak. He truly believed that this was a moment of grand importance. He welcomed us with a warm embrace. *Strange*, I thought, but at this point, I was willing to do whatever was necessary to be able and permitted to leave the gathering. Professor Rucký placed us in a small semicircle and started to pray. He prayed quietly as he moved from one to the other. Again, I was looking down at the carpet beneath me, not daring to look him in the eye. I closed my eyes and braced myself for whatever was coming. My mind and intellect were on high alert. There was a clear argument happening within my cognitive understanding. I was not ready to hop on the wagon of faith and religion. God did not exist; that I knew for certain. And even though this evening was pleasant and everyone here seemed authentic, this was not for me. Professor Rucký approached me. With my eyes closed, I could sense his nearness. He placed his hand on the top of my head and started to pray. I stood there bearing through the moment. As he continued to plead for me and on my behalf before the throne of God, as he put it, I recall only one thing. I resolved to demand of God that, surely, it would not be too difficult to prove Himself to me. I admitted my inability to believe in Him unless I was given proof that He was real and that He existed. In my ignorance, I requested of the God of the universe to meet my demands if this faith thing was going to go anywhere. I knew that this petition would never be answered, would never be met. Professor Rucký concluded with a loud amen, and to my surprise, so did I. We said goodbye and walked out. All three of us were relieved that this was behind us. We knew that we would never come back. I shared with both Petra and Marika my request of God to prove Himself to me. They thought that it was a clever move. Little did I know that the Lord took my proposal seriously and that a plan was already underway for the King of the universe to meet with me in a powerful and a life-changing way, demonstrating and declaring to me not only His existence but also, and more importantly, His passion and love for me.

Taste and see that the Lord is good; blessed is
the man who takes refuge in him.
—Psalm 34:8

52) Meeting the Hero

Life went on, only it appeared to align itself with a fast track of sorts. Engagements at the state theater became frequent and regular occurrences; late-night studying in the bathroom solidified as the new norm. Conversations with my parents over the phone were thankfully recurring more often as the Liberec Central Post Office building was located across the square from the theater, and every time I had a performance, I would stop by the office to call home. Once a month, I took a trip to Vítězná třída (*Vee-tez-naa tree-dah*) (Czech for "Victory Avenue"), where I had the privilege to collect my paycheck at the directorate of the State Theater. It was exciting to receive an income as I was completely dependent on my parents for every crown. Both schools were free of charge, but the room and board at the dorm were not. My parents gladly covered that expense. There was no immediate pressure for money, yet it was nice to know that extra income was coming my way.

That same springtime, in April of 1991, Mr. Pokorný gathered the students of the sophomore year of the state ballet school in the studio, stating that he had a special announcement to make. As we were used to being frequently summoned to receive special instructions, I did not think twice about what this could be about. "Hello, everyone, I hope that you all are doing well and everyone is doing fine. I wanted to let you know that I am extremely pleased with your efforts here at the conservatory but also applaud you for what you bring to the stage at the theater. I do understand the newness and the challenge of the task of dancing with the professional artists of the company, but I feel that it is essential for you to hear that you are doing well and your artistry and technique are growing increasingly as you become steadily more comfortable in the lights of the stage. I did not call you here today to pour my praises on you solely... I have brought you here to let you know that the president of the Czech and Slovak Federative Republic, the newly adopted postrevolution name of Czechoslovakia, His Excellency Václav Havel, will be coming to the Liberec region. The regional governor has requested that the State Theater participate in the entertainment for the president. After a conversation with the leadership of the theater, we concluded that showcasing the future talent of the city is what we need to present. I have been commissioned to prepare a short program for the president, and I selected your class to be those performing for His Excellency. This special appearance will be in two weeks at the Sychrov chateaux, just outside of the city, where President Havel will be stopping for a lunch during his visit to the city and the Liberec region. We will be performing the section from the *Špalíček* ballet where you are the featured artists. The State Theater orchestra will be playing live and you will be dancing in the courtyard of the chateaux, entertaining the president. I do not know the security requirements just yet, but we have two weeks to make sure that everything is taken care of and prepared, and to showcase the achievements of Liberec and of the academy. Questions?" There were none as we sat there feeling overwhelmed with excitement. In two short weeks, we would get to perform and meet the president of our nation. He was the hero of Czechoslovakia as he led the people through the Velvet Revolution some fourteen months prior. This was a great honor and a privilege, and we were willing to put in the extra rehearsal work Mr. Pokorný was surely to demand, to ready ourselves to be, and to do our best. It was more the desire to honor our leader than anything else. President Havel was doing a marvelous job of leading the republic toward democracy, as so many remains of the forty years of Communism were, sadly, prevalent in the society. It was a difficult and fragile task, but if there was one person who could do it, it was our cherished president, Mr. Václav Havel. In two weeks' time, we were bussed to Sychrov where the technical crew of the theater prepared and built a stage in the corner of the historic courtyard the night before. We arrived and immediately went through security scrutiny by the presidential secret service. Once cleared, we were led to a room that served as our dressing room, where we were watched by an agent of the presidential protective team. It was located on the bottom floor of the main chateaux building. I remember when the presidential limousine pulled through the neo-gothic gate of the castle, and President Havel stepped out of the car to be greeted by the leadership of the region and the city. We were peeking through the windows to catch a glimpse of the president. He and the first lady, Ms. Olga Havlová, settled in the middle of the first row of chairs, and we were summoned to the stage. The performance lasted a short twenty minutes. We danced with fervor and dedication. Afterward, the president applauded us, and both, he and the first lady, shook our hands. He was much shorter than I expected, but there was something special about him and his persona that made him appear larger than life. As he was greeting us, I was remembering all the accomplishments of this one man, who was willing to put aside personal comfort to be a tool in bringing liberty, democracy, and prosperity to the Czech land. Dancing for the president and meeting him that warm and sunny April day has remained a cherished memory in my heart and life.

I urge you then, first of all, that requests, prayers,
intercession and thanksgiving be made for everyone—
for kings and all those in authority, that we may live
peaceful and quiet lives in all godliness and holiness.
—1 Timothy 2:1–2

53) Running from Suez to Sucre

As the weeks and months continued to unfold, we were preparing for another public exam to graduate from the second level of the ballet school and be permitted to move up to the junior, or third level, of the academy. Written tests and oral exams at the gymnázium also increased in magnitude as we were nearing the end of the school year in June. This seems to be a great place in my storytelling to share about Professor Havlík (*Hav-leek*), the gymnázium faculty member responsible for teaching geography. Professor Havlík had the build of a marine. He was tall and masculine. He wore circularly framed glasses, too small for his face, defined by a strong jawline. His mustache indicated that he used to be redheaded. There was no hair left on his head, and his baldness only intensified his tough demeanor. He was passionate about geography and often ridiculed those who saw his subject as an easy breeze to a solid A. One time, he entered the classroom with a large amount of rolled-up maps. He asked us to hang them around the room and then sat behind the desk in front of the class. "Voborsky, how nice of you to join us today," he said with a tone of clear disapproval of my ISP. I suppose that he saw my choosing of when I would and would not be attending classes as something completely baseless and without merit. "Come up front here, please!" he continued. "Today we will see if the stamina gained from your 'dancing training' will help you secure a good grade in geography. That is, if you know some basic locations around the world, all included in the glossary I gave everyone at the beginning of the semester." By the time he finished stating all this, I was standing by the blackboard not knowing what was heading my way. "I have cards here with ten locations written on each one. All you have to do after you select one is to run to the appropriate map, find and point out the designated location, and then run to show us the next one. You will have sixty seconds to do that. For every missed location, your grade will go down. You miss four, and you have failed. Clear?" He looked at me through his glasses that could have used a bit of cleaning. I could tell that he was convinced that there was no hope for me and a failing grade was on its way. "Yes, Mr. Professor," I replied. It is appropriate to mention here that we had stopped addressing the faculty as "Comrade Professor" now that the Communist regime was obsolete. It was a difficult habit to break as all my schooling years I was drilled to say just that. As I stood there looking at Professor Havlík, a surge of determination to succeed was rising up within me. It felt like an arm wrestling competition. Only one of us was going to be the winner. It needed to be me for two reasons: firstly, to get a good grade and, secondly, to demonstrate to Professor Havlík that I was not easily intimidated by him and his teaching methods, even though the exact opposite was true. Just as I was preparing to prove my geographical knowledge of the globe, he pulled out a stopwatch to time my efforts. Professor Havlík also taught physical education, and today, I suppose, he was combining the two subjects into one grand experience, I thought. He fan-opened the cards before his face, and I selected the one in the middle. "And go!" he shouted as he pushed the button at the top of the stopwatch.

Denali was the first term on the card. I ran to the map of North America and, on the Alaskan peninsula, located the highest mountain of the continent.

Gobi Desert, a brushland located between China and Mongolia, was next. The map of Asia was hanging at the back of the classroom. And so I ran. All my classmates were cheering me on *silently*. I could sense their support.

Tasmania was next. *Tasmania, Tasmania*, I was thinking. Right, an island south of Australia. *There it is.* I hurried toward the map of the Australian continent.

"Rhine," I shouted next. *It is a river in Germany*, I thought. *Europe, where is the map of Europe?* I looked frantically around the classroom. *There it is.* I sprinted dodging desks, chairs, and my friends. Time was running quickly, and Professor Havlík was in his element of pure devilish enjoyment watching my striving.

Suez Canal is a narrow man-made channel dividing Africa and the Sinai peninsula. *Where is the map of Africa?* I was panicking. *There it is.* I started to run toward it, already eyeing the northeastern corner of "the Dark Continent" to locate the canal.

Burkina Faso is a small landlocked nation in Africa. At least I did not need to run anywhere this time, as I could point out Burkina Faso on the same map I just ran to.

Sucre. My eyes saw the clearly written word, but my mind was going blank. *Sucre, Sucre.* It sounded familiar, but I could not think of what and where it was.

Caspian Sea, that was easy. I returned to the map of Asia and pointed out the sea, considered to be the largest landlocked body of water in the world, located in Russia.

Andes Mountains... A long range of mountains running down the western coast of South America. Easy. As I ran toward the map of South America, I started to notice my perspiration. As I was pointing to the mountain range, my eye caught a glimpse of Sucre, the capital city of Bolivia.

"Sucre," I said as I pointed to the circled star, indicating capitals, in the middle of Bolivia. I was not sure if Professor Havlík would credit it to me or not, but there it was.

Lake Victoria was the last item on the card. I did not know what time I had left, but I ran back to the map of Africa to point out the lake on the western border of Kenya. "Here," I yelled as I pointed to the body of water.

"Impressive, Mr. Voborsky," was what he uttered, but I knew that he was not pleased with the result. "I do not think that I can give you credit for Sucre, so it will be a B. But other than that, you did well." I was satisfied with a B.

Then he called out two more classmates. It was much more enjoyable to watch them take this unique quiz than it was to be the one taking it. That was for sure.

The earth is the Lord's, and everything in it, the world, and all who live in it; for he founded it upon the seas and established it upon the waters.
—Psalm 24:1–2

54) Falling in Love...with Opera

The State Theater hosted performances at its historical building in the center of Liberec but occasionally toured throughout the country and abroad. These were fun excursions from the regular rhythm of life. During this second season at the theater, I was dancing in many productions of the ballet and opera companies. The exposure to new genres of art was an amazing gift that I cherished and enjoyed thoroughly. My favorite operetta, which in its nature is a prequel to musicals with spoken and sung words, is *Die Fledermaus*, also known under its English title *The Bat* by Johann Strauss. This fun-filled piece is brimming with incredible arias and a plot of comedy, misunderstanding, and fun. In the middle of it all is the famous waltz "A der schönen, blauen Donau," known as the "Blue Danube Waltz," often played by the Vienna Philharmonic Orchestra at New Year's celebrations, televised from the Staatsoper in Vienna, Austria. This almost eleven-minute waltz was an incredible workout but also extraordinarily fun to dance. My love for opera was awakened while dancing in the famous French opera by Georges Bizet, telling the tale of love of a cigar-factory worker in Seville, Spain. You guessed well—it was Carmen. There were so many opportunities for a rhythm-filled flamenco-style dancing all throughout the four acts of the performance. When I was not dancing, I would sit in the wings and listen to the high-caliber singing talent of my colleagues of the opera company. I heard once that opera is an art form that is either loved or hated. The very first exposure to its flavor is, therefore, crucial. It has been my recommendation to everyone, since these days at the State Theater that when in search through the opera world, one should always start with "Carmen," where the melodies are known, the music is captivating, and the production is well-balanced with action, singing, dancing, and, well, passion.

Sing to the Lord a new song, for he has done marvelous things.
—Psalm 98:1

55) Under the Alps

While in the second season of dancing as a corps de ballet member of the ballet company, the theater was booked to perform a series of shows in a beautiful city of St. Gallen, Switzerland. When touring domestically, the stage crew usually went ahead of the cast to set the stage with the lighting and production sets a day before the show. When we toured to Switzerland, however, it was all of us traveling together. I came to the theater building, which was our meeting spot fifteen minutes before the designated time. It was then, and still is now, a habit of mine to be ahead of the indicated time for a meeting or a gathering. I did not realize the sheer amount of buses and cargo trucks necessary to transport the full ensemble of the opera—ballet and the State Theater orchestra as well as all the other personnel, sets, and equipment necessary for a successful series of productions in St. Gallen. My classmates and I were designated to a bus transporting the ballet students, who were the youngest members of the cast, as well as some members of the orchestra and the supporting personnel members. I was glad to travel and sit next to people I already knew. It was during the ride to Switzerland when I witnessed a sad display of behavior by some of those with us on the bus. Language, coarse joking, inappropriate touching, and more were shocking to my classmates and me. We could only imagine how that would increase upon our arrival and settling in the hotel in St. Gallen. Sadly, we were right. It was not that my friends and I were pure in our actions and thoughts. We were already experimenting with lifestyles deemed inappropriate for someone of high school age, but these elders around us were modeling behavior that was immoral in so many ways. I realized then how easily persuaded we all can be. It doesn't take much for one to start mirroring actions that, otherwise, would not be thinkable, appealing, or desired to be a part of one's life or habits. It was not a conscious decision of mine to abstain from most of the invitations offered to me by those around us as well as my classmates. Now, looking back, I know that the Lord, in His mercy, was protecting me by granting me desires contrary to those around me. Why would I be given convictions others did not adhere to? Why was the Lord working in my life before I ever surrendered my heart to Him or before I had the slightest inclination to please Him? I do not know the answer, but I am thankful, extremely thankful, that the One I was yet to meet was already gracious and merciful to me in countless moments of my young life. I am filled with gratitude to have been protected from unnecessary heartache that I saw in the lives of the professionals and classmates around me whose choices led them to unforeseen consequences and pain. I am grateful.

Performances in St. Gallen were a huge success, and we returned back home with a sense of a mission well done. We represented our nation, our city, and the name of the Šalda State Theater well. I was blown away by the beauty of the city, which is considered to be the gateway to Appenzellerland, the Alpine region of Switzerland. The center of the town features a splendid baroque abbey of St. Gall, hosting one of the richest medieval libraries in the world. The whole complex is a UNESCO heritage sight and worthy to be visited and admired. The overall cleanliness of the city and the region was a sight to behold as Czechs had a long way to go in learning to keep our own surroundings in order. Switzerland was my second country of the former western block to have visited. What made the greatest impact on me, however, goes beyond the beauty of the city and its buildings, beyond the incredible display of the Swiss Alps. What impacted me most, what I pondered continually, was the manner of the citizens that we witnessed from both the personnel at the theater that we directly worked with and the regular citizens we met on the streets. There was an overwhelming calm exuberating from their lives. Their western mind-set was foreign to us, but it was extremely appealing and desirable. Would we, would I, ever be able to live a life marked with such unique quietness and peace? I was not able to even begin to imagine living without constant worry, overload, and stress. I was not sure what exactly the secret ingredient was that brought the seemingly balanced approach to life of the Swiss people, but what I did know was the truth that something in my life was missing. But what?

He will call upon me, and I will answer him; I will be with
him in trouble, I will deliver him and honor him. With a
long life will I satisfy him and show him my salvation.
—Psalm 91:15–16

56) Dwindling Strength

As water continues to flow under a bridge, so do the days of our lives continue to pursue their unrelenting course of never stopping, never slowing down. Every day brings new joys, new challenges, new difficulties. Every day offers its opportunity to be lived out just that one time. Then it vanishes, never to be lived again. I found myself striving more and more to maintain the image of one being fully in control, fully in charge. No one but I knew the deep striving of my mind, my body, my emotions. There were so many nights when I sat on the floor of the dorm's bathroom, hours passing, with my textbook opened but my mind wandering a million miles away, unable and too exhausted to learn, and with streams of tears flowing down my face. Was my load too heavy to carry? Will I fail to graduate? Did I make a mistake in choosing this field and this particular way to achieve it? There were countless moments when all I wanted was to be in our living room playing chess with my dad, strolling through Prague with my grandfather, eating my grandmother's delicious home cooking, or even arguing with my brother when charged with the responsibility of making sure he went to school on time with his teeth and hair brushed. What would I give to hear my mom's complaining about the teachings of Marx and Lenin that brought so much anxiety into my mind just a few short years ago? I would give anything to be home. But I was here—I had to be responsible, and I had to press through my feelings and do what I promised to myself and those I loved. Before I ever moved to Liberec, my dad held me by my shoulders and, with an intent look into my eyes, challenged me with encouragement—that he and mom were behind me but that the war I was choosing was going to be long and hard and that I need to win it by focusing on triumphing over one battle at a time. I wanted to make him proud, I wanted to be victorious, but I just did not know how. There was no strength left, there was no resolve, there was no desire. I was losing the fight.

Every morning, Professor Rucký, now also known as the pastor-teacher, still faithfully pulled his chair to the front of the ballet studio to steadfastly encourage us and share hopeful pieces of advice to all who were willing to listen. On several occasions, he mentioned the Christian gatherings that were happening at the Liberec Culture House. Believers and those searching for God gathered on Sundays at nine o'clock to worship, to hear a message, but above all to be encouraged by one another. We were all welcome to come and see for ourselves. This was some eight weeks after our disastrous visit to the youth meeting on that fateful Wednesday night, when I challenged

God to prove His existence to me. So far, He did not. I was not ready to step into another trap. But there was a thought nagging at me, perhaps a small wonder, if there was a possible answer to my longing for that which was missing. Could it be found in the fellowship of the Sunday crowd? I was unable to identify it, unable to pinpoint what exactly I wanted, but the pain in me was real, and I knew that time was coming when something radical had to change, or else, all was lost.

> *Come, all you who are thirsty, come to the waters; and*
> *you who have no money, come, buy and eat.*
> —Isaiah 55:1

57) Curiosity Wins

This was another weekend spent in Liberec. Saturday dance classes concluded around two o'clock in the afternoon. There were no scheduled theater performances that I was a part of, anyway, that weekend. It was me and the empty room in the dorm. I persuaded Petra to stay after school to go grab something to eat with me before we parted ways. She gladly agreed, and we found a place offering some good Czech cooking. Dumplings and sauce tasted delicious after the hours spent in the ballet studio. We were both famished. The fellowship with Petra was more and more enjoyable. We laughed together, we shared our feelings with each other, and we complained out loud together. She was a great friend, and I was thankful to have her. "Would you want to go to the gathering tomorrow?" I asked her before catching a bus to the dorm. "I am curious to see what it looks like and what all is happening there. I know the youth group was a disaster, but Rucký says that hundreds gather there. So, if worse comes to worst, we sneak out if we get bored. What do you say?" Petra looked at me, and her little frame displayed an enthusiastic response. "I was thinking about attending a Sunday service some-time," she replied. But I was nervous going alone. I don't know what to expect. My mom is opposing the idea and finds this whole 'church' thing absurd, but my dad is saying that it never hurts to explore new things. So I'll see you tomorrow at eight forty-five by the front entrance to the culture house?" she concluded. "Sure thing," I said. Petra ran across the street to catch her bus as I had a few more minutes before mine arrived. She hopped on, and I waved. After she left, I decided to walk to the dorm instead, to waste more time before arriving to the empty walls of the former monastery. I was excited to have something to do tomorrow, even though I had no idea what to expect or how to prepare for something so completely unknown and new, as a church service would most certainly be. I was glad to face the uncharted territory with Petra; that was a sure thing. I stopped to think a bit about my own parents' opinion about religion and faith. Everything I knew that indicated where they stood was based on the one awkward exchange we had during my over-the-weekend visit a few weeks ago. But I was not committing to anything. I was just going, really, to fill my otherwise empty Sunday. And there was no harm in that.

Give ear and come to me; hear me, that your soul may live.
—Isaiah 55:3

58) Divine Appointment

I woke up anxious. *Strange,* I thought. *Why am I nervous?* I decided to walk to the culture house instead of waiting for a public bus. The Sunday frequency of the public transportation was much slower than during workdays, and so it would take about the same amount of time walking as it would taking the bus and connecting to a tram. The culture house was located across the street from the ballet school, and so I knew exactly how long it would take me to walk there and meet Petra on time, before entering the building itself. It was a beautiful morning. The sun did a marvelous job of illuminating the early and quiet hours of the day. There were hardly any people on the streets, as the whole nation always enjoyed sleeping in and taking advantage of a "lazy" morning before the hustle of the week began the next day. Approaching the culture house, I noticed the sun splendidly reflecting from the angled glass structure.

Then I perceived the fairly large crowds of people flooding into the center of culture, a stark contrast from the empty streets and squares of the city. I arrived at the designated entrance and waited for Petra. She did not share the same dedication of being on time, and so I waited. And waited. And *waited*! I was growing frustrated, and then I thought, *She backed out or was forbidden to come!* There were no cell phones to text one another, and one was left to simply wait and see and grow unnecessarily upset. I was an expert at that, sadly having no sympathy for anyone who could not be on time. *Would I go in alone, or would I chicken out?* flashed through my head. Right before nine o'clock, I saw her leisurely walking from the direction of the bus stop located off Fügnerova Street, a three-minute brisk walk from the culture house.

"Ahoj," she shouted while waving her arm raised above her head. My ahoj had a completely different tone, as it clearly indicated my frustration with her delayed arrival. The fact that she gave me no explanation or apology simply ate me alive. But I had to get over myself as there was a bigger issue, a bigger deal at hand, to face. For both of us, we were about to step into a completely unknown experience of seeing people exercise their faith in a public gathering that would have been illegal to take place some two years prior. Mr. Rucký explained to us that the church had exploded in numbers of attendees after the Velvet Revolution. He was convinced that the forbidden fruit of "religion," now permitted to be explored and enjoyed, attracted many to come, and like us, discover whether a relationship with God would be something they relished tasting, figuratively speaking.

We entered into the culture house and followed the flow of traffic of people finding the large, "Main Events," hall. Again, it was music that we heard long before seeing the doors to the arena. *Why is it that they always start early?* I wondered. The three sets of double doors were opened. Ushers, or greeters, were stationed all throughout the building. The whole time as we walked from the first main entrance until we entered into the main hall, many of them would shake our hands and welcome us. This was already a mind-boggling experience. Czechs are not very social people when it comes to relating to strangers. People do not greet each other with a friendly hello when passing on the sidewalks. Everyone lives and functions in their own world, and others are simply unnecessary distractions and invaders into those spheres. I always encourage foreign visitors in Prague to, for the sheer pleasure of it, take a morning commute on the metro and watch the Czechs sit and stare as they travel to work. Their heads swaying to the rhythm of the moving train, clearly annoyed that they have to share their hometown with all these tourists. They are familiar with the other commuters as they daily share the routine and route, but they never cross the line of solitude to become acquaintances. Here, it was the exact opposite, and I felt uncomfortable. *I don't know you, and I am not sure I want to shake all these exuberant hands. Do I need to smile in return? Why would I? This is crazy,* was going through my head as I proceeded into the auditorium.

The large room had a stage at its end. On it, there were several musicians playing. There were singers singing with their eyes closed, each holding a microphone in one hand while the other was raised to the ceiling, as if trying to touch something that was either not there or beyond their reach. Both Petra and I were shocked to see such a large crowd in the room. Hundreds of worshippers were present and singing along with the leading team on the stage. A portable screen featuring projected lyrics of the songs, for those who would not know the words, stood in the corner of the stage. Everyone seemed to be familiar with them, I assumed, since their eyes were closed, and yet they kept singing. We found two available chairs one-third of the way into a row, and so we had to squeeze in as there were no chairs at the end of the linked up seats to sit on. Now we were surrounded by these singing enthusiasts. I noticed tears flowing down some of their faces. They did not appear sad, and yet they were crying. I was puzzled. What was absolutely unique in this experience, apart from these elements I just described that could be seen in a public concert of a pop star of sorts, was the incredible atmosphere in the room. I could not place my finger on it. It was authentic. It was inviting. It was, I would say, supernatural. I experienced a never-before-known fusion of being an alien yet feeling right at home in this large crowd of strangers. Without realizing it, my wall of defense that I erected to surround my mind and heart melted like wax. The songs kept coming, one after the other. I had never heard any of these, obviously, so the projected lyrics came in handy. I tried to pick up each individual tune and then sing with the crowd. Once in a while, I would simply just listen to the message the songs were communicating before I would join in singing. Some would tell God how amazing He was, some would be asking Him for His nearness, some would be *almost* acknowledging shortcomings in the lives of the singers, when reflected and compared to who He is. *Why were they stating that? I would think that they were here to sing praises to Him. That is more than what the rest of the sleeping population ever did to please God, if He were to be real. Surely, getting up on a Sunday morning and coming here and participating in the gathering would earn some benefits, score some points with God, if He existed.* These thoughts would pop into my mind on occasion as the singing continued; but the outpouring of the singers, both on the stage and off, was no doubt genuine. So I would stand and listen, stand and sing, and stand and close my eyes to perhaps receive something from the One all these around me assembled to worship.

"*Sit down, Jiri.*" *What was that?* I paused, my eyes closed. I continued to sing, tried to anyway. "*Sit down, Jiri!*" It was such a strange yet strong command. *Everyone is standing. Everyone is singing. Why would I sit down?* my mind protested. *I cannot sit down. That would be rude and draw unnecessary attention to myself,* I reasoned with myself. I remained standing. "*Sit down, Jiri!*" I could no longer resist this commanding sense. I know that no one was audibly speaking to me, and yet I was certain that I was as if hearing a voice. It was a soft whisper; and yet in the midst of the loud music around me, I heard it clearly and unmistakably. I sat down on the cushioned chair. I stopped singing and just listened to the words. My eyes remained closed. I dared not to open them. There was no desire to do so, as I started to recognize peace or stillness in me and around me. I rested on the chair in front of me, folding my arms under my forehead. The music kept playing, and the singing continued. I was drifting away. No, I was not falling asleep, but I was as if losing consciousness. The peace and stillness turned into a hush. I recall some hands being placed on my shoulders and back, and then *silence*. Everything faded away. Everything but this deep sense of serenity and calm. It was beautiful. It was unmatched by anything I had ever experienced before. I let go. There was no need for protection, no need for a wall to hide behind. It sounded as a voice so soothing, so loving and gentle, soft, yet powerful and commanding, addressing me directly. *"Jiri, you asked Me to prove myself to you. Well, here I am!"* I could not argue with the inward whisper, but in reality, I did not, would not, do that, anyway. This was the most wonderful and majestic sound I had ever heard as the voice of the Lord is uniquely inviting when our hearts are drawn to His presence. *"I am God, and I am here. I know you more than you know yourself. Before you ever drew your first breath, I was inaugurating a mighty plan of deliverance, to rescue you and to bring you to this moment of introducing you to Myself. I love you, Jiri, and My Son, Jesus Christ, has made this meeting possible. I will teach you everything you need to know. The one thing I am doing right now, in this instant, is granting you the gift of faith, necessary for you to believe in Me by the power of the Holy Spirit, Whom you have been already experiencing for some time now. Your eyes have been opened. Receive the gift of salvation. Like a hand placed over a small pebble, I am placing My mighty palm over you, Jiri. You are Mine, and I have a plan for your life. I love you!"* I came to my senses and opened my eyes. I was lying on the floor of the auditorium, with those around me praying for me. There was no more singing, just music playing and someone praying from the microphone. What just happened? I did not know the answer to the question; but I now knew without a shadow of a doubt that God is real, that He is near, that He is mighty, that He loves me. All the doubts I ever faced were simply gone. I believed. It was more than that; I perceived that the reality of a spiritual dimension was as real as anything I could see and touch. Both of these worlds, the natural and supernatural, were ruled by the Almighty God, Who created them both and delighted to share Himself with us and now with me. I did not know why, but I knew that it was the absolute and undeniable truth. I could not wait to find Professor Rucký to share with him what just transpired in my life. What was I to do next? I did not know, but I was overjoyed to learn more about the character of the

God I had just met. Professor Brother Evald was overwhelmed to hear what I had to share. He invited me to follow him in a prayer of salvation, as he put it. "Yes," I shouted. Both Petra, who heard everything I was sharing with Mr. Rucký, and I prayed that day for the Lord Jesus Christ to be our Savior and Redeemer, our Shepherd, and our Lord. This time around, I repeated every word Pastor Evald said with conviction and faith. This prayer was bigger than a statement, greater than a powerful speech; these few words caused one who was dead to become alive, alive forevermore, no longer an enemy of God but now His beloved child who was rescued and brought home. The Lord had chosen me to be His, and He orchestrated a way for me to meet Him and come to know the deep love Jesus Christ, the living Son of God, had for me. "Amen," came out of my lips, and I could hardly contain the joy that was, like a strong spring of a mighty river, spilling from the depths of my soul. That glorious Sunday morning, I realized that my name had been written in God's Book of Life long before I ever cared to meet and know Him. That inclusion forever sealed my eternal destiny. I was to overwhelmingly enjoy the presence of my esteemed Rescuer and King. That beautiful day, the Lord brought me from darkness into the light of His Majesty; and I realized the immaculate orchestration of all the previous events of my life that would be used to help me arrive at this junction, where I found my eternal salvation by placing faith in the completed work of Jesus Christ. Even today, He says, "Come to me all you who are weary, and I will give you rest." Come to Jesus. Taste and see just how incredibly good He is!

> *Salvation is found in no one else, for there is no other name*
> *under heaven given to men by which we must be saved.*
> —Acts 4:12

59) Lay Down Your Idol

Almost as quickly as we finished praying, Professor, and now Brother, Rucký looked intensely into my eyes and stated something that did not make much sense right there and then. With both hands placed on my shoulder, which he loved to do when something profound was to be communicated, he whispered, "The Lord God is the only One true King. But often we place other things or other people on the throne of our hearts and lives. This cannot—no, this must not—be. The Bible says that we cannot serve two masters. Jiri, ballet is a master of your life. It is an idol. It is a god. You must dethrone it and allow the Lord to be the One, the only One, who reigns and rules your heart. It is not going to be easy, and you cannot do it in and of your own strength, but as much as you need air to breath, you need to understand that ballet will choke you to death if you continue to serve it as your destiny, goal, satisfying source." Then he smiled at me and walked away. Petra and I stood there watching him leave the room. *That's it? That is the first instruction, the first helpline to this new chapter of our lives?* I thought. "How are we supposed to dethrone ballet?" Petra whispered. "Do we leave the academy and just focus on our academics?" she continued. "That is impossible, Petra. Maybe we can keep dancing but keep an eye on just how much we love it and make sure it does not get out of hand," I said while scratching my head. This was not going to work at all, but that was the only feeble plan my mind could think and produce at that moment. "Are you going to tell your parents that you prayed to become a Christian?" I continued. That seemed to me more pressing than anything else at the given moment. The ballet idol had to wait. This was crucial to be conversed about. "Are we going to go public with our newly found faith? What will our classmates, roommates, teachers, and parents think? What will they say? Will we be grouped into the same category of weak and pathetic losers, with Professor Rucký?" Almost as quickly as I would say that, a nudging feeling in my gut would remind me of the supernatural experience of being in the Lord's presence about an hour or so ago. "It was going to be all right. We just need to gage each situation as it arises, and the Lord will lead us through it," we were convinced of it. "*Griliáš*" (*Gre-le-aash*)? Petra said with a smile. This particular sundae was our favorite. For two ballet students, we were quite the regulars when it came to devouring one of these. And so, on that beautiful Sunday, we enjoyed splitting some ice cream as angels in heaven celebrated in the presence of God over these two sinners that, by the grace of Jesus, turned to Him in repentance and faith. Our lives changed completely that day. Only with time would we come to realize the full magnitude of His salvation and discover what the Lord prepared for us to do, find a way to serve Him, and bring Him glory through our two seemingly insignificant lives. After Petra and I parted our ways at the Fügnerova stop, I looked forward to walking to the dorm, enjoying the beauty of the day, and trying to comprehend what just happened, what just took place in my life.

I could not tell you if I met someone I knew; I could not tell you if the rain started to pour. All I could think of was my experience at the church gathering earlier that morning. I replayed that moment of being in the presence of the One I was so sure did not exist. His immense love and the permeating peace were unforgettable. Just as I reached President Edvard Beneš Square, with the imposing Liberec City Hall, I came to realize and was completely overwhelmed with the following revelation: back in 1987, when my world came crashing down as I was ripped out of the National Ballet Conservatory in Prague, God was already at work. Meeting Mr. Pokorný at the Regional House of Pioneers and the Youth was not a coincidence. The Lord was guiding me and orchestrating everything around me. The Velvet Revolution was already written on His calendar long before I first distributed the antigovernment pamphlets on the streets of Liberec. The Master was tearing down the seemingly impenetrable Iron Curtain to bring freedom and Christianity into the lives of the people locked behind it, people like myself. All those lonely times of sitting on the bathroom floor, wishing for that someone special to fill the longing in my heart, my Rescuer was right there causing the unquenchable thirst of my soul and preparing me to receive the undeserved rescue Jesus died to offer. The Messiah brought Professor Rucký to the academy as a messenger of His hope and of His grace. Through him, the Almighty God gently yet surreptitiously led my steps to the youth group meeting and, later on, to the Sunday church gathering. All along, He was unfolding His master plan. He chose me to be His and flipped the world upside down for me to realize it. How great and how deep is the love of the heavenly Father for His children. I did not search for Him; I did not ask for Him. I did not know I needed Him. I did not choose Him. No, my God—in His wisdom, in His power, and in His will—chose me. Later on, I learned that this is a passage of scripture written in chapter 15 of the Gospel of John, and it continues to say that the Lord appointed me so that I might go and bear fruit that will last. I did not know much that day, I did not know where to start to learn, I had no idea how my life trajectory would continue to unfold, but I was certain that there was a powerful God Who was personal and intimately interested in me, and He already knew how to answer all my worries and all my questions. I was at peace, a completely and powerfully overwhelming peace. I was born again. Thank you, Lord Jesus!

The next Monday felt as ordinary and as any other, prior to that—ballet class at six thirty followed by a mad dash to the gymnázium to catch the second period class there and then grabbing a quick school cafeteria lunch before running back to the conservatory for the afternoon dance classes... It all felt so normal. Hectic but ordinary. I don't know what my expectations were exactly now that I was a Christian, but life went on seemingly in the same tracks. The only noteworthy difference was my desire to learn more about Jesus—His character, His attributes. There was a longing within, a thirst of sorts, to be with Him in the day-to-day hustle and a desire for Him to be with me as I tried to face every challenge and difficulty life would throw my way.

The State Theater planned to include *Snow White* and *Coppelia* to its playbill in the next season, and we were to be included in both productions. The exact cast list and roles were to be designated in upcoming weeks and months, once again, based on our performance and effort displayed at the academy. It was thrilling to be included, and I hoped that I would be granted the privilege of dancing a significant role in one of these ballets. As Professor Rucký stated clearly to me, ballet was a big deal to me, too big of a deal, sadly to admit. I did not know how to change that reality. Was it wrong to want to be the best? Was it wrong to desire a notable role? I did not know how to battle the urge to steal the spotlight.

*In the same way, I tell you, there is rejoicing in the presence
of the angels of God over one sinner who repents.*
—Luke 15:10

60) A Diplomatic Fiasco

It had been over a month since I last visited my family and
another Friday with a schedule-permitting visit to Ústí presented
itself. I caught the five o'clock bus to my hometown. This was going
to be my first return back home since I claimed Jesus to be the Savior
of my life. I was unsure as to how to convey this milestone to my parents. A diplomatic approach was of utmost importance. Delicate and
gentle observation of the mood in the family needed to be yielded to
before any such information could be uttered from my lips. The joy
within my soul was continually bursting from me whenever I paused
to think and ponder the fact that I met Jesus. These thoughts led
to a big smile to appear on my face, often noticed by the frowning
populous of the Czech people. I guess they wondered if I was insane
to smile for no reason. I enjoyed the two-hour ride without doing
anything productive. I did not study, I did no homework, and I did
not read. I just sat there and admired the passing beautiful scenery
of Northern Bohemia. It was almost as if I knew deep down in my
gut that a day would come when I wouldn't be able to see this countryside whenever I'd wish. I watched it flow outside the bus window
until I fell asleep, only to wake after we reached the bus terminal in
Ústí. I never tired of coming home. It was exciting. The trolleybus
ride from downtown to my neighborhood in Ústí took about twenty-five minutes. With every passing stop, I would be more and more
excited to see my family and simply be home with them, even if just
for two nights. We reached Mírová (*Mee-ro-va*) stop, and I jumped
off the bus to walk the last five minutes on foot to reach the apartment. The days were getting longer as the spring season was advancing; and the air was fresh with frequent rains that caused the trees,
flowers, and even grass to reach their lush shades of green. My bag
was packed with dirty laundry, and I was desperate to get them clean.
Poor mom, I often thought. I reached Zvonková Street where my

parents' apartment building stood, overlooking the large park filled with playing kids, bikers, people walking their dogs, and the elderly sitting on benches fervently discussing the affairs of the changing society, as well as gossiping about what one said and did. They, like my grandparents, worried whether this new democratic government would continue to pay their retirement or whether they would be able to afford their groceries and medicines as the prices were steadily rising. Their generation often remembered the old regime and quietly wished that we could return back to Communism, not because it was good but because it promised them a certain level of security. My grandmother herself sat on a bench by the entrance to our apartment building. She rose to greet me with a sloppy kiss on both of my cheeks. "Yirka, Yirka," she would say, which is an adoring version of my name, as tears covered her face. "It is so good to see you!"

"Same here, Grandma. How are you?" I'd reply, still holding my bag in one hand trying to fence off her attack of smooches.

"We are well, thanks. But you know, times are hard. Things are changing… It's a bit scary to face the unknown and learn how to navigate this 'capitalistic' way of life… Grandpa and I are trying and doing our best…you know…but what about you? How are you?"

Did she just say "capitalistic"? I giggled in my heart. She was cute inside and out, with her little frame reaching barely above five feet, but she could get feisty and hold her own when it came down to it. "I am well, Grandma. I am really well, indeed! I am excited to catch up with you tomorrow! You and Grandpa need to come upstairs after lunch, and we can talk about life and everything," I concluded. She kissed me fervently on both cheeks again to welcome me home. I walked into the entry hall of the building and waited for the elevator. My excitement to see my folks was growing stronger still. The small elevator was designed to fit the bare minimum, but it would suffice to carry me and my bag of laundry. I opened the door and stepped out upon reaching the third floor and with enthusiasm rang the bell by my parents' apartment door.

"Yirka," I heard from behind it as my mom was walking to open the door. "Ahoj, ahoj, ahoj," followed as, now for a change, she grabbed my head to land some kisses of her own.

"Ahoj, Mom and Dad," I replied, trying to also acknowledge my dad, who stood at the end of the short entry hall, allowing my mom to complete the physical overflow of her emotions, done in the doorframe to the apartment. He and I kissed on the cheek. I stepped in to close the doors behind, and before I even took my shoes off, a European custom, I blurted out, "I became a Christian! I went to church on a Sunday a few weeks ago just to waste some time, and the Lord met me there. I surrendered my life to Him. It is amazing, and I cannot wait to tell you more." I could not believe that this just transpired. What happened to my plan of careful, balanced, and diplomatic deliverance of this touchy subject? I do not know what came over me, but the cat was out of the bag. The atmosphere in the little short entry hall changed drastically. One could almost cut the cumbersome energy with a knife. My dad lit the cigarette hanging from his mouth and continued to stand there leaning against the wall. My mom did not receive my proclamation the same way at all. The welcoming glee had long left the room. She was upset, angered by what I said and, I suppose, by what I had done. Her face reflected the rising tension within her. Like a volcano that is about to explode and spill lava and ashes across its surroundings, so was my mom about to explode into a response stated in a high volume and with a clear message of disapproval.

"I thought you were better than this! Religion…religion! Why God! I thought it was clearly communicated last time you brought the subject up when you were home? We do not approve! Are you that desperate to need this crutch in your life? Jiri, this is the greatest disappointment you could have done to us! Of all the things that you could have explored with the new freedom we have here, you had to dip so low as to follow some crazy lunatic into a religious sect! Unbelievable and so disappointing!" With that, she turned around and walked away. The problem was that the little apartment offered us no ability to seclude ourselves from each other to let the heated emotions subside. We had to face the elephant in the room every time one would show up. It brought the family closer together as we learned to get over ourselves and our sentiments and were forced to reconcile, forgive, forget, and move on in living life as a family where all members deeply cared and loved one another. This was no different.

My dad winked at me as he blew out a breath-full of cigarette smoke from his nostrils and said, "Welcome home, son."

"Are you hungry?" sounded from the kitchen. "I made dumplings and sauce and can warm them up for you on the stove." I guessed that my mom already moved on, as she seemed to worry about my dietary needs now, rather than panic about blindly falling into some kind of religious trap. "You have lost weight again, right?" followed from the kitchen. My dad walked to the living room to continue watching the Friday evening television programming, and I was left alone, still holding my bag, standing in the entry hall. I looked up toward the ceiling and whispered a quick "Thank you" to the Lord that this was behind me, not as planned perhaps but behind me!

As I would do every time I returned home, I dumped the dirty clothes into the laundry compartment hidden under the corner bench surrounding the kitchen table. "What is new, Yirka? How is it going with everything?" my mom continued. "Wash your hands. The dinner is almost ready." Here I was, sixteen years old, and my mom faithfully reminded me to wash my hands before I sat down to eat. I paused to watch her hustle around the kitchen counter as it was obvious that my coming home made her excited and happy. Even my "news" could not change that. And so I walked to the bathroom to wash my hands and sat on the bench to wait for the plate of hot dumplings to be placed in front of me. They tasted amazing! Right after that, my mom pulled out a freshly baked cake, my favorite of course, in an attempt to put some pounds of weight on my skinny body, over the next two days, before I returned to the food-deprived lifestyle of a dancer-student. I ate the cake in the living room as my dad turned the volume of the television set off. We talked about grades, schools, dancing at the theater, but also about Petra and my feelings for her. Míra returned home and joined us with his plate of dinner. He was growing up and resembled an anatomy book, opened to the page where each muscle of the body is clearly highlighted. There was not a gram of fat on him. Gymnastics was turning him into a powerhouse, petite but defined powerhouse. This was what I loved about my returns home. Sitting around, talking, playing games, and, yes, eating a lot. We did not talk about my faith any more during this or any other visits until a need to meet Brother Evald the following year arose.

The sophomore year came to an end. The premiere of *Snow White* was a success. This was the first time when the lead role was given to a student of the conservatory who, according to Mr. Pokorný, best fit the look of a young girl hated by her stepmother. All the stressful finals at the gymnázium were passed one after another, with a huge relief. The public ballet exams went without a glitch, and before one was ready, the two months of summer were upon us. The State Theater, as all professional theaters in the Czech and Slovak Federative Republic, closed its doors for the months of July and August. This was the time to fix and address any structural issues of the 108-year-old building and give all the artists the much-needed time to rest and regain inspiration for the following season. Our family spent a two-week vacation in Southern Bohemia in a small privately owned hotel with tennis courts and a lot of lakes all around— lakes where my dad fished, we swam, and, most importantly to my liking, we visited a variety of historic castles in the region. I also spent a couple of weeks at the International Dance Intensive, annually held in Prague, where I continued to learn and grow as a dancer. Dance teachers of diverse dance genres, from all over the world, gathered in Prague to teach and share their expertise with the students. Many former Czech dancers and choreographers who defected from Communist Czechoslovakia and built their careers abroad returned to give back to their beloved homeland and, through their presence, encouraged the growth and maturity of the Czech dance world to look away from the model of the Soviet ballet. I learned so much that summer. This was my first experience taking classes from English speaking teachers. The world around me was changing almost every day. The summer flew by, but I managed to enjoy it all, the hard work at the Intensive, the family vacation, and the simple rest at my parents' apartment. After the two months, I was ready to face another demanding year. I did not know that the Lord had so much in store for me to learn and to discover in this new season of life as September of 1991 rolled around and I moved back to Liberec.

> *The word is near you; it is in your mouth and in your heart,*
> *that is, the word of faith we are proclaiming: That if you confess*
> *with your mouth, "Jesus is Lord" and believe in your heart*
> *that God raised him from the dead, you will be saved.*
> —Romans 10:8–9

THIRD ACT

THE PLANS OF GOD

61) Unexpected Proposal

The fall semester started at full force. I returned to the academy with a renewed vigor to train hard and work diligently in all aspects of life. There was a slow spiritual growth starting to take place as I began to attend Bible studies. Every Thursday evening, there was a large room of a hotel rented by the church, where the members met to be led by believers who had walked with the Lord a bit longer than others. This is a great opportunity to point out that the overall spiritual age of the church was adolescent at best. The church congregation consisted of new converts, like myself, and then some who knew the Lord only a few months or years longer as most came to know the Lord after the fall of the Communist regime. There were several leaders—elders of the church who were believers for a longer while; but even among them were a great number of fairly young disciples. What transpired as an amazing strength among the members was the authentic fire of the newly found relationship with Christ. People were eager to grow and their joy truly was their strength. Brother Evald was busy teaching leaders as they would then teach others. Theologically speaking, a basic yet profound foundation of Christendom was being laid. Enthusiasm met with eagerness to learn was producing lasting fruit in the lives of this young church.

Here I was. I did not know anything. It might sound far-fetched, but I knew not that the Bible was divided into two testaments. I did

169

not know the story of Creation; I never heard about Adam and Eve. The Exodus meant nothing to me. I was yet to hear about David defeating Goliath, Noah building the ark, Abraham offering his son Isaac, and Joseph's conquering imprisonment only to rise to be the second-in-command of Egypt. I needed to be taught about the virgin birth of Jesus, His miraculous calming of the storm, the supernatural feeding of thousands with two fish and five loaves, His glorious entry to Jerusalem, the Last Supper, His trial, His conviction, His betrayal, His beating, and His death. I heard that He rose, but I was lacking the basic understanding of how the Resurrection directly benefited me and every believer, every Christian, all around the world. I did not see the big picture, the mosaic of a large family, where brothers and sisters all around the world sat united at a large family table. The chair at its head, a throne really, was employed by a heavenly Father, Abba Daddy, Who loved us all—a God Who desired to have us close and near. This Father was intentional, profoundly personal, and yet the King of all kings. Everything was hallmarked with a deep meaning, and I had no understanding. Not yet. I was hungry to learn, and I wanted to understand more. These Thursday evenings were filled with discovery and awe as I began to grasp a bit at a time of the magnitude of the God Who rescued me and set me free.

The state ballet school began to produce talent that shone brightly in the productions of the theater. In this third year of the academy, a broader divide between the students emerged. Some rose to the challenge of the curriculum, and some started to fall behind. There were both male and female students who started to catch a closer eye of Mr. Pokorný as well as of the general audience attending the performances. This rise of recognition did not go unnoticed by the senior members of the company. Three soloists, in particular, pushed back and pushed hard to let us know where our place was as young members of the corps de ballet. Nonetheless, Mr. Pokorný gladly featured the promising talent of the school. His effort was directly reflected in the casting of *Coppelia*, the next premiere scheduled for the season. The casting was posted in the stage entry of the theater. There were no hints given prior to the posting, and no one knew what to expect to see and find on the casting list. To my great surprise, I found my name as an understudy for the role of Franz, a young man who falls in love with a life-size doll, Coppelia, and leaves behind Swanhilda, his true love. A company soloist, Tomáš Brož, was cast into the role of Franz, but I was thrilled to learn and understudy the role in hopes that an opportunity to perform it would present itself. It was an honor, and I recognized the privilege and trust Mr. Pokorný bestowed upon me. I was also dancing the role of Franz's friend with another dancer from my class. It was going to be great fun.

As life would have it, another unexpected turn was coming my way. Brother Evald, Professor Rucký, invited both Petra and me to his office at the church. We did not know the reason, but we gladly agreed to come. Once again, we started to walk up a narrow Němcová Street to the small building at its end. Pastor Evald welcomed us and, for the first time, invited us to his apartment on the third floor of the church. His wife, Ruth, served us hot tea as we waited to hear what the meeting was all about.

"How are you, guys?" was a great start to a conversation that could go a million different ways.

"We are well, thank you," we responded almost in perfect unison.

"I have invited you here to ask you a question...no...not to actually ask you a question but to present you with an opportunity. You see, I know that you are working hard attending two schools and dancing at the theater... How is that going? By the way...keeping up with the challenges of it all?" He sipped his tea and took a moment, letting us struggle with the wrestling match between our imagination and our curiosity. Petra and I held our cups of tea, but neither one of us sipped any. "I have asked you here to let you know that I received a phone call a few days ago, a phone call from Vibeke Muasya." Our puzzled facial expression clearly indicated that we had no idea who that was. Brother Evald smiled at us, and his face became filled with that loving countenance we knew from the morning classes. "She is the artistic director of Eternia Dance Theater in Laxå, Sweden. Her company is currently touring with a production titled *We Want to Live*," he said, struggling to pronounce the English title. "The main couple in the company has requested a leave of absence for a few months, to deal with personal issues of settling documents for the Finnish wife to be able to move to America with her American husband in a year or so." Evald took another slow sip of tea and followed it with an investigative glance to see whether or not we were keeping up with the flow of information. "Drink your tea," came out of his mouth. Obediently, we took a sip without taking our eyes off him, anxious to hear more. "Anyway, Vibeke and I have been friends for a while, as I have been guest teaching for Eternia on occasion, and she called to ask if I knew of any dancers that could come and dance with Eternia for some time, while Jeremiah and Mona are absent. They are looking for Christian dancers as this is a Christian company; a part of a larger organization called Kreative Mission. You two came to mind, obviously, as you have come to know the Lord recently."

Silence filled the room the moment Professor Rucký finished speaking. I took a second sip of tea, only to bridge the slightly tense atmosphere between us all. "You would like us to travel to Sweden to dance with Eternity?" Petra asked first.

"Eternia," said Brother Evald.

"Eternia, I'm sorry," she continued, "but we are in school, and you said it yourself—we have a contract here at the theater. I just don't know—"

"For how long?" I interrupted. "Are we talking about a couple of weeks or a little bit longer… Mr. Professor?" My voice cracked a little as my nerves were experiencing a momentary overload.

"Three months…actually," he whispered while sipping his tea.

"Three months!" shouted Petra. "That is impossible! The gymnázium directors would never allow us to miss three months of school. Even with the individual study plans, we both have… There is no way… I don't think."

"I know that you both are young and, when it comes to faith, very inexperienced, but the Lord delights to move in supernatural ways. There is a biblical verse in the book of Luke," he continued, "that teaches us that with God nothing shall be impossible, and so I believe that God will make a way even where there seems to be no way. I cannot, and I will not, force you, but there is an opportunity for you to go and taste what it's like to use the talents and the passions you have been given and use them for the glory of God! And that will be priceless to discover!"

We had a lot to think about, no doubt about that. If the Lord God was in this, He would remove the impossible obstacles. There were three hurdles that we could name right away. The principals of both of the gymnáziums would have to give us permission, Mr. Pokorný would have to agree and excuse us from the conservatory, and the State Theater would have to pause our contract for three months. None of these seemed possible to come to pass. And then there were our parents, who would have to give us permission as well. *That's where the train comes to an end of the track*, I thought to myself. My mom and dad would never allow me to leave for three months in the middle of the school year, even if all the other impossibilities were surpassed.

"Sadly, we cannot go to Sweden," we concluded, sitting on the sofa in Brother Evald's living room. He looked at us. This man had prayed that the Communist regime would crumble and Jesus would be welcomed in this country. Evald believed that there would be a thriving and prospering church in Liberec when every building around him proudly displayed banners with a Communist propaganda slogans in both Czech and Russian languages. This man saw God move mightily when he officially requested to receive a permit to practice pastoral work at the Politburo in Prague after his resignation from the National Theater. He walked with the Lord through many difficulties, facing countless oppositions. He knew that there was nothing impossible for God to accomplish. We, on the other hand, were looking at the situation through our understanding. And that was very, very limited and, sadly, very worldly. "Let us pray," Brother Evald continued. "If we want to witness miracles happen, we must always start on our knees, and while fighting the urge in us to doubt, we ask the Almighty God to move in spite of our unbelief or doubt." He placed the teacup on the little round table covered with a crocheted tablecloth as he slid off the chair to kneel before starting to pray. Petra and I followed suit. There was a great desire to go and be a part of Eternia, but the doubt that the Lord would open these locked doors was alive and thriving at this very moment. Brother Evald was correct. We were yet to experience a supernatural move of the Lord—yet to walk by faith and not by sight, yet to trust beyond the cognitive reasoning of our minds. The Mighty God was about to teach us a lesson that would forever shift our understanding of Him. It started that evening on our knees as we requested for Him to move in power, to burst through the locked gates, to make a way in removing the heavy obstacles, should He desire for Petra and me to travel to Sweden. With closed eyes, we quieted our hearts and simply and honestly approached the throne of the living God.

Professor Rucký initiated the whole process by speaking with Mr. Pokorný, requesting a permission to leave the ballet school for the duration of our guest appearance at the Eternia Dance Theater. Mr. Pokorný called us into his office for a brief meeting.

"Sit down, please," he started, gesturing toward the two chairs on the opposite side of the desk. The tone in his voice was less than pleasant. Both of us noted that right away. "Professor Rucký spoke to me regarding your desire to work in Sweden during the Eternia Dance Theater tour this fall. I assume that you have given it a thorough consideration. I would have no problem letting you go and excusing you from the curriculum. Dance and stage experiences outweigh the studio-gained knowledge exponentially. What bothers me to no end, however, is your willingness to break the contract with the State Theater here to get a contract with another company. That really bothers me. Well, as the artistic director of the ballet company, I will revoke your participation in the *Coppelia* premiere. Jiri, you will not be understudying Tomáš in the role of Franz. You both might be permitted to dance corps de ballet parts, based on perfect knowledge of the choreography and staging, but any chance to do a demi solo work is simply out the window. The contract with the ballet will be paused and restarted hopefully upon your return... I am disappointed. Can I ask you a question?" The tone of his voice changed. "Is it true that you both became religious?" Petra and I looked at him, still processing everything that he said prior to the question he just asked.

"Mr. Pokorný," I started, knowing that I was treading unknown waters, "yes, both of us accepted the Lord as our Savior a few weeks ago. We do not mind you knowing, as we are not hiding that truth. We just did not see the need to talk about it here at the academy or at the theater…and, also, we were just as surprised as you were when the opportunity to go to Sweden was placed before us, recognizing the many challenges this will bring both here and at the gymnázium." I took a short little breath, giving Petra the option of chiming in with anything that could help the tense conversation. She did not. "And, sir, the contract with the theater would have to be resolved before we would go, and we understand that fully. If you do not release us, we won't be able to pursue the opportunity, and we are okay with that. We have not spoken to the gymnáziums' principals yet either, as we doubt that their permission will be granted…but we wanted to start with you." By now, a steady stream of sweat was running down my back. Petra continued to say nothing. In reality, there was not much more to be said.

Mr. Pokorný replied with a question, as if ignoring anything I just said, "Do you know the exact dates?"

"Not yet," Petra replied, "but once we have your permission, we will start lining up all necessary details and hopefully getting all the answers to you, to the gymnáziums' directors, and, of course, our parents. They do not know either, at this point."

"Well, if you are willing to forfeit the *Coppelia* premiere and any potential solo roles for the rest of the season, you have my permission to be excused from the conservatory for the time being. I will need a written letter from the director of the dance company to file with your records. You need to let me know details as soon as you know them. I will inform Professor Gabajová, and we will go from there. Is that good?"

"Yes, Mr. Pokorný, thank you," we said one after the other.

Walking out of that meeting, we knew that a colossal wheel was put into motion. It was time to approach our separate gymnázium directors and see what the outcome would be. If they are on board, which would be a miracle, to say mildly, then there is hope with our parents. But the whole deal is hinging on their decision. And what if my principal would say yes and Petra's said no, then what would we do? This was a pickle. We needed to schedule an appointment with them as soon as it was possible.

The next day, I rushed out of the morning ballet class the moment our final jumps ended. No resting, no listening to Professor Rucký sitting on a chair. Getting to the gymnázium pronto was my aim. Upon entry to the school building, I went directly to the office of the head principal, Dr. Kutínová. I knocked politely. A small part of me desired to hear no reply from the inside of the office. "Enter," sounded resolutely from beyond the door. I wiped my sweaty hands on my jeans and opened the door.

"Good morning, Dr. Kutínová. Do you have a moment for me to speak with you, please?" I stood by the door not sure how far in I was welcomed to enter her office.

"Please come on in, Mr. Voborsky. It is good to see you! How is everything going? I do receive a regular progress report from Professor Vondráček regarding you and your ISP, and as far as I know, you seem to have found a rhythm in balancing the load. I must admit that I am impressed." She sat down on her chair behind the large desk and motioned with her hand for me to take a seat as well.

"I have come here today, Dr. Kutínová, to request your permission to leave the school for up to three months. I am not exactly sure when and even for how long, but three months would be the absolute longest amount of time." I looked at her to find an older, wise woman sitting in her chair of decisions with a relaxed facial expression unmoved by the statement I just made. Either there was no way on earth that she would say yes, thus enjoying this moment of suspense, or it would be the exact opposite, and I stressed myself for no reason. She removed her round-framed glasses and leaned against the desk.

"And why would that be?"

"Well, another student and I at the state ballet school were given an opportunity to guest-perform with a professional dance company in Sweden while two of their dancers are on a leave of absence. The director of the academy granted us his permission yesterday, and I wanted to meet with you to seek your permission to interrupt the semester." I resolved to give the smallest amount of information, partially not wanting to get tangled in a net of confusing statements and partially because I was nervous to approach her with the request.

"I understand that we have structured our curriculum to prepare all our students for whatever the field of their future career might be," she said with a calm voice and demeanor, "and from the very first time I saw your file deciding to enroll you at our school, I knew that your path and career will simply be different than most. If going to Sweden will help you reach the goal you have set before you, I will not stand in its way. We will need to find a way for you to continue studies while absent, and Professor Vondráček will have to assist you with that, but you have my green light." After giving me some practical information and paperwork I needed to fill, I walked out of her office realizing that, simply put, the Lord was removing the obstacles swiftly and easily. I started to get overwhelmed and excited all at the same time. I whispered a quick prayer asking the Father for Petra's meeting to go as favorably as mine. The Lord answered that prayer beautifully. The last remaining struggle was to persuade our parents to see the opportunity the same way Dr. Kutínová did. Time would tell.

I knew that there were certain topics better not discussed over the phone. I discovered that my diplomatic skills grow in effectiveness when the receiving party sees my gestures and my overall body language during the exchange of information. Asking my parents for permission to travel to Sweden was one of those topics better hashed out in person. As it turned out, our departure for Laxå was much more urgent than we initially realized. I called home and asked my parents if they would be willing to come to Liberec for a day, as I had something very pressing to talk to them about. They agreed and promised to arrive Liberec the following Saturday just in time to pick me up at the academy after my classes. I was well aware of the fact that Saturday held several potential nuclear explosions in its arsenal. My parents were going to find out that I spoke to a line of different people about going away while keeping them both in the dark; they were going to meet brother Evald, whom they blamed for my religious disillusionment; and they were going to be asked to help pay for my flight to Stockholm and back. I don't know what they were thinking the reason for coming to Liberec was, but I knew they were not that creative to think up a plot of such large proportions in their minds.

My dad's little white Škoda was standing parked by the side-walk in front of the conservatory. I rushed out of the building with determination to be calm and collected when I saw them. *No need for unnecessary drama*, I thought. It was good to see them. It was always so good to see them. My dad recommended lunch, and I could not have agreed more, as I was hungry after dancing the past five hours straight. We walked to a restaurant nearby and ordered from the menu offering delicious specialties of the Czech cuisine, such as fried cheese, dumplings, schnitzel, *šopský* (*shop-skee*) salad, and more. We all ordered according to our liking and enjoyed some light conversation while waiting for the food. I knew that I needed to open up about the reason for their travel to Liberec and I needed to do it now. I was scared as I did not want to disappoint them, on this beautiful autumn Saturday, with telling them something they would see as a total baseless and unsubstantiated reason to travel to Sweden.

I cleared my throat indicating that I had something important to say. "Thank you so much for coming to Liberec today," I started carefully, "as I wanted to talk to you face-to-face about an issue that I am facing right now. *Issue* might not be the right word, but, hon-estly, what I am about to tell you is a huge deal, and I did not want to discuss it over the phone. Last week sometime, Professor Rucký invited Petra and myself to his home, where he presented us with an opportunity to perform with Eternia Dance Theater based in Laxå, Sweden. There is a need they have, looking for a pair of dancers to join their upcoming tour…and he thought that Petra and I would be a perfect fit—"

"Here is your lunch," said a waiter, approaching our table with three plates of hot food. I was not particularly happy about the tim-ing, as I was on a roll and did not want to restart the speech again. It was too late; the food was now served, and my momentum was lost.

"Thank you," my mom said, looking at the server. "Bon appé-tit," she continued, looking at my father and me. "You were saying?"

was her indication that she was not ready to respond until she knew more details of the pressing issue at hand. I took a deep breath to gather my thoughts and my courage to continue.

"Yes, yes…anyway, the company in Sweden needs two dancers, and the artistic director reached out to Professor Rucký asking if he could recommend anyone from the academy. He immediately thought of me and Petra and presented us with the opportunity. He then spoke with Mr. Pokorný, who met with us and gave us the permission to leave the conservatory, and even excused us from the theater contract as well…all this to say that we received the approval to explore our options…and then I—"

"Just a minute." My dad interrupted. "What about your academic studies? How would you go without falling too far behind? How long would you be gone?" I was not ready to talk about the length of the engagement until I presented all the supporting evidence and granted approvals. My dad was messing up my train of thought and my arguments to, hopefully, win the case. None of us were eating at the moment, and the food was getting cold. The tension between us started to emerge because I was getting frustrated; and my folks could tell, which, in return, caused tension in them.

"I met with the head principal, Dr. Kutínová, and she and I had a great conversation. She saw the potential struggle with an extended absence but also recognized my academic efforts and performance in the past two years at the gymnázium. She and Professor Vondráček were willing to work out a study plan that I could take with me to Sweden." I purposefully omitted the possible length of the tour hoping that my dad would not ask about it again.

"And you would have time and the will to study, to push yourself academically, when dancing and touring with the Swedish troupe?" My mom interrupted. I did not like the word *troupe* and would much more prefer the word *company*, but that was not what I needed to focus on at this moment. *Was my mom using the word* troupe *to belittle Eternia, or was there no preconceived notion in its use?* I wondered. "Yes, I would have to stay disciplined. Petra and I would keep each other accountable to study on target while in Sweden."

"What did her parents say?" my dad spoke again. "And you never told us how long this trip would last?" I did not know exactly what Petra's parents said and thought about the whole idea of us going, as she was having the same conversation with them just about now as well.

"She is speaking with them today before we all meet with Professor Rucký, who wanted to meet you all to share about the tour and answer your questions," I said.

"What did you say!" my mom said harshly. "You want us to meet Rucký? I don't think that's a good idea. We have nothing to say to each other... There is no way... This is..."

"*Bohunka, Bohunka,*" my dad said, placing his hand on my mom's. "When is the meeting supposed to take place?" He looked at me.

"At four. Petra's parents will be there as well," I said. My dad's face returned to his calm composure, that I admired so much about him.

"Well, we'll look forward to meeting him, won't we, Bohunka!" he continued while stating this rhetorical question. "Now let's eat before all this food is wasted, can we!"

"Um, hm," my mom mumbled, knowing my dad, and understanding that this conversation was over. I was relieved that I no longer had to keep all this in me. Now we just needed a good first meeting with Brother Evald, and that could be a challenge. I knew that there was no need to stress over something I couldn't influence, and so I shifted my focus to the plate of now-lukewarm food that I was more than ready to devour. After a short while, the three of us resumed talking about life back home as well as here in Liberec, conversing about Míra, my grandparents, my grades, and more. Yes, we talked with our mouths full, and for once, we did not care that it was impolite.

"Welcome, welcome...hello and welcome!" Professor Rucký was beaming with enthusiasm and joy. It was not fake, but it was atypical for a Czech.

Petra's parents, Franta and Marcela, were already inside the apartment on the third floor of the Moravian Church building. This was the very first time for my and Petra's parents to grace a church building, apart from visiting historic cathedrals for tourism reasons in the past. Brother Evald and his sweet wife, Ruth, were to be the very first Christians for our parents to meet. Evald recognized that they needed to meet each other, and so he introduced Petra's parents to mine and vice versa. *That was a good move*, I thought.

We sat to the side as he and Ruth served coffee for them to enjoy. There was no chitchat happening. I noticed that Ms. Grůšová, Petra's mom, shared the same resentment toward Brother Evald as my own mother did. Petra's father, Mr. Grůša (*Groo-sha*), did all the talking. I was not sure if he was sensing the awkwardness in the room and was trying to lighten up the mood or if this is simply how he always was. "Thank you for coming here today," Brother Evald started. "My wife and I both understand that perhaps being on the grounds of a church might make you feel uncomfortable or uneasy, but please know that we wanted to meet with you here, at our apartment, and offer you our heartfelt hospitality. I have enjoyed teaching Petra and Jiri and the other students of the state ballet school. I also felt compelled to share my faith with them all. I tried to do it honorably and without forcing anyone into anything. As you well know, there are thirty-two students in this class, but only three expressed an interest to know more and to even begin to explore faith. Jiri and Petra came to our Sunday church gathering where they professed their faith in Christ. This was His work and their decision, not mine." I was freaking out. If there was a way to monitor the tension in my mind and heart, the indicator would be off the charts. Brother Evald was sharing his faith to four devout atheists, whose children now also believed that God is real. I appreciated his openness. I saw it in the ballet studio. I experienced it in the different church gatherings when people, just like our parents, came in to question, or sometimes even argue, the existence of God. This was different. These were my parents, and so much was at stake. If this visit went south, it could potentially deeply wound my relationship with my mom and dad and perhaps forever diminish the potential for their own salvation. Here he was. Here they were. Brother Evald was beaming with the peace and the presence of the Lord. As he continued to speak, our parents started to relax, bit by bit. I could not say the same about Petra and me, but our feelings did not matter at this moment. Brother Evald shifted to the topic of Eternia Dance Theater and the opportunity that was presented to us to dance in the *We Want to Live* tour that fall and winter. He did explain that there would be no compensation. Provision of housing, meals, and all local transportation would be covered. Eternia Dance Theater was willing to purchase two roundtrip bus tickets to Stockholm for us.

"I researched bus options, and the quickest bus connection takes almost twenty-four hours and includes a ferry transfer over the Baltic Sea from Northern Germany to Sweden. I would recommend purchasing flights to Stockholm and back as that flight is just under two hours," Evald continued. He added that Kreative Mission was able to pay the bus fare amount, but most likely, remaining funds for the flights would need to be supplemented by the two families. He explained that he understood that finances might be a problem and a strain on the budgets and left the decision to our parents. He diplomatically moved from whether or not they would allow us to go to rather focus on the details of the proposition. The first parent to say anything was Petra's father. His personality was a perfect medicine for the tense atmosphere in the living room.

"I wanted to thank you for thinking that these young birds could handle something like this. I guess all of us are a little worried about the religious aspect. Do you know the organization up in Laxå well?" By now, Mr. Grůša was standing. His wild gestures and the tone of his voice made him a natural center of attention. "Both Marcela and I care deeply about our daughter as the Voborskys do about their son, I am sure, and the main question for us is not money for the flights or whether or not they will dance a lot. What we have been thinking about ever since Petra mentioned this to us is safety, both physical but almost more importantly emotional. We are not comfortable with the religious aspect of the whole proposition. I know that Jiri and Petra recently experienced some new 'faith,' but it is one thing to let them assess church and its effects on them here and another to send them to Sweden for who-knows-how-long without knowing much about the company there. Can you give us some assurances that they will not be forced into a religious sect of sorts?"

Brother Evald did not seem at all alarmed by the question Mr. Grůša just posed. I think deep down he was excited to be given an opportunity to explain and point out differences between religion and a relationship, an actual personal relationship with the Lord Jesus Christ. "That is an excellent question, Mr. Grůša, and I appreciate your concern for both Petra and Jiri. Ruth and I have three daughters, and as every parent would, we deeply care that they are well, safe, protected, provided for, and doing well physically, spiritually, and emotionally. I have personally visited Laxå several times. It is a small town in the middle of the country, directly between Gothenburg and Stockholm. The Kreative Mission, which is the parent organization of Eternia Dance Theater, has staff members from all over the world. The directors are a married couple from Denmark, and they have a long history of running this organization with integrity. Yes, they are Christians. They believe and have a relationship with the Lord, which might be a strange and unknown element to you, but as I have witnessed in my life and theirs as well, it only drives them to be people that adhere to and live by a higher standard of personal responsibility to God and to those around them. The dancers are all professionals, also from different nations, but all with professional experience of different theaters and companies from all over the world. They train hard and regularly, they spend hours in the studio preparing new productions, and then they tour around Sweden and Europe to present their programs. I believe—no, I am convinced—that not only would Jiri and Petra gain artistically from being around these artists, but they would also gain a broad new perspective for their personal lives that will be a source for them for years to come. I cannot fully satisfy all your concerns, but based on my experience while visiting Eternia, this is a safe place that will stretch them and give them a new platform to grow as two strong individuals!" This was a great answer that brought a much-needed relief in our parents' minds. Professor Rucký promised to connect with Vibeke the next day and gather all necessary information from her so that concrete plans of our departure could be arranged. He did ask both sets of parents to talk it out between themselves and let us know their decision soon.

The visit finished on a good note. My mom did not love Brother Evald and perhaps deep down still carried a questioning attitude about his motives, but she was a lot less apprehensive about him. For that, I was thankful. Upon leaving the house, both sets of parents spent a long time talking outside of the Moravian Church building. My parents conveyed their appreciation to the Grůšas for giving me a meal here and there as well as on occasions offering to wash laundry for me. Mrs. Marcela connected well with my mom as they spoke about us and our crazy lives of balancing so many things all at once. Then it appeared as if a time out was called, as they huddled into a tight circle. An arm gesture once in a while, followed by a short burst of laughter and a nodding of a head indicated that a serious conversation was taking place. Time seemed to stop or at least slow to a bare minimum, as Petra and I stood in a distance not knowing what was being decided and said, but we remained optimistic. We knew that being in this together was a huge help for the two sets of worrying parents. After a long while, the huddle ended. They shook hands and parted ways. Petra joined her parents, who walked down the steep street toward a public transportation stop, as I joined my parents walking to their car. "Well, it sounds crazy and insane, but we all agreed that, if anything, we want to be behind you guys and give you the permission to follow your dreams and do what we could never do growing up. We were locked in this country, not permitted to ever leave unless the government allowed us to receive passports and the departure slips necessary to cross borders. Times have changed, and we need to be—no, we want to—be flexible. Both the Grůšas and we have decided to allow you guys to go!" my dad said while his arm was around mom's shoulders. Her head was leaning against his arm as he was talking.

"I hope we won't regret this," my mom chimed in. I could not believe it! The Lord did it. He removed all the obstacles out of the way. One by one. He made a way, and we were permitted to go. Petra and I were going to dance with a professional company in Sweden. This was almost too much to gather and comprehend.

"Also," my dad continued while enjoying my visible and obvious excitement, "we all think that it is best for you guys to fly. Mr. Grůša will purchase the airline tickets at the Liberec ČEDOK (*Che-dock*) Agency (Czech Travel Bureau) once we know the exact dates from Mr. Rucký, and Bohunka and I will send him a payment through the Czech Post Courier. What do you say to that?" he asked me teasingly. I was completely overwhelmed with a thrilling and inundating joy. We were going to Sweden!

It took a full three days before we knew the departure date from Mrs. Vibeke. Due to the complex system of receiving money from abroad, it was decided that we would purchase the flights in Liberec and Kreative Mission would reimbursed us upon arrival in Laxå. The departure date was eleven days away, scheduled for the following Saturday, exactly two weeks after the meeting between Brother Evald and our parents took place. It was going to be a busy ten days to pack, to settle our ISP material, and receive the printed work we needed to complete while abroad, to officially interrupt my residence at the dormitory, and to get mentally prepared for the trip. Also, we were notified of the potentially freezing temperatures in Sweden. During the final conversation with Mrs. Vibeke, Brother Evald was informed that the trip would only be seven weeks in length, based on the final confirmed bookings of the tour, rather than the originally proposed three months. That was a huge relief to me and Petra. Mr. Grůša, Petra's father, went to ČEDOK to find the published fare of the ticket but then sent us with the money to purchase the flights ourselves. Here is a fun memory of how the system of securing a seat on a flight worked in a post-Communist country in the 1990s.

The Czech Travel Agency (ČEDOK) bureau was located on Revoluční (*Re-vou-looch-nee*) Street in Liberec's downtown section of the city. This street, like many in this town located at the foothills of Jizera Mountains, has a steep incline and serves as a natural treadmill for the sport-loving citizens of Liberec. Petra and I finished our morning technique class with Professor Rucký and decided to skip our gymnázium studies in order to purchase our flights to Stockholm. Back in the day, electronic ticketing was only in the imagination of the most creative thinkers, and we had to obtain a printed airline ticket consisting of several pages of fine print and information regarding our flight. We entered the bureau through a large set of glass doors and saw a sign pointing to the air-travel section of the travel agency. A lady seated behind a modern-looking desk smiled at us and politely asked us, "How can I help you today?" I am sure that she did not expect two young teenagers to actually do any business with her that day but treated us with respect, nonetheless. There were two chairs on our side of the desk, and we were invited to sit down.

"Hello," I started. "We have come here today to purchase roundtrip flights from Prague to Stockholm for the next Saturday, November 2, with a return on Friday, December 20, please," I said while looking at a small printed calendar I brought with me.

"Are you the two young dancers who are flying to dance in Sweden?" she replied. Petra rolled her eyes, clearly understanding that Mr. Grůša must have given the agent detailed information of the "immeasurable talent" his daughter and her friend have to be selected for such a unique mission. He was known to easily make friends with anyone he would meet and, with his great personality, be the center of attention anywhere and for pretty much an unlimited time. He was always fun to listen to as he had an unending supply of unbelievable stories from his life that he shared with the artistry of a seasoned Hollywood movie actor.

"Yes, we must be," Petra replied to the agent, obviously embarrassed by what her father must have said to her in the past.

"Okay, let me see what I have available," the lady said while pulling out a large folder from underneath the desk. "Next Saturday, you said, right? Just a moment…please," was her commentary as she was flipping large pages of the folder. Her voice was fading into a whisper as her mind focused on the task of locating the Czechoslovak Airlines pages. "Here we are… Prague to Stockholm… Just a minute…" Her finger was sliding horizontally across the page. There were columns for each day of a three-month increment of the year. Each day had an indication of the flights between Prague and the given destination, in our case, Stockholm. Then there was a number of the flight and a printed price of the ticket. Before we could purchase it, she had to call Czechoslovak Airlines' office in Prague to confirm seat availability for the designated day and flight. CSA, the airlines' abbreviated name, conducted two flights between the capitals every day of the week, and so there were two numbers to choose from. "Would you like to travel in the morning or in the evening?" she asked us, lifting her head from the page but keeping the finger firmly on the located number.

"Morning, please" I said, remembering that we would also have to drive four hours to Laxå once clearing the Swedish customs, locating our baggage, and meeting whoever was going to pick us up at the airport. Without any reply, she picked up the phone and dialed the number of the CSA reservations in Prague.

"Hello, ČEDOK Liberec here, I am calling to request a reservation of two seats for OK490 on 11/02 and two seats on OK491 on 12/20… Yes, yes…thank you! Very good." She looked at us with a smile. "I have been able to reserve two seats for you, and once we complete the transaction here, I will confirm it with CSA over the phone again. I will need to see your passports, please," she continued. Every time she paused to speak, a little well-rehearsed smile appeared on her face. "CSA uses Tupolev 134 aircraft on the route to Stockholm. There are two seats on either side of the single aisle, and you guys can decide who would like to sit by the window. For practical purposes, I will reserve a window for Miss Grůšová flying to Stockholm and for Mr. Voborsky flying to Prague. Is that okay?" She waited for us to nod our heads while she smiled again and then proceeded with the reservation. She was typing fervently, putting enormous amounts of information into a massive computer placed on her desk. A sidenote here about the Tupolev airplane mentioned. Czechoslovak Airlines, as many former East European air companies, was only allowed to use Soviet-made airplanes in their fleets during the Communist era. It was not until the late 1990s when these were being retired and exchanged for Western-made planes, such as Boeing and Airbus models. Today, only North Korean airline, Air Koryo, uses this type of airplane. When I flew to Milan in 1987, I also traveled on Tupolev 134. "The total fare for the two airline tickets will be twelve thousand, five hundred Czechoslovak crowns, please," she said and smiled again. Petra pulled out the money from her bag and paid the lady in cash. Credit cards were in existence then but primarily used by foreign tourists visiting Prague from the West. The Czechs did not begin to use them until much later in the process of transitioning from Communism. Once we had paid the travel agent, she inserted more information into the computer and pushed the print button. Thin pieces of paper were pushed out of the printer. While that was happening, she picked up the phone and redialed the CSA number in Prague, confirming the conclusion of the transaction here in Liberec and dictating to the agent on the other end of the phone line the ticket number located on the bottom of the preproduced document. Then she assembled the printed papers and inserted them into a cover booklet of Czechoslovak Airlines. Both tickets consisted of a separate page for each direction of the flight from and to Prague, as well as pages breaking down the total fare of the flight and pages displaying detailed personal information. Also included were pages for our checked baggage for each flight. The last page included our rights as passengers and an overview of the itinerary. They were all stapled into a cover booklet. Part of me misses having a fancy airline ticket in hand when I fly today, but the ability to purchase a flight from the comfort of my home is something that was unthinkable before the Internet and Wi-Fi existed in the last decade of the twentieth century. With a smile, the agent handed us the printed booklets, saying, "Your flights are booked. Thank you for flying with Czechoslovak Airlines and for using ČEDOK to purchase your tickets today. Enjoy your trip!" We took the tickets, and before we left the bureau, we carefully flipped through the booklet—not to make sure that everything was correct necessarily but simply to admire this literary masterpiece in our hands, securing two seats for a flight to Stockholm and back. We were able and ready to fly to Sweden.

The next week prior to our departure was filled with preparations for written and oral tests, quizzes, and exams that we needed to complete as a part of the agreed arrangement with the gymnázium professors. The amount of information of the twelve subjects was difficult to keep separated in my mind, as I struggled to prepare for as many appointments with the individual professors as I could. I always felt much more comfortable in oral testing than I did in a written one, but I needed to do well in all of them as my ISP was hanging in the balance and was crucial to be maintained. But the upcoming trip was a great motivator during the hours of studies and reading I needed to do. By God's grace, I did well on all of them. The Wednesday before the departure, I had to travel to Ústí to pack good winter clothes I did not have with me in Liberec and exchange Czechoslovak crowns for the Swedish ones in the bank. I used the couple of days to visit with my family and my grandparents before my parents drove me to Prague early Saturday morning. I also turned seventeen that Friday and was able to celebrate my birthday at home. Every birthday celebration consisted of eating a large store-bought Harlekin (Harlequin) chocolate cake with an extravagant amount of whip cream on its top, and this year was no different. I was excited and so looking forward to the adventure of traveling to Laxå the next day.

May the favor of the Lord our God rest upon us; establish the work of our hands for us—yes, establish the work of our hands.
—Psalm 90:17

62) Sverige

I did not know much about Sweden. I knew that it was, and still is, a kingdom. I knew that it was a part of the Scandinavian portion of Europe and that Swedish is its official language. I knew that winters were cold and snow covered the ground for much of the winter days. We were met by Jeremiah and James, dancers with Eternia. Both of them were Americans, and their accent was fascinating to us. We liked them almost immediately as they made us feel extremely welcomed and at home in a country that received them as foreigners as well. The drive to the small town of Laxå was enjoyable watching the beautiful scenery along the road leading in a southwestern direction from Stockholm. If there is anything that I recall after all these years as my first impression of Sweden, it would be the trees. Everywhere, all throughout the drive, were tall trees in huge quantities. We stopped in a larger city, Örebro, to pick up groceries and supplies for the Kreative Mission base. Neither Petra nor I minded helping the guys to do some shopping. Then it was a short drive to Laxå, a town with a population of three thousand authentic Swedes, a warm and welcoming group of people who speak the funny-sounding language of Swedish. Kreative Mission was a complex of buildings surrounding a large open grass area, almost resembling an athletic oval-shaped field. There was a large structure to the right, holding the offices and directorate of the organization. Large meeting and dining rooms and a huge industrial kitchen were also located in the same building. The following building was also large. It had enormous windows in its front. One could tell that it was designed and built to be a gymnasium, but it was converted into a ballet studio furnished with mirrors, ballet barres, and a sprung dance floor. The size of this studio was much larger than the studios at the state ballet school, or even the State Theater back home. Other buildings surrounding the field looked like duplexes, each with a second floor. James led me to one of these. It was occupied with three male members of the Mission. James was the only dancer of the company living in this particular house. Some duplexes were occupied by married couples, as others were filled by the single members, split up by gender. These houses were peppered around the base. It was a Kreative Mission policy to have everyone associated with the organization living here on the base. It took me a while to get familiarized with everyone in my duplex, but right off the bat, everyone seemed just as welcoming and warm as Jeremiah and James were when I met them at the Stockholm airport earlier that day. I was given a room that I had all to myself. This was the very first time in my life when this was the case, and I was glad to be able to stay up as long as I needed to do all my assignments and studying. The room was on the bottom floor of the duplex. It was simply furnished with a bed, a desk with a chair, and an IKEA chest of drawers for my clothes. There was a "welcome" note on my bed. I felt blessed to read that the whole team was excited to welcome me into their big family. They also expressed their gratitude for Petra and I to come and step into the roles that Jeremiah and his wife, Mona, danced in the repertoire. A common living space was just outside of my bedroom, as was a small kitchenette with a microwave and a fridge. There was a full bathroom on each floor. The large squared window of my room faced toward the woods that stood some fifty yards away surrounding the whole base. I felt at home pretty much right away. I wanted to wash up, and then I realized that my stomach was strongly signaling that it was time to feed it. I asked James about some food, only to be told that there was a corporate dinner at six o'clock, which was about now. On the way to the cafeteria, James explained to me that there was a large food pantry and everyone could eat there or even take some basic groceries to his duplex. Dinners were done corporately, being enjoyed together, and every member was assigned to cook for the base and/ or be responsible for cleaning the kitchen when it was their turn. It did not take long to walk from the duplex to the cafeteria, and I saw many slowly gathering for the dinner feast.

Petra and I were introduced to everyone, and we tried desperately to remember at least a few of their names. I enjoyed the warm meal. The fellowship was overwhelming, though, as I recall. Everyone spoke fast and over one another. There were so many dialects of English used, and my mind was quickly reaching its limit. I was getting tired, and with that, I was getting a little frustrated. That is, sadly, normal for me. I did not want to be trapped here answering many questions. I was also intimidated by the fact that I was a young Christian, and whenever a biblical reference was made, I felt lost. My exhaustion assisted me in saying, "Good night," and leaving the cafeteria. A hot shower felt amazing, and shortly after that, I was in my bed knowing that it wouldn't be long before I was a goner. The snow was falling outside my window. It was a beautiful winter night. Almost as a lullaby, the snowflakes were slowly putting me to sleep. With my head resting on the pillow, looking up. I started to pray. "Thank You, Lord Jesus, thank You for Who You are. Thank You for bringing me and Petra here to Laxå safely. Thank You for all these fantastic people. Thank You…for Your grace to choose me to be here… Thank You, Father…" I never finished that prayer as I drifted to a deep sleep. I knew that my Lord was watching over me and that He brought me to Sweden to serve Him and to grow me in my understanding of His character, heart, and even purposes throughout the time spent with Eternia. I was humbled by that thought, and I was grateful.

It was an incredibly powerful growing experience, working with the company of the Eternia Dance Theater. There was such a unique and, to me, completely new loving atmosphere among all the dancers of the company. Everyone worked in joyous submission and with a deep respect toward each other. I often wondered, *How could this be?* I understood that Jesus and everyone's love for Him here was to be seen. I did not know just how much and how powerful that love truly is when lived out and how visible the invisible God can be when displayed in the life of His people. The artistic director, Vibeke, entered the studio each day with a clear mission to accomplish precisely everything she deemed necessary to complete each day. Her determination, strictness, and yet love reminded me of Brother Evald, and I wondered if he was inspired to do so by her or whether she saw that quality first in him when he guest-taught here in the past. The expectation for Petra and I to learn our parts was high. Time was short to learn the full production, and there was no time to waste—no time to wait for us to board the train of "I am not sure what this step sequence is." Everyone around us already knew their parts. We were expected not only to learn the steps but to fit into the style of the company as well as to be able to dance with clean technique and compelling artistry. What struck me as most powerful was the attention paid to the artistic side of the production. *We Want to Live* was a composition specifically created and written for the Eternia Dance Theater. The creator of the musical score was a British composer, Adrian Snell, whose inspiration for the project was a poem entitled "Fear," written by a little Czech Jewish girl, Eva Picková.

This fourteen-year-old girl was imprisoned at the Terezín (*Te-re-zeen*) Concentration Camp during World War II. Her riveting cry, captured in the words of the poem, profoundly paints the horror and the dim hopelessness that were hovering over this and every Nazi concentration camp across Europe. What is so interesting about this is the fact that Terezín, also known under its German name of Theresienstadt, is a small Czech town located eighteen miles from my hometown of Ústí. I performed at this former concentration camp with the Kvítko ensemble several times growing up, when annually the government of Czechoslovakia organized peace celebrations of the allies' victory over the Nazi Germany in 1945. On the grounds of the Terezín concentration camp is a brick-built fortress, originally constructed in the eighteenth century as a link in a chain of fortifications of Bohemia. The starlike footprint of the city and the fortress layouts are unique and architecturally one of a kind. The main entrance gate to the camp had alternating black-and-white decor stripes around its edge that send chills down one's back when entered. Sadly, it was used time and again as a military prison and, during the war, as a Jewish ghetto and a camp that housed over thirty-two thousand prisoners. I knew that children were imprisoned in Terezín, as there are wings set aside specifically for them, but I never knew one by name *not* until I was given a copy of the poem during a rehearsal in Laxå.

> Today the ghetto knows a different fear,
> Close in its grip, Death wields an icy scythe.
> An evil sickness spreads a terror in its wake,
> The victims of its shadow weep and writhe.
> Today a father's heartbeat tells his fright
> And mothers bend their heads into their hands.
> Now children choke and die with typhus here,
> A bitter tax is taken from their bands.
> My heart still beats inside my breast
> While friends depart for other worlds.
> Perhaps it's better—who can say?—
> Than watching this, to die today?
> No, no, my God, we want to live!
> Not watch our numbers melt away.
> We want to have a better world,
> We want to work—we must not die!

Only in God's omniscience would this poem become the cornerstone to Snell's powerful musical creation; Vibeke's choreography, and, exactly fifteen years later, a piece of my own ballet, *Hiding Place,* telling the story of Corrie ten Boom. If one tried really hard and poured all his efforts to be creative and pertinacious in every moment of their life, they could never match the creativity, knowledge, wisdom, reign, and power of the Almighty God, a God Who works all things together in such illustrious and powerful ways, as to bring a Czech dancer to Sweden, introduce him to a letter written eighteen miles away from his hometown by a girl in 1942, and then allow him to use the talent of dance, and later choreography, that He Himself imparted. My God is that glorious.

Petra and I poured all our strength into meeting Mrs. Vibeke's expectations and, in one week, rose to the level of readiness to be able to leave Laxå for a tour around Sweden. I was dancing the story of Benjamin, a young Jewish boy who fought the oppression of Nazi Germany against him and his people, sadly, to no avail. Benjamin and his friend Eva died at the end of the ballet, as did nearly six million Jews during World War II. Their remembrance is carried in the lives of those who bravely, through many creative ways and means, retell the story of one race trying to erase another, as they understand the importance of remembering and never repeating this horrendous error again.

> *For if you remain silent at this time, relief and deliverance*
> *for the Jews will arise from another place, but you and your*
> *father's family will perish. And who knows but that you*
> *have come to your royal position for such a time as this.*
> —Esther 4:14

63) It Does Not Matter How Many

Eternia Dance Theater traveled in a bus furnished with bunk beds for the dancers. It was a comfortable way to travel from city to city, from performance to performance, dancing night after night in many communities, large and small, all throughout Sweden. I do not remember them all, and I do not remember many details from these tours. There is one show, however, that stands out in my mind as unique. It was a long through-the-night drive from Norrköping, following a performance the previous day. These travels through the night were my favorite. There were not enough beds for everyone on the bus. Some would sleep on the sofa, and some in the seats. Dancers would take turns sleeping in the bunks, but no matter where I found myself drifting off for the night, I loved waking up to a crisp snow-covered morning in another part of this beautiful country. Nights were long, and daylight short, as Sweden covers the very northernmost part of the European continent and during winters it does not see much of the sun. But whenever the sun decided to rise, I got to witness the birthing of each new day as the Creator God painted the skies with countless gorgeous colors, never repeating Himself but always offering a fresh assurance of His nearness and love. Breakfasts often consisted of a stop in a fast-food restaurant where a warm breakfast and a strong cup of coffee supplied the needed energy for whatever was yet to come that day.

We arrived at Kristianstadt around ten o'clock in the morning. It was always very entertaining to watch whoever was driving at the time to find and locate the performance venue. This morning was no different. We were scheduled to perform in the Kristianstadt Theater. Most historic opera and theater houses are usually located on a square with a fountain located in front of these temples of culture. It took us a while to locate the main square of the town, but there was no theater there to be found. The driver, still clearly displaying the overnight drive in his visage, peeked out of the window and, using his rapid Swedish, asked a local resident for help. Kristianstadt is a smaller city that is bordered by a river on its western edge. There on its banks lies a beautiful sprawling Tivoli Park. The Kristianstadt Theater, also known as Tivoli-Teatern, is located in the middle of the gardens of the park. This 1906 horseshoe-shaped building was designed by a local architect who also designed and oversaw the building of the Royal Opera House in Stockholm. As we would do on most performance days, we first located the backstage loading docks and started to set up for the evening performance. Dancers would take turns in showering as everybody else continued with the technical setup. I was not only replacing Jeremiah in the performance itself, but I was also substituting for his setup duties and had to quickly learn the nuts and bolts of what that meant. In the Liberec State Theater, there were people responsible for the technical aspects of each performance, and the performers never helped nor were permitted to be around when setups were taking place, and so my knowledge was limited. But I was eager to learn, and everyone was a great mentor and teacher, assisting me in this new endeavor. We would usually have a moment after lunch to walk around the vicinity of each performance venue, and this was no different. The air was cold but clean, and the falling snow was almost always a guarantee. I walked around the Tivoli Park for a little while before returning back to the theater. As I would do every performance day, I stepped on stage when everything was ready and done and reviewed the whole show, marking through choreography sequences and getting familiarized with the new space. The whole company would gather before the performance to worship together and lift up the audience before the Lord in prayer. Then about thirty minutes before the beginning of the show, the doors would open, and the audience members started to settle in their seats in anticipation of the performance. This day followed that formula to the smallest detail. Daylight was long gone, and the streets outside were illuminated by the street lamps and the bright winter stars in the skies. The magnificent interior of the Tivoli-Teatern was also brightened by the fancy chandelier and the lighting fixtures all throughout the auditorium. Doors were open, and ushers were in their places. The dancers were in the dressing rooms preparing for the top of the show. Time was running. Everything was culminating toward the nineteenth hour, when the doors would be closed and the chandelier would be dimmed. Everything was going just as it should. There was one element missing, absent from the normal rigor of the day. There were no people. There was no audience. My English was not that good to fully grasp and understand everything that was being communicated between the company members and the technical personnel in the front of the house. Petra and I were trying to catch on; but all we knew was that there were no people coming in, no audience flooding the seats, and no hustle around the box office. Jeremy Van der Pant, the tour director for Eternia, originally from Great Britain, did not seem alarmed as I saw him walking away from the backstage toward the foyer of the theater. The time now reached the nineteenth hour of the day, and normally, we would take our places to begin the performance. We waited. This has never happened before, as we were told. Everyone waited for Jeremy to return and let us know what would happen next. He came a little after the top of the hour and, with his beautiful and commanding British accent, ordered all of us to do what we knew to do: take our places. Then everything proceeded like it did every night—the work lights dimmed, the preshow announcements were played, and then the pause between them and the first notes of Snell's music filled the building. I calmed my heart and my nerves as I waited for the curtain to open. The show started with me seated at the family table with my sister and our parents ready to do the Jewish Shabbat dinner. Music started to play. Light slowly started to shine from the left side of the stage. The velvet curtain lifted, and we started to dance. It is always very difficult to see into the audience as the front lights shine against us while dancing. We gave it our all. We danced and sweated. We told the timeless story of Benjamin and Eva. The ninety minutes went by quickly. There was no applause coming from the audience during the evening. That was not unusual, as the European audience is generally much less expressive during a performance and applause typically happens at the end of the night. The ballet concluded, and the curtain closed. The cast lined up for the bows behind the closed heavy velvet fabric. The lights relit, and the curtain opened. As we stepped through the proscenium, we saw the audience members—standing and applauding, visibly moved by the story they just watched. There were not thousands in the Tivoli-Teatern that night. There were not hundreds nor even fifty nor thirty. No, that particular evening in Kristianstadt, Sweden, four people came to watch the show seated in the front row. As we concluded the bows, and it did not take very long, the curtain closed for the last time that evening. As we would normally go to our dressing rooms to change out of our costumes and prepare to strike all the equipment, Jeremy called us all to gather. "This was one of the most exciting performances I have ever witnessed," he started. "These four people, these four souls, were privileged to find themselves in the presence of the Lord, Who poured His love on them, just them, for the whole hour and a half tonight." He paused as his eyes filled with tears. "Every other ballet company would cancel. Everybody else would send them home. Jesus did just the opposite. Tonight, He delighted to introduce Himself just to them, and He used you all to be the messengers of His grace and love for these people. It is not our responsibility to worry about how many He will bring. It is our responsibility, however, to always, and I mean always, honor Him with our best and leave it up to Him to do the rest. He made that crystal clear when I walked to the foyer at seven o'clock tonight. God brought us to Kristianstadt for these four, and He accomplished His purpose because we were willing to be Jesus's vessels. Thank you for trusting me in this. Thank you for loving the Lord like this. Now let's get moving and clear the theater as quickly as we can." I was moved by his words. I realized that I had so much to learn about the kingdom of God and about how my Savior works His purposes in often very unique and extraordinary ways. I was humbled to be a part of His work.

> *But the plans of the Lord stand firm forever, the*
> *purposes of his heart through all generations.*
> —Psalm 33:11

64) God Morgon!

It would not be an accurate retelling of the story capturing my first visit to Sweden, if I had not shared the following rendezvous. To help better understand the irony of it, I must first confess that I am a city boy. Very much so. All the way. My dad took me fishing growing up; and as I shared earlier, I only managed to survive these trips to nature because I focused on building forts and fortresses out of mud, rocks, and sticks in the woods. Many find themselves refreshed when they take a walk through the forest. For me, it is the exact opposite. I leave the companionship with the trees completely exhausted and drained. My dad tried to teach me to differentiate between the different kinds of birds, mushrooms, trees, and fish, only to give up after I would call a cuckoo bird a woodpecker, a freshly caught zander a carp, and a spruce tree a maple. On the other hand, a stroll on Paris' Champs-Élysées, for example, fills me with vitality and life. I guess I better relate to the crowds of people and the vigor-filled busyness of the city than I do to the quietness of the countryside. But here I was, sitting in the middle of Sweden, in a small town surrounded by nothing except wide spread woods all around. The company would return to the base every ten days or so, only to leave again after a short rest lasting anywhere from forty-eight to seventy-two hours. During these days, I focused on catching up on schoolwork as there was no real time to do so on tour. My large window would be kept open as I felt stimulated by the clean crisp air. Though the room was chilly, I sat at my desk by the window diving wholeheartedly into studying while wrapped in a blanket and wearing a pair of thick knitted socks my grandmother made for me.

The sun was shining brightly as the grounds around the Kreative Mission were blanketed with white unblemished snow. I was deep in thought pouring over the work that I was given by Professor Vondráček. Time was short, and there was so much to do. It was sometime between nine and ten in the morning as I sat there determined to have a lot of the work completed by the time my stomach growled for lunch. Not paying attention to anything but the schoolwork, I did not notice that a large moose decided to pay me a visit. He slowly approached the opened window as if trying to glean some science knowledge for himself. And then he breathed. Through his nostrils, he exhaled and, with the warm air from within, let me know that he was interested in a short visit. I looked up slowly, not knowing what kind of beast this was, and the last thing I would want is to upset it. As my eyes met his, the moose pushed his face through the window into the room. His head was enormous. There were antlers that looked like large, extralarge to be exact, hands flipped upward as if one was asking, "What's up?" They stopped the entrance of the head as they collided with the frame of the window. He kept breathing. "*God morgon*," Swedish for "good morning," was the only thing that would make this an even more unbelievable circumstance. I was frozen. My mind went blank. If I learned anything that morning, all of it most certainly and abruptly rushed out of my mind, and my memory bank, perhaps never to return. There were, but a couple of inches between the beast and me. Then I noticed his eyes. They signaled warmness and peace. I was not about to become brunch. His nostrils, large and shaped as crescent moons, kept smelling me. It was a good thing I showered that morning, partially to help me wake up and partially because the showers were occupied the night before. *Should I touch it?* There was no way that I would actually do that. *Would I dare?* These thoughts were running through my mind. Everything in me was uptight, but my breathing was calm. In all honesty, though, I was freaking out. Yes, silently but truly freaking out. Then the moose exhaled again and pulled his head through the window frame. I got to see his full beauty. The antlers, his massive body, and the beauty of his fur, also called velvet, masterfully reflected the sunshine of the day. He looked at me again, as if saying, "Goodbye, friend. Study hard!" and then slowly and casually walked away. I sat there looking after him as he disappeared into the forest. I could not believe that this just happened. It took me a moment to be able to, again, fully focus on the work in front of me. I pondered whether or not to keep the window opened. I did, and deep down, I hoped that my newly made acquaintance would return. That, he did not do.

In his hand is the life of every creature and the breath of all mankind.
—Job 12:10

65) The Rearview Mirror

Before long, it was time to return to the Arlanda airport in Stockholm and fly back to Prague. It was not the flight I worried about; it was the fear of returning to the normal rhythm of life, school, dorm life, State Theater, exams. There were only three days before Christmas Eve, and yet I felt that so much had to take place. I needed to see if there were any performances I was scheduled to dance in anytime between Christmas and the New Year. My parents met me in Prague to take me to Ústí, and I asked Petra to call once she had the opportunity to review the performance roster at the theater. There was nothing scheduled right around the Christmas holidays, but there were a few operettas posted toward the end of the year. That was a typical programming strategy of the state theaters around the nation, to draw people in by offering an unexpected twist in the productions for the New Year celebrations. Petra called to let me know that there were two shows scheduled two days apart from each other for December 29 and 31. I had a dilemma to solve, as the dorms were closed for the winter break. I asked Petra if it would be possible for me to stay with her family but was declined, as there was no room in her family's apartment, which I completely understood. I needed to mitigate the problem of not having a place to stay. Professor Gabajová had offered me a place to stay in the past, when I had to remain in Liberec and the dorms were closed for the weekend. She lived in a large historic apartment in Liberec, with an empty bedroom; and being a widow, she often spent time at her cottage in the garden section of the city. There she poured her energy into gardening and knitting, leaving the apartment vacant. I never accepted the offer until now. I called Professor Gabajová with hesitancy as I understood that it could be potentially awkward to ask her to stay with her right around the holidays. She answered the call and, to my unexpected surprise, sounded excited to speak with me. She asked about Sweden and my time there. She was not interested in the artistic content of the performed repertoire but was extremely interested in knowing the details of the Eternia Dance Theater technical style used in the daily ballet class, as well as in the production's choreography. She gladly offered me the empty room and told me where I would find the spare key to unlock the apartment. She was going to spend Christmas with her son Peter and his wife and would not be there, anyway.

I enjoyed Christmas that year. As I listened to the familiar LP records that my mom played all throughout my childhood, the lyrics of the Christmas carols were speaking so profoundly and impactfully to me, as I now understood the true meaning hidden in their message. I was moved by the proclamations stated through the old Czech carols that somehow escaped the political censorship of the Communist regime and, miraculously, remained to be listened to by the general public, even during the strictest era of the mandated socialist propaganda of the past. As the music filled our small flat, my heart was somehow deeply moved by the music and its message, much more profoundly than ever before. I realized that my spiritual ears were opened and the Spirit, Who now resided within me, was connecting with the truths of the songs. I was impacted profoundly with my emotions overflowing with gratitude and worship. I reflected on the fact that 1991 was the year when I became alive, born again, and was filled with exuberant joy of the found Savior. I was saddened knowing that nobody else in my family truly heard the lyrics like I did and knew the source of their message, King Jesus.

I left for Liberec to take a company class and to rehearse to prepare for the performances. It was good to see all my classmates as well as friends from the company. Some welcomed Petra and me warmly as some had a hard time overcoming the feeling of jealousy and even envy of our experience in Sweden. The reality to be back was as real as I expected it to be and as challenging as I feared. I had to focus on remembering these productions' choreography and, through dedication and hard work, reassure Maestro Pokorný that he did not make a mistake by allowing me and Petra to travel to Sweden. The demand was formidable, and by God's grace, we both rose to its challenge. The December 29 performance was the sultry operetta, *The Countess Maritza*, by a Hungarian composer Emmerich Kálmán. The three-act masterpiece was filled with captivating rhythms and melodies inspired by his native country. It was always a thrill to perform as it was a delight to watch the audience enjoy Kálmán's adventure-filled musical gem. The last performance of this, personally revolutionary year, was Strauss's *Die Fledermaus*, my favorite. Glasses were flowing with real champagne as the cast celebrated the old year and, through this melodic performance, welcomed the year to come. Thinking about everything that transpired in the past 365 days, as if peeking through a rearview mirror, my heart was overwhelmed and grateful.

You turned my wailing into dancing; you removed my sackcloth and clothed me with joy, that my heart may sing to you and not be silent. O Lord my God, I will give you thanks forever.

—Psalm 30:11–12

66) Goodbye, Dorm Life

The New Year began with a great start. I was refreshed after the winter break and, with a gusto, dove into the second semester of my junior year. There were more opportunities to perform in more productions of the State Theater, and studies at the ballet school as well as the gymnázium were going well. One big change that I had decided to undergo, and received my parents' blessings for, was to move permanently to Professor Gabajová's apartment to rent the empty room there. She would spend more and more weekdays and almost all weekends at her cottage, and so it was a welcomed change to have an apartment to myself with the freedom to study and stay up as long as I needed, and not to have to worry about disturbing my roommates in the process. I also no longer needed to worry about where to stay when the dorm would close for the weekend, as happened from time to time. There were several occasions when Mrs. Gabajová and I sat around the kitchen table to let the hours go by while we sipped hot tea and talked about life. She would wear a thick large wraparound scarf on her shoulders or lower back, no matter what temperature the thermometer would show. She always moved around slowly and carefully but always with elegance and the graceful posture of a ballerina. There were a few evenings when the light fixture above the kitchen table stayed on for a long time as we would play cards together. Professor Gabajová never spoke much of her husband except for one evening, when, after a quick game, we remained in the kitchen talking. She boiled more water for another cup of tea and offered me some as well. I knew that I should devote some time to studying, but I sensed that there was almost a need, or a desire, in Mrs. Gabajová's heart to reminisce. I gladly agreed to another cup of chamomile tea and listened as she started to share her stories. Then, suddenly, she walked out of the kitchen and into her room at the end of the hall. I was not sure as to why, but I sat there and waited. She returned clutching a large photo album against her chest. The look in her eyes clearly indicated that to open the book of memories would most likely unlock a flow of emotions and perhaps even tears. I was not sure if I was ready to be the comfort she might need; but

I wanted to see—no, I was dying to see—some pictures from her dancing days and from her life spent in the spotlights of the National and State Theaters. She gently placed the album on the kitchen table and brushed the dust from its cover. It was clear that many years had passed since she last saw what was about to be opened before us. She sat on the chair next to me and readjusted the scarf around her shoulders. Slowly, she opened the album. It was filled with black-and-white photos of both personal and professional lives. There were pictures from La Bayadere, Giselle, Swan Lake, and from ballets more known in the Russian ballet world such as Rimsky-Korsakov's *Scheherazade* or Boris Asafyev's *The Fountain of Bakhchisarai*. There was a large collection of posters, playbills featuring her as the principal ballerina for different ballets, newspaper articles about her, and interviews done with her. There were solo photos from her career, as there were also pictures with different dance partners. Mrs. Gabajová flipped a page and then paused. Her eyes filled with tears. There was an aged photograph of her and a man who appeared to be taken during a pas de deux in the second act of Tchaikovsky's *Swan Lake*. Her fingers gently brushed across the photograph as if trying to remember something or someone special. She did not say anything at first. I was not sure who that was, but he must have been special to her. "This is my husband, Eduard," she said quietly. "He passed away just three years ago, and I am trying to move on… It's just difficult." She paused for a moment, her eyes looking at me. "He was too young to go, too young to leave me, too young to die!" I was not sure what to say. I did not know much about her personal life, but I saw that the pain in her heart was real and still very fresh. "I am glad you are here to bring life back into these rooms of the flat that Eduard and I shared together for all these years. Thank you, Jiri." I was almost embarrassed to be thanked, as I was the beneficiary of the affordable and comfortable housing, but I was happy to bring some companionship to Professor Gabajová. Often, during our conversations over a steaming cup of tea, I would share the hope of Jesus and the comfort and love I found in Him less than two years prior. Though there was no direct rejection, there was also never a direct embrace of faith in Mrs. Gabajová's life. I rented the room from her until I graduated from both schools, in June of the following year.

As the school semester approached its culmination, we were in full swing of preparations for the public ballet exam coming up in June, as well as learning choreography for yet another ballet, *From Fairytale to Fairytale*, scheduled to premiere in March. I do not recall the exact time frame, but around April or early May, Brother Evald approached Petra and me with an invitation to return to Sweden in the summer and to participate in the annual Creative Arts Festival. It was going to be a full monthlong intensive focused on the performing arts, held in Laxå. Right away, we were excited to go and see all our friends there as well as meet new Christian artists from around the globe. Brother Evald offered to choreograph a piece for us that we could present at the festival. We would need to find time outside of the already packed schedule to learn the choreography, but we were willing to do so as we desired to bring a piece that we could perform in Laxå. Professor Rucký selected Antonín Dvořák's third *scherzo* from his Ninth Symphony, "From the New World," that this Czech composer wrote while serving as the director of the New York Conservatory of Music. This particular piece is almost eight minutes long. Professor Rucký envisioned a boy wandering through life who meets the Holy Spirit, Who helps him find the path to eternity. I was to be the boy, and Petra was to be the Holy Spirit. The selected piece of music is more or less an allegro that called for great stamina and endurance. The cry for help was very real once I reached the culminating last few counts after jumping, spinning, and partnering for the duration of the choreography. It did not take us terribly long to learn the steps. It was made clear to us that, in order to tell a conveying message, our hearts must be fully on display and artistry to be the featured element, riding on the back of brilliant technique. *No pressure*, I thought sarcastically as I knew that a painful process of achieving Professor Rucký's expectations was about to come our way. The semester's end arrived with a lot of stress and hard work as completion of all academic exams required sleepless nights and countless hours of studying, always reintroducing the familiar overwhelming feeling of incomprehensible and unsurpassable amount of knowledge to be attained. But, by God's grace, I finished the junior year successfully in both the academic and artistic fields. Summer break was here, and we were scheduled to depart for Sweden in the middle of July. We were prepared to participate and prepared to perform. Professor Rucký gave us his approval and blessing. I could hardly wait to return to Sweden.

My grace is sufficient for you, for my power is made perfect in weakness.
—2 Corinthians 12:9a

67) Crucial Appointment

Am I the only one who sees certain life appointments more important than others? To put it differently, are there apparent turns on the path of our life that seem more crucial or more important, turns that we cannot afford to miss? These unexpected derailments often lead us onto horizons that truly lie beyond our wildest imaginations, horizons where the will of the Lord awaits to usher us into the chapters of life yet to be read. For me, one of these divine rendezvous—one of these radical turns off the projected and, frankly, expected road—was in the Master's manual scheduled for the summer of 1992.

Petra and I arrived in Stockholm after taking a twenty-four-hour bus ride, traversing many miles of long highways, passing many towns and cities in Germany and Sweden, and crossing the Baltic Sea. We arrived on schedule and were met again by two staffers of the Kreative Mission. The drive to Laxå was almost too much for the body to handle. All those hours of sitting in very restrictive seats of the bus and then a minivan were about to break us. Or so we thought. We arrived at the base early in the evening. The accommodation arrangements were different from the previous winter when we came to dance with the company as there were so many participants registered for the festival. It was overwhelming and exciting all at the same time. I could not believe to see all these Christians, so many young people, desiring to serve the Lord with the talents He has given them. Often, we see ourselves being the only ones; and we forget the bigger, the global, the kingdom perspective. Here we were. We were gathered into the large room for a quick orientation. We were introduced to the faculty that traveled to Laxå from all over the world, coming here to pour into us and to inspire us to love Jesus firstly and completely.

We stayed in large dorm rooms, each furnished with six bunk beds. Divided by gender, we were assigned to rooms and encouraged to meet our roommates. So many summers have come and gone since then, and to be honest, I do not remember any one particular brother who shared the room with me that year. During the day, we went our separate ways to learn from the staff in our individual classes. Petra and I would join other young dancers and dance all day enjoying the challenge brought our way by all the phenomenal artists. The big performance was scheduled for the first weekend of the festival. Petra and I found an empty studio on several occasions to rehearse our pas de deux. It was astonishing to me just how quickly one's stamina and built-in strength fade. It was a real struggle to push through rehearsals to the end of the dance. Frustration and strife would find a way between us. Both Petra and I knew that we needed to pull together, to encourage one another, to be standing in unity. It felt as if a battle or sorts was taking place. Being young believers, we had no idea that spiritual warfare is a real thing and that the enemy tries devotedly to bring disunity among God's people. We pressed through and felt ready and prepared by Saturday afternoon. We were scheduled to be the final number of the first half of the evening. The performance and all Saturday activities were held outside. The Scandinavian sun rarely sleeps in the summer months. The days are long, and the temperature remains warm, as it wars a prevailing fight, resisting the incoming coolness of each night. The white nights are a real thing, and they have a profound ability to affect one's mind over a period of time, as the real nightfall never fully comes. "Representing the Czech and Slovak Federative Republic, we have Jiri and Petra, a pair of students from the state ballet school in Liberec. They will present for us a piece titled "New Life." The choreography is by Evald Rucký, and music is by Antonín Dvořák," sounded from the speakers. The Swedish announcer had obvious difficulties pronouncing Evald and

Dvorak's names. Petra and I looked at each other. We knew that there was no looking back. We had to step on that stage and simply dance! I took my pose in the middle of the stage and fought hard not to hear Brother Evald's words in my mind, whispering suggestions and encouragement to me. I asked the Lord to speak through me and, also, to me during these next eight minutes. The music started to play, and as every dancer does, I stepped into the choreography. I had a story to tell, a message to convey. I started to dance and slowly, as if supernaturally, Jiri started to fade away; and the lost boy of the story, the one who did not even have a name, started to emerge. The initial two minutes or so were a solo work, depicting the unsure purpose of my life. I had a vast amount of experience to draw from, many moments of feeling useless and without a direction. High jumps landing in low poses, staccato abrupt motions, deep cambrés when one's back arches deeply, sharp movements of the head—all these were to paint the picture. The message was simple and yet so profound. I was "lost!"

Then the music changed; and on the horizon, on the edge of the stage, appeared a silhouette, a girl in white. I noticed her immediately, but I was skeptical at first. She reached out to me, and I responded to her invitation. There was something so very different about her. She was not of the world; she could not be. She spoke of the Lord and of His love. Her message was too good to be true. Could a solution to my longing be that easy to be gained? The choreography was alternating between us dancing individually and us dancing together. Slowly, I found myself captivated by her message that led me to the source of true salvation. Two minutes remained... My body was for sure experiencing deep side pains. Why is dancing in the studio so different from dancing before the crowd? Is it adrenaline? Is it nerves? Sweat was pouring down my back. My brow, like a mirror, reflected the sun that still shone with brightness and intensity above us... Petra danced performing rapid piqué turns around me, while I was expressing the exchange between Jesus and the nameless boy in the center of the stage. Then she ran off, and I had the last sixty seconds to express the jubilant joy of the newfound life. The last note hit the audio waves, and I collapsed as if in the presence of the living God. A total exhaustion echoed through my body, and the pain followed shortly thereafter. The audience sat there completely silent and then erupted to a wild applause. I stood up and invited Petra to join me back on the stage. We bowed as we were trained to do by the state ballet school staff. We bowed again and slowly exited the stage. The moment we stepped off the stage and found a place to find privacy, we both swooned to the ground, resting against the wall. Professor Rucký would be proud of us, not because we danced flawlessly but because we gave it our best and left it all there on the outdoor stage. As my breathing started to normalize, a deep sense of change was starting to surface in my heart. I had to focus, as if trying to hear the still voice of the Lord that whispers, when He is giving us an important word. My mind was calm and still as my body was catching up to the same. I closed my eyes to block out all distractions. And then, suddenly, I understood. The Lord used the dance with its pain and through its message, to set me free from the idol, ballet held in my life. I remembered the moment after I first met the Lord, in the spring of the previous year, when Brother Evald warned me of the dangers serving the "muse of dance." It took all this time for the Lord to do it. But as clearly as I could know, I was certain that I was no longer a dancer who loved Jesus, but I was a lover of Christ who happened to dance. I was overwhelmed by this immense gift of God and how He made me feel so special when presenting it to me. Wow! The festival was off to a great start. What else did my Father prepare for me?

"This was amazing! Great job! Hello, my name is Randall Flinn. I am really blown away by what I just saw. That was powerful, you two!" "Thank you very much, sir," was all I could get out. My body was still recovering from the effects of the performance, signaling pain and fatigue, and my spirit was momentarily immobilized by the revelation of what God just did inside of my heart and soul, setting me free from the bondage to the blinding desire for fame and recognition as a dancer. We had the privilege of taking Mr. Flinn's contemporary class earlier that week. There was something so special about him. His American accent only added to the power of his modern class. We studied Graham technique class at the academy, and though its elements were very similar in style, there was a component radically different. The last portion of each of Flinn's classes was devoted to learning a piece of his contemporary choreography. Mr. Flinn was a passionate teacher and, apparently, a very gifted choreographer. His style felt natural to do. The way he connected sequences felt like a therapy to the body. There were creative elements popping out of nowhere, and the flow of his choreography seemed seamless. There was a strong emphasis given to the connection between the dancers and the Lord, woven into the fabric of the movement. I was a ballet dancer hesitant to ever label myself as a contemporary dancer, but in his classes, I experienced a natural ability to do what was asked of me. That summer evening, Petra and I connected with Randall on a deeper, personal level. We ended up eating dinner together. Little did I know that this was the beginning to a lifelong friendship. There was not a day when we would skip his class. There was a great equipoise between the strict requirements of a ballet class and the freedom of movement in Flinn's contemporary choreography. The longer the festival lasted, the deeper our friendship grew.

It is for freedom that Christ has set us free. Stand firm, then, and do not let yourselves be burdened again by a yoke of slavery.
—Galatians 5:1

68) Heavenly Repairman

It was a sunny day. Petra and I spent the morning picking blueberries in the vicinity of the base. Sweden's climate must be ideal as these berries grow in huge amounts and sizes. We were given massive brushes designed specifically for easier collection of the fruit, and with their help, there were buckets full of blueberries in no time. After returning to the dorms, I had no real plans for the rest of the day. It was a day of rest, and no scheduled classes were on the roster. Knock, knock, knock, sounded on my door. It was Randall. "I borrowed a boom box and wanted to experiment on you with a piece of choreography, if you would be interested," he said while lifting his arm with a shiny gray boom box.

"Fancy," I said, not knowing if I should be more excited about having something to do that day or by the invitation to work with Mr. Flinn one on one. "Give me a second to throw some dance clothes on," I said as I looked around the messy room for some dance attire. There were several dancers staying in the room, and we found it to be a challenge to keep our stuff organized and separated from each other's.

"I'll meet you in the studio," he replied as he was already on the move. I was excited to follow him there and start working. "There is a Mighty Spirit...," sounded from the studio, "shining out across the sky... He is calling out the weary...to green pastures, 'Come and lie.'" The voice of the singer sounded powerful and compelling. "Call me Randall," was the first thing that Mr. Flinn said, extending his hand to me.

"My name is Jiri, but you may call me Yirka, which is the nickname version of my official name." We shook hands, and I knew that I made a friend.

"Okay, Yirrrka," Randall started, trying really hard to roll the *R* in my name, as a native Czech would do, "five, six, seven, eight..." He started to move showing anywhere between eight to sixteen counts of movement at a time. "Do it," he said, looking at me while taking a step back to observe. "Hm, how about this way?" He would demonstrate an alteration to the steps he just scrapped. I was not sure if it was me and my dancing that he did not like or if he was not fully satisfied with the proposed choreography. "Yeah, yeah, yeah... I like that better...nice...deeper...and smoother...nice," echoed through the studio. "Let's try this with the music... Five, six, seven, eight... and..." The music started to play, and I moved. Randall would stand by the boom box with his feet turned out resembling a classical dancer rather than a contemporary one. His right hand would beat the rhythm to his thigh. "Good, good, good," he said, pausing the music and, in his thoughts, diving into a place where he would find inspiration. He would play a section of the song, rewinding the CD back and forth to find the right spot to continue. I used the time to review the choreography, ready to do more. "Okay, now from this point, try this." Randall would demonstrate another section of the dance. Large gestures were alternating with grand movements on the ground. "Now with music, please," he said while I took the starting position. "No, no, no, let's do it from the second verse... You are over there, right?" He pointed to a spot on the studio floor. "Let me find the music," he said as he pushed the "rewind" and "forward" buttons on the top of the boom box. The music sounded distorted while it was being located by the laser inside of the machine. "Here? No," he said as he gave a quick listen to the song, "but almost... Ready?" I was in my place to begin the second verse. And then...silence. The machine stopped working. "What happened?" Randall asked while looking intently at the piece of expensive equipment.

"I am not sure," was my response. "Is it plugged in?" I asked as if the machine suddenly decided to unplug itself from the outlet in clear demonstration that it was done with our "back-and-forth abuse."

"Yes, the light indicating that the power is flowing in is on," he said while pushing the "on" button on and off repeatedly, assumingly hoping for that to be what will fix the machine. But it did not. The boom box was broken. The "on" light flickered as if saying goodbye to Randall, and then it went out. "I can't believe this," Randall continued, his voice clearly resembling the saddened mood of his heart. "I borrowed the boom box from the guys promising to return it in good condition, and I don't have the money to pay them for a new one. What am I going to do?" I had no idea what to say, no inspiration for how to encourage my friend, as we both sat on the floor of the studio looking at the machine. "Jiri, I know what we need to do... We will pray for it to be healed and fixed," he said, looking at me with a spark in his eye.

"Say what now?" came out of my mouth. "Pray for the equipment?" My mind was racing trying to keep up with this man who, like Brother Evald, had a faith that was standing on all his previous experiences with the Lord, bolstered by the miracles he has seen God do during the many years of walking with Jesus. But I was a young Christian and believing like that, believing practically, was not yet customary for me. I did not mind praying with Randall, but I worried that my unbelief that God would repair the boom box could cause Randall's prayers to go unanswered.

"We need to lay our hands on it, Yirka…to demonstrate our faith… It's biblical, and I believe that it honors the Lord," he said as seriously as he could. His hand was already placed on the top of the equipment, and I followed suit. It was not because I knew to do that. It was not because I felt led to do that. I placed my hand on the boom box because I did not want to disappoint Randall with my lack of faith. I placed my hand on it, and we both closed our eyes. "Lord, You are a big God," Randall started, "and we are calling on You, Mighty Father, because we have a need—a big need right here in this studio." I was trying to pray along, but with all honesty, I must confess that my mind was winning the "intellect versus faith" fight. I knew that this was an opportunity to grow in knowing Jesus better, and I was about to miss out on it and mess it up. I did not want to fail the test and have to relearn it elsewhere. I asked the Lord to help me believe that He could and, in actuality, would repair the boom box. Randall continued, "This piece of electronics is broken, Lord Jesus. We cannot fix it, and we cannot replace it. We ask You, Lord God, to extend Your mighty hand, and as we are in faith placing our hands on it, we pray that You would do the same and heal it. Yes, Lord Jesus, we pray that You will heal this boom box and make it work as if it were brand-new! We believe in You, and we pray in the name of Jesus. Amen."

"Amen," I added. We opened our eyes, and I could tell that Randall's fear was replaced with peace. My unbelief was not replaced with faith, per se, but my heart and mind were definitely filled with excitement to see if God would answer our plea.

"Well, it's still plugged in, and the light is not shining, but let's power it on and see. I think it will all be just fine," he said with almost a joyful noise in his voice. Randall looked at me, and then he pushed the button. "There is a Mighty Spirit. Crossing barren land. He's sowing love unceasing. Fresh fruit spring from the sand," sounded as clearly and as powerfully from the two speakers of the boom box as when we first started to use it. Randall shouted, "Hallelujah!" and did a little celebration dance as I sat there in a complete awe of the

Lord. The Lord showed up in the studio not to fix a broken machine per say, He showed up in the studio to teach me that He is interested in every detail of my life and that there is absolutely nothing too insignificant or too small to be brought before the *mighty throne* of God through prayer. It has been some twenty-eight years, but I still remember learning the lesson that day. Father God was preparing me to continually build upon the work He had already accomplished in me. We could hardly wait to share the "Heavenly Repairman" story with our friends and the participants of the festival. This unique episode, of having to trust Jesus like this, brought Randall and I close. At the end of the festival, he extended an invitation for Petra and me to travel to Houston upon our graduation from the academy the following summer. He promised to assist us with the necessary paperwork to be able to go to Texas for the summer, take classes there, see Houston, dance some with his company Ad Deum, and simply visit America. We could not believe what was happening. It was too much good news to contain within us. We were thrilled to do whatever was necessary to make this invitation a reality and be able to spend three months in Houston. The Lord planned a great meeting among myself, Petra, and Randall Flinn, an American choreographer from Houston, Texas, who believed that our God works in mysterious ways, often using silly things like a broken boom box, to powerfully display His power and unquestionably demonstrate His sovereignty. Hallelujah!

Everything is possible for him who believes… I do
believe; help me overcome my unbelief.
—Mark 9:23–24

69) Marathon

The summer always seems to pass by with an incredible speed and almost in a hurry. The summer of 1992 was no different. Before I knew it, the time to move back to Liberec had come, and it was time to get on the 5:40 bus connecting the two Northern Bohemian cities. I was relieved that I was no longer required to live in the dorms but had the freedom of renting a room from Mrs. Gabajová. As the bus pulled out of the Ústí terminal, I knew that the senior year would be filled with challenges as well as crucial life decisions. As early as the school year began, I had to choose my graduation subjects. These are four courses that every graduating senior selects to complete an oral exam at the end of the school year. The examination is done in front of a committee of professors and can be attended by a small number of guests. The graduating grade score will place the high school senior into a lineup for the entry to university study. The university entry exam results are combined with the student's graduation grade point average and collectively place them into the final queue for the selected college. The first thirty or so applicants are then invited to attend the chosen institution of higher learning. By law, Czech language and one foreign language are mandatory subjects for the graduating exams at all gymnáziums in the country. By my senior year, I had studied Russian for eight and English for seven consecutive years. I felt that in the changing world of democratic growth and progress in Central and Eastern Europe, it would be of a greater benefit and value to select English. So I did. I made a decision to graduate in philosophy and music in addition to the two languages. I also had to successfully complete the graduation exam from the state ballet school. Typically speaking, the state academic graduations take place in May, and the conservatories, or performing arts schools, graduating performances are scheduled for June. I was soon to find out that my graduation performance was planned for June 6, 1993. I also had to find time to audition and secure a position in one of the professional ballet companies in the nation. As I was sure that I could continue to work for the ballet company of the Liberec State Theater, in my heart, there was simply no desire to do that. All this to say, I was leaving Ústí with my mind racing and my soul sending a series of short prayers to the Father for clarity, guidance, assistance, and His will to be made known to me as each fork in the road came my way.

Ever since I can remember, I function best when I line up all the hurdles before me in a mental sequence and then focus on conquering one at a time. That way, I would avoid feeling utterly overwhelmed and avalanched in the process of concluding my studies in

Liberec, and concluding them well. I lined up on the proverbial start line, with my feet placed in the blocks of "discipline" and "resolve," my fingers placed on the turf of "opportunity," and my internal ear ready for the gunfire signaling the start of the race. I knew that I had to approach this year in a steady and systematic way in order to come out on the other side with grades that would make my parents proud, a ballet graduation to enjoy and to feel good about, and, Lord willing, a secured contract with one of the nation's leading professional companies. It was time to buckle up and do my best. This year was going to be a long-drawn-out marathon, and should I choose to run it like a sprint, I was for sure to run out of stamina and end up failing terribly.

The first semester was filled with hard work in every aspect of life. The intensity in the gymnázium academics was high; the ballet school's classes were filled with expectations of the faculty for us all to work hard while being mindful of the exam performance at the culmination of the year. The roster of performances and premieres at the State Theater was packed to the rim. The one positive, and a huge one at that, was that for the first time in six years, I was not required to take a chemistry class. This alone was a guarantee of a much easier year, academically speaking. And for that, I was thankful.

Cast all your anxiety on him because he cares for you.
—1 Peter 5:7

70) Velvet Divorce

The nation as a whole was also going through a dramatic season in its existence. A brief glance across the history of the nation clearly indicates the unity of the Czech and Slovak people, who shared so many commonalities among them. In the more recent chapter of history, Czechoslovakia emerged at the end of World War I as a democratic republic in 1918, when the Austro-Hungarian Empire ceased to exist. The unity among the two nations was strong. Yes, there were some salient differences, the most obvious one would be the Czech and Slovak languages, but the love between the two nations was brotherly and strong. By 1933, Czechoslovakia was, de facto, the only functioning democracy in Central Europe. Its economy was one of the strongest in Europe. The ingenuity of the Czechoslovak people was second to none. That was true until 1938, when the nation was sold out to the rising Nazi Reich in the Munich Agreement, in Czechoslovakia known as "About Us, Without Us, Munich Betrayal," a pact signed by the governments of the United Kingdom, France, and Italy. In this agreement, a portion of Czechoslovakia, known as Sudetenland, a region heavily populated by German-speaking minorities, was given to Adolf Hitler as a scapegoat, guaranteeing his appeasement and assuring evasion of another conflict in Europe. Hitler did not stay true to his word, and World War II affected every continent of the world because of it. The hardship of this cataclysm brought a challenge to the union of the Czech and Slovak people, but the love one for the other brought the nation through the war to its glorious conclusion in 1945. Sadly, the victory of the Soviet-backed Czechoslovak Communist Party in February of 1948 established a regime that brought hardship, fear, persecution, suffering, and pain to the Czechoslovak people for the next forty-one years. Even then, they persevered to be one nation coexisting and living in harmony, one force fighting the oppression of the socialist ideology. The collapse of Communism in 1989 was a promising beginning to a life filled with the joyous and hopeful future of the people. Not long thereafter, voices crying for a dissolution of the federal republic into two peacefully coexisting but completely independent nations started to be heard. In 1992, everywhere one would look, signs of a divorce were clear. Every Communist nation in Europe that was comprised of several nations within one border was marked with bloody ethnic wars marking their separations. Czechs and Slovaks desired to divorce peacefully, nonviolently. All the paperwork was being drafted, and preparations were underway. In the fall of 1992, I knew that my beloved country was about to change, once and for all. And so it did. The Czech and Slovak Federative Republic officially split into the Czech Republic and Slovakia at midnight on December 31, 1992. When we woke up the following morning, the Velvet Divorce was done, and I was now a citizen of the Czech Republic, never to be called a Czechoslovak again.

*He makes nations great, and destroys them; he
enlarges nations, and disperses them.*

—Job 12:23

71) Study, Study, Study

The spring was filled with preparations for my graduation exams. The intense review of the Czech and English grammar structures with their rules and exceptions, endless essay writings, vocabulary studies, literature reading, and authors' biography memorizations were all a part of getting ready for the graduation test. Equipping for the philosophy exam was difficult as well. The philosophy professor, Mr. Adamec, was strict. A deeper study of the reasoning and cognitive approach to struggles, existence, purpose, and meaning of life often directly opposing the views of God, of the Bible, and of faith was a must. Endless rounds of critical discussions, systematic persuasions, debates, and intellectual arguing among the students were greatly enjoyed by the professor. Me, on the other hand, not so much. Then there was music. One would think it would be easy to prepare for an exam of such an art form. We had to learn to distinguish between the slightest differences of the Romantic and Classicist music; know the distinctions between a pitch and a melody; and learn to group composers by era, style, and the type of their work. We were taught rhythms, tone colors, and textures of music. We also had to identify, name, and title the composers of fifty different compositions. The music exam would also consist of an instrument performance. I had five months to prepare for this most difficult and crucial exam of my life. Then there were all the other subjects I also needed to do well in, in order to be permitted to graduate from the gymnázium. One of the most time-consuming assignments was to read Fyodor Dostoevsky's Преступление и наказание, known under its English title of *Crime and Punishment*, in its original language, Russian. Finding the time to do so was extremely challenging and demanding.

During this long marathon of the senior year, I often lifted my eyes to see if the "finish sign" was starting to emerge on the horizon. With each passing month, that was more the case. It fueled me with much-needed strength and motivation. One thing was becoming more and more clear to me as the year was moving on. If the Lord granted me the privilege of concluding my studies here, I would never go to school again. The amount and the weight of the carried load while progressing through two schools and working a part-time job at the theater was taking its toll. It was breaking me slowly and systematically, forever diminishing a desire to study further. To graduate was my goal. That I had to focus upon.

In the ballet school, the graduation repertoire was announced with pomp and circumstance. The importance of this first graduating class, and its superb presentation, was clearly and repeatedly highlighted to us by our class professor, Mrs. Gabajová. Casting into roles also took place in early January. Everyone had plenty to focus on and plenty of time to prepare to shine in front of the audience and the panel of experts gathering at the theater in June. The class was to perform a segment from Tchaikovsky's *Swan Lake*, the cornerstone of all ballet repertoire, at the beginning of the evening. Petra and I were to perform a pas de deux and the principal variations, where I would be Prince Siegfried and Petra, Odette. The conclusion of the evening was to feature a suite from *Romeo and Juliet*, Shakespeare's drama, danced to the music of Sergei Prokofiev. This was to be a spectacular, fast-moving, and hopefully captivating depiction of this well-known love story, crossing the forbidden line of edict and culture. The bar was set high, and the potential for the graduating exam performance to be either amazing or a complete disaster was real.

> *But blessed is the man who trusts in the*
> *Lord, whose confidence is in him.*
> —Jeremiah 17:7

72) Groundhog Day

The springtime was also filled with frequent calls and mail communications with Randall Flinn, seeking a way to obtain the visas necessary for travel to America for the summer visit in June. Randall sent us all necessary documentation for the tourist visa. Back in the day, one had to go to the embassy of the United States and simply hope that there would be an opening in the consular department's schedule for the applicant to be interviewed by an employee of the embassy. Petra and I decided to go on a Monday morning. We thought that it would be good to be there as early in the morning as possible. We caught an early bus out of Liberec scheduled to arrive in Prague around eight o'clock. The Florenc bus terminal is a busy place as bus connections from the whole country as well as other European destinations all culminate there.

We jumped off the bus and hurried to the metro. There is a subway stop conveniently located at the bus terminal. The days when I lived in Prague attending the National Dance Conservatory taught me to navigate the public transit system of the Czech capital. Line B was a short ride to the transit stop at Můstek (*Moo-steck*), a busy hub filled with thousands of fast-moving Czechs and about the same amount of foreigners, often helplessly attempting to read the Czech signs in desperate need of finding their way in the underground train system. From there, it was a quick two-stop ride to Malostranská (*Mah-lo-stran-skaa*), a station located in the Little Quarter section of the historic city, nestled underneath the famous Prague Castle, the largest castle complex in the world. From there, we had an option to take a tram or a short walk through the narrow streets of the Little Quarter. We opted to walk and did that with speed and precision, arriving at Tržiště (*Tr-zhish-te*) Street, where the splendid building of the Schönborn Palace is located. In this historic baroque-style residence of the Schönborn aristocratic family, the embassy finds its home. The flag of the United States is proudly flown above the large entry gate, indicating to all that this is a property now belonging to the United States. We walked up to the main gate of the diplomatic post and, to our surprise, were the only ones there. Petra and I looked at each other knowing that something was not quite right. There was a sign posted behind the glass of a small display window, stating in both the English and Czech languages the following:

> Due to President's Day, an official holiday, the embassy is closed and will reopen on Tuesday, February 16.
> Z důvodu Dne prezidentů, státního svátku, je Velvyslanectví zavřeno a znovu se otevře v úterý 16. února.

We could not believe that we would choose to travel to Prague on the one day in February when the embassy would be closed. We were discouraged. The excitement combined with nerves and slight hesitation of the interview with the consular officer at the embassy was replaced with sadness and even frustration, that our trip to Prague was in vain and would have to be rescheduled. We wanted to undergo the interview as soon as we could in case of any unforeseen complications that could arise. We decided to return to Prague the next day.

It felt like Groundhog Day, as we repeated everything in the same identical manner the very next day. An early morning bus ride from Liberec, followed by the transit on the metro line B, transfer at Můstek, a quick ride on line A to the Malostranská stop, and a brisk walk to the embassy building put us to the destination right around eight thirty. This time, however, a long line was already formed, following the facade of the building. People in the line, like us, were holding folders filled with the necessary documents needed for the interview. And like Petra and I, everyone there had the same expression indicating nerves and hesitation on their faces. One by one, the guard at the gate allowed the visa applicants to enter the metal detector and cleared them to access the premises of the embassy. Once Petra and I did the same, we were directed to take a sharp right-hand turn to enter a holding room. From there, people were called to a window to be registered for the interview and, based on the nature of their desired business at the embassy that day, were directed to sit and wait to be summoned. After a certain number of people were counted to be in the building of the embassy, the doors were closed, and everyone left outside was informed to return another day. We were glad to come early and be among those permitted to enter. The wait was long. Nobody talked. Everyone waited for their name to be called. "Jiri Voborsky!" sounded in perfect Czech as the lady at the window was a native speaker hired to work at the embassy. I glanced at Petra, indicating through the silent look that I was panicking and nervous not wanting to jeopardize the interview and be denied the visa. I walked through the door, buzzed in by the lady seated behind the window. A narrow staircase led me upstairs to the second floor, where a large rectangular room opened up before me. The interior was modern in stark contrast to the historic building of the palace. Large windows lined up the left side of the room. Ornate iron bars added extra protection to the facility of the embassy. On the right side were sections divided by partitions. Each section had a consular officer seated behind a thick bulletproof glass of dark-green tint. A microphone assisted the communication between the applicant and the officer. I was invited to sit down on a chair facing the lady behind the glass. She wore a scarf around her neck, tied into a knot with two separate tassels hanging down splitting her left shoulder. She wore a business suit, with a jacket over a lightly colored blouse underneath. There was a table attached to either side of the thick glass. A mechanical opening under the glass allowed for the required documents to be submitted. The officer's side of the desk was designed to hold a computer and a telephone and provide space to review the submitted documents.

"*Doub-ree den*," she started, using Czech to communicate with me. I detected a heavy accent; and though I was impressed that she knew the language, between using a microphone, a thick glass between us, the accent, and my nerves, it was very difficult to understand what she was saying.

"*Dobrý den*," I replied and then continued in English, offering her to communicate with me in her native language.

"I see that you are applying for a tourist visa. Share with me the purpose of your trip to the United States." I was not quite sure what the word *purpose* meant, but I put two and two together—that she needed to know the reason for which I desired to travel to Houston. I explained how Mr. Flinn invited me and a friend, who was also applying that day, to travel to Texas for a visit during our summer break upon concluding our studies and before starting a new job in September. "Do you have a job secured?" was her next question.

"I do not, but I am scheduled to audition for the Moravian National Ballet next month," I replied with confidence.

"I see," she said as she looked through the documents I handed her. "Are you planning on working in the United States?" was the next question.

"I am not," I answered truthfully. I had no plans to look for a job during my stay in Houston.

"I see that Mr. Flinn will provide housing and food for you and that your parents are willing to assist you with the plane tickets as well as additional cash for the trip… That's good. I do need to inform you that you must purchase a round-trip ticket. Should you attempt to travel to the United States on a one-way ticket, you will be denied entry into the United States. On a B1/B2 tourist visa, it is illegal to be traveling to the United States for the purpose of making money. Should you decide to seek employment of any kind, you will be deported from the United States and not permitted to return. For that purpose, a different visa would need to be applied for. Is that clear?" Her eyes looked at me with a stern focus. Her rigid jaw line underlined the seriousness of the statement.

"I understand," I responded.

"One more thing you need to know, and that is, even if I grant you the B1/B2 visa today, it will be up to the immigration officer upon your entry into the United States to allow you or possibly deny you to enter." Then she smiled at me and told me to return back to the embassy at 1400 hours to collect my passport with the tourist visa issued in it. I could not believe that I was approved, and the only thing that I worried about now was for Petra to be authorized as well. She was, and we both were leaving Prague with freshly issued visas printed in our passports that cold February Tuesday. This hurdle was behind us. Now we could start looking for airplane tickets for the transatlantic flight to Houston. That was going to be another miracle in the making; I had a feeling in my gut.

Nothing is impossible with God.

—Luke 1:37

73) Auditions, Take 3

It was early April. As it's common for the climate of central Europe, April in Czech is often a blend of warm, sunny days, occasional snow flurries, cold rains, and even strong thunderstorms. Overall, nature beautifully displays its desire to leave winter behind and demonstrate the newness of life through the colors of blossoms, by the vibrant green color of the leaves, and the chirping birds in the air. As it is with the creation around us, mankind also holds within himself the desire for freshness in life, and even a new beginning, spurred by this season of the year. As my academy studies were approaching the final stretch, I had to figure out what my next chapter of life would look like, as every senior around the world does, and where I would be able to continue dancing. It had been a great privilege working for the company of the State Theater in Liberec over the past four years, but as surely as I enjoyed it, I knew that I had to move on and try to audition for another professional company somewhere around the country. When I paused long enough to be honest with myself, I always came to realize all over again, the enormous struggle the employment at the theater had been. There were many different elements of influence making marks on my heart, deep wounds in my soul, and a strain on my overall well-being. I knew that I would not be able to find the same loving camaraderie and a family-like environment in the secular professional ballet companies, as I found in Sweden. I was hoping to find a company where the dancers inspire each other to work together, to present high-caliber professional productions, and to aspire to bring joy and deep cultural experiences to the audiences before them. I knew that the larger the theater would be, the more likely this would be the case. I needed the Lord to guide me. I knew that without Him, no matter where I would dance, eventually, I would find myself dissatisfied and frustrated. I was torn as I felt that perhaps the career as a whole was a hopeless task. The profession of a ballet dancer is marked by building oneself up, to receive accolades and applause, and therefore difficult to be one where a Christian can be used for the glory of God. The comfort in these moments of frustration was found in remembering how I was rescued so very unexpectedly by God, Who, in His wisdom, guided my footsteps in bringing me to Liberec and, through the orchestration of events, saved me from eternal condemnation. Surely, this same Lord had a plan for me that went beyond the senior year of high school.

I lifted a prayer in my heart. "Lord, I believe that You are wise. I believe that You reign in accordance to Your will and wisdom. Father, guide me. You see the best fit, as I look for the theater You would have me work and dance for. I desire to be submitted to Your lead. There is a larger plan and larger picture that I forget to ponder and remember, a plan You ordained and designed. Help me walk in Your peace as I audition for different companies. Lead me to the place You prepared for me, in which I can honor You. I trust that, once again, Your purpose in my life will be accomplished as I walk through the open doors before me. I love You, my Jesus."

There was a large vitrine at the entry to the theater where all internal and external announcements were displayed. If any ballet company or other art organization held its auditions, their communiqués were posted there. We were strongly encouraged to check the bulletins often and submit applications for companies that sounded good to our liking. Out of all the options displayed, the ballet company of the Moravian National Theater in Brno, Czech's second largest city, sounded like the best fit for me. I made a phone call, and before long, I was on a train, Brno bound.

Brno surprised me. Growing up, I read about and came to know a lot regarding its history and prominence in the nation. But seeing the city in person, I was blown away by its size and beauty. A large fortress, Špilberk, sits on a hill overlooking the city, as does the Saint Peter and Paul gothic cathedral. The cobblestone streets of the city, all hustling and bustling with life, were busy with traffic, trams, cyclists, and pedestrians. I purchased a map of the city and followed the route from the main train station to the operations building of the Moravian National Theater. The auditions were held in the ballet studios there. As I walked through the doors, nervousness came upon me like a blanket thrown over a body. It was not the fact that I did not know anyone nor that I never auditioned for a professional ballet company before. What made me nervous that day was that I was about to find out firsthand how my talent and ballet technique abilities compared to the others gathered here to audition. Would I be able to compete and measure up to them? I did not know what to expect. The all-familiar sense of simply doing my best and applying myself kicked in. I entered the studio boldly and confidently, knowing that, above all, my God held this moment of time in His hands and His will would prevail. The ballet master and artistic director, Jiří Kyselák (*Kee-se-laak*), entered the ballet studio and introduced himself and his assistants to all that gathered. He acknowledged the piano master seated behind the grand piano in the corner of the room. The assistants seated themselves around the studio, with pieces of paper and pencils in hands, carefully observing the dancers. The class started. A simple plié combination gave us a chance to warm up and ease into the class. I knew that technique was one element necessary for a successful audition, but all throughout my conservatory studies, I was taught that artistry is what sets one dancer apart from another when both possess a strong technique. I danced, and even enjoyed, myself that day. The April sun was filling the studio through the windows located high above the mirrors on the wall. The pianist played as if to inspire us to fill his music with our technical bravura and individual personality, giving us a chance to stand out and make an impression. As the barre portion of the class concluded, some dancers seemed overwhelmed and nervous, as others seemed to be bolstered in confidence. I tried to stay focused. The center was more organized as we were asked to dance in smaller groups. A quick déjà vu feeling flashed through my mind from my auditions to the Prague Ballet Conservatory, when I was twelve. This time around, my mom and dad were not seated in the hallway, nervously tapping their feet against the floor. I was here all on my own. The class was moving in a quick succession. Once in a while, I noticed Mr. Kyselák whispering to the lady seated next to him. He pointed to a dancer, and she made a note on the paper at hand. Before long, the class was nearing its end, and with the last combination, the révérence, we acknowledged the ballet master who led the class. "Thank you, everyone," Mr. Kyselák said, standing and applauding the dancers in the room, "We enjoyed watching you dance. I would like to speak with some of you before we dismiss today. We will read a list of names of those I need to see. It won't take long. I just need a moment to talk with those named. The conversation does not indicate the results of the auditions. I simply want to have a conversation with some of you. The Moravian National Theater will send you an official letter with the results of today's auditions within a week or two. It was a privilege meeting you all today, and we look forward to seeing some of you in September when the 1993–1994 season begins." He asked his assistant to read the names. Mine was included. In a private meeting with Mr. Kyselák and the leadership of the company, a short conversation took place. I was not sure exactly what the purpose of these meetings was, but I gladly answered all questions asked and enjoyed the personal connection. I was leaving feeling good about the day. I did not know what the results would be; but I had peace, a strong prevailing peace, that my Father was working all things out, just as He desired. The letter arrived in less than a week. It was sent to my address at Mrs. Gabajová's apartment. The envelope had a printed seal of the Moravian National Theater in the upper-left corner as my name was typed in the addressee section. I took a deep breath before I opened the envelope. I did not know what I was about to find stated within. I closed my eyes as if to calm myself down and then pulled the folded letter out. The message was short and to the point.

Mister Voborsky,

It is my privilege to inform you that you have been selected to join the company of the Opera Ballet of the Moravian National Theater for the 1993/1994 season as a corps de ballet member. Please confirm with us your acceptance of the position in a written statement before the end of this season. A contract will be signed at the beginning of September. I look forward to hearing from you. Congratulations!

Sincerely,
Jiri Kyselák
Opera Ballet Artistic Director
Moravian National Theater

Wow! I made it. I landed a spot and had a position with the MNT Company for the next season. I was excited and thankful. I could not wait to get to a phone booth and call my parents to let them know. The year was shaping up well. There were some significant hurdles before me yet to overcome, such as the gymnázium and state ballet school graduation exams, finding and purchasing an airline ticket to Houston, and finishing reading the *Crime and Punishment* novel in order to receive an A grade in my last year of Russian. That took a lot longer than expected. I was blown away to see the obvious guidance and provision of the Lord in all the aspects of my life. I was hoping to be a strong witness for Jesus in Brno the next year and, until then, to focus on doing well, with His assistance, in overcoming the remaining hurdles before me.

He guides me in paths of righteousness for his name's sake.
—Psalm 23:3

74) A Chuckle

It is an interesting thought to pause and think just how much the world has changed. There are elements of life that will never be like they were ten, twenty, or thirty years ago. My children will never know a day without being able to communicate with anyone around the world from a handheld device, rather than wait for a sent letter to arrive. They are accustomed to instantly find needed information on the World Wide Web instead of spending hours in a library researching the given matter. It is the norm for them to find and purchase anything with a simple click of a button that replaces long lines in stores. They know that any and every movie can be found and watched from the comfort of the home and one does not have to dress up to venture out to view the only one movie presented in a single-screen cinema, as was the custom growing up. These, and many other advances of technology, have been gained in the last few years. As great as these are, there is a lost charm of life, washed away in the progress around us. What was it like to sit with a close friend you have not heard from in a couple of days and, over a cup of coffee, talk face-to-face about life's struggles and joys? What was it like to watch a teacher write on a blackboard with chalk dust flying in the air as he fervently explained a math formula? What was it like to hold a copy of an older book and catch the aroma of the paper while reading? I understand that headway will happen and there is nothing I can do to stop it or slow it down, but as I recall and remember my youth and childhood, I miss the wonder of life that, I fear, my children will never know, life that disappeared with the modern way of living.

I already shared about the process of securing a flight to Stockholm, when traveling to Sweden. I want to tell the story of purchasing my first transatlantic ticket for my trip to Houston. This was before one could sit at a home computer, with a cup of coffee at his side, and search the Internet until the best flight option was found. As our American visas had been issued, Petra and I knew that we were facing an enormous challenge of finding and securing our flight to Texas. After a visit to a local travel agency in Liberec, it became apparent that we needed to venture to Prague and visit individual airline offices there to purchase the tickets in person. The options were limited as only a handful of companies served both Prague and Houston. Czech Airlines proudly connected Prague with the JFK Airport in New York, even under Communism, but offered no additional connections throughout the United States. We needed to find an airline that did. We decided to visit three main carriers, namely Air France, KLM Royal Dutch Airlines, and British Airways. It was such a trip down memory lane for me as I cherished the remembrances of visiting Prague with my grandfather as a little boy, peeking with curiosity into the shopping windows of foreign airline companies. Back in the day, I hoped that, maybe, one day even I could step aboard these aircraft and travel to places far away. Now I was actually looking for an offer from these companies to do just that. My parents, as well as Petra's, offered to fund the tickets for us. My father and mother were willing to sacrifice many years of savings to make this trip possible, as it was an enormous amount of money to purchase a transatlantic flight back in a day. I am sure that the same was true for the Grůša's. Our mission this day was to find the best option and price for the ticket and then return back to Prague with the cash to buy it, as our families had no credit cards and all transactions were purchased solely with cash. Air France and KLM were located on Prague's famous Paris Street, an avenue connecting the iconic Old Town Square with the Vltava riverbank. We were able to receive a print out of the flight connections and estimated prices from the ladies decked in sleek dresses of the respective airlines. Both trips required a layover in Paris or Amsterdam, respectively, and then offered a nonstop connection to Houston. British Airways office was located on the Old Town Square itself, occupying a second floor of a historic palace, thus signaling its wealth and prestige. British Airways offered us the most affordable ticket, and we knew that we would be returning to Prague to purchase our flights with the United Kingdom's national carrier. That was exactly what we did just a few days later. Both Petra and I purchased the flights and received a printed booklet, similar to the one Czech Airlines issued for our flight to Stockholm. In it, we found our boarding passes and baggage tickets to fly from Prague to London, where we would connect to a flight bound for the Intercontinental Airport in Houston for June 24 and then return to Prague on August 28, 1993. I cannot recall how many times I looked at the ticket on the way home. It was difficult to believe that I was going to America, that slowly but surely all the ducks were being lined up, and that only a few months were dividing me from sitting on board of British Airways' Boeing 747, flying across the Atlantic Ocean to the United States. As I recall the wonder of it, I chuckle knowing that my children will never know what it's like to be dreaming and longing to, one day, travel to faraway places.

They have already crossed the big pond on numerous occasions; and the magic of it, that comes after desiring something for years, was never experienced.

> *As for God, his way is perfect; the word of the Lord is flawless.*
> —Psalm 18:30a

75) Graduation Exam

The little desk calendar, featuring a Czech castle on its left side and the days of each month on its right, was flipped to the month of May. I had lived through seventeen of these in my life. Early on, they were signified by the May 1 parades, celebrating the successes and achievements of the Communist regime. An interesting memory revolves around the mandatory decoration of all private and public windows with Czechoslovak and Soviet flags. Even our apartment windows came equipped with specific metal holders on either side of the frame for my parents to insert the flags. I do recall one year when panic spread around our apartment as my parents were unable to locate the rolled-up flags. An official reprimand was given to anyone who did not participate in the festivities by displaying the friend-ship of the two nations, represented by the Czechoslovak flag of the red-and-white field intersected by a blue triangle, waving in the air next to red Soviet Union flag with a yellow star, sickle, and ham-mer in the upper corner of a bright-red field. A quick trip to the store averted the official scolding that one year. The months of May were also remembered by the May 8 and 9 celebrations of victory and of the conclusion of World War II. Large military parades were annually taking place at Letná, a large portion of Prague, where the Czechoslovak Army and its Warsaw Pact allies demonstrated their strength by displaying its newest military equipment and, by doing so, indirectly flexing their muscle against the worst enemy of all, the imperial North Atlantic Treaty Organization. Annually, also in May, flowers were placed beside the Tank Monument in Prague. After the war, the Soviet Red Army tank number 23, the first tank that reached Prague during its liberation in 1945, was placed on a pedestal in a square renamed to the Square of the Soviet Tank Commanders. Yes, I know, what a name. The tank remained displayed there until 1991. During the Communist era, the Tank Monument was a place where the gratitude of the Czechoslovak people to the Soviet Union was exhibited and where flowers and wreaths were annually laid by the government officials. School trips were taken to the monument to instill appreciation in the Czechoslovak youth, mine included, for our big brother, the Union of the Soviet Socialist Republics. Every May, large gatherings of the Czechoslovak Pioneers took place, when songs of freedom and happiness were sung, celebrating the beauty of the socialist and Communist ideals. Songs were sung in Czech, in Slovak, and in Russian. Delegations of Soviet comrades often visited these large assemblages and brought words of encouragement to inspire our devotion to the teachings of Lenin, Marx, or our own comrades who led the nation to a "brighter and more prosperous future." I loved the month of May and all these celebrations, for as a child, I bought into everything I was taught, trusting that the people were leading us well. As a young Pioneer, my devotion was unwavering. I blindly accepted everything I was asked to believe. I was sold out. Now that I was older, that was no longer the case. Through the Velvet Revolution, the true faces of Communism and socialism were uncovered. The pain and suffering in the lives of so many who were imprisoned and even killed because they did not agree was a powerful tool in opening the eyes of the nation, especially of my generation.

Politics aside. The month of May 1993 was significant for a completely different reason. This year, I was going to graduate from high school, and in order to do that, I had to successfully complete the graduation exam in the Czech language called "maturita," as if it were a maturity test, and in doing so to conclude my four years of grueling secondary education. As I stated earlier, my graduating subjects were Czech, English, philosophy, and music. It is appropriate to think of this exam as the test of maturity, as it requires an enormous amount of focus and exemplification of knowledge and wisdom often way beyond the years of an eighteen-year-old student, displayed in front of a panel of professors...

The preparations for the exam begin by receiving a list of fifty questions per subject. These questions are gathered into a hat on the day of the exam. One per subject is then drawn out, and for twenty minutes, the student presents the response for the panel to grade and, if needed, to further examine the student by additional inquiry. To sum it all up, each graduating student arrives on the day of his "maturita" with roughly four thousand minutes of knowledge in his head, hopefully.

I received my questions along with all my classmates. The list was long. We had to assemble the information for each question, information that we received sometime during the course of our studies at the gymnázium, and then simply memorize the amount of knowledge prepared to present the response and deliver it eloquently and with a convincing manner on the fateful day.

That day was May 28. I woke up early. Papers were spread out all over my rented room. There was no longer rhyme nor reason to the mess around me. I fell asleep the night before over notes that became increasingly blurry as the night went on. Slobber on my face clearly indicated that I simply passed out from trying to read late into the night. I took a quick shower, a cold one at that, to perk myself up. Breakfast was quick that day. A cup of black tea with two spoons of sugar was my hope for the necessary boost of energy. I had an ironed blue dress shirt hanging on the back of a chair, ready to go. The one tie I owned was tossed over it as well. I got dressed while reviewing some questions deemed critical or struggle-some. I had to be at the gymnázium by nine forty-five for the exams to start at ten o'clock sharp. My plan was to walk out by nine thirty at the latest. Around nine o'clock, I was out the door. I could no longer stay in the apartment, as my nerves were going wild. I felt as if I retained no information. Everything was blending and coalescing in my mind. I was, simply put, anxious.

There were twelve of us assigned to graduate that day. We all arrived at the school well in advance of the required tenth hour of the day. Everyone was as nervous as I. Precisely at ten o'clock, Dr. Kutínová summoned our small group to one of the classrooms rearranged for the graduation week. The necessary setup of the room consisted of a large long table covered with a white tablecloth at one end and a chair by a small desk with a pile of white papers, a pencil, and an eraser nicely organized on it at the other. "Welcome, everyone," she started, once again wearing her round-framed glasses on the tip of her nose while looking over them at us. "You have worked hard the past four years preparing for this day, for this moment in time, to come here and present—no, to showcase—your knowledge to the panel gathered here. I want to introduce you to Dr. Novotná, who will be the chair of the graduation committee today." It is required by law that every high school invite a principal of another school to be the overseer of the graduation exams. "Hello, students." Dr. Novotná took over. "It is my highest honor to be here today with you, with my colleagues, and with Dr. Kutínová to witness your superb presentation of knowledge and wisdom you garnered during the past four years of studies here. Today, you will be summoned into this room one at a time. You will then select a question from the box." She motioned toward a box placed at the end of the long table. "You will have twenty minutes to make notes on the paper at your desk and then orally present your answer for another twenty minutes. Should your presentation end before the twenty minutes are up, any one of us here can ask you additional questions until your time is complete. Then you will be asked to leave the room and prepare for the next subject. We will do this until all twelve of you complete all four exams. I just wanted to add that yesterday's group of graduates did not do as well as we expected, and I hope that today, you all will rise to the occasion bestowed upon you by the gymnázium and by the requirements of the Department of Education. With all this to say, good luck, and we will call the first student back here in just a few minutes." Drs. Novotná and Kutínová both tried to smile a little, but they appeared just as nervous as we were. We walked out of the room, sat on the bench against the cold brick wall, and in silence waited for the door to open and the first name to be called. I was called in third. As I walked in, Renata, the student who was called in second, was ready to do her presentation. Walking in, I passed the first student, David, as he was leaving the room. His pale face clearly signaled his own disapproval with his performance that day. The first graduating subject was Czech language. The question drawn from the box could possibly be of a grammatical nature, it could be poetry, it could be a literary movement, or it could be a question pertaining to the life and work of a Czech writer. I stepped to the box, looked away, and reached in. *Lumírovci (Loo-mee-rov-tzee)*—this one typed word was all the little piece of paper stated. I had twenty minutes to sit down and prepare my presentation of this movement of Czech writers gathered around the *Lumír (Loo-meer)* periodical published in the '70s and '80s of the nineteenth century with the aim to lift Czech literature to a European level. I sat behind the desk and for a moment looked at Renata, who was copying a complex Czech sentence to the blackboard in order to demonstrate the grammatical analysis of it. Her right hand was writing while her left hand was wiping the accumulated sweat against her spring-themed dress. I shifted my focus on the blank paper and prayed a quick prayer for the Lord to help me recall anything about the object of my presentation. I do not know if the Lord was busy answering other prayers, but His assistance was not as quick and as thorough as I had hoped. *Lumírovci, Lumírovci!* I was trying hard to visualize my notes. Slowly, I started to remember. As the disjointed thoughts started to flow, I jotted them down hoping to make sense of them while verbalizing them. Again, I am a much better oral-exam taker than I am a written-test taker. The twenty minutes were up. Renata was leaving seemingly relieved, and I was invited to stand in front of the committee to present my answer. Before I could start, another student was called in to draw his question and prepare to respond.

"Well, what did you pull out?" Dr. Novotná asked, seated in the middle of the panel, with three professors on either side of her. "Lumírovci, I pulled out Lumírovci," I answered as if saying it once was not enough. The piece of paper in my hand was shaking, descriptive of my nervousness. *Breathe, Jiri, breathe*, I reminded myself. I looked in the direction of the committee, and while not really looking at anyone in particular, I started to speak, occasionally peeking into my notes. The longer I spoke, the more relaxed I felt. We were drilled to speak slowly and clearly and, even if unsure, to present the answer with confidence. So I tried. I covered everything that was in my notes and even beyond. There were a few crack in my memory of the Lumírovci movement. Those were obvious. Once I concluded, to my shock, there were seven more minutes of allotted time. Two professors asked additional questions, and with two minutes still to go, I was released. I walked out trying to replay what just took place and how well, or not, I did. We were not given the grades right away, as they had to be agreed upon by all members of the panel. The grades were given to us at the end of the long day, after the last student concluded his exam. Renata and David were already deep in review of other subjects, as I could not believe that I had to do this three more times. It was good to have one portion of the maturita exam behind me, for at least I knew what to expect. Philosophy was next. If there was a potential for my graduation exam to be a failure, philosophy clearly presented the danger. If a student received a failing grade in one graduating exam, they could retake that subject in August. Their ability to take an entry exam to a university was no longer possible for the following year, but the graduation diploma would still be awarded. If a student received two failing grades during the exam, they had to repeat the senior year of high school and retake the graduation exam the following year. That was not an option, as I could not imagine prolonging my studies in Liberec for another year. I had to do well. I opened my philosophy notes and poured all my efforts into avoiding a potential disaster. I did. Again, I left the room feeling that I did not do perfectly, but I was pleased with my presentation of Value Theory of Aesthetics. English language was third, and least of my worries. The last subject was music. My mind and my body were running on empty. The tie around my neck caused me a huge deal of irritation and discomfort. My shirt clearly showed perspiration seeping through the fabric. I stepped into the classroom, again following Renata. The first part of the exam consisted of recognition of a piece of music. I worried, but the presented piece could not have been any easier to identify and to elaborate about. Czech composer Bedřich Smetana's "The Moldau"—the second movement of his symphonic poems celebrating his, and my, native land—was played from the LP record player. I recognized it instantly. I was also able to recall other interesting notes about this most famous of Smetana's work. It was a great start to my music exam. After this, I poured all my fervor into answering the drawn question, Leoš Janáček, a Czech composer belonging to the group of modern nineteenth century writers, known for his original approach to composition and unique melody style. It was a breeze. I concluded my twenty minutes with a short presentation of Tchaikovsky's Moderato from the second act of *Swan Lake*. As I played, Professor Vondráček, who assisted me countless times during my struggles with advanced algebra and calculus and helped me navigate my ISP, clearly indicated his pride and approval of my last moments of the graduation exam's saga. I played as well as I could seeing the proverbial finish line approaching, my graduation, and the conclusion of the gymnázium studies within reach. Late, around five o'clock, in the afternoon, we were summoned again into the classroom and, with lots of drama, were presented with our graduating grades. "Jiri Voborsky, grade point average of your combined grades of the written and oral examinations of the Czech and English languages, philosophy, and music is 1.5, therefore graduating with honors. Congratulations." There was a ceremony at the Liberec Historic City Hall, held on May 31, 1993, when, in the presence of my family, I and all seniors who successfully completed the maturita graduating exams received an official diploma from the hand of the city mayor. It was hard to grasp that, after these long four years, I was finally finished with all the tedious and necessary work that brought me to this point. All that was left to do was conclude my graduation performance and receive a diploma from the state ballet school. That performance was now six days away. It was time to devote all my attention to preparing to take the stage at the State Theater. My maturita was a success, at least officially on the paper. I guess the Lord was listening and answering my prayers after all.

Being confident of this, that he who began a good work in you
will carry it on to completion until the day of Christ Jesus.
—Philippians 1:6

76) From Behind the Velvet Curtain

"Again, again…try harder!" My back was aching. "Greater gestures, Jiri, and longer neck! Remember that you are dancing for those on the third balcony of the theater, those who could not afford to buy the expensive tickets at the orchestra level. And they cannot see anything if your gestures are too small, clear?" The tensions were running high. Both Professor Gabajová and Mr. Pokorný wanted us to look our best. There was no unnecessary drama, just a huge amount of practical last minute instructions, helping the thirty-two seniors put on the best graduation performance possible. The Sunday matinee was approaching quickly. And no matter how much we practiced, we felt nowhere near ready. The *Romeo and Juliet* suite was coming together well, and I was able to really step into the character of Romeo and convey the longing of his heart for his forbidden love. *Swan Lake*, on the other hand, was a struggle. Very few people know that the actual Moscow premiere of *Swan Lake* in 1877 was a big failure. The original choreographer, Julius Reisinger, is not to be blamed, at least not fully, but the audience did not care to see and enjoy a tragedy of unfulfilled love written into the original script. The remake of the ballet for the Saint Petersburg premiere in 1895, choreographed by Marius Petipa and Lev Ivanov, was just the opposite. Their version was a hit, and the ballet became the cornerstone of the classical ballet repertoire and, in essence, a household name. Their pure classical choreography has been passed down without major alterations since the 1895 premiere. Now it was our turn to present an excerpt of this jewel and do it justice, remembering that experts, dance critiques, professional dancers, and the general audience would be watching and critiquing our every move. It was hard to approach it with ease. We did not want to repeat the Moscow fiasco.

Due to the regular State Theater performances, we were unable to rehearse on the actual stage until Sunday morning. The dress rehearsal was scheduled for ten o'clock, but around eight, we all started to arrive at the historic theater building, giddy and clearly nervous. The rehearsal went well as we were all familiar with the stage from the performing we had done there over the past four years.

Mr. Pokorný had done a great job communicating with the technical crew as well as the stage manager in regards to the technical aspects of the performance. We went to grab lunch, yet none of us really ate a whole lot. Our focus was on the velvet curtain ready to open at five o'clock that afternoon. This was an unusually hot day. Beautiful, sunny, but abnormally warm. The shifting shadow of the Renaissance city hall was moving across the façade of the theater house standing next to it. I took a moment sitting on the bench, and while admiring the two imposing buildings, I was recalling some highlights of the past four years of life that passed so quickly. So much happened. Some things were expected, but most were a complete surprise. I came to Liberec in hopes of doing well at the gymnázium, only to pour all my energy and efforts into thriving at the state ballet school. The unexpected turns in the path of life that God preordained for me to take, as I came to realize, were what made these four years well worth every tear, every lonely moment, every late night spent over an open textbook, every painful rehearsal, every self-denial, and every sacrifice my parents and I made when I moved away at fourteen years of age. It was through all these that the Lord masterfully worked, at first behind the scenes as if veiled and then gloriously in the open. It was here in this beautiful city of Liberec where I came to find my Savior. Sitting on the bench, I was overwhelmed with gratitude, and thanksgiving words were inadequate to describe. That afternoon, while looking at the 1883 ornate building of the State Theater, I prayed to offer the graduation performance to the Lord Jesus Christ as a thanksgiving for all that He had done.

The time had come, and we all gathered on the stage. Everyone was ready, at least in the physical sense, to deliver what we rehearsed. Looking around the stage at my classmates, I saw the magnificent white headpieces wrapping around the tightly secured ballet buns of the girls. Then there was tulle. Lots and lots of tulle jetting away from the tight waists of the ballerinas creating the famous classical tutus. The gentlemen were dressed in costumes reflecting the individual characters of the story. These costumes belonged to the theater, and it was apparent that hours of detailed work went into creating every single jacket that we wore that night. Black-and-white tights covered our legs, resembling the classical style of the opening portion of the performance. This was as real as it gets, I thought. Mrs. Gabajová walked into the midst of the dancers and, with the charm and elegance that accompanied her every move in and out of the ballet studio, requested our attention. "Listen, everyone, please, listen... Thank you. Before we start tonight, I wanted to take a moment to tell you that it has been an honor to teach you these past four years. Not everyone gets the chance in life to watch young lives grow in so many different elements, ways, and aspects as I and all the staff of the academy were able to witness. You learned a lot, no doubt about that. And as true as that is, I am convinced that we have laid but a foundation—a foundation onto which you will continue to build. You came as students, four years ago, and this afternoon, you will demonstrate that you are leaving as artists. Yes, young but artists with much potential and talents to still grow and utilize. When this beautiful red velvet curtain opens tonight, there is a full house of excited spectators, ready to watch you do what you came to the academy to learn and to earn. You came to learn what it means to be a professional-level dancer. Tonight, you will earn their recognition for accomplishing that goal. So, as the curtain flies open, don't just do beautiful steps. Tell them a story, move them, impact them. Enjoy one another, and with this performance, let the world see that dance is a moving art form that has the power to deeply affect the emotions of the audience. I will be watching, and watching with pride. Let's do this!"

I was grateful for Professor Gabajová and the friendship I was given while spending long hours conversing about life over steaming cups of tea. She was right about what she said, but there was a small element that she knew nothing about. It was during my touring with Eternia when I learned that, indeed, dance is a powerful art form that can impact the emotions of the crowd; yet and more importantly, I learned that God can use dance to impact their hearts. That is why I wanted to continue dancing. I did not know how exactly I was going to do that in Brno, but that was the Lord's problem, not mine. My side of the deal was to be obedient and be submitted to His guidance and leading. I hoped that as the velvet curtain opened that evening, the audience would perhaps see something different about me and about Petra.

The whole performance went as well as it could. I truly enjoyed all my classmates, knowing that I will never dance with all of them again. We crossed many miles together, and it all culminated right there and then. We received great reviews by the experts, by the newspaper, and by the audience. After the graduation ceremony concluded, we walked out of the theater to a large crowd of waiting family members, friends, and even colleagues from the company. It was overwhelming. I looked intently for Brother Evald as I wanted to say the last goodbye, not knowing when I would see him again. He smiled at me whispering into my ear to remember and never doubt that the Lord had a plan for me and to always joyfully submit to it. "He will use you, Jiri, for His glory. Just you watch!" he said. He hugged me and walked into the crowd. My parents and grandparents were beaming with pride. I was glad to see them also. I had to spend a few more days in Liberec to pack the rest of my stuff, receive my conservatory diploma, and then go home to prepare for Houston. The class held a party celebration at the theater café that night where I was able to properly part with my friends. Some were staying in Liberec, dancing on a full contract with the State Theater. There were some moving abroad to Greece and Germany, some were going to pursue modeling, and others auditioned for musicals in Prague. It was a happy bunch that night, sitting around a long table sharing memories and telling tales of the past. I was soaking it all in. It was a bittersweet moment, to say the least, but deep down, I was ready for the next page in the story of my life.

He will be an instrument for noble purposes, made holy, useful to the Master and prepared to do any good work.
　　　　　　　　　　　　　　　　　　　—2 Timothy 2:21b

FOURTH ACT

INTO THE NEW WORLD

77) Across the Pond

As I sit behind the lit screen of the laptop and through these pages relive the story of my life, I have come to realize how encouraging and uplifting its content is to me, first and foremost. I do not see my life as anything special. I was compelled by my friends and by the Lord to simply tell my tale, not to exalt myself in any shape or form but to remind myself and the readers alike that the Lord, indeed, has a unique plan for each of us. As this tapestry of His will unfolds, a masterpiece emerges into a bright light that spotlights the One and only Creator God, the all-wise and all-knowing Ruler of the universe and everything in it. We all are privileged to be players on the stage called history that, time and again, points to the One Who deserves all glory, all honor, all praise, and all devotion. Every fiber of our effort is meant to do just that; and yet, sadly, so many times we miss the point, we miss the purpose, we miss the mark. Simply said, we forget that this, indeed, is His story, not ours. As I continue to testify to what God has done, I pray that the following pages would continue to be a reminder that God is for us and that His plans are already stored in His plan-book and will come to pass, every one of them, at His perfect timing. Be encouraged!

At the age of eighteen, I hugged my parents at the Prague airport, to board a flight to London where I would transfer to fly across the Atlantic Ocean. After a year of communicating with Randall, getting all the paperwork in order, I will finally arrive in the Lone Star State of Texas and finally see America for myself. These next two and a half months were going to be rich in experiences, in enriching our lives, in encounters of the Lord in the land of the free. Petra and I could hardly contain our excitement. We checked in our large pieces of luggage, and with one last glance at the two sets of parents, we vanished into the hustle of the airport. The date was June 24, 1993.

We arrived at Houston Intercontinental Airport midafternoon, right on schedule. It took a while to off-load the superjumbo jet full of tired travelers. Petra and I followed the flow to face the immigration process for the arriving tourists and visitors. I clearly recalled the warning of the consulate worker at the embassy in Prague, who strongly stated the full jurisdiction of the immigration officer upon the point of entry, who can grant or deny admission to the visitor into the United States. I knew by then that my mind can be imaginative when it comes to creating a large spectrum of possible scenarios in my head as to how things could develop in a given situation. This time, it was no different. The immigration process was slow, and the designated area set apart for foreigners entering the United States seemed small and underestimating the incoming number of travelers. Petra and I stayed close to one another. As the line moved on, all of a sudden, we were separated into two lines. As I was not alarmed by the unexpected separation, the fact that it occurred did not help in easing my apprehensiveness in facing the entry interview.

"Next," was the call of the officer. I calmly stepped to the booth and placed my passport and all the required documents on his desk. "What is your purpose for the visit?"

"Hm, tourism," I said with conviction.

"Can I see your return ticket, please?" the officer continued.

"Yes, yes, yes," I said as I was frantically locating the British Airways booklet consisting of my return ticket. "Here...sir," I said as I handed the ticket to him.

"I see that you will be staying in the United States until August 28. Let's see here," he continued as he was looking for the page with the tourist visa printed on it in my passport. "Here... I see that you were granted a three-month tourist visa by the embassy in Prague.

That should cover the length of your stay here. May I see the invitation letter, please?" The invitation letter was one of the requirements requested for the issuing of the visa and apparently for the admission to the United States. Petra and I both had one from Randall addressed to each of us individually. It simply stated that Randall would provide for our housing needs during our stay in the US. The officer carefully read the letter beginning to end. "All right, I see that everything is in order. I must remind you that it is illegal for you to be earning money while visiting, and should you do that, you will be deported. It is also crucial for you to know that you may not overstay your allotted time. If you do so, you might jeopardize a future return to the States. Clear?" he said, looking at me intently. "Yes sir, clear," I replied. "Welcome to the United States, and enjoy your first visit to America!" He flashed a friendly smile and fervently stamped my passport, and after he handwrote something over the stamp, he closed my passport and returned it to me. Petra was also permitted to enter. We were in. We crossed the painted line as if crossing a visible border and stepped toward our experience-filled visit of the "Land of the Free." We collected our checked bags and stepped into the arrival hall trying to find the friendly face of our American buddy and friend, Randall Flinn. He was waiting for us, standing in a turned-out position, clearly not being able to hide the fact that he was a dancer. As we saw each other, we embraced him gladly and knew that we could relax now. We were here, and Randall was prepared to welcome us to Houston. As we stepped outside the airport, both of us were shocked by the intense heat of the day. Even though it was close to five o'clock in the afternoon, the temperature was high, and the sun was clearly dominating the time of the day. It did not bother us. We were in Texas, and that was all that mattered. The adventure was well underway, and we were going to love and enjoy every moment of it and boldly embrace whatever it would bring our way.

The Lord himself goes before you and will be with you; he will never leave you nor forsake you. Do not be afraid; do not be discouraged.
—Deuteronomy 31:8

78) First Impressions

Randall was a man on the move. With his long legs, he walked with determination and purpose. That we knew from Sweden. Now we were on his turf, and it became clear we needed to move quickly in order to keep up with our American friend. As we piled into his two-door car, he asked us briefly about the flight and about the immigration process of entering the country. It became obvious that the crossing of the Atlantic Ocean was a much bigger deal to us than it was to him, as he had done so many times in the past. As he continued to talk, he also managed to pay the parking ticket and merge into the flow of traffic heading toward the city of Houston. This is when our eyes grew wide open despite the jet lag that started to show its effects. The following will narrate the perspective of two young teenagers who, for the first time, experienced and were moved by their impressions of America's fourth largest city. These two kids grew up in a country whose progress was stifled by socialism and the heavy push back of the Soviet Union. There were vast differences between the two nations, cultures, and peoples. We came here to discover as much of these as possible. That discovery started right away, whether we were ready or not. Czechoslovakia had one motorway connecting Prague with Brno before continuing to Bratislava, the capital city of Slovakia. This highway had two lanes heading each direction. Exit ramps were often short and very sharp, requiring the driver to slow down greatly before exiting. The interstate here was just the opposite. Long multileveled entry and exit ramps and multi-level intersections assisted in moving the heavy flow of traffic swiftly through the city. Randall was driving fast, commenting on the large distances that needed to be crossed daily in this city of 2.5 million. There were five lanes leading the travelers toward the skyline of tall buildings emerging on the horizon. Petra and I have never seen a skyscraper before, but that was about to change. Randall seemed to be entertained by our wide-eyed bewilderment of what we saw. And so he allowed us to soak in the sights before he resumed the flow of conversation. I had never seen so many cars. I had never seen traffic that heavy. I had never seen billboards lining up the road competing for one's attention with neon lights and flashy images. There was so much to look at, and all that while one was driving. I found that to be an overwhelming element. As the road went on, Randall informed us that we would not be staying with him but that he found a family who was willing to host us for the next two months. "The Hesters are amazing people. You will get to see a typical life of an American family that loves the Lord, a family that homeschools their children and that lives the 'American Dream.'" He let go of the steering wheel to do the quotation marks. "You will love them! They live in a house that is in the southwestern portion of the city. It will take us a while to get there, but they are looking forward to welcoming you to their home." Petra and I were stuck on the "homeschooling" word. We did not know what that meant exactly. Did some kids continue to learn at home after they return from school every day? That sounded a bit too much. And so we asked Randall to explain to us what "homeschooling" meant. As he started to convey the vision and purpose of it, we were floored. We never heard of such a concept, and it was going to be remarkable to watch a family do just that, teach their children at home instead of sending them to school. It was becoming more and more difficult to keep our eyes open, as the seven-hour time difference between Prague and Houston started to overpower us. "We are here!" woke me up abruptly. "We are here, guys. This is the Hesters' home." Our eyes opened, but the eyelids were heavy, nonetheless. Meeting the family perked us up as there were two adults who right away beamed with such great Texan personality; three children who were full of life and joy; and a dog that could hardly be kept back from overpowering these two strangers, who, to its delight, probably smelled badly after traveling for almost twenty-four hours. They welcomed us in, showed us our rooms, served us a hot meal, and asked a few basic questions before it was apparent that we needed to take a quick shower and then rest our heavy heads on the pillow for a good night of sleep. There was no way of letting our parents know that we arrived in one piece, as there was no Wi-Fi allowing us to do so, no WhatsApp to be used, no Facebook or Instagram to be utilized to send an instant message. Phone calls were costly, charging a high dollar per every minute of conversation; but phone calls, fax messages, and a good old mail service that took about two weeks to bring a letter back and forth were the only way to communicate across the Atlantic. We decided to solve that predicament the following day. We thanked our new friends for opening their home to us, hugged each other, and parted our ways to walk to our own rooms and sleep. As my head hit the pillow, I could barely thank the Lord for His traveling mercies and guidance before I drifted into a deep sleep. I was about to spend my first night in Houston, in Texas, in the United States, in North America. I could not believe that this was happening to me. Exhausted and with a little smile on my face, I drifted off to a much needed rest.

The fear of the Lord leads to life: Then one
rests content, untouched by trouble.
—Proverbs 19:23

79) Houston

Our days turned into weeks. This was a strong indicator that we were having a great time in Houston, soaking in so many new experiences every day. From the family life at the Hesters, to taking ballet classes at the prestigious Houston Ballet Academy, to watching Randall's Company, Ad Deum, work with a deep heart desire to honor the Lord with every performance, with every presentation, every rehearsal and even every class. As time continued, there were some stark differences surrounding us on every side. One significant difference between a European way and an American way of life, that both Petra and I found to be hard to overlook, was the absence of human contact. It is normal in Europe to always be surrounded by people. Most of the time, these are strangers whom one meets on the sidewalk, commuters squashed and pressed together in a crowded public transportation vehicle, or a large group of loud children playing on a playground of a park that was converted into a battleground, at least in their imaginations while playing a game of make-believe. In Houston, everything seemed to be the opposite. It did not take but a week for us to notice the lifestyle of operating from one's car. One could go to the bank, the restaurant, the cleaners, the pharmacy, the post office, and more without ever once leaving the comfort and solitude of the car. Even on the busy highways, packed with thousands of vehicles, I realized, when a closer look was taken, that most of these only had one person in them. Before too long, this started to have an effect on me. I never realized that being with people I did not know and did not care to know was the normal way of life and when taken away it was deeply missed. I had to whisper a prayer of repentance for every time I complained about a tram being too packed and crowded, for every occasion when a bicyclist almost ran me over while walking down the street, or for quickly judging a passerby who displayed a dislike of life through the frown on his face. How I wished to meet one now.

Another huge challenge was being surrounded by fast talkers. The American English combined with the Texan accent and conversation unfolding in a fast successive manner was overwhelming at first. I felt like a broken record when requesting for people to repeat statements time and again, asking them to speak slower. Often, I built the meaning of a sentence on the few words that I understood and simply imagined the rest. To combat this, I was prepared to agree. All the time and everywhere, I prepared to say yes in case of doubt of what was being said. This led to many funny situations and moments along the way when yes was the least logical response to a question often causing people to question my sanity. "Would you like a bagel for breakfast?" as an example, is a simple question where yes would be adequate. But when it's followed by "Aren't you sick of eating bagels every day?" and again my reply is yes, a potential rudeness could be perceived by the one asking. But then when the conversation continued and I was asked, "What would you like instead of bagels for breakfast, Jiri?'" and I replied yes, they started to wonder a little whether I was totally normal. As a perplexed look appeared on their faces, I realized that they knew that I did not understand, which led me to become nervous, and to resolve the situation, I'd smile and say, "Yes!"

Simply let your "Yes" be "Yes," and your "No," "'No."
—Matthew 5:37

80) Learning a New Word

Petra and I would often speak to each other in Czech to relieve the pressure of always communicating in English. Often that presented itself with funny or embarrassing moments, such as this one: It was a beautiful, sunny, and very hot day. The Texas heat was challenging the two young Europeans, not used to such high temperatures, to their limits. It was a Sunday, and after finishing a church meeting, Randall took Petra and me to Pappadeaux Seafood Kitchen, a fancy Cajun establishment known for delicious food often accompanied by good fellowship of friends and families enjoying the spicy cuisine experience. Upon our arrival, we were escorted to a long table where so many friends of Randall's were already seated and conversing. The restaurant was busy that day as it usually welcomes hungry worshippers who built a good appetite in church services across the city. Petra and I were seated close to the middle of the table. We initially spoke with those seated next to us and across the table from us. Often we had to answer the same sort of questions like "Where are you from?" "How do you like Houston?" and "When are you returning back to Russia?" as many did not know the difference between the Czech Republic, a small country located in the center of Europe and the largest nation in the world spanning the eastern portion of the "Old World" before dominating most of geographical Asia. To them, it was one and the same. Eventually, though, their conversation would turn to those they knew, and Petra and I could then speak with each other. As we started to talk, we naturally switched from speaking English to speaking Czech. The noise in the restaurant was clamorous and loud, as many were talking, the ceiling fans were spinning, background music was blaring, and the waiters were hustling to serve the many guests. Though seated next to each other, Petra and I had to speak loudly in order to hear one another. Occasional laughter added to the level and volume of our conversation. We found ourselves engaged in conversing, almost forgetting everyone else around us. We did not realize just how loud we were. "Yo, fuct!" I shouted. In Czech, this means "Yes, for a fact!" but when said in an English-speaking country, the meaning is completely different and quite offensive. We didn't know. The moment I yelled, "For a fact," in Czech, trying to convey my point to Petra, the whole restaurant froze, and everyone stared at the two of us. All the noise, apart from the ceiling fans, ceased to exist, and we wanted to do the same. Randall, being the Texas gentleman that he is, stood up and gestured his apologies to the restaurant guests motioning for them all to resume their eating and fellowshipping. He approached the two stunned Czechs and explained to us what just happened and the meaning of the word that we spoke, not spoke but yelled, across the whole western hemisphere. We were sorry not knowing how to explain what just happened. I felt terribly for all those seated directly next to us, as they might have felt judged by the sharp looks of all in the restaurant, signaling that it was their fault that we misbehaved so rudely. We regretfully learned another English word that day, one that we were not taught at our English classes at school, for obvious reasons, and came to understand that often a word in one language can have a completely different meaning in another. It was an embarrassing moment then. It is a funny story now!

The words of a man's mouth are deep waters, but
the fountain of wisdom is a bubbling brook.
—Proverbs 18:4

81) VHS

There was so much to do in Houston, and our guests invested a lot of time to entertain us way beyond our expectations. Trips to watch Houston Ballet performances, shopping sprees at the Houston Galleria, and occasional offers of phone calls with our families are just some examples of us being spoiled so greatly. Afternoons were spent by the family's pool under the hot Texas sun, allowing us to get a nice tan that was going to be envied upon our return home. Even though we were busy, occasionally, there was not much to do. One of these days, Randall handed us a VHS tape for us to watch. Yes, this indicates how long ago this was. "You guys watch this and let me know what you think. I bet you will enjoy this!" he said and went to run another set of errands. *A Symphony of Movement* was the title of the video. There was a ballerina in a white dress with colorful lights in the background on the cover. Many images were joined together in a unique design reflecting the 1990s. At the bottom of the front cover, it stated, "Ballet Mag-ni-fi-cat," as we struggled to read and understand the meaning of the word. But if Randall recommended it, it must be worth the while to watch. And so we placed the tape into the VCR player and waited for it to be pulled in and lowered into the machine. Locating the correct input on a TV set was easy in the day as there were usually only two options. Initially, the tape

appeared damaged, as the video seemed jerky and not synchronized with the audio. After a couple of seconds, however, it started to play. Dancers in bright-red costumes ran onto the stage to an orchestrated prelude of Beethoven's "Ode for Joy." Instead of a choir singing the famous Schiller's German version of the poem, a young classically trained voice of a contemporary singer started to sing "Joyful, Joyful, We Adore Thee." The dancers were breathtaking. Sharp. Technically clean. Professional. Strongly unified in movement. The choreography was classical, challenging, swift, and progressive. But above all, there was something that captivated us more than anything—joy. There was a powerful, overwhelming, contagious, captivating, true, honest, youthful, glorious joy pouring from the TV screen. *What is this? Who are they? Wow!* Petra and I were completely drawn in. Song after song, and many times without us understanding the lyrics fully, these jewels of beautiful and anointed art impacted us deeply. We were moved and found speechless. Tears flowing down our faces indicated that Randall was wrong. We did not merely "enjoy" this, as he guessed; we were moved beyond enjoyment, beyond words, stirred deeply in our hearts and souls by these incredible artists that we knew nothing about. We could not wait to see Randall the next day to ask him about these dancers on the tape. For now, we came to realize that dance and worship in particular can be used powerfully to effect the viewer, the audience, and bring them into the presence of the living and glorious God.

Ascribe to the Lord the glory due his name. Bring an offering and come before him; worship the Lord in the splendor of his holiness.
—1 Chronicles 16:29

82) Discovering More

The next day, the sun was faithfully demonstrating its power and dominance with intense heat. Petra and I were picked up by Deana, one of Randall's close friends, to be driven to our morning technique class at the Houston Ballet Academy before we were to meet Randall later that day. HBA is a great center devoted to excellence in training and dance education. Petra and I both took classes from Mr. Freddie, a teacher who displayed great devotion to challenging his students in every class. He reminded me of Brother Evald in that immensely. What differed, however, was the absence of Christ in Mr. Freddie's life. The whole academy was very much a place where the light and hope of Jesus did not shine and darkness, almost sadness and despair, clearly marked most, if not all, there. The faculty and the students alike revered and honored the founder and the director of the Houston Ballet, Ben Stevenson, who would daily walk through the school to bring encouragement and inspiration to everyone there. We were grateful to be able to learn so much during our time at the academy, but with every class, it became more and more evident that the secular world would be a challenge once I returned back home and started my contract with the Moravian National Theater in the fall.

We met Randall early in the afternoon and followed him to a Whole Foods Store. This place was a sanctuary to him, though he would never admit that verbally. I do recall the bewilderment when Petra and I saw a grocery store for the first time. All we knew from home were stores much smaller and much simpler in the selection of products sold and the somewhat limited choices in brands. The stores here were just the opposite. I do recall the toothpaste selection specifically, as Petra was simply unable to choose one out of the display of so many. This was what we imagined about the American retail world, but seeing it and experiencing it for the first time was simply beyond words.

This particular day, we bought our lunches and sat in the area designated for eating, much more than for fellowship. It did not matter to us, as we could not wait to ask questions regarding the videocassette he lent us the day before. It was obvious to him that we loved what we saw as our questions started to come quickly. "I knew that you would love it!" Randall said. "It is clear that your academy training is much more classical in nature than my vision for Ad Deum and where my expertise and strengths lie. Ballet Magnificat is a professional Christian ballet company started by the lady that you saw on the tape, the one who also shared her testimony in the middle of the video. Kathy Thibodeaux is an accomplished ballerina that was radically saved by the Lord at her husband's band concert in the late seventies, I believe." Pieces of lettuce were falling from Randall's wrap as he continued to convey what he knew about the group while trying to enjoy the warm food. "She started the ballet to be the first Christian ballet company set apart for the glory of God. I guess that was obvious to you guys when you watched it, right?" "Yes, yes...yes...it vas...big, no...no...tzat's a rong vord. It vas amazing!" Petra started to reply. Randall smiled as she was looking for words to describe to him what we thought about what we saw and paint a picture of how it impacted us. All that with somewhat limited English vocabulary when it came to describing something unusually powerful and moving as this VHS was. Randall continued. "This company is based in the city of Jackson." "They are not here in Texas?" I interrupted. Another piece of lettuce fell off the wrap as Randall held it close to his mouth, giving me an evil eye for not letting him speak without being heckled. "No, Yirka, they are in Mississippi." "The river?" I said, totally declaring my ignorance when it came to knowing the individual states of the Union. Europeans, typically speaking, are well acquainted with states such as California, Texas, and Florida, as there are some cities which names are familiar to most Europeans such as Chicago, Dallas, Miami, and, of course, New York City. Jackson and Mississippi did not fall into either of these categories. I had a lot to learn. "Would you be interested in visiting Jackson and meeting Kathy and the dancers?" "Yes, totally, please! Would that be possible?" Petra and I were shouting over one another. "I'll call to see if we could take a trip there." This was amazing. We would take a road trip to visit another state and meet the amazing dancers from the video. That is exactly what happened. Randall had already mentioned Petra and me to Ballet Magnificat as he worked on trying to obtain our visas and even attempted for us to be able to participate in the annual Summer Dance Intensive in Jackson. As all our paperwork took much longer than initially anticipated, we missed the deadline to be registered. None of this was known to the two of us. But we appreciated Randall's efforts in making our visit to the United States as eye-opening as possible. When he reached out to them, calling to see if a visit would be possible, they responded with a resounding yes as they were able to secure a host family for a ten-day visit. It was a done deal. Petra and I were going to Mississippi.

I will instruct you and teach you in the way you should go; I will counsel you and watch over you.

—Psalm 32:8

83) Crossing the River

It was the first week of August, and we were in Randall's car heading out of Houston. We did not know how far Jackson was from Houston, nor did we know how long it would take to get there. Neither Petra nor I had our driver's licenses, so Randall had to do all the driving. Hours on the road spent in watching the countryside pass us by were exciting. Before long, we came to a sign announcing "Louisiana." Then it happened. A large metal construction started to appear on the horizon. "What is that?" I asked Randall as I pointed to the apparent towers rising before us. "We are about to cross the mighty Mississippi," he said, enjoying our excitement. As we approached the bridge, we could hardly take it all in. The river was something we learned about in our geography class, but seeing it for the first time was thrilling. Randall even allowed us to take a picture as he exited the interstate to find a good view of the bridge and the river. We drove on, crossing the river that signifies the divide of the nation, and eventually passed a sign that welcomed us to the "Hospitality State of Mississippi." I was surprised to see all the green trees along the road. Everywhere, large, green, almost never-ending sight of trees. It reminded me of Sweden as I recalled our drive from Stockholm to Laxå a year ago or so. As I do not care much for nature, I admit that it was pleasant to the eye to see the vibrant verdant scenery all around us. We were getting excited. The plan was to be dropped off and picked up again in ten days to go back to Houston to have a few more days there before flying back to Prague. We were ready to enjoy every minute of our visit to Jackson, to Mississippi, and every moment of meeting the dancers of Ballet Magnificat. After seven long hours, we started to see the skyline of Jackson's downtown. To our surprise, Randall drove us to the local theater, back in the day called the Municipal Auditorium, where it was prearranged for us to attend a performance of Ballet Mississippi, a professional Jackson company. They were presenting an evening of three shorter works and featuring Fernando Bujones, a world-class Cuban-born dancer who also served as the company's artistic director at that time. Petra and I had no idea that we were going to attend a performance and were not dressed appropriately. We learned quickly that it did not really matter as much since we were going to see a matinee show when the attire is more relaxed. We parked the car by a large concrete building with massive columns and a balcony facing the street in front of it. We got out of the car, only to notice the humidity. Sticky, hot, wet humidity. "Welcome to Mississippi, guys." Randall chuckled. "This is normal. You will get used to it, or you might not!

But this is the norm most of the summer months here!" We were looking at the quiet streets around us that were, in the same manner as the streets of Houston, completely void of pedestrians. As we were stretching our legs, two young and skinny girls, beaming with energy and enthusiasm, skipped toward us. "Hi y'all, my name is Tara, and this is Christina. Welcome!"

"This is Kathy's daughter," Randall explained, "and you are?" asking the other fair-skinned girl he did not know.

"I am Christina, and I take lessons at the Ballet Magnificat School of the Arts. Tara and I are close friends, and we will be watching the performance with y'all today." Christina's voice was quiet and had a little Southern accent. Tara, on the other hand, sounded much differently from the people of Texas. One thing that confused both Petra and me was the word *y'all*. Randall was laughing hard watching the initial exchange among the four of us. The excitement of the two locals, met with the hesitation of the two visitors, struck him as hysterical and entertaining. By then, a gentleman approached us and shook Randall's hand. "This is Michael Cadle, and he works for Ballet Magnificat. Michael used to dance with the company and now pours his efforts into the business side of things. He is the one who found the host family for you guys to stay with." I recognized Michael from the video. I could not believe that we were in Mississippi already meeting people who impacted us so profoundly through the video presentation.

"Welcome to Jackson. Tell me your names again," Michael requested. We introduced ourselves, slowly trying to articulate our names as clearly as possible. We learned that to be helpful in Houston, as "Jiri" and "Petra" are not common names in the English-speaking world. "We are excited to have you here for the next ten days or so. The company is currently on tour in Canada and will be returning home in three days," he continued. "Tara here is excited to have her parents back, right?" Michael said, looking at Tara, who stood a few feet away still talking fervently to Christina. "I won't be watching the performance this afternoon, but I will be back afterward to take you to your host, the Husbands," Michael continued. It was funny to me that in Houston, we stayed with the Hesters and here we were staying with the Husbands. We politely thanked Michael for everything he already did for us to be able to come and visit Ballet Magnificat. Randall said his goodbye as he needed to return to Houston to be there to attend to his responsibilities, and he promised to see us in ten days or so to pick us back up. We placed our bags into Michael's car. Michael and Randall hugged, and they both got into their cars and drove off. Tara and Christina were gracious hosts during the afternoon. That evening, we were driven to the Husbands' home. As it was in Houston when we met the Hesters, the Husbands were amazing, hospitable people as well. They shared with us how they loved the Czech Republic and the Czech people as they had gone to Prague for several short-term mission trips. When they heard that there was a need to house two Czech dancers for a short time, they immediately offered their home to become our place of refuge during our visit of Mississippi. We were excited, so excited, to be here ready to soak in everything the Lord prepared and stored for us in the Hospitality State.

And my God will meet all your needs according
to his glorious riches in Christ Jesus.
—Philippians 4:19

84) Suspenders

It is astonishing to think how fashion keeps experiencing strong and often profound comebacks. It is apparent that if one would not cave to the pressure of being ridiculed and ostracized when wearing a particular piece of clothing that was in style yesterday but is long out of style today, he would find himself back in the "in" crowd once another cycle of the fashion world completed its circulation. I fall into the category of the one who waits for the repeated season to come back, as fashion and clothing are not my priorities. I am one that prefers and enjoys wearing clothes that are comfortable and familiar in spite of them not being current or fashionable. Back in 1993, as I came to the States with one suitcase filled with flannel shirts and pairs of corduroy pants, customary for the post-Communist era of Eastern

Europe, little did I know that, fast-forward almost thirty years, flannel shirts would be back in style. Another typical addition to my fashion lifestyle were suspenders. To this article of fashion, I want to say, "What was I thinking?" Lastly, I wore large-framed glasses that accompanied a puffy hairstyle. My faithfully thick hair needed to be trimmed regularly, especially in the Mississippi humidity I must add, to avoid the look of a loser. But here I was, at the age of eighteen, wearing my flannel shirt, corduroy pants held up by brown suspenders, large glasses, and puffy hair as the Ballet Magnificat Company arrived after their 2,300-mile journey from Edmonton, the Canadian city in Alberta. We were so excited to finally meet the dancers we watched on the tape. Shoulders pushed down, necks stretched, stomach pulled in. We were ready to make a great first impression. Tara and Christina, as well as the office staff who got to know us over the past couple of days, enjoyed watching the two starstruck Czech dancers trying to strike a good fancy with Kathy and the dancers. The large Silver Eagle bus pulled into the parking lot in front of the building adorned with the "Ballet Magnificat" sign on its front wall. The doors opened, and the dancers started to appear, emerging from the interior. The nonstop two-day journey was visible on their visage. We did not care. Tara could hardly wait to embrace her mom and dad as she ran toward the bus to give them both a warm Mississippi hug and welcome. I don't know about Petra, but I was nervous. Finally, the dancers started to enter the building after collecting their luggage and dance bags, loading them into their personal vehicles, and checking to see if any pieces of mail arrived during their absence. Tara made sure that we met Kathy. "Hello, I am Kathy... It is so nice to meet y'all!" she said, sounding tired but genuine. "Mama, Mama...he can do a really nice '*saut de chat*,'" Tara yelled, pulling on her mom's arm. I was embarrassed that the first thing Kathy heard about me was how I could do a ballet step rather than anything regarding my personality or character. Other dancers briefly introduced themselves, but the desire and need for a good rest was clearly the dominating thought on their minds, much more so than meeting these Europeans dressed as if they stepped out of the history textbook of the 1970s. Until this day, my wife, Cassandra, who also stepped out of the tour bus that day, recalls seeing this Czech boy standing by the entry doors with his large glasses, puffy hair, and suspenders. Emoji with an open hand hitting a face would be appropriate right here. It is a good thing that at the end of the day, what we wear does not matter as much as who and whose we are.

The Lord does not look at the things man looks at. Man looks at the outward appearance, but the Lord looks at the heart.
—1 Samuel 16:7b

85) Invitation

A few days of rest and the dancers were back in the studio to prepare for another tour coming up. Petra and I were invited to take classes with the company and observe the rehearsals. Every day started with a time of worship and communal prayer, much like we saw in Sweden. There, as well as here, this was not approached as something that Christians should do—it was clearly foundational for every day—to connect with the Lord and to make sure that centering on Him came before anything else. Watching these brothers and sisters pray and pour out their hearts before the King of kings made me realize just how much I myself needed to grow in daily connection with Him. I loved watching them open their Bibles, often marked through and through with highlights of favorite or profound passages. There were pages exemplifying the wear and tear of daily use. I wondered how that must please the Lord to see one reading His love letter that much, that the paper carrying His message was not able to withstand the repeated use. By this point, I still did not own my own copy of the Bible. There was a growing desire for one, but I simply could not afford to purchase it, as my finances were almost completely exhausted. We loved our time in Mississippi. The experience with these precious people was having an overwhelming impact on us both. The classes were challenging, and Kathy was clearly the one in charge. There was a desire for technical excellence driving each dancer, no doubt about that. But the rehearsals were my favorite part of each day. What was so striking about them, beside the moving aspect of worship, was the unity of movement among the dancers. When I say unity, I mean a complete matching of every single movement, gesture, placement, arm height, head position, intensity, and timing of one dancer with the others. Countless minutes were spent on perfecting this unique element that I had never seen anywhere else. Kathy explained to us simply stating that the physical unity directly correlates to the spiritual unity among the company artists. It was obvious and impactful to watch them dance with such submission of one to the other.

Days in Jackson were turning fast, as it is always the case when one loves being in a place or doing something they truly enjoy. During the second week of visiting Jackson, while sitting in the corner of the studio watching a rehearsal, Kathy approached Petra and me with her eyes intently looking at us, signaling that there was something on her heart she wanted to convey. "Your time to go back to Houston is coming up, am I right?" she started. "Yes," we replied. "Have you enjoyed being here?" was the next question. Kathy did not even wait for us to reply, as it was more of a rhetorical question. Our enjoyment of the time in Mississippi was clearly obvious in us both. As our heads nodded, she continued, "I would like you to pray about staying here with us longer. The others and I are sensing that the Lord might be calling you both to Ballet Magnificat. I don't know what that would mean and what all He would need to do to make it possible, but often the call of the Lord comes first, and with our yes on the table, God begins to move and guide us down a path we did not know existed. Would you all pray and seek Him with us? Time is short, but if this is of Him, He will gladly make the answer clear." She smiled and, with the natural grace of a world-class ballerina, walked back to directing the rehearsal. Petra and I were stunned. Naturally, we first thought of the obstacles in the way, obstacles that were larger than life and impossible to overlook. Our natural man was rising up, and our young, inexperienced spiritual man was drowning in shadows of fear and doubt. We wanted to stay; there was no question about that. Ballet Magnificat was a perfect fit for us to combine our love for the Lord, our desire to serve Him, and our talent of dance being an offering used for His glory and purposes, much like we saw in the dancers of the company. But there were impediments, obstructions, constraints that we could not have imagined being moved out of the way, even by the Almighty God, we thought. Visas to stay, money to have, places to live, permission of our parents to be given, contracts to fulfill, tickets to return home to use… The list of why this was only a wish, only a dream never to be realized, was long and mightily convincing. But Kathy was right—we could not say no if we did not spend time on our knees asking the Father for His direction and will. We resolved to do just that, in our separate rooms independently, to approach the throne of God and humbly ask Him for the answer. This time, however, in order to be able to submit to His answer, no matter what it might be, we needed to ask Him without preconceived terms, without predetermined decisions, and without prearranged plans in our minds and hearts. God was going to speak, and we could not afford to miss His message. This was crucial, possibly detrimental, and of utmost importance. Our future was hinged on getting this right, and for young Christians who walked with the Lord for less than two years, the fear of being able to do so was overwhelming. It was time to pray like we never prayed before, hoping that He would be gracious and understanding of our limited experience of hearing and knowing His voice.

Lord, you have assigned me my portion and my cup; you have made my lot secure. The boundary lines have fallen for me in pleasant places; surely I have a delightful inheritance.
—Psalm 16:5–6

86) Guidance

That evening, after a delicious dinner at the Husbands, we shared with them about the invitation we received and asked them to pray for us to hear from the Lord. They promised to do that, and I have no doubt they did.

The room was dark, only a lamp shining onto my bed brought a small amount of light into the room. I borrowed a Bible, and not knowing where to turn to open it, I asked the Lord to guide me.

How does one hear the Lord? How does one differentiate between the voice of his own mind and the voice of God? I was hesitant. No, I was afraid—fearful that I would mess up the plan of the Almighty because I was too immature to know how to pray and seek Him, unable to find the path preordained for me. Even so, the Lord was moving forward prepared to spend a moment with me to teach me, firstly and most importantly, that He is for me and not against me. He is an intimate Father delighting to teach me to hear His voice, training me to trust Him, showing me His loved-filled deep regard for me, and demonstrating that He chose me and that His sovereign plan is just that, sovereign. After that, in the second tier, there is where my answer would be found. Answers from the Lord are secondary to His desire for us to be intimate with Him. I needed to learn that before the Lord would lead me to know His will. The Bible was closed, placed on the carpet. My knees were bent, hands clasped together, and eyes closed as my heart approached the presence of the Lord.

"Father God, Jiri here. Lord, I am entering Your presence. I have a heavy question on my mind and heart, and I need You to guide me to know Your will. Before I ask You to answer me, Lord, I want to simply tell You how amazing You are and how amazingly gracious You have been to me. I recognize it, Father. I count it all a privilege. I believe, Lord, that You brought me to Your kingdom. You chose me when I was not looking to choose You at all. This is all Your work. And it is splendid. You are glorious, wise, loving, gracious… oh, so gracious, merciful, incredibly faithful. Who am I without You? I do not know why You chose me, but, Lord Jesus, I thank You that You did. As I come before Your presence tonight, Lord, still my fears, quiet my worries, push away all distractions. Captivate me with Yourself, I plead. I need to know Your plans and will, yet more than that, I want to be with You tonight. Now, Lord, I will wait for You to take over and meet with me, Lord Jesus…" The room was silent, the light was shining, and I was not moving. I was waiting to see what the Lord would do next. Then suddenly, as if speaking directly into my heart and mind, the Lord asked me to recall and remember how He moved when we were called to go to Sweden—how incredibly

He ordained all the "unsurpassable" elements to make a way where there seemed to be no way. I was being flooded by faith to believe the unbelievable. I was reminded also to recall when He called me to be His and how He orchestrated that moment to be so unique and life changing. I was flooded with peace. He reminded me when he broke the chains of slavery to the "muse of dance" in Sweden. I was flooded with trust. My God was here, and I was in His presence.

> *Those who know your name will trust in you, for you,*
> *Lord, have never forsaken those who seek you.*
> —Psalm 9:10

87) The Answer

As my heart was so deeply and profoundly impacted by the presence of my heavenly Father right there in the simple room where no single element met the criteria once required by the living God when His meeting place, the temple, was built; right there in a room where I was embraced by the Lord, Who through the torn curtain of that very temple made it possible for me to enter in; right there in the room on Poplar Boulevard in Jackson, Mississippi, God answered. I had a sense to pick up the borrowed copy of the Word of God and, in it, find and read a message that was going to be used this one night to unveil the plan of the Lord before me. I opened the Bible to Isaiah 41:

> *But you*, Israel, my servant, Jacob, *whom I have*
>   *chosen*,
> you descendants of Abraham my friend,
> *I took you* from the ends of the earth,
> from its farthest corners *I called you*.
> I said, "*You are my servant*";
> *I have chosen you* and have not rejected you.
> So *do not fear*, for *I am with you*, do not be dis-
>   mayed, for *I am your God*.
> *I will strengthen you and help you*; I will uphold
>   you with my righteous right hand.

For I am the Lord, your God, who takes hold of
your right hand,
and says to you, *"Do not fear; I will help you."*

I kept reading as it became more and more clear to me what the Lord was calling me to do. My eyes were flooding with tears, as I knew that the Lord was right there with me. The peace in my heart was louder than all the noise of rationality, and then I came across the following lines that pierced my heart and soul:

I, the Lord have called you in righteousness;
I will take hold of your hand.
I will keep you and *I will make you to be* a cove-
nant for the people
And *a light for the Gentiles,*
To open eyes that are blind,
To free captives from prison and to release from the
dungeon those who sit in darkness.

Then as if a light switch was flipped, the tangible presence of the Lord was gone. His dealing with me was concluded. The Lord spoke, and I had no choice but to stand on what I believed He challenged me to do. I was to stay in Jackson longer, trusting that He will come through and open the gateway to make it possible. I was thankful, excited, and totally in panic all at the same time.

I saw Him perform some radical maneuvers in the past, but this was a whole new level of needing to see the Lord move mountains. My eyes were getting heavy, and fighting to stay awake was difficult. I believed that the Lord would somehow confirm to me that I heard him correctly. I knew that there was nothing else I was going to accomplish that evening. I climbed into the bed and, with a sense of calm, turned the little lamp off, quickly drifting into a deep sleep.

I will praise the Lord, who counsels me; even
at night my heart instructs me.

—Psalm 16:7

88) The Barrage of Confirmations

As I woke up the next day, I was unprepared to receive all the confirmation the Lord was ready to pour out before me. Confirmation is not always guaranteed to be given, as there are many heroes of the Bible that only received the call and never the confirmation, only to find themselves in countless difficult moments and seasons when running hard after God. Why would I be different? It's simple. I was not as mature as these heroes of faith, and the Lord knew that a confirmation would provide a much-needed and great aid. As I look back, I wonder if the Lord was smiling as He watched me grab the doorknob and, with the simple twist, open the door to the barrage that was coming my way, a barrage He knew would overwhelm me completely, like an avalanche rushing down a steep mountainside. Laura, my host, was the first person I saw that day. There was a slight smirk on her face, I thought. *Did I miss something?* I wondered.

"What did the Lord say last night, Jiri?" she asked while continuing to focus on the homemade pancakes she was making for everyone in the house.

"I *think* the Lord said… I *believe* the Lord said yes!" I replied, trying to sound confident in my answer.

"That would make sense, since He told Wayne and me to keep you in our house past this week!" As I stood there bewildered, Petra came into the kitchen with her face pale and colorless.

"Good morning…everyone… How are you…? I don't… The Lord said yes," finally came out of her mouth. By then I had to sit down.

"Petra, I was just telling Laura the same thing, and I was hoping that you heard the same answer from the Lord… I cannot believe it… This is…well… How will we do this?"

"I don't know anything, and I could not really sleep much. My mind was wondering the whole night," Petra continued. "All I know is that to leave would be disobedience, but to stay is asking for some serious challenges to face and overcome… Just the thought of telling my folks that I am not coming back is… Can you imagine?" By then she was also seated. The pancakes started to burn a little as Laura was captivated and distracted by our conversation.

"The Lord is a big God, and He will make it clear as He will guide you one step at a time. You will see," she said, turning back to the stove.

"My mom will have a heart attack," I whispered as I pictured her reaction on the other end of the phone line. "To hear that we are staying in America to join a Christian ballet company without money, without an airline ticket, without visas… Wait, the visa! We have to leave the country before our visas expire at the end of August, or else we will remain here illegally. Oh my goodness!"

Laura turned the stove off and turned back to us. Her Southern accent was cute and friendly, but her message sounded resolute and strong. "The Lord will make it clear to you one step at a time!" Worry not and eat, y'all!" So we did. When we arrived at Ballet Magnificat, the company dancers and the staff all gathered for the morning devotional time. Kathy asked us if we heard from the Lord. I requested to borrow a Bible to be able to read the passage I found to be so profound the previous night. I was nervous reading out loud, but that did not matter. There was a decision to be made, and they all needed to know how the Lord spoke to us specifically. Reading the Isaiah passage was powerful even the second time. The dancers' eyes were closed as they were listening and praying all at the same time. I concluded and I knew that, had this been a court hearing, my case would be closed. John Vandervelde, the company minister, picked up his guitar and started to play a song. Everyone sang and praised the Lord. After, he went into a powerful prayer asking the Lord to open every door that we did not even know existed at the moment. He requested of the Father to manifest His profound power in every step. He prayed for the Lord's divine provision for us and everything we might need as this seemed to be the will of God for us to stay in Mississippi a little while longer. He concluded by thanking the Lord for confirming to Petra and me what the leadership of Ballet Magnificat sensed the past couple of days, that is, the placing of the Lord's call on my and Petra's lives to join the ministry of Ballet Magnificat. We called Randall to speak with him and seek his advice. "I knew this was coming," he said right away upon hearing our statement. "The Lord did not bring you to Himself to dance somewhere in a secular company for the glory of ballet. He has much better plans. I don't know what this means exactly, but you guys have my blessings. Look not to the left or right. Keep your eyes on the Lord, and He will make His path clear before you," he concluded. "There is a I-94 card in your passport that should have a stamp from the immigration officer, received when you landed in Houston. Check the date on it as that is when you must leave the United States," he continued. "Sometimes these are similar to the date when your tourist visa expires, but other times, these are issued for a much later date. The stamp trumps the visa, if that makes sense. My advice would be to check the date, and should it be later than the visa date, the Lord has made it clear. Then call the airline and see if you can switch your return flight. I am excited for you guys, and I am excited to see what else the Lord has planned to do with you all here in America." Petra and I thanked Randall for being such a great and godly friend to us both, for believing the Lord with us, for encouraging us with the Word and with his wisdom. We hung up the phone and looked at each other. "If Randall is correct, the date in our passport would be a strong confirmation that we heard the Lord correctly. We needed to find the piece of paper, the form—what did he call it?—I think…I-94, yes, 94…and check the date on it." We always carried our passports with us as it was the only adequate form of identification we could present while in the States. I pulled my passport out and waited for Petra to bring hers. We sat at the table and looked at each other. "Ready?" I asked her. "Not really… I am nervous to find out, nervous of the implication this could have…but let's do it. On the count of three?" she suggested. "Yo," was my reply. "Raz…dva…tri," I counted. We both opened our passport to the page with the printed US visa page. It was there where the I-94 document was inserted by the immigration officer. We did not know the document's significance at the time and did not realize its potential power in allowing us to remain in the country beyond the validity of the visa. Who would have thought? The paper was easily legible. Very basic information such as the first and last name, passport number, country of citizenship, and such are located on this arrival record. The visitor is requested to submit it when they check in to depart the country. There on it was a large oval stamp stating "Immigration and Naturalization Service of the United States of America" around its edges. The all caps word ADMIT is located below. Underneath it is a line on which the officer writes the type of visa, in our case B1/B2, and then the date stating the expiration of the permitted visit to the United States. And there it was, the same on both of our documents, even though we were processed by two different officials; the date was "Dec 24, 1993." With that one glimpse, we realized that the door to stay in America was opened until Christmas of that year.

Randall's words from the phone call rang in my mind, "The Lord has made it clear," as if Randall was speaking prophetically. We could not believe it and to take a moment to let it settle was an absolute must. "Now what?" Petra asked. "Petra, the most difficult challenge will be the conversation with our parents. Can you imagine what they'll say, how they'll react?" Petra did not respond as she visualized the conversation in her mind and pictured the many different scenarios that could be its direct result. "Oh my," were her only uttered words. Her eyes were locked in a deep stare, and no movement accompanied her subtle breathing. "This will be hard," she added. She was right. The office director, Jeff, gave us permission to call home. Back in the day, it was a costly and expensive thing to do, and we appreciated his willingness to let us do so. I calculated the seven-hour time difference between Jackson and the Czech Republic to realize that it was around six o'clock in the evening. I needed my dad to be home as I did not want my mom to have to convey the news to him alone. I asked the Lord for my dad to be there. It was that simple. I picked up one of the office phones as Petra was doing the same on another. I dialed my parents' number and waited for the ring on the other end of the line to start.

"Haló!" a Czech for *hello*, echoed on the other end. "Hi, Mom, how are you?" I started.

"Ahoj, ahoj, how are *you*?" she replied, and we had a brief conversation. I asked if dad was home, but by then he was already pressing his ear to hear me.

"It's great to hear you guys. I don't have much time, as this is so expensive, but we are here in Mississippi, as you know." I informed them of the trip to Jackson during our previous conversation and I was grateful that I did so as I did not have to explain why I was not in Houston. "We have had an incredible time visiting the ballet company here." I purposefully used grandiose words to describe our experience to help my case I was about to present. "Long story short, Kathy, the director of Ballet Magnificat, invited both Petra and me to extend our visit and stay in Jackson longer. We just found out that our visas permit us to do so as well. There are many details to be figured out, but I wanted to speak with you guys to hear your thoughts about the possibility of extending the visit in the States." I was used to delivering challenging information to my mom and dad over the phone, from my years living in Liberec, and they were accustomed to receive them in that manner as well. Petra's parents did not have that "training," and I saw Petra struggling on the other phone. Our glimpses back and forth brought encouragement as the conversations continued.

"Oh my, Jiri, this is huge. A great opportunity but also a huge decision. How much longer would you stay there?" my mom continued.

I knew that she was about to drop the phone when I said, "Through Christmas. We don't know much, but if you guys would give me the initial okay, I would gather more information here and let you know soon."

"Son," my dad entered the conversation, "we are always standing in our support of you, and you know that. This is an opportunity that could potentially change the course of your life. I am just wondering about the practical aspects like your position with the National Theater in Brno, your scheduled flight back, how would you support yourself living in the States, where would you live, and such. If you think that you can justify these concerns, maybe not right now on the phone but before your flight back, then we are behind you. We just want you to be sure that this will not mess up your job opportunity here. You know how competitive the dance field is, and finding another position with a good ballet company later might be difficult down the road. Please think and consider it all. I know this call is expensive and we might need to let you go. We love you, Yirka. Let us know how things develop there. Does that sound good?" I could visualize my dad as he was speaking to me. I also pictured my mom looking at him while they were crowded by the phone in the corner of the kitchen, appreciating the leadership skills she saw him always acquire and display in the right manner and moment.

"Yes, sir! I love you both. Ahoj…oh, and thank you!" With that, I hung the phone and checked if Jeff was okay with the length of the call. He was paying no attention to either of us. Petra was still speaking a little while longer.

"My parents want to know what your parents said," she asked. I gave her a thumb up to signal their temporary permission, as a detailed explanation would do more harm than help. The Grůšas reluctantly agreed firmly stating that they will be in direct contact with the Voborskys to figure everything out there. It was a satisfactory conclusion to us both, and with that, Petra said her goodbye and hung up. We were relieved as that was behind us. It was not a green light, per se, but it was not a red forbidding light either. We looked at each other, walked to a bench at the entry hall of the studio, and sat on it; and while looking at the floor, I said, "Now what?"

And without faith it is impossible to please God, because
anyone who comes to him must believe that he exists
and that he rewards those who earnestly seek him.
—Hebrews 11:6

89) Moment in Time

Time is an interesting element that is a part of everything that is normal to us. We cannot imagine living outside of the structure of time or living without its direct influence and presence in and on our lives. There are times when we love how quickly time runs, as something exciting might be on a horizon approaching and we cannot wait for it to finally be here. We cannot speed up its coming; we simply have to wait and be patient. The excitement in the midst of the waiting can produce much-needed character building within us. Then there are times when everything seems to be moving in a slow-motion manner and we find ourselves as if swimming against a strong current resisting the progress. Being in an unpleasant moment or circumstance often causes us to desire for it to simply be over and for us to be able to return to what we enjoy. Again, there is absolutely nothing we can do to expedite the process, and simple waiting is the only solution or remedy to move onward. What brings peace in both of these scenarios is to know that God is not limited by time and that He is faithfully at work in every circumstance. He is the only one who can influence time and everything that comes our way in its flow. God is above the time frame of time as He is eternal, always existent, able to step into the process of time, if He so desires, and/or view it as a snapshot in one singular picture. One can be frustrated with always desiring to be somewhere else or to do something else, and never appreciate the "right here and right now" and miss the precious moments granted to be enjoyed. On the other hand, if one only sees the very moment he or she finds himself or herself in and has no aspiration or plan for progress, frustration and a sense of lack of productivity are guaranteed to eventually arrive, move in, and have a deep effect. The answer is found in trusting—trusting the Lord for both the present, in which we honor Him by appreciating the gift of it and knowing that He is with us; and asking Him to guide us as we pray and plan for what is yet to come and, in it, find the sense of participation in His plans being fulfilled knowing that we serve a greater purpose, mainly God's.

After the phone calls with our parents, we remained in Jackson not really knowing how things would develop. We did not know the full time frame; we did not see a clear path before us. We could be frustrated or even fearful in that, or we could trust the Lord and joy-fully accept everything time was going to bring to our shores, in His timing. And so we slowly settled down with the fact that we won't be going back to Houston, and most likely won't be flying to Prague at the appointed time. Our British Airways tickets, costly tickets our parents purchased in the spring of that year, came in a fancy booklet with a shiny cover page displaying the airline's logo, including the royal crown, and an image of a British Airways jumbo jet, just like the one that carried us westward across the Atlantic, soaring through the clouds. As elaborate as the tickets were, we came to find out that they were not changeable. In other words, we had two options, either to utilize the return portion to travel back home or to let the remainder of the ticket expire, leaving us on this side of the ocean without a secure way of getting home. It was Friday, August 27, 1993, and Petra and I sat in the living room of the Husbands' home after we returned from the ballet studio. As it is usually the case, the weather was hot and humid that day. Powerful rain showers would come and go, only to intensify the humidity and one skin's reaction to it. We took quick showers; mine was much quicker than Petra's, and we then met in the living room. Laura knew that this day was crucial. It was clear to her as it was clear to us. This was the day when the final decision was to be made. We brought our airlines tickets to the room with us and opened them up. The tickets for the flights from Prague to London and from there to Houston were already gone leaving only a tiny strip of the perforated paper close to the spine of the booklet. The baggage vouchers were also torn out and utilized. The page that was next to be used stated BA196 IAH Houston Intercontinental to LHR London Heathrow flight reserved and purchased for the next day, August 28. We knew that we could hop in the car and still make it to Houston to catch the flight. Wayne kept reassuring us that should we decide to do that he would be more than happy to drive us to Houston, anytime of the day or night. Another powerful rain started to erupt outside, and forceful waterfalls of fresh rainwater flooded the yard behind the house. It felt as if the Lord took the beauty of the day away to prevent it from persuading us in our decision making, potentially based on the sunshine flowing through the living room window. Laura took a seat on the loveseat next to us, silently displaying her support, as Petra and I held the opened flight booklets. Petra had tears in her eyes, and I was not surprised. The decision before us was as real as it could be. There were almost constant streams of scenarios running through our minds, of the possible consequences of missing the flight. But as loud as these were, there was also the always-present peace of the Lord silencing one worry after another. "I think we need to declare verbally our trust in the Lord," I said, looking at Petra. I was hoping she would not look at me, as that would be easier to handle, but the opposite took place. "I am scared, Jiri! I am really scared, but I cannot ignore the peace of the Lord, or whatever it is that is resonating in me, whispering that this is what He has for us!" "Yes... He proved Himself in many different ways to us both, Petra, confirming His will to you and to me, and now is the time for us to stand by faith on every single one of these declarations," I whispered. "I know, Yirka. I know," she replied, nodding her head. Laura chimed in to remind us of the greatness of God, the Father Who cares deeply for His children, whether they are strong or whether they are weak. His love never changes, and He promises to be with us always, even in moments when great decisions are being made. She was right. The peace of the Lord was evident in the room. It was undeniable. We both knew what He was calling us to do.

"Lord, we thank You for this moment. The reality is, You knew that we were going to be here, sitting and worrying, fearing to make a wrong decision, fearing the unknown. The reality is that You, the God outside of time, already see everything that is before us— including every provision, every obstacle, every joy, and every regret, every victory, and every defeat. This afternoon, we close these tickets to declare that we place our feeble faith and trust into Your mighty hands, Lord. We know that You are calling us to stay in Jackson. We don't know much more than that, but You made this one thing clear. We do not want to miss it, and we don't want to mess it up. Have Your way, Lord. We believe in You and Your goodness toward us. What a plan, what a challenge, what a God! We rest in Jesus, and in His name, we prevail! Amen."

I opened my eyes and saw Petra's ticket already closed. "I had to do it. I could not wait any longer. I had to close it," she said, smiling with a residue of tears still visible on her cheeks. I was proud of my friend, and I followed suit. The next day, August 28, came and went. We never boarded the Boeing 747 jetliner that Saturday. Instead of going home, we joyfully and expectantly looked forward to the adventures God had in store for us in Mississippi and beyond, still to be realized.

> *Commit your way to the Lord; trust in him and he will*
> *do this; He will make your righteousness shine like the*
> *dawn, the justice of your cause like the noonday sun.*
>
> —Psalm 37:5

90) Journey Continues

Words. Words are used to communicate. They can be powerful. They can encourage. They can wound. Some are simple. Some are complex and beyond our understanding. Words are the building blocks used to structure and convey messages. They are used to teach us, to entertain us, to correct us, to assist us in expressing our feelings and our emotions. Words come in through sounds of countless languages and dialects, often closely knit to the culture and the people who use them. I love languages, and I enjoy words. From a young age, it had been exciting to hear foreigners speak and communicate, especially as they marveled at the beauty of Prague. I belong to the group of nerds who did not mind learning grammar structures, drilling vocabulary, spelling, and sentence structures. I loved it all. The ability to communicate beyond my native language of Czech was a great motivator to study, to practice, and to press through frustrations that face everyone learning a foreign tongue. The reward was when a successful exchange with a Russian student, often a Pioneer, happened; when ice cream was ordered in Deutsch on our vacation in Germany; during the basic exchange that happened in Español with a believer in Bolivia; when translating a message from a friend in Poland not able to speak English, who communicated his heart with the company on tour years later. It is then when the reward for every minute spent learning is greatly satisfying. Words build a powerful bond among mankind. They are a gift of the all-wise God, Who allows us to exchange and verbally interact with each other, a privilege no other creature experiences to such degree. And yet there are experiences, moments, feelings, sensations, visions, dreams, and even thoughts that are beyond adequacy to be conveyed and communicated fully with a clear meaningful element of speech, a word. My experience in Jackson, namely with and through Ballet Magnificat, falls into such a category. It is on my heart to retell in the following pages and describe the growth I experienced, the treasures I discovered, the encounters I witnessed, the provisions I gathered, the challenges I overcame, the blessings I received, and the friendships I built since I closed the airline booklet and purposefully missed the flight back home. As I do that, I am fully aware that words are simply not able to truly convey the gratitude of my inner man who was deeply altered by the faithful and tangible hand of the Lord. As you continue to read the account of His work and plan preordained for me, may you be personally spurred on in your own experience with Jesus, an experience that you will find difficult to convey with paper and ink. Should you find yourself not knowing the One this book desires to glorify and yet sense a stirring in your heart, do not wait, open your heart, and receive His gift of salvation, whose value also falls into the category of "beyond description." What a Savior, and what an adventure it is to be discovering the prepared treasures of Jesus, carefully selected for you and for me. Find yourself speechless!

No one is like you, O Lord; you are great, and your
name is mighty in power. Who should not revere you,
O King of the nations? This is your due.
—Jeremiah 10:6–7

91) Birds and Sparrows

Foreigners. Both Petra and I were strangers, visitors, foreigners. We followed the call of the Lord, being completely dependent on Him for every provision, great and small. We learned quickly that, most of the time, He meets these needs through His people. They benefit as they serve while we benefit being served. Altogether, God gets the glory in the process. This is the kingdom of God that we were learning about while navigating the initial waters of life in Mississippi. The Husbands offered a sacrifice of hospitality as they extended the invitation from ten days to almost three months. We had a roof over our heads until the beginning of November. Every day, rain or shine, a teacher at the Ballet Magnificat School of the Arts, Lauri Worrill-Biggs, pulled up to the house in her red two-door sports car exactly at eight forty-five. Never a minute early and never a minute late. Without ever asking for a penny, Lauri drove us to the studio and often would bring us back home. What a generosity lived out in a practical way. We enjoyed a great Christian fellowship in a local church, initially going with the Husbands as we felt almost as members of the family. We never went hungry, we never went dirty, and we never went without. God was gracious to provide faithfully and abundantly during these six months in Jackson.

Shortly before we were to move out of the Husbands, allowing them to return to the regular rhythm of a family life without the two strangers living under their roof, another two families opened their homes for us until Christmas of that year. Petra would move to a house with an older lady, a widow, providing her some much-needed fellowship and company; and I would nestle into a pink room with a large dollhouse dominating the space in a family with young children. Never before had I slept with Barbies all around me, but I was grateful for the provision. It was November 1, 1993, and I was to celebrate my nineteenth birthday. The Husbands used the occasion for a great goodbye party. We shared stories, we laughed, and we ate a birthday cake. It was special. I was not expecting any gifts as the family has given us so much already. But it would not be Laura and Wayne to not have something for me regardless. "We got you something little," Laura said, holding a wrapped gift in her hand. "It's not much, but we wanted to make this birthday memorable for you, being away from your family and country, a foreigner that became a dear friend. We pray that this small present would bring you much joy!" I don't like—let me rephrase, I hate—being the center of attention in a gathering of any kind. Everyone in the room was standing quietly with their gaze glued to me. I was embarrassed and uncomfortable, and yet I was blown away to be receiving a gift. I took the gift form Laura and placed it on the table. After the initial struggle with the string around the box, demonstrating my nerves in front of the guests in the room, I managed to get the gift open. Inside a box, I found a maroon leather book with my name engraved on the bottom-right corner. I was given and I humbly received my very first copy of the Bible. I briefly remembered when a copy of the Word was handed to me in Liberec, during the visit of the youth meeting three years ago, when I saw a printed copy of the Holy Bible for the very first time in my life. Now I owned my own, and I was overwhelmed. It was deeply thoughtful of the Husbands. The Bible was beautiful, it was special, and it was mine! I was excited to start reading it and explore its hidden treasures firsthand. My first Bible came with a yellow highlighter, and I wondered then if it would one day resemble the Bibles of the company dancers I saw at the Ballet Magnificat studio. Until this day, I continue to love discovering more and more of the hidden wealth and riches of the precious Word of God, that so profoundly reflects the heart of its Author.

Your word is a lamp to my feet and a light for my path.
—Psalm 119:105

92) Would You?

"For unto *us* a Child is *born*…unto *us* a Child is *given*, unto *us* a Child is *given*…" This cornerstone of Christmas music, known and recognized as the Handel's Messiah, has been sung on numerous occasions all around the world, performed in countless renditions and arrangements. It was only the middle of September; but this day, the company would not rehearse the usual repertoire, prepared and polished for the upcoming tour. Instead, a series of Christmas carols would flood the audio waves in the studio. As it is the case in most of the corners of the dance world, Ballet Magnificat is no different in that the preparations for the Christmas performance, held in December, commence early in the year, when the regular world still enjoys the warmth of the sunny weather and Christmas is nowhere on anyone's mind. I was excited to watch the company rehearse something new. It was thrilling. But then the unexpected happened. Kathy approached me and stated that I would be included in the Christmas performance. It might not have been a big deal to her, but my world just got rocked as if with a shocking earthquake of sorts. I could not believe that I would be granted such a privilege. *A Christmas Festival* was the cornerstone of Ballet Magnificat's seasonal celebrations of the birth of the Savior, Jesus Christ. This piece of the repertoire required clean technique as it was solely ballet-based choreography. I enjoyed the challenge of it, and I absolutely loved connecting with the powerful lyrics of each song in this production, as my heart and soul correlated with their message. That December, I was honored to join the company on its Christmas tour. Setting aside the nerves associated with stepping on board the bus I first saw pulling into the parking lot in August, I was looking forward to the experience of the tour and for the first time seeing the impact this dance company and performances with a Christ-centered message would have on the lives of the audience. The tour was short, about ten days or so; and, yes, the audiences seemed to be touched, even empowered by the personal connection with the Lord during each performance. The deepest impact, most certainly, happened in me, the young Czech boy who was chosen, rescued, guided, bought, called, and equipped by the Lord to be a part of a team that danced not for the glory of man but for the glory of God. It was humbling, and until this day, I wonder why the Lord chose me, out of all the dancers of the world, to be used as a dancing ambassador for the King of kings. I will never know.

The ballet graciously purchased round-trip airfare for Petra and me and sent us home for Christmas with the hope of us returning in January. Our tourist visas were expiring on December 24, and we needed to adhere to its strict requirements and guidelines in order to be able to return, and leaving the country before the given deadline was the most important of them all. We also needed to obtain another visa in Prague. There was a hope that an "R-1 religious worker" status could be granted. Along with our personal belongings, therefore, Petra and I carried files of documents to be presented to the Consular Department of the US Embassy back home. Time was short. We only had a couple of workdays between Christmas and New Year's Day and a couple of workdays at the beginning of the New Year to hopefully receive the visas. We celebrated a sweet reunion with our families upon landing in Prague, and we knew to soak in every moment with them throughout the holidays. Petra and I were going to meet in Prague on Tuesday, December 28, to face the complex bureaucracy of the consular process, hoping that the vast volume of documents we brought with us was going to suffice for the questions and requests of the "corps diplomatique de l'ambassade" (the diplomatic corps of the embassy).

> *But blessed is the man who trusts in the*
> *Lord, whose confidence is in him.*
>
> —Jeremiah 17:7

93) Not So Fast

The meeting did not go as planned. The lady sitting behind the bulletproof glass of the consular department of the US mission in Prague was not moved by the documents we brought with us. After we officially applied and filled out an application for the R-1 Religious Worker visa that day, submitting the paperwork to her, she simply looked back through the glass and said, "May I see your seminary diplomas certifying your eligibility for such status, please?" We explained and presented our graduation diplomas from the state ballet school and carried on to elucidate that, though we do not have seminary education, Ballet Magnificat is a recognized religious organization and we, as Christians, hope to qualify for such immigration status. I will never forget the expression on her face that was signaled through the viridescent thick glass. "Unless you are a priest, a nun, a certified religious or charity worker, unless you are a pastor, a bona fide member of a registered religious organization, there is no way for you to be able to receive such status. Being ballet dancers is not, and never will be, adequate for such a grant." With that, she placed the application back into the drawer beneath the glass and returned it to our side for retrieval. "Could we, in that case, apply for another B1/ B2 tourist visa please?" I asked as my brain was spinning and working hard to reconcile the given predicament. "Yes, but because you applied for an R-1 status today, I cannot allow you on the same day to also apply for another type of visa. I am sorry." I could tell that her mind was miles away, perhaps thinking of her own family in America she might not get to see over the holidays because of her duties at the embassy, and these two Czechs were not her concern. She was also bound by the bylaws and regulations of the United States government, which gave her an easy way out of this unpleasant conversation. We needed a miracle. "Thank you very much," we said humbly and walked toward the doors leading to the staircase and eventually to the exit from the premises of the embassy. I was hoping that at the last minute as we reached for the doors, she would call us back and reconsider her position. She never did.

"Prayer is our only option at this point," Petra suggested. "I know, Petra, but the door seems to be shut and locked, bolted, forever closed, and I don't see how this will change…but what else can we do?" This attitude and mind-set, sad to say, is a typical outlook of a Czech person. The precious people of my beloved homeland, myself included, are marked with a strong negative outlook, even spirit, that defines them as one of the most pessimistic nations in the world. "The glass is absolutely and always more than half empty," could be our national motto. As Christians, we are taught by our Father to have faith, to pray continually, to stand on hope; and I had a long road ahead of me to walk on, leaving the defeatist Czech norm behind and instead, with eyes set on Christ, grow in the expectant nature of a Christian.

We were walking through the cobblestone streets of the city, slipping and sliding, as they were slick from the snow that covered them. The wonder of Prague's beauty was shadowed by the bad news we just received. We left the city without a specific plan apart from spending a lot of time in prayer and connecting over the phone as to what we sensed was the leading of the Lord. I have a vivid recollection of standing outside of my parents' apartment building a few days after the faux pas at the embassy. It was a cold but clear winter night. The snow on the ground reflected into the darkness of the night. As I walked our dachshund, Peggy, that night, I looked up as I started to pray. It was difficult to do so inside of the apartment as there was no privacy for an uninterrupted prayer. Outdoors suited me much better. I was talking to the Lord, simply asking for a clear guidance or direction going forward. I am not sure how I was hoping to hear from Him that chilly winter night. The snow resounded with a clear crunch under each step I took. The dog was my only companion as there were no people outdoors due to the chilly temperature of the evening. I could see my breath rising with each spoken word.

"Lord… I see the vastness of the sky, and it reminds me of the vastness of You! Nothing is impossible for You—that I know. What I do not know are the plans You have for me. There is a draw, a desire, to return to Jackson and continue to be a part of Your work there. Is that of You? Last summer, You spoke so clearly as You guided Petra and me into the next chapter. Is that chapter over? Are you bringing us back home to serve You here? Right now, the door to return is closed and…" *"Stop, Jiri!"* The strong sense in my heart was undeniable. *"Son, I know your personality and tendency bent toward fear and unbelief. It might not come naturally to you, but a frequent replay of the things you have seen me do in the past will build stronger faith in your heart and mind. It is time for you to take a step onto another level of faith. Recall and be encouraged. Do not lean on your understanding. It is tainted and easily influenced. Instead, remind yourself of what I have done in you, around you, and what you are learning about me from the pages of the Bible. Then pray without doubting, and you will see me move powerfully!"* I knew that the Lord brought this correction because my initial response to the situation at the embassy was hopelessness and doubt, rather than sound trust and faith in the Almighty God as the prevailing voice in my heart. I received His correction humbly, and I knew that an adjustment in my spirit was a must. I started to pray differently that crisp winter night. I started to pray expectantly. Only a couple of days later, a peace greater than any doubt, surrounded me during another walk with Peggy. In it, I sensed that the "bolted door" would be open and our return to Mississippi would be possible. I felt encouraged and bolstered by the Father's tangible presence. How would He make it happen?

I was able to celebrate the coming of the New Year, 1994, marking the completion of the first year of the new Czech Republic.

The midnight fireworks displayed above my hometown of Ústí nad Labem were spectacularly arrayed against the starry winter night and reflective off the white snow below. The Czech national anthem played on the television featuring images from around the country. As the noise of the fireworks carried on, President Václav Havel delivered his speech to the nation following the conclusion of the anthem. He focused on encouraging the people in the hopeful expectation of the bright future for the Czech Republic, now starting its fifth year of democracy. I was encouraged listening to the president as it reminded me that my God, much greater and mightier than any earthly power or authority, is able to shift any obstacle and open any door. Shifting my focus back to the fireworks outside, I had an urgency to enjoy the view as I was not to stay here in Ústí or in the Czech Republic long term.

Petra and I connected, only to find that both of us were gathering identical stirrings in our spirits. We decided to return to the embassy on Tuesday, January 4, only five days prior to our scheduled return to the States, and submit another application for a visa. Upon our meeting in Prague, we followed the familiar passage to the embassy, proudly displaying the flag of the fifty stars in a blue field and thirteen stripes of red and white alternating top to bottom. Moments before entry, we asked the Lord in joint prayer for His favor. The freezing temperatures caused us to pray swiftly and to the point. Everything was in God's hands, and we trusted Him completely. This time, we applied for a tourist visa, and without any problems or delays, our passports were ready to be picked up later that afternoon with a six-month multi-entry visa issued. We were not returning to Jackson with permission to work, as the R-1 visa would have allowed us to do, but we were returning.

> *Then you will call upon me and come and*
> *pray to me, and I will listen to you.*
> —Jeremiah 29:12

94) Homeless, Not

Upon our arrival in Mississippi, the drastic contrast in weather was undeniable—bright sunny blue skies pierced with beams of bright light were beautifully bedecking the January days. These were much different from the gray clouds so typical for a winter climate of Central Europe. I did not mind leaving the freezing temperatures behind, honestly stated. Initially after our return, Petra was taken to stay with the older widow who promised to keep her for some time before Christmas. I was graciously welcomed to stay for the first week as well.

We dove into the hard work of getting back into shape after three weeks of lounging and feasting on our moms' cooking. I was invited to start touring with the company, starting with the West Coast tour at the end of January, as Petra was invited to train at the school of arts as there was no opening for another female dancer at that time. I could spend countless pages attempting to describe the vast array of emotions within me, ranging from sheer joy to overwhelming hesitation, as I came to realize that I would be a permanent, unofficial and unpaid, addition to the Ballet Magnificat touring company. There was an overwhelming sense of pressure to be a benefit rather than a burden to this small yet powerful group. These were talented and devoted missionaries, called to proclaim the greatness of the Lord through the medium of dance, dedicated to His glory and honor. As excited as I was about venturing out on such an exciting journey of touring and dancing with Ballet Magnificat, I had to solve the immediate and pressing circumstance. Starting the following Monday, I had no place to stay. It is a benefit at times to not know what the future holds. If I knew how prolonged and difficult it was going to be to find a permanent roof over my head, I wonder, would I give up? As the month of January continued to pass with every new day that I knew the Lord had made, I commenced walking down a long eighteen-month path through a season of being without a home. I would bring all my belongings to the ballet every day and awkwardly wait for whoever would invite me to stay with them that night. The ballet has a strict code of conduct in place, forbidding being behind closed doors with members of the opposite gender; and as wise and necessary as this rule is, it made my situation even more difficult, as many members who would be willing to house me for a night simply could not. Sometimes, a dancer who was married took me home for one night, often as a surprise to the spouse, I suppose. It was difficult to add me to any family setting as the dancers of the company lived on a limited income. Every extra mouth to feed was a significant disruption to the budget, and I was extremely grateful for every meal and every bed provided for the night. My deepest gratitude goes to John and Karin Vandervelde, who already had seven children of their own with very little extra to spare, and yet they trusted the Lord to provide as they extended their invitation. Another couple was Rick and Rose Faucher, who often invited me to stay with them for several nights in a row. What a luxury! Touring was a great help as I did not have to worry about food or housing while on the road. I was appreciative and thankful. As this humbling situation continued, I learned to depend on the Father for everything. There was not a single night when I had no place to sleep, nor was there a single day when I went hungry. Kathy's mom, Mary, to all known as Mamaw, hosted me on an occasion. A company dancer, Cassandra, was renting a room from Mamaw already, and by now, Petra also permanently lived with her as well. An extra room in the back of the house became my refuge when no other option presented itself for the night. Finally, in the summer of 1995, Christina, the young fair-skinned friend I met the first day in Mississippi, came to the ballet studio letting me know that her parents, Tom and Barbara, had been in conversation with Ballet Magnificat to offer me a room in their home, open-ended. I was thankful and joyful as I no longer had to depend on the Lord in this particular manner, and I worried that I would become undisciplined in exercising my faith. But the joy and gratitude in my heart were enormous. I lived with the Hudson's for the next two years.

The lions may grow weak and hungry, but those
who seek the Lord lack no good thing.
—Psalm 34:10

95) Touring

There is no count to know the amount of times I crossed the mighty Mississippi in the next many years of touring with the company. As I remember vividly the very first time I saw and crossed it on the way to Jackson, I have lost the wonder of the vastness of the river since then, unfortunately. My very first tour was a journey from the lush Mississippi to the deserts of Arizona and New Mexico, the great state of California, and even Oregon, if I recall correctly. It was a task and a half to keep up with the swift and grueling pace of the tour. At times, there would be sequences of four or even five performances in a row, each in a different city, before a long drive only to do another run of four in a row. Through-the-night drives only added to the exhaustion of it all. The dancers of the company were also the technical crew often entertaining the professional stage hands techies as they marveled watching the thin ballerinas with work gloves display the expertise in knowledge of the technical aspect of theater. I was quickly summoned, trained, and immersed into the setup team. I had a lot to learn. As a foreigner, I loved seeing and experiencing different corners of this beautiful country spanning majestically across the North American continent. From the Grand Canyon to the Hollywood sign, from Mount Whitney to Cape Canaveral, from Chicago's Magnificent Mile to the Grand Tetons, from small towns to large cities alike—all of them were electrifying for me to see, visit, and experience. The performances ranged from shows in theaters, churches, and large arenas, to gymnasiums, auditoriums, and outdoor venues. Ballet Magnificat was busy fulfilling the mission to present the gospel to the largest possible audience and I was privileged to be a part. I loved it all. Often, while on tour, the company would be accommodated in family homes rather than hotels. This brought another exciting element of my American experience into the mix. Like a collection of stamps, the hosts came in different shapes, sizes, personalities, and many levels of gifting in hospitality. Rich and poor, great and not so much, welcoming and overwhelming, outgoing, overly hospitable, curious or disinterested, nervous as well as joyful, we have seen it all. We have stayed in five-star hotels but also in trailer parks, cabins, and campers, sometimes in large mansions, other times in studio apartments, guest houses, basements, bedroom suites, living rooms, and even kitchens. I slept on pull-out sofas, waterbeds, bunk beds, king-size beds, twin-size beds, on the floor, or on soft inflatable mattresses. Some hosts hated animals as some were animal lovers, and a wandering cat or a loud parakeet would only add fun to the experience of spending a night or two with the family. Some were pilots, and an occasional flight in a small single-engine Cessna would be a diversion from the demand of the tour. Some were pastors, entomologists, lawyers and inventors, art collectors, farmers, teachers, doctors, designers. You name it, we stayed with them all. As I'd step into their homes and lives, I was touched by their hospitable spirit. Sometimes, eight short hours concluded the visit, as other times we would stay for days. I have seen and experienced an array of situations and scenarios with the hosts, over the touring years, and several stories to share, stories that could fall into the "no way that happened to you" category, come to mind. I will only share the two most memorable of the bunch.

As it is written, "How beautiful are the feet
of those who bring good news."
—Romans 10:15b

96) Spread Them!

Dallas—one of the first American television series that graced the Czech living rooms following the overthrow of Communism, with a huge popularity may I add—was the saga of the Ewing family and its struggles handling their oil empire. As one can imagine, this dramatic series was a fascinating window to peek through, particularly for a postsocialist society, and create for itself a terribly misguided view of America and the American way of life. Czechs would faithfully return to the television screens, with anticipation and wonder, to watch the soap opera unfold. I myself was influenced in imagining the city of Dallas to be a utopian-like metropolis where all were rich and streets were paved with gold. During my first year of touring, Dallas was one of the company's tour destinations. I was excited. We were scheduled to perform a day after we arrived in the Dallas—Fort Worth area. Picked up by my host, I was driven to a large house and enjoyed a delicious dinner and conversation with all gathered around the table. They were fascinated by my life story as they were also entertained by my expectation of what Dallas truly looked like, anticipation based on the television series. They laughed, and I wondered why. The host—whose name I no longer remember, but for the sake of the story, let us refer to him as Bobby—offered to take me to see downtown if I would be interested. "If I would be interested?" I repeated the question. "Yes, yes, yes…please," I added. We hopped into his truck, which reminded me more of a massive armored vehicle sitting high above the ground, and drove toward the center of the city. When I first started to tour, I desired to purchase a postcard, a lost art form by now, in every town we visited. I purchased them to send a warm greeting to my family back home, allowing them to follow my adventures in the "New World," and I was hoping to find a postcard of Dallas this day. The daylight was vanishing with the setting sun, and after a good twenty minutes of high-speed driving on fairly empty highways, the skyline of the city started to appear in the distance. My anticipation grew. No, the streets were not paved with gold; but Dallas, with skyscrapers and ambiance on every corner, was a true American city. It was built on a perpendicularly intersecting grid of one-way streets, much different from the city layouts back home. Lights were lighting the streets, and the city was buzzing with evening life.

As we drove around, Bobby could hardly speak fast enough, as he was thrilled to dazzle his new Czech friend by proudly presenting his hometown. My reaction and enthusiasm, reciprocated back, only fueled Bobby's pride and joy. He was a Texan, after all, and, boy, was he proud of his Lone Star State. "Is there anything you would be interested in seeing or doing?" Bobby asked. That night, I was wearing a pair of shorts with pirate symbols, including a set of small skulls wrapping around my right leg, a hand-me-down that I should have graciously refused, thinking retrospectively. I was not dressed up to go anywhere, as the original plan was to merely drive through the city and be amazed by it from the comfort of the truck. "The only thing I would like to find would be a postcard to send home, but I am not sure if that's possible since it's late and shops are already closed…but that would be the only thing, thank you," I responded. Bobby drove for a while and then stated that there was a hotel that might have a gift shop open twenty-four hours a day. "They would most likely have a dazzling postcard of the city," I pondered. Hyatt Regency Hotel, interestingly featured in the opening credits of the *Dallas* saga, was a jewel to behold. It was magnificent, overflowing with a sense of luxury, wealth, and comfort. I was embarrassed to walk in wearing my pirate shorts and a T-shirt. My tour guide, Bobby, assured me that we'd be quick—in and out, as he put it. We were told that the gift shop was located on the second story of the large atrium of the hotel. Rising high above the ground level, the balconies of each floor were disappearing into a slim viewpoint, creating an illusion of a structure higher than it actually was. The young Czech boy continued to be marveled by all he saw as the Texan host continued to swell with pride and contentment, witnessing the wide-eyed face of the European. The golden elevator took us to the second floor. It was a little past eight o'clock, and the gift shop was already closed. Bobby seemed more disappointed than I was as he was unable to deliver and fulfill the small wish of his guest. "That is all right. Thank you for trying to do this for me. I loved seeing the hotel as it is beautiful and very impressive." Bobby continued to apologize as we were waiting for the elevator to take us back down. Just as the doors of the lift opened, we saw smoke pour out of one of the balconies high above us, high above the ground level of the hotel. "I am not sure what that is," Bobby said as we stepped into the elevator to ride to the floor below us. As we exited the elevator, we looked up, only to see that the smoke had intensified and something odd was happening up on the high floor of the hotel. We spent a couple of minutes observing the developing situation. We were approaching the exit doors as the lights of police cars and fire trucks flashed through the entry glass. The exit doors opened before us. By now, Bobby lost his Texan calm and cool as he intensified his speed, now running out of the building. I kept up with him; I was trying to, anyway. Just as I thought we made it out all right, I was suddenly grabbed by my neck and thrown against a brick wall leading toward the entrance. "Spread them. Spread them!" Whoever grabbed me and threw me against the brick was now kicking my inner ankles apart one from the other. At the same time, someone else was spreading my arms apart and pressing them against the same wall. As they continued to repeat the same command, prodding my legs further apart, I wondered how far and low they wanted me to go. Being a dancer, I could have gone lower than anyone else they ever attempted to subdue, but I am sure that was not the point. I figured that this was a common practice of intimidation: to yell and create fear and discomfort for the one being submitted. I knew not to fight back and let them do what they thought was necessary. By then, a firm hand of the gentleman, moments ago kicking my inner ankles, started to pat me down. There was no body part exempt from this sudden and thorough search. I started to worry a little, even though there was nothing on me that could be perceived as a weapon; I am sure my "pirate's shorts" offered no assistance to my innocence. The other gentleman was continually holding my wrist and pressing them against the wall. *Where is Bobby?* I was wondering. I had no idea. After I was thoroughly searched, I was suddenly turned around, now facing my attackers. The Dallas police officers were all running around. The two of them holding me called, "We've got them. We've got them!" *Oh my*, I thought, *this is like a movie, an American action thriller of sorts, and I am the bad guy...cool!* "Tell me your name. Tell me your name!" the officer screamed in my face. I was wondering if it was a protocol for everything to be repeated twice, but I replied as calmly as I knew how, "Jiri Voborsky." The puzzled look on the officer's face clearly indicated that he did not get either of the two names. Continuing to be the dominating one in the exchange, I supposed that asking me to repeat it was below him. And so I rolled with it. "Where are you from, and how did you start the fire?" I started to realize and see the whole picture. The police presumed that I was the one who caused the smoke that Bobby and I saw a few minutes ago. "I am from the Czech Republic, and I am here on tour with a ballet company. I did not cause the smoke, sir." I looked him in the eye as I was responding and defending myself all at once. By then, Bobby was brought to my side of the entryway after his interrogation was over, I assumed. "I am so very sorry about all of this," Bobby started. "No worries, no worries at all… This is like a movie… I can't believe that this is my first experience of Dallas… What a thrill," I replied. Bobby was shocked to see me loving this unexpected drama as he was also hugely relieved that I was not experiencing a trauma of sorts. "Is this gentleman… Ji-ri Vor-bos-ky," the police struggled to read my name on my passport, "truly a ballerina, ballerino? What do you call yourself?" He paused in his inquisition of my Dallas host, frantically searching for the proper title of my occupation. "Ballet dancer," I relieved his anxiousness. "Is he really a ballet dancer?" the officer continued. Bobby replied favorably as he also added the place and the time of the performance the following day. "You should come and see for yourself, Officer," I added. "I just might, you know, to verify your information… I am not that much into ballet… I have never met a ballet dancer before, but first, we have to see how all this pans out here tonight, gentlemen," the policeman continued. My arms were still above my head, and my legs were in a wide split position as I was leaning against the wall behind me. It started to become more and more difficult to keep my arms in such an awkward position above my head as the blood flow struggled to make regular circulation. "I think you would enjoy it tomorrow, if you came," was my attempt to convince this tough-looking Texan to come see, no doubt, his very first ballet ever. Just as we were finishing our conversation, a small group of officers walked out of the hotel with a fellow in handcuffs reluctantly walking in their midst. "We got him, guys," was being announced time and again as progression was made toward the open door of a police car. "I guess you didn't do it after all, right?" the officer said while gesturing for me to relax my arms and legs, thank goodness may I add. Bobby replied, "No, Officer, we did not do anything," as he was getting a bit frustrated at the situation. On the way to Bobby's house, he continued to make sure I was okay. This whole episode was a great thrill to me, and I enjoyed it all. We never really found out what happened to cause the smoke and the fire alarms to go off at the Hyatt. As it was a huge disruption to all the guests that evening, to the Czech boy, this was an unforgettable and thrilling adventure. I did not purchase a postcard that evening, but I gained a story to share. The greatest conclusion to it all is the fact that the police officer brought his wife to watch Ballet Magnificat perform the next day, as he came to "verify my facts." I was reminded how all events, no matter how random they might seem to us, are carefully planned by the all-knowing God to unfold in accord to His sovereign will.

> *I will come and proclaim your mighty acts, O Sovereign*
> *Lord; I will proclaim your righteousness, yours alone.*
> —Psalm 71:16

97) A Lady with a Smile

Touring encompasses great experiences as it does challenging ones. One evening could be spent dancing on the stage of a large state-of-the-art facility in a large city, only to try to fit the performance onto a small wooden platform of the local community center the next day. There were times when the company would be housed in a five-star hotel towering over a busy downtown, only to be housed in a trailer home with a family who barely fit into the crowded space of it the following night. But no matter what the setting, I learned quickly that the approach toward every given scenario makes a world of difference in what it is going to be. As the years of touring flowed like a quick stream of a mighty river, most of the experiences fade into a mesh of forgotten events. But then there are few that do not. The following describes another memory that I will, most likely, never forget.

The company was scheduled to perform at Baylor University in Waco, Texas. Baylor was a frequented stop on the touring calendar, and familiarity with the routine of a performance there felt like a well-rehearsed drill. This particular time, one element of the Waco stop was a bit different. John, a company dancer and colleague, and I were directed to wait for the hosts to come and pick us up as we were to stay with them for the next two nights. Staying with complete strangers has its unique charm, at least at times, and it does require a bit of getting used to. Both John and I were completely comfortable to stand on the sidewalk awaiting the arrival of our host. All other dancers were long gone as John and I kept standing and waiting for the ride to our host home. About thirty minutes after everybody else left, an open jeep started to approach us. The music playing through a large speaker attached to the car was felt long before the car was seen. A young teenager jumped out of the jeep after it came to an abrupt and screechy stop. "Are y'all with the choir?" was the opening line of a young man dressed in blue jeans, cowboy boots, and a flannel shirt. "My aunt sent me to pick up her guests," he continued. John and I looked at each other, and with a surprised expression on our faces, we nodded and loaded ourselves and our luggage into the car. "Cool," the young man said as we started to move. I was blown away by the acceleration speed from zero to a hundred in less than a millisecond. Both John and I subconsciously grabbed the frame of the jeep and held on for dear life as the cowboy must have thought that the choir boys were looking for a rodeo ride experience of their lives. I have only seen John's face depicting such sheer panic one other time. It was during a wild taxi ride when on tour in Malaysia a few years later. That resulted in John bribing the taxi driver with double the pay if he would slow down. Here in Waco, no bribes were offered. After a short drive, we arrived at the "aunt's house" and unloaded; and before we could say anything, our driver was disappearing into a cloud of dust, driving away to perhaps something more exciting than introducing two "choir boys" to his aunt. Grabbing our bags, John and I walked toward the house and rang the doorbell. No one came to open the door. We tried a few more times and then decided to simply walk in. As we entered the house, we could not believe the amount of people present within. It felt a bit as if we stepped uninvited into someone's party. As we stood there with our bags in hand, we watched the busyness of the house as people walked in and out of the house and in and out of the entry hall that opened into the living room. "Hello," was John's attempt to catch someone's attention. Finally, a lady holding a glass in her hand spotted us and, with a big smile on her face, gave us a grand Texas welcome. "We are with Ballet Magnificat, and we were brought here to stay for the next two nights. We hope that this is the right place," John continued, clearly expressing his doubts by the tone of his voice. The lady kept smiling as she listened. "So you are with the choir, right?" followed. *Oh my! We jumped into a wrong car—that is for sure*, I thought. John tried one more time to explain that we were ballet dancers, not choir members. Smiling, the lady said that there would be a square-dancing party later that night and that we would be welcomed to join in since we were "dancers" as her fingers gestured quotation marks in accompaniment of that word. "Meanwhile, throw your bags in your room," she continued. "It is upstairs two doors on the right from the staircase." Relieved that we were at the right house, John and I went up the steps. As we started to approach the second floor, we saw a rabbit run across the room. The smell clearly indicated that animals were present, and their droppings were too. Thick carpet made a thorough cleaning difficult, apparently, and we just moved on continuing to search for our designated room. The second door to the right from the staircase was "decorated" with two yellow police tapes crossing in the middle of the frame. On it, we read, "Do NOT CROSS," being repeated over and over. "Interesting welcome sign, ay?" John said as he tried to make the situation appear better than it was. We recounted to make sure we were not about to open the wrong door and then proceeded to do just that. At least we tried. The door was obstructed by something behind it, and swinging it open was impossible. With a good push, while ducking under the police tape, we managed to open it enough to enter the room. Shockingly, the floor was covered with everything imaginable. The one single bed in the corner was a clear sign that one of us would be sleeping on the floor, after some much-needed clearing of adequate space to do so. Being younger, I offered the bed to John, who was visibly struggling to maintain a positive outlook on the given situation. We cleared the floor and went back downstairs to see if receiving dinner would be possible. Our tour schedule indicated that the hosts were to provide it for us. John and I checked a couple of times to make sure that was the case, at least on the paper. As we walked into the kitchen, there I saw something that was appalling and utterly gross. Right there on the kitchen island we saw a large dead deer. Wondering whether or not it was supposed to be an impressive centerpiece to the presumably celebratory occasion of some kind or whether it was a gift brought in by one of the guests, we were unsure. But the bloody beast was sprawling across the kitchen counter, and its smell was filling the room. I am not a hunter, John was, but to us both, this was an unusual sight to see a wild animal simply placed in the middle of the kitchen. We proceeded to ask the lady with the smile whether or not we could get something to eat. She offered us what looked like a "unique Texas version" of pasta Bolognese, served from a large pot on the stove. It tasted great, as both John and I were famished, but what took away from the enjoyment of the food were the small dried pieces of the previously served food glued along the edges of both of our plates. It appeared that the dishes were never thoroughly cleaned but rather just rinsed. I never struggled as badly to eat a plate of food as I did that evening in Waco. People were coming in and out of the kitchen area, but nobody spoke to us. We felt invisible and unwelcome. We were not in anyone's way; it's just that everyone was busy enjoying the occasion for which they had gathered and the two "choir members" did not belong to the group of acquaintances. We washed our plates, and it was a chore to try to detach the dried-up pieces of food from them, and then we returned to our room as it was going to take some time to make it inhabitable. I nestled on the ground, said my "good night" to my fellow traveler, and tried to close my eyes to get some much-needed rest before the next day. It was going to be busy with the setting of the stage, dancing, striking the equipment, to complete the ten-hour workload. Just as I was finally able to drift into a deeper sleep, a sudden loud banjo music awakened me abruptly. The party had shifted to the backyard; and under some string lights, people started to enjoy a good authentic Texan square dance, accompanied by loud celebratory singing. It was a challenge to fall asleep as the country-styled music continued into the night. Waking up the next morning exhausted and not feeling rested, we ventured downstairs again to see if breakfast could be obtained. The house was quiet. The deer was still there, with one eye looking sternly into the kitchen, and the after-party attestation was evident all around. No one was to be found to assist us, and so we simply helped ourselves. John's need for a morning cup of freshly brewed java developed a skill within him to seek out coffee no matter where the given host would possibly hide it. We did not mind the peace and the stillness of the house, following the excitements of the previous night, but a slight worry about our transportation back to Baylor started to surface. The same young man from the day before pulled in just a few minutes after the scheduled pickup time, and with speed easily doubling the given pace regulations of the individual streets, we arrived at the university just in time for the set up. "See y'all tonight," was the only sentence that came out of him as he sped off out of the parking lot. We were excited that he was planning on coming to see the performance that night hoping that he would not be disappointed that, instead of singing, dance and ballet would be the art forms on display. Our worries were proven unnecessary, as no one from our mysterious host family came that night. The young Texan was talking about when he would pick us up again at the end of the night to take us to his "aunt's house" when he had said, "See y'all tonight." He did just that. We returned to a house increasingly smelly with the lifeless deer in the kitchen. We helped ourselves to whatever we could find to eat and went upstairs to our "Do not cross" bedroom for a hopefully good night of rest. Neither John nor I struggled with sleeping well after a performance. We prayed a short prayer thanking the Lord for what He accomplished that evening, and before long, both of us were snoozing and fast asleep. Our young "cowboy" friend took us back to Baylor the next morning to meet the rest of the company before we ventured onto our following destination of the tour. As miles were passing us by, riding our tour bus down the road, the dancers would often share some fun stories and experiences from the hosts. This time, John and I simply could not say anything, as our words would most likely sound ungrateful and maybe even complacent. No, we did not stay at the most hospitable of places; but we did have a roof over our heads, hot water to shower with, and a cup of black coffee to get us going. The lesson I learned in Waco that time was to search for the blessings possibly hidden under the obvious difficulties. We never met the "aunt" our driver kept talking about unless the lady with the smile was her. We will never know.

The cheerful heart has a continual feast.

—Proverbs 15:15b

98) Cassandra

The air-conditioning was not working, once again, and the bus was getting hot and sticky. The scenery outside the windows was passing by, and the company was heading out of town to start another tour. The dancers were all gathered in the front of the bus, sitting on the large sofa and the eight original seats, structured in four rows of two. This day was no different from all the other first days of tour as we gathered to worship, pray, read a Bible passage, and together dedicate the trip to the Lord and to His glory. The only difference that day was the heaviness of my heart. The day before we were scheduled to leave, I received a call from my parents telling me that my beloved grandfather passed away, suddenly and without warning. My grandpa loved buying produce at a farmer's market. The trip to the "paradise of aroma and color" always had a twofold purpose, to get the freshest goods for my grandmother's cooking and to entertain the merchants with his witty commands and occasional jokes. He knew many of the merchants by name, and he was liked by them all. He had no enemies, only good friends he knew for a number of years. This particular Saturday, he left as he did every week; this time not to return home. While he was in the store, congestive heart failure claimed his life abruptly. I was devastated to receive the news, as to my best knowledge, my grandfather did not come to receive the free gift of salvation, provided through faith in Jesus Christ, before his earthly life came to an end. Another burden lying heavy on my heart that day was the tremendous distance between my family and me and not being able to be present for grandfather's funeral and burial. The 5,100 miles separating Jackson and Ústí might as well have been a million light-years. I was unable to go home to walk through this difficult moment of loss with my family and be there to pay my respects to the man who loved me in such a special way. There was nothing I could do about it.

Emotions were challenging to be kept at bay as waves of sadness and pain flooded my heart that day while riding on the tour bus. My precious sisters and brothers were doing their best to bring me comfort and encouragement as there was so little anyone could actually do for me. We started to pray. Passages of scriptures speaking truth and bringing comfort resounded with such clear and powerful peace administered to me by the Lord Himself. The rhythm of songs alternating with prayers and scripture readings was supernaturally effective, and slowly I was being comforted. I prayed for my loved ones as my friends joined with me in knocking on heaven's door, that my family's pain would be used by the Lord to open their blind eyes to see the fragility of life and to start pondering eternal perspective, mainly everlasting life. I was praying earnestly. Even though I am yet to see these prayers answered, I believe with all my heart that the Lord heard my cry that day. Many years after this special prayer time, I learned that the Lord had used those few moments to touch the heart of one of the company dancers and turned them to see me differently from that point on. I learned that Cassandra was deeply moved when she saw my brokenness for my grandfather as well as my fervor of desiring my family to be saved. A cornerstone to a great friendship was laid that day. Nobody but the Lord could see then what all was yet to come through it. Time would tell.

It was tremendously heartbreaking to lose my grandfather without being able to say goodbye. It was difficult being so far away when everything in me wanted to be right there, by my grandmother's side to bring her comfort. But in everything in life, we have a choice. We can choose to regret and wish that things would transpire differently, or we can embrace each challenge with the hope and trust that our God works all things together for the good of those who love Him, as He works all things for His glory and purposes.

And we know that in all things God works for the good of those who love him, who have been called according to his purpose.
—Romans 8:28

99) Visa Miracle

It was the summer of 1995. By now, I had lived in the "Land of the Free" for almost two years. Officially and in the eyes of the government, I was a tourist and a visitor; that was my status. In my heart, I started to adjust to a new country and its culture, customs, and people. I fully embraced the work I was called to do, joining the vision of Ballet Magnificat, that filled me with an overwhelming sense of purpose and joy. Around January of that year, after Petra and I returned from our mandatory trip out of the United States as dictated by the B1/B2 visitor visa regulations, Ballet Magnificat initiated the process of applying for an adjustment of status. The time had come for us both to begin the tedious process to obtain a legal work status in America and start to support ourselves. We needed the Lord to open that door and provide a nonimmigrant work visa

that would permit us to do just that. There are many areas of life in which knowledge or understanding are limited or even nonexistent. Then, when a circumstance arises, often unexpected, we are thrown into an overwhelming process of acquiring the knowledge that was lacking. Think of a diagnosis of an illness you have never heard of that all of a sudden pressures you into a research of its impact, prognoses, and treatment in order to know what steps to take to bring healing and restore normalcy of life. The adjustment of status was just that for the ballet and for me. The immigration laws of the United States are complex and can be difficult when attempted to navigate through. Like crashing waves of a stormy sea that overwhelmed a boat that seemed sturdy and safe a short moment ago, so were the unexpected discoveries of the intricacies of the immigration statutes that seemed incomprehensible and daunting for the limited staff of Ballet Magnificat. A call to an immigration lawyer—and, yes, there are some who build their whole career on helping people find the right course of action when facing an immigration predicament, brought us to an understanding that the "best bet" would be for us to apply for an R-1 religious worker nonimmigrant visa. Immediately, I knew that the road forward just got a bit more likely to require a miracle of the Lord. The R-1 status was the one Petra and I applied for at the embassy in Prague in 1993, when the lady with a scarf gracefully tied around her neck informed us that unless I was a monk or a pastor and Petra a nun, we would never qualify for such a work permit. Neither of those happened. We were simply dancers who believed in using their God-given talent for the Lord, and Ballet Magnificat was the place we were led to do so. In my mind, this was not going to happen, and my tenure in America was, therefore, coming to an end, as my tourist visa was reaching its last season without a possibility for an extension. As Ballet Magnificat continued to tour, there was a moment taken in the middle of each performance, when Tim Dryden, the tour director at the time, humbly approached the audience with a request to pray that "a miracle would happen and Petra's and Jiri's visas would be granted." After countless shows, audience members I had never met before would approach me and her to lay their hands on our sweaty shoulders and pray to the One Who is present in all places at the same time to make a way where there seemed to be no way. Time went on, and the deadline for a farewell departure was approaching quickly. The immigration attorney, Barry Walker of Tupelo, was working tirelessly proving that we, indeed, qualified to be the first-ever ballet dancer to receive such status. Endless documents needed to be submitted. My graduation diploma from the state ballet school as well as my contract with the State Theater provided the needed support of my qualification as a professional. The key element needed to be proven was the connection of our faith, of Ballet Magnificat being a government-recognized religious entity, and of the need for these Czech dancers to be employed here. As it is often true with the Lord, the approval came at the eleventh hour. Two envelopes came to the ballet addressed to me and to Petra. When I opened my letter, I pulled out a document that featured the torch of the Statue of Liberty at its top. It stated the following:

> R-1 Petition for a temporary nonimmigrant reli-
> gious worker
> The above petition has been approved.

Additional information was also printed, but I did not read it in detail, as I was overwhelmed with the basic opening line that took a real fight, fought on knees of prayer, to receive. "Thank you, Lord! Once again, you provided a miracle. I recognize it, and I joyfully acknowledge You for this provision and victory," I prayed. I looked at the document in my hand and read it once more. A line stood out to me that informed the recipient that the approval notice is not a visa. The visa needed to be received at an embassy or a consulate general of the United States. Those are always located outside of the country, obviously; and so for Petra and me, another trip to Prague was inevitable. Upon reaching the building of the US embassy there, my stomach tightened, expressing the nerves I was feeling as I stepped onto the premises of the complex. The long wait on the bottom floor was followed by the calling of my name to progress upstairs to the room with the bulletproof glass where I would face the consular employee of the embassy. I did not know what would follow, and a hefty file of documents was, therefore, in my hand. The one difference was the petition approval I now had that was nonexistent before. I approached the window and saw the same lady—this time without a scarf but wearing a similar, if not identical, business suit—sitting on the other side of the glass. I handed her my passport and the approval notice. She took it, reviewed it, and then started to fervently type on her keyboard. I could not see the computer screen to know whether she was inputting information or researching some. Time seemed to pause. My knees were shaky, and my stomach continued to growl. The lady reread whatever just popped on the screen and then looked at me. "You did it, I see. There has never been a dancer who was approved for the R-1 visa, did you know that?" she asked through the microphone attached to her station. "I assumed so, ma'am," was my to-the-point reply. "I, and many others, have prayed for this miracle to take place," I added. The lady paused as if pondering my statement. "Well, God must have heard and answered your prayers. Congratulations! Please come back around two o'clock this afternoon to retrieve your passport and your new visa." And so that day, Petra and I were officially government-recognized religious workers who did not preach with their words but shared the gospel of Christ through the medium of dance.

Call to me and I will answer you and tell you great
and unsearchable things you do not know.
—Jeremiah 33:3

100) Wild Provision

I often wonder if I am the only one that experiences prolonged seasons of silence from the Lord. Initially, those thoughts kept me wondering if there was a recurring insufficiency in me that faithfully disqualified me from the attention that, I believed, God gladly granted to every believer. The mentality based on the ask-and-immediately-receive principle reflected on my spiritual immaturity. In my early years of walking with the Lord, this phenomenon was much more profound in my life than it thankfully is today. I recognize the patient work of the Holy Spirit in me, Who, while highlighting many personal shortcomings, teaches me that God's briskness to answer my prayers is not hinging on me but solely on Him. The Lord works His will in His perfect timing. I am still learning to trust Him when prayers seem to be slow in getting answered. I know that my God is in control.

Complete dependence. As one growing up in a city with a vast public transportation network, I was unprepared to come to Jackson, where such a matrix of buses does not exist. To get anywhere, I was dependent on the gracious gesture of others to drive me. I needed a way to gain some independence in that manner; I needed a car. Now that I was able to receive a paycheck, one would assume that a loan would be possible. That might be true, but the size of my initial pay forbade me from even thinking about purchasing a bicycle, much less a car. Fifty dollars was my starting salary. I was able to stretch those five thousand pennies far, but a purchase of a car was simply not an option.

It was the latter part of October. The leaves were showing off with a display of bright autumn colors. The company was on a tour of the mid-Atlantic portion of the country with its final stop in Baltimore, Maryland. Cassandra was born in the "Charm City," and her family lived in the small town of Jarrettsville, located some thirty miles north of Baltimore. Cassandra invited me to stay at her family's house and meet her parents during our three-day stop. Again, put me on a stage and I am in my element; put me into a room of strangers and I am a fish out of the water, desperately trying to find a way out of the awkward situation and back into the safety of the known environment. But it was an opportunity to meet the parents of a coworker whom I enjoyed getting to know more, and so I accepted the invitation. Upon our arrival in Baltimore, we were met and greeted by Cassandra's mom, Cristina. Though of a smaller build, this gray-haired lady was overflowing with joy, enthusiasm, grace, and bold countenance of Jesus, greatly flowing out of her small frame. Loaded into her car, we advanced through the winding roads of the "Old Line State," passing picturesque farms with bands of horses roaming amidst white fences, clearly defining the boundaries of each property, and countless fields that in the springtime must have displayed bountiful harvest. Forty-five minutes had passed before we started to approach Cassandra's hometown. Judging by the excitement that was rising in her countenance, we must have been near. We arrived at a farmhouse located downhill from the main road. The farm consisted of two family homes, a larger-than-life barn, and a small pond. A cornfield gently wrapped around the property's line, only to finish the movie-like setting, totally mesmerizing the city boy from the Czech Republic. Cris invited me to step into the house that breathed history, character, and uniqueness of style. This was where Cassandra and her three younger brothers grew up. A church steeple was rising beyond the cornfield, as I looked out the window. "That is where I came to know the Lord," Cassandra said, pointing toward

302

the church. "Good ole Baptist pastor's preaching of the fire and brimstone brought me to realize my need for a Savior… It was effective," she concluded, laughing lightly at the statement she just made. The house was rather small and compact. What it did not possess in size, it surely held in charm. A brief tour gave me an idea of what it must have been like to raise four kids here, considering the busy morning house traffic, especially the rotational use of the one and only bathroom by six people, for example, and the scheduling it would require with activities and hobbies that demanded driving out of Jarrettsville into surrounding towns, mainly Baltimore and Bel Air. Cristina served coffee and hot tea as we sat at the family table and engaged in a light conversation. As time went on, I was growing tentative, knowing that Cassandra's father, Harry, was about to step through the door after a long day of teaching at the Towson State University. Born in Warsaw but raised in Austria during World War II, Harry grew up observing a much different world from the one I grew up in, or the one Cassandra herself knew to be the norm. All I knew of him prior to our first meeting was the fact that he was a history professor, smart and witty; held his PhD with expertise on Eastern Europe and the Soviet Union; and, according to Cassandra, did not know the Lord. The moment came, and the long anticipation finally came to an end as the door opened and Harry returned home. We cordially introduced ourselves to each other. He did not say much but did ask a lot of questions about the situation back home, keeping a close eye on the European development while desiring to compare the media message with a firsthand account. As the evening continued to unfold, it became clear to me that Harry was a strict teacher who expected every student to put in the required work in order to receive a good grade in his class. I learned that he was also an author writing college-level textbooks, as he also did research on the Vietnam War, among other things. It was a pleasure meeting him that day, but I knew that I could never keep up in a debate of any kind with a man who owned such vast knowledge and that should a discussion arise, it would only lead to embarrassment and defeat. "Keep Harry at a safe distance," was the strategy I adopted quickly. The next day was the performance day, and we spent most of the time preparing for it and gearing up to deliver the last show of the tour. Cris and Harry both attended the performance. After the performance, I was to spend the last night of the tour, hosted at the Piotrowskis. It was a late hour of the night by the time we returned back to the farmhouse. Harry was still up, watching sports on the television. A quick conversation took place about the performance while Cassandra and I ate a late dinner. Harry asked basic questions, but it was apparent that he did not want to engage in a deeper conversation regarding faith and spiritual things. He asked about my current visa and monetary situation as he experienced being an immigrant himself, when his family first resettled in America. I shared briefly not knowing how much Harry really wanted to know. Then he asked me if I had a dollar. Puzzlement on my face clearly indicated that I was confused about the purpose of the question. "Yes, I do have a dollar." Harry looked out the window of the house, peering into the darkness, and continued to speak with a calm voice. "I own a two-door Isuzu. Do you know that line of Japanese cars?" I had never heard of it, and I admitted that to him. "Well, I have an older model parked outside, and it has been a great and dependable car. The problem is that, due to the sodium chloride used on the roads here, during the winter seasons, its frame has some rust on it, and the car no longer passes the technical inspection in the state of Maryland. If you are interested, I will sell it to you for one dollar, it really being a symbolic price, because I know that it will pass the technical inspection in Mississippi. Are you interested?" I could not believe it. This man I just met, a man with whom I had very little in common, would show me such generosity. "Do you know how to drive a stick shift?" Harry continued. I just received my driver's license a few months ago, but I had never driven a car with a standard transmission. "No, I don't," I said, not knowing if that was going to change his offer. "Well, you will have around a thousand and one hundred miles to learn." He chuckled. Surely enough, the next day, I drove away from the cute farmhouse in Maryland in a car, my first car, a beautiful two-door Isuzu. Initially, my skills were rough, navigating the shifting of the gears, but the seventeen-hour drive to Jackson provided me with plenty of opportunity to not only learn but conquer this skill. Cassandra and I followed the ballet bus back to Mississippi, and I must admit that as long as the drive was, it did not provide enough time for me to fully gather and grasp the magnitude and the goodness of the Lord, manifested in this little Japanese white wonder. Little did I know then that the Lord was going to provide six other free-of-charge vehicles in years to come. How great is our God!

Every good and perfect gift is from above, coming down from the Father of heavenly lights, who does not change like shifting shadows.
—James 1:17

101) Cassandra's Visit

I recall reading and examining poetry in school. It is fascinating to think that a huge quantity of time could be spent on tearing apart a written work of a poet and discussing their intentions, feelings, and message for hours. Often, I must admit, the quantity of the spent time did not produce the quality of the gained knowledge the teacher hoped for and expected. I dreaded all of these "unnecessary" strenuous exercises of the mind. Then several years later, I was in the process of discovering the beauty, power, depth, and direct benefit of the Bible as I started to have daily morning devotional times. Early on I learned that in order for this reading and studying of the scriptures to take place, it must happen moments after I first wake or it won't happen at all. I  cannot get up and get my cup of hot and aromatic Earl Grey tea, as I cannot get up and take a cold shower to perk me up due to my undisciplined nature. I must pick up my Bible right when my eyes first open, run to the Lord before anyone or anything else, and then and only then enjoy the above mentioned amenities of my spoiled morning routine. If the reading doesn't happen first, sadly, it will most likely not happen. After I received my first Bible, as the parting birthday gift of the Husbands, I dove into the reading and studying of it. I discovered the Word of God to be an overwhelming source of information, inspiration, and teaching combined with a deep content and profound personal message. I would skip books such as Leviticus and Numbers to focus on passages more relatable to my immature spiritual age. As I kept reading different books of both testaments, I came across a book of poetry, and if I could, I would roll my spiritual eyes. *Great, poems!* I thought. *I hope they won't be as boring as those we perused in school.* My attitude was to be quickly corrected as my eyes glided across profound pieces of truth found in the opening chapter of the book of Psalms, flowing from the heart of their writers, that immediately connected with my own spirit. "Blessed is the one who does not walk in step with the wicked (1)... Serve the Lord with fear and celebrate His rule with trembling (2)... But you, Lord, are a shield around me (3)... Lead me Lord in your righteousness (5)... If there is guilt on my hands (7)... How long must I wrestle with my thoughts (13)?" These pieces of poetry are beautiful. Rather quickly, I realized that David, Solomon, Asaph, and other authors of the psalms were greatly relatable and their writings expressed joy, sorrow, fear, faith, acknowledged sin, demonstrated repentance, portrayed seasons of rejoicing as well as seasons of desperation. Slowly, I came to realize that this book would be one that I would keep returning to as my own life continued to unfold before me. I do not build friendships easily, nor do I have a desire for having many friends with whom I might have shallow relationships. I would much prefer to have few friends whom I know deeply and who know me the same, friends who are willing to speak into my life faithfully, profoundly, and continually. As I kept being inspired by the psalms, I would use them to communicate to the Lord about the deep feelings of my heart. I would relate to David and use his words to pour my gratitude at the feet of Jesus or there before the throne of God express a hesitation or even fear I was experiencing in different seasons of life. I was also reminded to offer thanksgiving to the Lord for Who He is, what He personally means to me, and for all that He has done. One of the objects of my rejoicing was my friendship with Cassandra. I was recognizing her small but continual gestures of kindness that made a deep impact on me. The Lord was using His faithful servant to be the one who went out of her way to bless me and to reassure me that the Lord saw me, that He was near, and that He was for me. I was deeply appreciative of Cassandra even though I did not exactly know how to truly express the extent of my gratitude. Not until Christmas of 1995. Five years prior, Cassandra spent her senior year of high school in Oldenburg, Germany. Harry, her father, was offered a position teaching at the Carl von Ossietzky Universität, and the whole family moved to Germany. This one year spurred a love for Europe in Cassandra's heart. In 1995, she and her family planned to return and spend Christmas in Germany. I was excited to extend an invitation for Cassandra to travel to Ústí, to meet my family and to experience the beauty of Prague dressed in a blanket of newly fallen snow as it meets the sweet aroma of freshly baked cinnamon swirl pastries filling the streets. Petra also invited Cassandra to visit Liberec, and before long, the trip was planned to the last detail. I was excited to have Cassandra come!

It was a dreary day, as the Delta plane touched down in Prague. The Ruzyně airport was virtually unchanged since the Velvet Revolution and sadly displayed the elements of socialist architecture, known to focus on its function and completely omit beauty. The heavy concrete skeleton of the building was decked with gray marble stones on the ground and on the walls, and every arriving traveler was welcomed with the gloom of the terminal's cold atmosphere. Fortunately, the jet lag mixed with adrenaline and excitement of the trip assisted in overlooking this gateway to the Czech Republic. My dad and my grandmother came to meet us in Prague as my mom and Míra stayed in Ústí. Petra's parents were there waiting as well. The hugs and kisses given and received between all of us became the new norm of the arrival ceremony. Cassandra was thrown into the mix of it without any prior warning. Mr. Grůša, Petra's dad, believed in the theory that a foreigner will understand Czech if the native shouts it loudly. And so he did. Cassandra was kissed on her cheeks more that day than ever before; that is for sure. The plan was to start

Cassandra's visit in Ústí. A week later, a trip to Prague would reunite her with Petra, who would escort her to Liberec, where the rest of the Piotrowski family would also arrive that day to enjoy an authentic Czech Christmas.

My dad was the best tour guide. On the way to Ústí, we stopped at the chateaux of Libochovice. This four-wing baroque residence—surrounding a courtyard with two stories of balconies, decorated with arched colonnades—remained to be one of the most visited and popular castles in the country. Beautiful red frescos decorated the walls of the structure, and large English gardens completed the magic of the grounds. The snow-topped trees and bushes added a unique atmosphere, and the short stop there was a great start to the visit.

Cassandra was to be accommodated in my grandmother's apartment on the bottom floor of the building. Grandmother spoke no English and also bought into the belief that loud Czech will be miraculously understood by the foreign visitor. She was the perfect host, and I wish I could have been a fly on the wall to watch the two of them communicate. Czechs do not often open their apartments to guests, as the premises are too small to accommodate overnight company, and I worried that the language barrier and the small quarters would provide difficulties for Cassandra and my grandmother as well as for my parents. The opposite was true, and they all did well in making Cassandra feel welcome. My mom and dad took an immediate liking to her, and a barrage of questions about our relationship was almost endless. It mattered not how many times I explained that we were only friends; my parents were not buying that to be true. One of the greatest memories of the visit was when my dad took us to his favorite lake, where he spent countless hours fishing during the year. It was frozen over, and Cassandra and I were gliding and sliding on the ice surface while he took pictures. The week went by fast, and it was time to say goodbye. My parents both truly enjoyed meeting this young American lady. Cassandra was also a representative of the kindness and gentleness of the Lord, shattering and eradicating their post-Communist and atheism-influenced preconceived ideas of what a young Christian would be like. All that to say, Cassandra won their hearts. As it was hard to part, the time had come for Cassandra to travel to Liberec and meet her own family there and, in that circle, enjoy the celebration of the humble coming of Jesus, the Savior of the world.

> *Praise be to the Lord, the God of Israel, because he*
> *has come and has redeemed his people.*
>
> —Luke 1:68

102) Move Over

As I sit in my favorite chair—Bob as we call it, tucked in the corner of the family room and situated by a large window peering into the courtyard of our beautiful home, a courtyard decorated with festive lights creating a cheerful atmosphere—I continue to write my life story the Lord has allowed me to live and share. There are countless memories to choose from that could serve as topics for this next chapter. I am tempted to write about a trip to Dresden, Germany, when I lost all my documents and money. I am entertaining the idea of writing about a performance in Abilene, Texas, when a bald-faced hornet flew into my costume, relentlessly crawled under my jacket, and stung me repeatedly while I kept smiling and focusing on the choreography. I am wondering whether or not to tell a story of my first West Coast tour, when I was accommodated in a large Los Angeles mansion and led to a room featuring a king-size bed situated in the middle of the room and surrounded by floor-to-ceiling mirrors on all four walls… There is so much to choose from, and yet I feel that the following story is one that might bring you encouragement.

I was a free bird. At least I felt like one. With my new Isuzu car, I had the freedom to roam around the city of Jackson as much as I wanted. I was independent of others and could go to places as I pleased. The days between tours were few in number; and I enjoyed them by exploring Jackson, often driving around the capital, paying $0.99 per gallon of gasoline, and finding neighborhoods and old Southern plantation homes hidden in unexpected places. This one particular day, I took a ride, only to be interrupted by my stomach strongly protesting the long time without any intake of food. I had been given a coupon for a Whataburger chicken sandwich, and so I ventured to this previously unknown franchise establishment located on a major business and shopping street of the city. I pulled into the parking lot and parked the car facing the building of the restaurant. I ordered the free sandwich without fries or a drink and sat at a table facing the window. My pride and joy, the white Isuzu, was facing me "looking in" as I sat down and pulled out my Bible. I closed my eyes to thank the Lord for providing such a fine meal. There were very few other guests in the restaurant, which was perfect, as I wanted to enjoy reading and studying the Word before I went home for the night. As I took my first bite, my mouth was filled with the flavor and the juices of the sandwich. I thought it was delicious! I knew that this was going to be a fine hour spent with my Lord. I was in the gospel of Mark at that time. My bookmark was carefully placed at the end of the tenth chapter. As I dove into the next segment, I started to read about the Lord commanding His disciples to untie a colt, precisely found at a perfectly described place, to be used as Jesus entered Jerusalem while the crowds were singing "Hosanna" and waving branches before Him. I continued to read about Jesus spending the night in the village of Bethany. The story continued to tell of the Lord passing a fig tree the next day and, while not finding any fruit on it, cursing it. I felt the sauce running down my fingers as gravity was working its magic, and I was too slow combating it due to my careful reading of Mark's account. I took another bite and cleaned my hands some, only to return to the reading. I read about Jesus overturning the money changers' tables at the temple, about the teachers of the law looking for a way to kill him, which I thought was a steep penalty for causing some ruckus in the courtyard... This was my first time ever reading the four Gospels at the beginning of the New Testament, and I was soaking them all in. The story continued to mention the withered fig tree, cursed by Christ just one day prior. Peter was captivated by the finding of the withered tree and pointed it out to the Lord. Jesus responded to Peter and the other disciples standing by saying, "Have faith in God. Truly I tell you, if anyone says to this mountain, 'Go, throw yourself into the sea,' and does not doubt in their heart but believes that what they say will happen, it will be done for them. Therefore I tell you, whatever you ask for in prayer, believe that you have received it, and it will be yours." I stopped reading, as there were several words that stood out to me strongly from the text. I was young in my faith, but I believed with a childlike faith that the Lord could do anything. *"Have faith, do not doubt, believe, whatever you ask, it will be yours."* I was getting excited as my heart was being fueled by the encouragement from on high. The Lord was allowing me to experience His presence right there in Whataburger, sitting by a table and looking onto the busy street. As I continued to ponder the reading, I saw that my Isuzu was parked next to an empty parking place. "You can tell the mountain...," was echoing in my heart, "and it will move." I was looking at my two-door wonder parked outside, and while the sandwich sauce continued to drip on my fingers, I closed my eyes to pray. "Father God, thank You for this time here. I love how You are not limited by any place to meet with Your children. Even here in Whataburger. What an amazing God You are! Lord, I feel the boost of faith. It is electrifying and difficult to put into words. But I desire to ask You, Lord, to demonstrate Your power to me, Father... Lord, my faith is strong, young perhaps but strong, standing rooted in You... Lord Jesus, I ask You, sitting here, to please move my car, for which I give You praise again. Move it to the next spot over. I know this is a crazy request, but I know You can do it, Lord, and I just finished reading about the challenge You presented to Your disciples. Lord Jesus, would You please move my car... Thank You! In Jesus's name...amen." My eyes were closed shut. The sauce started to harden on my fingers, but it did not bother me one bit. I believed that when I opened my eyes, either the car would already be in the slot next to where I parked it, or I would see it shift itself over.

Before I continue with the story, I want to take a little detour to challenge you, the reader, with a simple question. How big is your faith? Do you believe that the Lord only works within the frame of "reason"? Do you view the power of God as something only fitting for the yesteryears? Is God able to part the sea today as He did in Moses's era? We are strongly influenced by the loud voice of the world around us continually challenging us to move away from believing the unbelievable. Our God is the same today as He was in the garden of Eden with Adam and Eve. His power is not limited nor outdated by the advancement mankind has made; and every reason that speaks against the principle, the authority, the Kingship of God—denying the sole provision of salvation through faith in Jesus Christ—will one day be silenced and deemed wrong. The Lord is just as able to perform miracles today as He was able to perform them in times gone by. Healing, provision, deliverance, protection, and above all salvation are taking place daily all around the world. It is erroneous to view these works of God as ordinary. We must recognize the pull the world has on us, on our behavior, on our thinking, on our opinion, on our faith. We must beware of the popular current stream of dangerous water that continually lures us into menacing zones of unbelief. We must be reflecting the faith of the disciples and continue in believing the improbable, the extraordinary, the supernatural power of our God and of His Christ.

Can you guess what I saw when I opened my eyes? Can you imagine the overflow of my emotions as I saw the miraculous shifting of the parked car? If you can imagine it, that makes it two of us. As I opened my eyes, the Isuzu was parked exactly where I placed it. I watched it intently for another moment or two, hoping that it would start moving sideways from one slot to the next. It never happened. "Lord, I don't understand," was the opening headline of my protest. "Why did You not move the car? Did I not believe enough? Did I not pray earnestly enough? I am not asking for a mountain to move, Lord. I just wanted a car, my car at that, to move one parking slot over. Why did You not do it, Father?" As I sat there in Whataburger, complaining to the Lord about the epic fail of this spiritual experiment, I sensed the Lord speaking to my spirit. Suddenly and to the point. *"Jiri, it was not your lack of faith. It was not My unwillingness to answer your prayer either, son. I only have one question for you: If I went ahead and moved the Isuzu over, would you glorify Me in the miracle, or would you be glorifying, directly or indirectly, yourself and the power of your faith?"* I was surprised to be asked that question. Initially, it felt unfair, but as I allowed the Holy Spirit to deal with me, I saw clearly that this "experiment" was much more about me than it was about my Lord. As I finished my soggy sandwich, I packed my stuff and started to walk out to my car. As I opened its door, I realized that the value of the learned lesson was much greater than the wonder of the would-have-been-shifted car. With that, I started the engine and drove home, grateful and thankful for the patient teaching of the Lord in my life.

> *I tell you the truth, if you have faith as small as a mustard*
> *seed, you can say to this mountain, 'Move from here to there'*
> *and it will move. Nothing will be impossible for you.*
> —Matthew 17:20–21

103) Another Revolution!

I am going to fast-forward on the invisible timeline of my story. Pretend to be with me in the year of 1999. Six years of working with Ballet Magnificat have gone by rather quickly. I had grown comfortable with the way of life easily defined with the phrase "Why thoroughly unpack if we are about to leave again!" People at church were accustomed to see me once or twice a month, and our conversation almost always circled around the simple, sadly identical, conversation:

"Hey, Jiri! How was tour?"

"It was great, thank you!" was my reply, sparing them the details of the trip as the passing in the commons of the church rarely permitted for a deeper conversation to take place.

"Great, when do you leave again?"

That usually took me a moment to figure out, but an answer of sorts, "Next Friday," would be my reply.

"Wow, and where to this time?" would be the concluding element of the exchange, followed by my answer of "I am not quite sure… I am sorry."

I lived in a studio apartment on the tenth floor of a high-rise in downtown Jackson at the time. The view from the two windows, sprawling across the entire wall of the apartment, offered a view of the Beaux Arts rotunda of the 1903 New Capitol Building, the classically styled limestone building of the Supreme Court, as well as overlooking the Midtown section of the city. The governor's mansion was located a short walk away. I loved living downtown, experiencing that side of life in America. My apartment was small, but it was my place away from the hustle and bustle of tour. As I pointed out at the beginning of the chapter, the year was 1999. There were no really affordable cell phones, I had no television, and I could not afford landline service. I called this season "living in the tower." The time at home was spent in reading, Bible studies, drawing, and finding creative ways in my kitchen while living on a fifteen-dollar-a month food budget. Great times. I had a plethora of time to think, pray, and listen to what the Lord was saying and communicating to me. I need to confess to you that I was not pleasant to be around that much back in the day. I could be moody, pretty moody, *actually* very moody at times. My low food budget causing malnutrition is my excuse; but in reality, and in all honesty, my self-centeredness is to be blamed. I loved being alone, disconnected from anyone and everyone. My thoughts were my only company, and I could follow them down some troublesome paths of imagination. I was convinced that I never wanted or needed to get married. I thought that I was "just fine" on my own. I was afraid that I would be a burden to a potential wife, and to exclude the notion of marriage was a whole lot easier than addressing my attitude and my heart.

But, God! Yes, the Lord, faithful and patient shepherd, never leaves us unattended, especially when the god of "me" starts to replace the true God on the pedestal of my heart. The Bible tells us in the book of Deuteronomy, "For the Lord your God is a consuming fire; He is a jealous (impassioned) God [demanding what is rightfully and uniquely His]." If I am a child of God, then not some of me but all of me belongs to Him, and my self-centered attitude must bow its knee in submission. If I am unwilling to do it the easy way, learn the lesson and pass the test, the Lord is more than able to intensify His tactics and methods to open my eyes and break my stubbornness. I was a slow student, I suppose, and the Lord was planning to do just that—change me whether I was willing or not. The church I attended at that time, Cornerstone, was led by Pastor Dan

Hall, a powerful and passionate preacher who believed that the Lord deserved to be loved, obeyed, and honored through every aspect of a believer's life. I met Dan and a few other brothers for a weekly Bible study in the Quarter, a French neighborhood of Jackson modeled after New Orleans. Our gatherings would consist of a quick fellowship followed by a deep and long dive into the Word. We followed a Bible study plan and a book written for men who were stubborn, like me. One Thursday in early February, we all gathered for a study, and as usual, we enjoyed some great encouraging manly fellowship. Dan was in his element of poking at us with his witty jokes. Then he transitioned with the statement, "All right, fellows, today we cover a chapter on marriage. What do you think about that!" His brown laser-like eyes looked at us sitting around the table. This was a group comprising of brothers who are single like myself, engaged, married, and even divorced. The response to Dan's statement clearly indicated the overall disapproval of the idea to talk about something that personal and potentially uncomfortable. "Well, I did not come up with the idea and the layout for marriage. God did…and if He did that, it lends itself to be a topic worth exploring. I have no doubt that He will speak to us all. I am convinced of that!" With that, we prayed and started to unfold the basic foundation the Lord instituted for the covenant relationship between a man and a woman. I was dying. Nothing in me wanted to be there, and nothing in me wanted to "waste" time on a topic that was a done deal in my mind. "Marriage is not for me. What is there to study?" was my resolute attitude hidden deep in my mind. I was scared of Pastor Dan, and I knew that if I were to tell him how I felt, he would tear me to pieces in a theological debate that I was for sure to lose. The lesson was over in a flash, and I was leaving the Quarter unchanged in my view and opinion. The Bible study came with significant homework, and surely enough, there was a bounty of material to be covered at home, including filling in blanks, answering questions, and reading a vast amount of Bible verses. I sat in my studio apartment looking at the study and fighting my ego. "I don't want to. Oh, I don't want to… This is crazy…and pointless… Lord, I don't want to do this!" God would not have any of my attitude. His authority was clearly present in my room, and His direction was unequivocal. The Lord desired for me to go through the marriage chapter, and that was the end of the discussion. And so I did. There were six short homework assignments under the umbrella of the chapter, and I reluctantly started to face one at a time. It was an eye-opening experience to read and study the very structure of the marital covenant God had ordained and orchestrated. What was mind-blowing, however, was the deep reflection of the earthly covenant relationship to the heavenly one. I was floored! As I kept plowing through the chapters, I was humbled once again and all over again by the inclusion of myself into the kingdom of God. What an amazing privilege to belong to the Royal Family of Christ. I was a member of the church and, therefore, directly a part of Jesus's bride. It was a bit too much to grasp when I saw it from this point of view, but I was overwhelmed with gratitude nonetheless. Then came the fifth day of the homework. I no longer protested to do it. I was faithfully looking up verses and filling in the blanks. As my hand wrote the answers onto the designated lines, my eyes saw that, though most of my scribbles were not legible, my heart was experiencing a revolution of a kind. As firmly as I knew that I had no desire to get married prior to the "marriage chapter," I now knew that there was a genuine longing for a wife and a family in my heart. I was shocked and utterly surprised. I was certain that it was not a change of heart per say but rather an experience of uncovering a treasure the Lord had "prehidden" a long time ago. This discovery threw me for a loop, but I was excited to discover this element of my heart's desire. I was lying on my futon sofa, looking on the lighted rotunda of the capitol realizing that Jiri Voborsky was, indeed, called to give up the selfish "leave me alone" way of living and step into a life of partnering with a bride, a companion, a wife. But who? Who would want to marry someone like me, a man who is and requires such a high maintenance? This one I had no choice but to leave it up to the Lord. I needed to step out of the way before I would mess things up. And so I did!

*I have been crucified with Christ and I no longer live, but
Christ lives in me. The life I live in the body I live by faith in
the Son of God, who loved me and gave himself for me.*
—Galatians 2:20

104) White Nights

It had been almost six years since I came to Jackson, and I had
the time of my life. I was happy in my role at Ballet Magnificat,
using the gift of dance to bring hope to so many different people all
over America. I was living a dream, and I loved it. I was reminded
almost daily that it is not my talent that makes a difference in anyone's life; it is solely the Lord Who accomplishes all alterations of
the human soul and heart, and I am simply privileged to be the tool
in the Master's hands. That was just fine with me. I was much more
effective as a tool than I would be as a carpenter. Submission to my
Savior brought me joy! I was honored to meet so many different people while on tour. It was almost overwhelming to keep up with the
names and titles, careers, and callings of all these wonderful people.
While touring, I got to share my story time and again, and every
time I did, I was reminded of its rarity and wonder. During one
tour stop, I met Vietnamese Christians who served as missionaries
in Saint Petersburg, Russia. We connected after a performance, and
before I left the next morning, we exchanged phone numbers and
e-mails. They invited me to come and visit them in Russia. What was
unique about the invitation was the fact that it was not my first one
that spring. I was also invited to go on a mission trip with New Tribe
Missions, an organization devoted to reaching secluded Indian tribes
in the Amazon Jungle of South America with the gospel of Christ. I
was thankful for the invites, but I just could not picture how any of
them would come to pass. Again, I had to learn that when the Lord
moves, we don't argue, we don't complain, and we just follow His
lead. Before I knew it, I was permitted to take a three-month sabbat-
ical from Ballet Magnificat. I had the ticket and the visa to Russia
and a fully paid confirmation for a spot with the New Tribe Missions.
Everything was lining up beautifully, and I could not have done a

better job planning it myself. I decided to utilize both trips with purposeful prayers about my future—particularly focused on marriage, the timing of it, but most importantly seeking the will of God regarding the biggest question of all, the bride. The day of my departure arrived. The plan was to spend two weeks in Saint Petersburg, one week in Moscow, one week at home with my family, and then five weeks with the Yuqui tribe in the jungles of Bolivia. Cassandra offered to drive me to the airport. There was sadness in her eyes seeing me leave for Europe, and I must admit there was sadness in my heart also. We were close friends and treasured our friendship as a gift from the Lord. We hugged, we said goodbye, and she drove off.

I flew to Prague, only to connect to a flight to Saint Petersburg. Spring in Europe is my favorite. Everything is green and lush, flowers and trees are blooming, temperatures are perfect, and the air is fresh. Springtime landing in Prague always offers a view of endless fields of bright-yellow rapeseeds stretching across endless horizons. It does not matter how many times I traveled to Prague; coming home has never lost its wonder and its beauty. I was once asked in a newspaper interview where I felt more at home, in Czech or in America. I answered simply and honestly: "When I am flying to Prague, I am going home, and when I am flying to the States, I am coming home." But that's a rabbit trail. I transferred to my flight to Saint Petersburg and with excitement waited to see this city that I had read about since I was a little boy. This was going to be my very first visit to the Russian Federation. I could not wait. The plane landed at the Pulkovo Airport, and after clearing customs, I met my Vietnamese friends. They drove me to an old apartment in the center of this metropolis of four million inhabitants. My exhaustion from the travels was overcome with the excitement of being in Russia. The drive from the airport was filled with untiring soaking-in of everything we passed along the way.

Saint Petersburg is a breathtaking city overflowing with many monuments of epic proportions. From the Winter Palace to the famed Nevsky Prospekt, Tsarskoye Selo, the Mariinsky Theater, St. Isaac's Cathedral, and many more. The city is truly a wonder, nestled near the Finnish Gulf, and located some eight hours northwest of

Moscow. I was excited to work with these missionaries, who taught English in Petersburg's public schools and used this doorway to share the hope of Jesus. I was able to connect with many students, and I was honored to dance on many occasions, using dance that is such a cherished art form of the cultural fiber of the Russian people. I assisted in food distribution to families that had needs beyond my imagination. All of this was such a privilege. I had many hours to myself as well. I spent some of them wandering around the city, watching "дедушки" (*de-dush-key*) or grandpas playing chess games in parks. I saw the Kirov Ballet, named one of the best ballet companies in the world, perform Don Quixote. I visited the Hermitage Museum; but more than anything, I walked around the city, sat in cafés sipping black tea, and watched the locals go about their days and lives. This is my favorite thing to do wherever I travel, by the way. I also spent hours upon hours in my apartment; and while the white nights, when the sun refuses to yield to the night, kept me from being able to sleep well, the Lord was speaking soundly and clearly to my heart. It did not take but three sleepless nights before I knew that Cassandra Teresa Piotrowski was the one for me. We were friends, best friends, but we never dated. One reason was the limited time outside of the busy tour life. The second reason was the potentially awkward tension a dating relationship could bring between us and into the company, but most importantly, I did not know that she was the one for me until the Lord whispered the news to me in Saint Petersburg. I was so excited and could not wait to let her know. I needed to know the timing of how everything was going to unfold. In this matter, the Lord was as silent as a grave. I loved my time in the city formerly known as Leningrad and my weeklong visit to Moscow. Before long, I was boarding a Czech Airlines flight to Prague, ready to spend a week with my parents. I had something important to share with them. The two-hour flight time to Prague was going by slowly, allowing me to give thanks for the past three weeks of serving the Lord in Russia, touching the people with the love of Jesus, love that many of them had never heard of, never tasted, never looked for.

*"Я очень любил свое время служить Богу в
России!"* ("I loved my time of serving God
in Russia!")
*"Two are better than one, because they have a good
return for their work" (Eclesiastés 4:9).*

105) What!

I landed in Prague welcomed by another fairytale wonder of a gorgeous day. The weather could not have been better. The excitement of seeing my family again was through the roof, and I could not wait to share the great news. It was strange to be arriving at the Ruzyně airport without Petra and not receive her family's enthusiasm in welcoming us back home, but my parents substituted adequately as kisses and hugs flowed in abundance. I was home, indeed. We traveled to Ústí, once again taking the all-familiar road home while passing the bright-yellow fields, greeting gothic castles rising on high cliffs, and zipping past small villages filled with authentic Czech charm. This road from the airport was so familiar to me and, without fail, was just as exciting this time as it was the first. I never tire approaching the Ore Mountains clearly dividing the Czech Republic from our northern neighbor of Germany. The interstate connecting Prague and Ústí was progressing in construction but was nowhere near being finished, and so our white Škoda exited at the end of the road onto a small path leading toward the regional capital while closely following the river basin of the Elbe River. I knew that in twenty minutes time, we would be crossing the city limits as the ruins of the Střekov Castle would welcome me home.

I knew that a week would fly by at a great speed. My desire was to find an engagement ring for Cassandra while I was home. The fact that she did not know what the Lord was telling me to do and how He was guiding me was a bit of a potential problem. The fact that we have not dated at all could also be an element that could cause some troubles down the road. But I was not leaving the Czech Republic without a ring, and that was that. I sat my parents down and briefly shared about my time in Russia and about my plans for

Bolivia, particularly about working with the Native Indians in the Amazon Jungle. My parents did well trying to hide their apprehension regarding the trip especially as I was not one to love the outdoors and "roughing" it out in the wild. To hear that this was a mission related work was not necessarily helping either. The conversation was stalling a bit, and I was ready to kick it up a notch. "Well, also, there is one more small bit of news I would like to share with you that has nothing to do with my upcoming travel plans," I started rather broadly, "and there isn't an easy way to say this, so here I go... Hm, hm." I cleared my throat. "Well, I will be getting married!" My dad, for once, had nothing to say. There was no outpouring of encouragement as he would often do when my life was resembling a sinking ship. He sat there silently in his recliner chair reaching for the pack of cigarettes to light one to calm himself down, I suppose. *Great*, I thought, *even my dad is against the idea.* I waited for the bit more dramatic reaction from my mom. She did not disappoint.

"To whom?" was her short but sweet reply.

"To Cassandra... Ha...the thing is," I stumbled to articulate, "well...she does not know it yet. The Lord told me in Saint Petersburg, but He has not told me when to marry her just yet." I followed the statement with a hesitant smile.

"What!" my mom continued. Now that was more the reaction I expected in the first place. "Are you crazy? Are you guys dating right now? Please don't tell me that you are not dating! Don't tell me that you are just going to ask her to marry you out of the blue?" Now that she said that, I was relieved as I did not have to bring that small little nugget of information out into the open myself.

"We are great friends, and I know that she would be open to it and will respond positively once I propose... I think."

"You think?" my dad continued, exhaling the cigarette smoke heavily. "What if she'll say...you know...*no*, then...what? You, you will be so embarrassed...son... Rethink this please," he concluded.

"I appreciate your concerns. I really do, but this has been a long process of God breaking me in this area already, and I cannot say no to Him. That is for sure." I started to feel sweat rolling down my back. "I know that it must be difficult for you both to understand when I mention the Lord speaking to me, but He is, and He is guiding me down this path. He does not speak to me audibly, per se, but He whispers to my heart. Tomorrow, I would like to go look for an engagement ring, and I thought it might be nice to do it together." I presented a small diplomatic peace offering in the given situation.

"Have you guys been together?" my mom continued, still in an obvious shock.

"Actually, we believe that we are not to be together until we are married. That is the biblical approach, and we will honor this principle."

"What! What if it does not work out between you two? You know what I mean," she continued, visibly worried.

"First, why would it not work between us? Secondly, remember she doesn't even know that I am contemplating a proposal and marriage… It will be just fine!" My tone had intensified, and my parents gathered that this conversation had crossed the line of propriety. They sat there for a little while longer while my dad's cigarette just burned away without being smoked.

"So when are we going shopping?" my mom asked to end the awkward silence.

"Tomorrow, after breakfast, how does that sound?" I responded.

"All right, we will take the car since we might be going from one shop to another," my dad added. That is exactly what we did. It was a lot having my folks ring shopping with me as their styles were so different from each other's as well as different from what I wanted to find. I was looking for a green emerald, small and delicate to fit Cassandra's style and personality. My mom pictured a large diamond ring, and my dad pointed to a ring with seven stones, way too large and far away from delicate. I returned to downtown Ústí two more times, this time without them. On the third day, I found exactly what I wanted. That day, I bought a piece of jewelry that could potentially forever change my life. I was excited and grateful that the Lord guided me to find it and provided the necessary funds to be able to purchase the ring! My parents loved the ring when I brought it home. Now all I needed was for the bride-to-be to say yes when I knelt before her. I had no idea when that would be, as the

Lord did not make it clear to me just yet, but whenever the green light was given, I was ready, with a delicate green emerald ring in my pocket, to kneel and "pop the question." Mission accomplished!

> *And the one who sat there had the appearance of jasper and carnelian. A rainbow resembling an emerald, encircled the throne.*
> —Revelation 4:3

106) The Jungle

With my big purchase secured, I could say goodbye to my family and leave Prague with a lighthearted excitement focused on the next big adventure, the jungle. The routing of my flights led me through Jackson, where I had a four-hour layover. Cassandra came to the airport, and we enjoyed a nice lunch together, courtesy of the airport restaurant. It was so great to see her again after four weeks of being in Europe. As much as I wanted to say something to her and indicate the leading of the Lord in my heart, I knew that sealed lips were the better option. Four hours were not enough time to convey my feelings accurately, while allowing a few minutes for Cassandra to react and to respond, before catching my next flight. No, no, no, now was not the time to indicate anything, and that was the end of the story. I shared about my time in Russia and in Czech, as well as expressed my increasingly pressing worry about the upcoming trip to the Amazon. We enjoyed the short visit, and before long, it was time to board my flight to Miami. I hugged Cassandra hoping that by the time we were to be reunited in five weeks, I would know more details of God's plan for her and me. Now I had to focus on the task at hand.

All the team members were to meet in Miami for a day of orientation before flying to La Paz, Bolivia. That was all I knew, and I was eager to gather more information before the adventure began. I arrived at the designated hotel in Miami, as planned. I got to meet the other twenty members of the team and the four leaders who were going to escort us down to the jungle and, Lord willing, bring us all back to the States. There were Americans and Canadians on the team, and then there was me. New Tribe Missions served us a welcome dinner before we left for our rooms for the night. I was exhausted from the transatlantic flight to Jackson, from visiting Cassandra, and from flying to Miami. By the time my head hit the pillow, I had been traveling for almost thirty hours, crossing seven time zones westward before crossing one time zone eastward at the end of the day. I could barely spell my name anymore, and a good night's sleep was my hope in bringing some relief to my physical body. The next day was to be spent in being educated and equipped for something none of us had ever done. As the day progressed, and the reality of the mission was clearly painted before us, I started to wonder if this trip might be just a bit too much for a city boy like me. We were told that after our initial flight to La Paz, we were to take a domestic commercial flight to Cochabamba, Bolivia. There we and our baggage would be weighed, divided into smaller groups of six and flown into the jungle. Housing was to be primitive, food scarce, water not fit to drink, and poisonous snakes all around. A supply plane with a food stockpile and mail was to come one time, roughly twenty days into the trip. We were going to be assisting the missionary couple in whatever they would ask us to do, most of which was to require hours of hard physical work. All day, while listening to the instructions, I was wondering just exactly how I managed to end up here and why in the world I would volunteer for something like this. That evening, I called Cassandra to share some of the details I learned earlier that day. This was going to be my last communication with anyone outside of the team for a long while.

The next day, as much as everything in me protested to board another international flight, I did just that. The flight to La Paz was a breeze. So was the domestic flight to Cochabamba. After our landing there, we were greeted by the workers of the New Tribe Mission and officially welcomed to Bolivia. The process to weigh us was tedious as the two small planes had to be carefully loaded and calibrated for each hour flight to the jungle. I was in the second group and had two hours to wait at the Cochabamba airport before my time to fly had come. Then it did. One more step on a scale and we were airborne, leaving all traces of civilization behind us. Before long, as far as one could see, we saw trees, trees, and more trees. The

Amazon is lush, vast, and overwhelming to take in. I had no idea that it was possible to fly for an hour and see nothing but trees. I started to grasp just how far away from any civilized place we would actually be. The pilot, a missionary himself, prepared us for the landing coming up. The small eight-seater plane was not landing at a small airport somewhere; this time, we were to land on a grassy opening that suddenly appeared between the sea of trees. The meadow was short and the landing rough. The moment the plane came to a stop, the door opened, and before I knew what was happening, I was being wrestled by one of the Indians. What a welcome. The crowd of locals gathered and created a circus-like arena around us as we rumbled. The other teammates stayed in the plane watching the spectacle. The Indians cheered loudly. Was I to fight back? Before long, another team member was also pulled out of the plane and fought. I started to fight back, at least try to anyway, realizing that this might be a good preparation for what the next five and a half weeks were going to be like, a fight for survival. Both my teammate and I were defeated by the two Indians who resembled pictures from an anatomy book. Every muscle was clearly sculpted and defined. The small piece of clothing covering their manhood was not helping us feel comfortable during the match. Another shocking element was the heat. The air was filled with hot sticky humidity that immediately soaked every piece of clothing I was wearing. It was difficult to draw a deep breath. We were in the jungle. After our defeat, we were greeted and welcomed by Philip, the missionary who has dedicated his life to reach these Indians with the love of Jesus. He and his wife had lived among the Yuqui Indians for fourteen years, we were told. They had three children who had just recently returned back to the village from a boarding school specifically built for the children of the South American missionaries. The planes made two more trips to bring the rest of the team. The wrestling welcoming ceremony repeated itself every time the planes returned. I enjoyed watching the next two matches much more than I enjoyed being in them. The nightfall covered the village much sooner than we expected. There was no electricity, only flashlights and matches to illuminate the night. We slept in primitive huts on sleeping bags under mosquito nets. The whole night long, the buzzing of the mosquitos prevented most of us from sleeping well. The first morning was beautiful. The intense sun brought daylight onto the village. Philip gathered the whole team in a large wooden structure. We all expected a nutritious breakfast, only to receive a bowl of cereal and milk we brought in with us from Cochabamba. Philip welcomed us again and shared a bit about himself and his family and talked about the vision of the NTM to reach as many Indian tribes scattered throughout the Amazon Jungle as possible. He said that after fourteen years of living among the 115 Yuqui Indians, one came to know the Lord. Just one. He continued to explain that the locals do not believe in sin. "Stealing, for example, is a good thing as one gains when he or she steals. As gaining is good, stealing, therefore, must be good as well." He warned us to be careful as our personal belongings would be stolen only to be offered back to us for an exchange for something else. I found this to be ironic being in the middle of nowhere and yet forced to keep a close eye on my stuff. Who would have thought! Philip continued to explain the kitchen routine. "There are supplies that you have brought with you. We will have to use them sparingly as they must last for the next twenty days. That is when the supply plane will deliver more. The Indians will offer us meat as they hunt daily, but everything else must be prepared by us. Water supply is limited, and dehydration cannot be avoided. The river flowing nearby is the only source of water for the village. In order to drink or use it in any way, the water must be boiled for twenty minutes after it is fetched and brought into the 'kitchen.' To reach a boiling point takes about an hour, as the pots are placed over small flames. By the time the water is ready to be used, most of it has simply vaporized, and the remaining amount will only fill a handful of small cups. You will find this process extremely frustrating and difficult, but your thirst will drive you to keep fetching, boiling, and preparing the water no matter the price and exhaustion. To substitute for the lack of water, hand-squeezed tangerine juice will be provided daily by the team members assigned that day for that task alone. The rest of you will be assigned to work around the village. The main plan for the next forty days is to build new houses for the Indians to encourage them to understand the importance of dividing themselves into family-like groupings. There is no real understanding of family structure. Marriage does not exist among the tribe. The construction consists of creating concrete pillars and then building wooden homes on top of them. It will be difficult mainly due to the extreme humidity and heat. Also, I can guarantee that every single one of you will get very sick. You will experience diarrhea and vomiting, but it should not last longer than a day or two. We wish we could prevent that from happening, but the conditions here are simply that harsh. You will be asking the Lord to take you *home*, but He will not answer those prayers." Philip chuckled. "Once you'll make it through this 'jungle baptism,' you should be fine for the rest of your time here. Be aware of large ants, snakes, poisonous spiders, and never venture into the jungle around the village alone. Please, hear me when I say, venturing into the jungle is a matter of life and death. Is that clear?" I was shocked. So was everyone else on the team. This was going to be much rougher than we ever expected it to be. There was no turning back. We were here, and onward was the only way. Phillip took us around the village to help familiarize us with the layout and its proximity to the river, happily flowing about a half a mile away. That was going to be hard to carry water that far, I thought. The Indians seemed calm and not at all interested in us being there. The men were out hunting as the women were in the village cooking and handcrafting ropes for the large hunting bows, we were told. The time had come for us to start boiling water as thirst started to loudly shout from within all of us. We also utilized the rest of the day and daylight to situate our sleeping quarters better before the next nightfall swallowed the village and us with it. We finished the first day sitting around a large campfire, singing songs of worship, and praying for the next long 39 days. The increased attacks of the mosquitoes forced us to seek cover in our small nets. Bible reading under a small flashlight concluded the day. I lifted a prayer of thanksgiving and requested help and protection for me and the team. I also prayed to the Lord for Him to speak to me regarding the timing of my proposal and marriage to Cassandra. With the prayers still rolling from my tongue, the heaviness of my eyelids overpowered me, and I drifted off to a dreamless night of rest.

I know what it is to be in need, and I know what it is to have plenty. I have learned the secret of being content in any and every situation, whether well fed or hungry, whether living in plenty or in want. I can do everything through him who gives me strength.
—Philippians 4:12–13

107) Among the Yuqui's

There are days in our lives that seem to turn quickly; weekends, holidays, vacations, to name a few. Then there are days that seem endless as each hour progresses in apparent slow motion and the day's end is nowhere in sight. Days in the Yuqui Village were the latter of the two. The promised cycle of sickness circled through the team; and as far as I know, all of us begged the Lord to simply take us home as the pain, fever, and gastrointestinal flu were of significant propor- tions. Kitchen duty quickly became the dreaded option as lugging and boiling water was strenuous and squeezing the tangerine juice made the finger- tips raw and tender. Missing personal objects became a daily routine, and as Philip had warned us, they reappear again  in about two days' time as they were offered back to us by the Indians. We bathed in the river, which was tricky, trying hard not to get any of the water splashed into our mouths. Every time we decided to wash, there was a faithful group of villagers being entertained by our attempts to stay civilized, shaven, and clean. Pouring shampoo on our heads provided much laughter and joy as the Indians simply did not understand the purpose of it all. Dehydration was as real as one can imagine. The never-ending sweat was pouring out of us at all times as the humidity of the jungle puts its Mississippi cousin to shame in intensity and discomfort. As tough as it was, we had a great time as well. Complete isolation from the outside world was difficult at first but in a couple of days it truly caused us to invest in each other and try to build bridges and relationships with the Yuqui people. The men taught us to shoot five-foot arrows. That was much more difficult to do than it appeared when demonstrated by the Indians. Freshly provided meat became the highlight of the day. They were truly skilled hunters. A loud shout filled the village one afternoon as we experienced the attack of a teammate by a poisonous snake. Philip came to the rescue with the antidote; and in a day, the group was back together, just a bit more vigilant. A toe infection of another teammate called for a surgery of sorts. I stepped into the role of a surgeon as I prepped a knife over an open flame, and with four guys holding the "patient," I cut the toe open and with all my might squeezed the infection out. The scream of pain must have been heard throughout the jungle.

One last memory worthy to be shared here was the warning we received from the Indians that footprints of a jaguar were spotted on the bank of the river. Some laughed; some panicked. The advice was to never go to the river alone. Prior to this warning, we ventured to the riverbanks alone when fetching water; but wisdom mixed with a desire to live beyond these five weeks, and not become lunchmeat, was a strong motivation to always go to the river with at least one other person. Then one day, in the early afternoon, the village was filled with a jubilant noise and celebration. The men were approaching the village singing and dancing. Everyone gathered to see the reason for such unusual joyful noise. As the dancing men cleared the way, we all saw four men carrying two large sticks between them; and on these, there was a freshly slaughtered jaguar, killed by several arrows discharged in a carefully planned ambush. I felt my knees shake and weaken as the reality of the proposed danger was visibly before us. The reality that we were truly in the middle of a jungle sunk in as the sense of adventure skyrocketed.

Twenty days passed, and the supply plane landed around two o'clock. The very sight of the plane caused a sense of an immediate connection with the outside world. We knew that more food was brought in, and we did not complain. But the most exciting element was the mail. None of us knew if any mail would come, but the hope that someone remembered us filled our hearts with anticipation and excitement. There was nobody that did not receive at least one piece of mail, but little did I know that I would receive more mail that day than in all my previous life combined. Cassandra had sent me a card or a letter every day since I saw her in Jackson some three weeks ago. I was embarrassed to receive the largest amount, but I was thankful that I did. As I opened one of the cards, a photo fell out. On it, Cassandra was holding a bouquet of flowers that she caught at her brother's wedding. As I flipped the picture, I read, "Do you know what this means?" I was not then, nor am I now, an expert on American customs, but I knew exactly what Cassandra was indicating with these six words. *What a confirmation, Lord! You have a great sense of humor!* I thought. The remainder of the time in the village was spent in continuation of the found rhythm of working hard serving the Yuqui people and the missionaries, boiling water and squeezing tangerine juice, and spending a lot of time in conversations with each other and with the Lord, Who did not have to compete with the distractions typical in the life of a Westerner. As difficult as the beginning of the time in the village was, we were all leaving the jungle changed and built up in our faith. I was ready to fly back to the States, go through the debrief in Miami, take a long and hot shower, and finally arrive back home in Jackson. I had so many stories to share; but one thing had to stay hidden, that I now knew that I was to marry—marry Cassandra Teresa Piotrowski. All I needed was a permission to ask her to marry me. I had the engagement ring in my car at all times, just in case the Lord's command to propose came, but I said and indicated nothing to Cassandra nor to anybody else. After the time spent with the Lord in Saint Petersburg and in the Yuqui Village, I was now ready to take this step. God is faithful in diligently working in our hearts, changing and growing us in accord to His will and plan. Isn't that amazing!

> *There is a time for everything, and a season*
> *for every activity under heaven.*
>   —Ecclesiastes 3:1

108) Will You?

As I continue to tell the story of the grandiose work of God in my life, sadly, I come to realize that a tendency to fill my days with the danger of a continual striving for thrills is alive and well. This danger is challenged with a never-satisfying newness apparent in every season of my life. As thrills are fun to be experienced on occasions, we are not meant to live on the edge of endless search for excitement and fun. If these short-lived rushes are not present, we find ourselves unfulfilled and feel that life is, plainly put, boring. The opposite is true as every day presents a fresh opportunity to find the Lord in that day and seek to enjoy the fellowship with Him through these twenty-four hours that will never be repeated. Should a day present an exciting experience, or a circumstance, it is a gift to be enjoyed as we understand that the next day again might return us back to the known and "normal" routine of life, also to be valued and cherished. Returning from the jungle was an adjustment to return to the normal life of a Western culture, where abundance and ease of life were present on every corner. I returned to the routine of dancing and serving the Lord at Ballet Magnificat, attending my church, pressing through more Bible studies, growing, and touring.

A friend from the Czech Republic, Kamil, was visiting America and expressed a desire to stop in Jackson to spend some time with me. I looked forward to welcoming Kamil in Mississippi, hoping that time spent with me and my friends here would challenge him to seek the Lord and perhaps even recognize the need for his own salvation. We had a great time together as he is outgoing and meeting new people has never been a struggle for him whatsoever. Finding activities to fill our days in Jackson could be a challenge, as the laid-back nature of the Mississippi people and the city of Jackson is quite different from other parts of the States and a European visitor might quickly find himself in search of things to do. A friend of Cassandra's, Patti, a lady who, along with her husband, Paul, had taken Cassandra under their wings when she first moved to Jackson; owned a medium-size motorboat. I thought that an afternoon of floating on the Jackson reservoir would be a memorable outing for Kamil, Cassandra, and myself. I called Patti to see if the boat would be an option for all of us to use; and Patti suggested Saturday, August 14, as a possibility. I was glad to have found another venture to make Kamil's visit to Jackson as fun as possible. Cassandra was also excited to join us. This was going to be a great day. We were scheduled to meet Patti at two o'clock in the afternoon. Prepared to face the heat of the summer sun, we had our suntan lotion packed and ready to go. As I was eating Saturday breakfast while chatting with Kamil about fairly insignificant things, as clear as day, the green light to propose was given from the Lord. *"Today is the day, son,"* was a simple yet clear direction from Him. With my mouth full, I looked at Kamil and said, "I am going to ask Cassandra to marry me while we are on the boat this afternoon. What do you think?" Kamil's excitement was off the charts. "Yes, yes…that is a great idea… I have a camera, and I can film it for you all to have…you know…forever!" I became sparky. "We have a lot to do, then, as I need to get flowers and prepare my 'speech.' Oh my goodness, this will be epic!" I picked up the phone and called Patti. "Good morning, Patti, how are you? I am calling to check that we are still on for this afternoon and also to tell you something," I started the conversation. "Everything is ready to go, Jiri, and it is a beautiful day today. It will be a lot of fun," Patti replied. "I know, it is a beautiful day. Patti, I am calling to let you know that while we are on the boat, I will… I want to…the Lord told me… Shoot, this is nerve-racking… Today, on the boat, I will ask Cassandra to marry me, and I wanted to…" I heard Patti's phone hit the ground. As I kept repeating her name, I heard a loud jubilation scream come and go as Patti ran around her house rejoicing over something that has not even happened yet. She returned to the phone and with heavy breathing apologized for dropping the phone. "No problem, Patti. You are something else! I wanted to ask if I could come to your house and drop off flowers that you could hide somewhere on the boat." Patti responded in an accelerated manner as her excitement was great and needed to be tamed a little. "I need you to act as normal as pos-sible please," I requested of Cassandra's dear friend. "I will do more yelling and rejoicing before I see you all so I don't give anything away," Patti promised. To her own testimony later that day, she did several rounds of loud uninhibited, joyous celebrations prior to our two o'clock rendezvous. Kamil and I went to purchase the flowers and help Patti hide them and get everything ready. Patti hugged me clearly expressing her emotions. She had several conversations with Cassandra about marriage and the when, the who, the how would that be, knowing of course that she and I were close friends who enjoyed spending time together a whole lot. Everything was set, and Kamil and I drove to pick Cassandra up and arrived at her house around one thirty. Cassandra came out with a bag strapped over her shoulder. Before she placed it in the car, she gently knocked on the window of the car. "I have invited Vladimir to come with us since he has nothing to do and is all alone. I hope you don't mind," she stated. Vladimir was a Russian dancer who joined Ballet Magnificat after completing the Bolshoi Ballet Academy in Moscow, desiring to dance for the glory of God rather than his own. I did not mind having Vladimir with us. I just was not prepared to have such a large audience gathered there for the proposal. But what's another person? "Sure, sure, sure…yeah…that is great… Vladimir…let's bring him along," I said, trying to hide that I was getting nervous.

We all piled into my car and drove to meet Patti at the reservoir. Patti was already in the boat ready to set sail. I am convinced until this day that Patti should have received an Academy Award for her acting that day. She seemed as calm and collected as one could be. There was no trace visible that she knew something exciting was coming up. Bravo, bravo, Patti! Truly an "actress professionnelle!" We gathered into the boat, and I pretended to introduce Kamil to Patti as if for the first time. We also welcomed Vladimir on board, and before long, we were pushing away from the shore to enjoy the afternoon and the large body of water. The signal between Patti and I was set, and she was patiently waiting for it to come. I performed before many large crowds countless times prior to this day, but I was as nervous as I could be. "Patti, could we turn the motor off and just enjoy the water and let the boat drift please?" I said suddenly. "That is unusual, but I don't see why not," Patti replied, shrugging her shoulders while turning the ignition key. This was our agreed signal. The waves were gently crashing against the boat, rocking it back and forth. Vladimir was looking into the distance, Kamil was pretending to record the scenery, and Cassandra and Patti were conversing about life. I checked that the ring was in my pocket, for the millionth time, and I pretended to show something to Kamil to have an excuse to stand up. Then I "noticed" that my shoelace was untied, to have a reason to kneel. Doing that on a rocking boat was an element I was not prepared for, and balancing was to be a challenge. I decided to kneel on both knees to be able to focus on what I was saying rather than on trying not to fall over. Cassandra had no idea what was coming. Patti started to get excited, and I knew that I needed to make the move. I grabbed Cassandra's hand and, without any further ado, said, "Cassandra, I have been seeking the Lord a lot over the past four months to know whether or not He would allow me the privilege to ask you to be my wife. When I was in Russia, I sensed Him confirm that you were the one, in Czech I bought an engagement ring, and in Bolivia the confirmation was given through the photo from Matthew's wedding where you caught the bouquet." Kamil was filming the moment, Vladimir just realized what was unfolding before him, Patti was giddy as a little girl, and Cassandra seemed, well, let's say, surprised at first. "Cassandra Teresa Piotrowski, would you marry me and be my wife?" I cut to the chase. Cassandra's eyes lit up brightly as a smile appeared on her face. "Yes, I would. I'd love to… It's about time!" She laughed as she intently looked into my eyes. Looking right back, I pulled the ring box out of my pocket and opened it up for her to see. Cassandra did not hide the utter shock that I actually bought the ring in advance, as if expecting a dating relationship first prior to a proposal. But she loved the ring and pulled it out of the box. Whether it was nerves or the Mississippi humidity, the ring did not seem to fit. "Oh, I will make it fit. That is for sure," Cassandra said, pushing the ring onto her small and delicate finger. We hugged as our friends, mainly Patti, cheered, and applauded. I pulled out the hidden flowers, and that was what "broke the camel's back." Cassandra started to cry. "No, no…these are tears of joy," she was assuring me. "I just did not expect this at all, and I mean at all! You did seem nicer to me ever since you returned from Bolivia, but I was just not prepared for this." Little did

I know at the time that Cassandra had previously shared with Patti, opening up about her feelings she had for me, that she carried in her heart for the past five years. Five years! As a good and godly woman she is, Cassandra turned to the Lord for advice. He spoke through His Word, specifically through the wisdom of King Solomon, who said, "Do not awaken love *until* it so desires." The good and gracious God He is, He translated the verse to her, saying, "It will be a while for Jiri to wake up, so be patient." And so she was, thankfully! Patti went on to describe her emotions since the moment I called her that morning, Kamil shared about our breakfast and planning of the event, and Vladimir just sat there to soak in the moment with the reserved calmness typical of a Russian man. We returned to the shore and went to Cassandra's house, where we shared our news with Mamaw before calling Cassandra's parents. I knew that I needed to ask Harry for Cassandra's hand, and I must admit that the order of doing so was a bit backward. As I asked him whether or not I could request for his daughter's hand in marriage, I was met with a long pause. "Does she really want to marry you?" followed on the other end. "Yes, sir, I believe she does," I responded, fumbling through my words. Another long pause followed, and I wondered if we got disconnected, which would be a better option than him saying no. "Congratulations, then!" was his response. I was relieved and nodded to let Cassandra know that his approval was given. Cassandra spent a few more minutes speaking with her parents and then hung up the phone. We also called home, waking my parents up to let them know that their firstborn was engaged. They were genuinely happy for us both. That evening, Cassandra and I went to visit company dancers and a few friends to let them know and share the engagement story. Many of them said what Cassandra hinted on the boat, "that it was about time," as I laughed in complete agreement. What they did not know was the journey of God's preparatory work of my heart and soul that started through the February Bible study of a "dreaded" marriage chapter. I can be pretty stubborn and a slow learner, I discovered; but praise be to God, Who is more patient—God Who prevails no matter how much one tries to resist His will.

For great is his love toward us, and the
faithfulness of the Lord endures forever.

—Psalm 118:2

109) Returning, for the First Time!

Do you dream of dreams that seem to take a long time to come true? Sometimes we never see them fulfilled, sometimes they simply take a long while, and sometimes they require us to be patient. One of my dreams that I carried in my heart from my very first experience with Ballet Magnificat was the desire to bring the company to Europe, specifically to the Czech Republic. In August of 1999, during my engagement-ring-shopping week, I also visited the North Bohemian State Theater in Ústí. I simply walked in and requested to be seen by the general director. He—along with Mrs. Honsová, who was responsible for the economic functions of the theater—sat down with me to listen to my proposal of inviting the American ballet company to the city of Ústí nad Labem for a one night performance. I presented them with promotional materials of Ballet Magnificat, explained the purpose and vision of the company, and included how unique it would be to be coming "home" as an active dancer of the group. They loved the idea, and the seed was planted. I also contacted Petra, who had returned from Mississippi and moved back to Liberec in December of 1998, asking her to see if the Šalda State Theater there would be interested in hosting Ballet Magnificat. Long story short, after many years of praying and asking the Lord to open the locked gates, I simply nudged them that summer, and before I was even prepared to hear the individual decisions, positive responses and invitations for the tour started to come in. After six years of dancing for the Lord in America, I was now able to bring Jesus to the Czech people. Performing arts are a natural part of the European lifestyle, and the fact that an American ballet company was coming in for a one-night show caused complete sellouts in all of the venues in five cities of the Czech Republic as well as in Brussels, Belgium. Ballet Magnificat was scheduled to, for the very first time, travel to Europe to share the hope of Jesus Christ through a night of dance, worship, and storytelling.

It was a picture-perfect late-October day as the company touched down in Prague after a nonstop flight from New York. The colors of the fall were vibrant that year. Our very first performance of the tour was scheduled for Liberec, dancing in the very State Theater where my professional career first commenced. Many former colleagues from the ballet company and classmates from the academy, as well as Professors Pokorný, Gabajová, and Brother Evald, were sitting in the seats that night. I was a nervous wreck. The evening started with a ballet titled *Unveiled Hope*, an album by Michael Card, a powerful set of music empowered by the life-filled lyrics directly derived from the book of Revelation. We stood in a formation in the center of the stage. The historic velvet curtain opened to  unveil history in the making, as for the very first time ever on this stage, in this theater, and in this nation, artists of a professional Christian ballet company were ready to worship the King of kings with everything they had. The shafts of the lights flooded the darkness of the auditorium. We began to dance. The opening song finished with a climactic ending that was typically followed by a large applause in the United States. Not here. There was not a slightest noise to be heard. We moved on and finished the entire opening portion of the night. The audience continued to be silent. Kathy was worried. "Jiri, they don't like us!" "No, Kathy," I said, "they are blown away by what they are seeing… I think." We had no time to discuss this further, as only a quick costume change separated the opening set from the second one: *Basic Instructions* by a contemporary Christian band Burlap to Cashmere. Their Latin-rhythm-filled music was to be an unexpected surprise for the reserved European crowd. The bright-red dresses and tightly fitted jackets shone brightly in the lights, standing in stark contrast against the black curtains of the theater. The music was impossible to not be enjoyed, and the rapid speed of the choreography started to break the walls around the Czech hearts. At the end of the fifth piece, as the dancers hit the final pose and their chests inflated and deflated in response to the stamina the set required, there was a moment of another complete silence. But then an outpouring of a vigorous and loud applause rushed through the crowd. "Bravo, bravo…bravo," sounded from the orchestra level of the auditorium as well as all three balconies. They were not only clapping; they were also whistling. But that was not all. The crowd stood up and started to stomp loudly. Stomping is considered to be the greatest expression of appreciation in many European nations, Czech included. The crowd was won over. We took our bow and waited for the curtain to close. After an intermission, we presented a story entitled *Savior*, telling the biblical account from Creation, through the fall of Adam and Eve, all the way to the powerful movement entitled "Cross of Love." This was, without a doubt, the very first time many, if not all, of these people saw the story of God's love for His people expressed in a powerful combination of dance, music, and costuming. Above all, the presence of the Holy Spirit powerfully descended into the theater that night. At the end of it, I picked up a microphone, and to the shock of many sitting before me, I spoke in Czech. I shared briefly about my ballet career starting right here on that very stage nine years ago, only to return with the privilege to share the hope of Jesus Christ with the people of my beloved homeland. They sat there and listened to every word. I was emotional, and keeping it all together was not possible. Tears were flowing down my sweaty face as I exhorted them all to listen to the Spirit of God, Who had already touched them throughout the night. It was such a powerful moment as the company stood behind me and, in silent prayers, called on the Lord to move in power. The evening concluded with us meeting the crowd in the foyer of the theater. Everyone was visibly moved as they were leaving. Their encounter with the living God was undeniable. The very next day, we found a full-page review written about Ballet Magnificat's first European performance. It stated the following:

> We witnessed a once-in-a-lifetime perfor-
> mance at the Šalda State Theater last night as
> the American Ballet Magnificat took the stage.
> Our own dancers technically compare to the art-
> ists we saw dance yesterday, but the power that
> flowed from the stage when Ballet Magnificat
> danced was unlike anything we have ever seen
> before. The whole night was divided into three
> sections all filled with technique, artistry, and
> the outpouring of the hearts of these dancers.
> The highlight of the night was the second piece
> of Latin rhythms that was met with an eruption
> of applause. The end of the performance was a
> moving story telling God's story from creation
> through the crucifixion and resurrection of Jesus
> Christ, unique to the Czech audiences. The
> whole performance was greatly received by the
> sold out crowd who left the Šalda Theater deeply
> moved. Bravo Ballet Magnificat!

The Lord used this ballet performance to introduce Himself to those gathered there that night. This was an incredible start to the first European tour. There were many other memorable and moving moments. I would like to share just two more with you. Dancing at the State Theater in my hometown of Ústí with my nonbelieving parents, aunts, uncles, friends, and dancers of the state ballet company sitting in the sold-out theater was a highlight for sure. I could not believe that the Lord would use Ballet Magnificat in this unique manner to be a visual tool delivering the power of God to thousands of Czechs. Most of them, professing atheists, would witness the love of Jesus, love expressed through the horror of the Cross, where the freedom from sin was won for them just as much as anyone else around the world. Seeing my mom and dad after the performance, as they rushed in to hug me and all the other members of the company, was my greatest reward, apart from them personally receiving Jesus's salvation that is yet to be realized.

Lastly, I want to briefly share another moment of the tour. We were in the city of Brno, the one in which I auditioned and was contracted to dance after graduation. After the conclusion of the performance, as I was finishing the verbal presentation of the gospel, I sensed the urgency to invite Traci, our tour director for Ballet Magnificat, to come to the stage and sing "Amazing Grace." This was not planned but the pressing of the Holy Spirit was strong. Traci was hesitant, but being the worship leader that she was, she understood that this was a moment like no other, and disobedience to the Lord was not an option. Traci took my microphone and gently cleared her throat. "Amazing Grace...how sweet the sound...that saved a wretch like me... I once was lost...but *now*...am found... Was blind...but *now*... I see..." As Traci continued to sing the following verses of the song, all of a sudden, audience members started to stand up. Not all, just some. At first, I thought they were going to leave. Instead, they joined in and sang with her. There were harmonies echoing throughout the venue as these Czech believers, who were peppered through the crowd, worshipped their Savior with Traci. It sounded heavenly, truly divine. If hours of practice were spent in rehearsal, one would think that the singers were great, but to realize that all this was spontaneous improvisation made the moment truly from on High. The Lord was displaying His presence throughout the theater—nobody left; everybody stayed. Some closed their eyes to soak it all in. Others were wiping tears from their eyes. A national radio journalist was there and did a short interview with me afterward. It was almost comical to have her ask questions while searching for an explanation of what she experienced a few moments ago. Through the radio waves, by her own testimony, the name of Jesus was proclaimed and honored that evening. As long as I live, I will never forget the first European tour—seeing God move in power and might. Every stop was special, every performance unique, but the common denominator throughout the tour was the faithful outpouring of the powerful Holy Spirit every night in every city in both nations. Little did I know that this was the beginning of the international touring of Ballet Magnificat that would span across five continents and over forty nations. God is an amazing planner. Being a part of His plans is the greatest privilege of life.

I might not be standing in the center of the stage anymore, waiting for the velvet curtain to open, but the call on my life to serve the Lord Jesus will continue as long as there is breath in my lungs. May we all continue to run hard after Him wherever and however He might lead us!

> *Declare his glory among the nations, his*
> *marvelous deeds among all peoples.*
> —Psalm 96:3

110) I Do!

"No, not possible. We are in Florida," said Tim, the tour director. "How about March, any weekend in March?" We kept our fingers crossed. "No, there are no openings on any weekend in March either you guys," Tim continued. "The only available weekend is April 1 or a date in November as everything in between is either a weekend on tour or vacation times when everyone is out of town visiting family. Oh, and also, if you choose Saturday, April 1, you need to know that we leave on tour the following Wednesday."

Cassandra and I looked at each other knowing that we did not want to wait until November to marry, and so April Fool's Day was our only option, giving us a little over seven months to get the wedding planned. Cassandra is a natural planner and thrives in organizational challenges, and seven months was more than enough time to line up all the "ducks" just fine. Meanwhile, we had decided to "upgrade" our physical expression of our love to holding hands. We felt strongly about waiting to share our first kiss only after being pronounced husband and wife. After our engagement, Cassandra left her church family that she had been a part of since first moving to Mississippi, to join me in attending Cornerstone Church. Our pastor, Nick Irons, was an excellent teacher during our premarital mentoring sessions. The biggest takeaway for the two of us was our conversation regarding "culture." Pastor Nick led us to consider the possible cultural differences two households living next to each other might have and to think how much more contrast could be true for us who grew up on two continents, in two political world systems, in two very different cultures and countries. It was also to see the distinct ways we valued and celebrated holidays and birthdays, the way we spent weekends and vacations, and see the influences of our families that shaped us to be who we were that often we didn't even realize. All these aspects needed to be talked about and pondered. He was absolutely right, and Cassandra and I took a significant time laying a foundation for our future family and discussing the possible tensions our own families might have upon us and our marriage. Another treasure gained from our meetings with the pastor was the "relational triangle." Pastor Nick explained to us that the physical side of the triangle and the emotional hypotenuse that grows on the opposite side are together dependent and need to be rooted in a vibrant spiritual relationship with the Lord in order to climb to new heights. As long as our spiritual side is strong and healthy, the other two will naturally grow and all together create a safe protection around our relationship and our marriage, with Christ being in its center. Our wedding was a blast as we celebrated our union in an international Czech-American style.

The church ceremony, communion, prayer, and a first kiss were followed with a sit-down dinner of divine mashed potatoes, Wiener Schnitzel, and a refreshing cucumber salad. The only disappointment was that my dad was unable to travel to Jackson for the wedding. More about that a bit later. On our big day, we were blessed to celebrate the goodness of the Lord with family and friends. With excitement and joy, we stepped into the next chapter of our lives, for better or worse, for richer or poorer, in sickness or in health, to love one another until death do us part, and, now as one, to serve the Lord however He would summon us to serve. We did leave on tour just four days later, but it did not matter to us. We were loving this newness in our lives, and every day seemed to present a fresh opportunity to find a way to love each other and those around us. We might have never dated, Cassandra might not have been prepared to be proposed to and asked to marry a knucklehead like me, but our individual love for the Lord combined with our genuine friendship for each other gave us everything we needed to face life with all its unexpected curves brought our way on the path of living it out. I planned a surprise honeymoon to sunny and exotic Morocco during the company's May break. It was great fun to take my bride on a trip where dancing shoes were not a necessary item to be packed. Both of us enjoyed the culture of the Middle East combined with the flair of the North African markets, history, customs, and beauty. It was there, in the Medina of Marrakech, where I was offered two camels in exchange for Cassandra. As tempting as the offer was, I could not figure out exactly how I would get the camels back home. I turned the offer down as both Cassandra and I laughed about it then and laugh about it still. She is worth much more; I know that full well. It was great fun to be alone, far away from the hustle of our busy lives, and spend two weeks focused on one another and on building great memories together. Our marriage was off to a great start, and both Cassandra and I knew that we were incredibly blessed and cherished by our Abba Father, Who had brought us together, allowing us the privilege of pursuing Him as one. The Bible states that "Blessed is the man who finds a wife as he receives favor from the Lord." I know that I am not one to deserve anything, let alone a wife like Cassandra. The Lord is so very good to His children, me included. I am a grateful man!

He who finds a wife finds what is good and
receives favor from the Lord.
—Proverbs 18:22

111) This Is the Way to Go!

As I mentioned earlier, my dad was unable to come to Mississippi for the wedding. He was forty-nine years old when he was diagnosed with a rare form of bone cancer. The pain that rapidly spread throughout his body prevented normalcy of life for him. Cassandra and I both wanted to visit him as soon as we possibly could, which was December of 2000, some nine months after the wedding. During the visit back home, we loved our time together, really enjoying every moment as we did not know how many more there would be. My  dad was a trooper as he hid the pain he was experiencing so well during our visit. We laughed, we talked a lot, and we played games. We simply sat together in the small living room visiting with my mom, my dad, Míra, Cassandra, and Peggy, our dachshund dog. We cherished every moment of this Christmas holiday. I once again shared with my dad the hope I found in Jesus. I even gave him a Czech translation of the Bible. I understood the absolute urgency for him to meet his Savior as his earthly life was coming to an end so quickly. My dad promised to give the Bible a chance and to read it after we left to go back home. It was with a heavy heart that I boarded the transatlantic flight from Prague to New York after the holidays ended, not being sure if I were to see him again, and being 5,100 miles away did not bring any ease into the situation. Cassandra and I prayed for my dad as the airplane rushed down the runway to take off and leave my homeland and my family behind.

I love long-haul flights. I enjoy settling in, making myself comfortable and using the hours to read, to relax, to watch a movie or two, to spend uninterrupted time with the Lord far away from text messages and phone calls. And, yes, I enjoy the airplane food as well. Flying with Cassandra is entertaining. She has a great talent and ability to fasten her seat belt before taxiing and takeoff, and with a slight complaint about the misery of the long flight yet to come, she falls asleep. Cassandra only wakes for the food service, quick use of the restroom, and then returns back to snoozing while calmed by the sound of the engine and the ever-so-slight movement of the fuselage. I average about twenty minutes of sleep no matter how long the flight might be, as my better half manages about twenty minutes of being awake during the same. This particular flight was to be a bit unique. We were seated in the front of the business class, courtesy of the collected frequent flyer miles, flying on the wide-body Airbus 310–300 Czech Airlines aircraft. We were somewhere over the Atlantic as the crew just finished serving us the gourmet lunch and a fancy dessert comprised of a vast selection of cakes and pastries. Cassandra, seated by the window, was fast asleep again, as the cabin crew started the duty-free service. Then out of nowhere and without any warning, the flight hit massive turbulence. Turbulence is defined as a rapid fluid motion characterized by chaotic changes in pressure and velocity. That is exactly what happened. The massive aircraft filled with approximately 220 passengers was being tossed back and forth like a toy. The massive drops of the plane followed by sharp right-and-left calibrations caused huge panic on board. The flight attendants, who just a moment ago resembled well-put-together "models," were thrown to the ground as merchandise, newspapers, and dishes were tossed about the cabin. I was strangely at peace. It was surreal. I experienced no hesitation, no worry. I was thankful to have had my seat belt loosely fastened across my lap, but should we have crashed into the waters of the Atlantic, I was at peace knowing that *"it was well with my soul,"* to quote the famous lyrics of Horatio Spafford. As the chaos and fear crippled a majority of the fellow travelers, I looked over at Cassandra, only to find her peacefully asleep, not hearing the ruckus of the cabin caught in the unexpected turmoil. *This is the way to go meet Jesus,* I thought as I decided not to wake my darling up. It was better to be asleep and miss the potential crashing of the aircraft. The turbulence lasted a couple of short minutes, but the emotional recovery lasted for who-knows-how-long. Most of the passengers around me were Czechs believing firmly that God does not exist, just as I did myself prior to my radical meeting of the living Jesus Christ; they were suddenly crippled by the fear of dying. Now that their lives were in danger, where was their hope, I wondered! In whom or in what did they place their security? As the plane recovered and passed the rough patch in the air, the crew started to clean up the bedraggled cabin, making sure that everyone was all right. *That is going to be tough*, I thought. Cassandra unexpectedly woke up and saw the mess all around her. As she looked at me, with her sleepy voice, she asked, "Is everything okay? What happened?" I just squeezed her hand, smiled, and simply said, "You missed quite a show, baby doll!" "That is too bad," she replied as her eyes closed, and she returned to continue her forty-thousand-foot-elevation nap. I have experienced emergency landings, mechanical malfunction while airborne, as well as many turbulences during my frequent flight travels, though this one was by far the worst; and yet I love to continue to fly, especially on long-haul flights. One thing I discovered on this particular Prague-New York route is the fact that I am not afraid of dying. I don't look for it, but whenever that moment comes, my soul is ready to finally meet my Maker, to fall on my knees in adoration and worship before Him, knowing that

> My sin—oh, the bliss of this glorious thought
> My sin not in part, but the whole
> It is nailed to the cross and I bear it no more
> Praise the Lord, praise the Lord, O my soul.

Jesus sees me forgiven and clean, holding me firmly in the palm of His mighty hand. He will guide me through the valley of death whenever I must traverse through, and He will welcome me *home*. This is not because I am perfect. No, this is because He is! He chose me, called me, saved me, and now holds me—eternally. Is He holding you?

> *I write these things to you who believe in the name of the Son*
> *of God so that you may know that you have eternal life.*
> —1 John 5:13

112) What Do I Say to the Pain

"Be fruitful and multiply." This biblical command, though given to Adam and Eve, applies to all mankind. We are called to bring forth another generation that will be taught the biblical principles and be the light and the salt of the earth. We also read that children are a blessing from the Lord. Now and at times, there are moments when a strong temptation to disregard this verse as true rings loudly. As the last string of patience and self-control has been broken by my own children's deliberate disobedience, I leave my godly character behind to react out of anger and frustration while wondering, *Where did my ugly outburst come from?* But, in reality, children, indeed, are an enormous blessing that cannot be measured in value, in cost, in energy output; they simply are.

Many young couples desire to start a family after they enjoy their first season of married life to the fullest. For Cassandra and me, this season was going to be fairly short, or so we thought. We had the benefit of entering marriage after knowing each other for a long number of years, serving together, touring together, working together. Both of us were a bit older as well, and we knew that the energy of running after a kiddo or two would far exceed the stamina required for a two-hour performance. After much prayer, we strongly felt to be led by the Lord to use a "natural family planning" method and allow Him and His timing to reign supreme. The desire to have children was strong in us both; and we simply never pondered that reaching parenthood could be anything but a great and fun journey through thinking of names, purchasing the first stroller, and learning how to change diapers.

It was the spring of 2001. As Cassandra stepped out of the bathroom, there was this unique glow all over her. *What in the world?* went through my head, and as a typical man, I simply did not put two and two together. Yes, everything has to be spelled out for me to arrive at the "I get it" station. As she saw and gathered the slowness of her husband, not for the first time I must add, Cassandra handed me the pregnancy test with two strong lines marking its result. Yes, we were pregnant! Like a flashing of a bright light in the deep darkness, emotions of joy, stress, excitement, and worry promenaded and flooded my mind. *Am I ready to be a father? How will we dance and tour with a child? Will it be a boy or a girl? Am I ready to play Barbies and have tea parties?* I could not answer yes to any of these questions, and yet I knew that this child growing inside of Cassandra is a human being knitted together by the awesome hand of God, Who is always in control. We started to get overwhelmed with such peace and joy as the days turned into weeks.

Due to my dad's illness, we traveled to Europe as often as we could. Going to visit my parents while having such great news to share with them of expecting a baby was a perfect combination that would bring some encouragement to a house marked by pain and discouragement as the prognosis of my dad's cancer looked dim. Once again, we landed in Prague to a beautiful and color-filled spring. Trees, flowers, fields, the sun—all of it was a picture-perfect vacation to be had. Cassandra, being the organizer that she is, planned some fun activities for just the two of us but also left plenty of time to simply visit my parents, sit, tell stories, and be together.

It was a Wednesday, and we planned to take a train out of town and do a bit of outdoor tourism in the countryside of the Czech Republic. We were catching a midmorning train out of the main train station. Our backpacks were packed with bottled water, unique Czech snacks that Cassandra learned to enjoy with me, and the must-have freshly baked poppyseed pastries bought hot in a small bakery. We grew in excitement of the day and the memories we were going to make. As we stood on the platform awaiting the arrival of our train, Cassandra handed me her backpack as she needed to visit the ladies' room. I do not think that I am the only man whose experience of waiting for a wife's return from a bathroom seems eternal in length. Being the good husband I was, I waited patiently even though the arrival of the train was imminent. Cassandra appeared from the underground escalator with a pale look on her face. Immediately, I knew something was wrong. "I have a lot of spotting, and I think we should skip the trip today," she said with a conviction in her voice that I was not going to argue with. "Let's go home, and you can lie down and rest," I said as nothing else came to my mind at the moment. By the time we arrived at my parents' apartment, the bleeding had intensified, and we knew that a trip to a hospital was a must. As we rode to the large state hospital, I knew that my fears were rising, and my imagination was running wild, producing an array of scenarios in my mind and heart. I was fearing for my wife and for her heart being broken and devastated should something unexpected take place. The swiftness of the admission, even though she was a foreigner, surprised me. Before long, the answers started to come in, and they were as devastating as I had imagined. Cassandra miscarried a few days ago already, and an immediate procedure needed to take place to remove the embryo and prevent further complications, such as infection or further damage to her uterus. Nobody spoke English, or at least nobody tried to communicate with her. Cassandra felt and was as alone as one could be. The procedure, titled dilation and curettage, is common following a miscarriage, we were told. This was an unexpected detour into a world I knew nothing about. Cassandra spent one night in the hospital, and I was not permitted to be with her. I was furious, and I felt helpless. I prayed hard and long for her that night asking the Father for His peace and presence to be in that cold hospital room. I also started to pray for His guidance as I knew that this was going to be my first valley of difficulty to lead my wife through. I needed His help, His wisdom, His love. The Lord was so incredibly faithful in those following moments and days. Both of us knew that an eternal life was created, and even though our little baby never saw the light of this world, it went to be in the light of the presence of its Creator forever more. One day, we will get to meet our first child. We never lost our hope in Jesus; actually, the opposite was true. We learned that it is moments like these when our human strength falls short and our dependence on Christ is the only way to grow in our love for Him. It does not, and it did not, push us away. But like a magnet, this pain of a miscarriage pulled us closer to Him. His plans are sovereign; we knew that already, but we learned that no matter how much we plan and prepare, God truly directs our steps in accord to His wisdom and understanding. We know that human life cannot be produced, ordered, created, or even killed and destroyed by man's will alone. Human life, from its very first moment, belongs to the King of kings. And whether it ever walks on the face of this world, it is an eternal creation forever dancing around the throne of God. As much as we were hurting, to have lost this first baby, we knew that God was in control, and we had faith and peace that one day we would experience the moment of seeing our child come into this world and with awe look into its eyes and chubby cheeks. What we did not know then was the fact that there would be yet another miscarriage just a few months down the road. That one was much more difficult to overcome as fears had moved into my heart and settled in for years to come. We knew that we could *get* pregnant, but we just did not know if we could *stay* pregnant. Our focus and our prayers shifted to praying in accordance with our needs, that is, for the Lord to sustain the life of the child in Cassandra's womb until it's time to be born has come. The Lord answered our prayers, and on May 14, 2002, Benjamin Isaiah Voborsky was born. Everything we dreamed for this moment to be like faded in comparison to the actual experience of holding this little baby, full of red hair, with big hands and big feet. That day, we imagined the wonder of God's plan for his life. What is the path God laid out for Benjamin to walk on? What is the mission the Lord ordained for him to do that no other person can fulfill? We are eighteen years into that journey, and it has been beautiful. Benjamin is a man with a great heart for the Lord and for people, especially those who do not live a life marked with ease and opportunity like he does. It has not always been easy, as Ben had to overcome many physical obstacles in his life, but we know that he is firmly held in the hands of his Creator and of his Lord. The story is continually being written, though in God's books, it had been planned out completely before the very first day of it ever came to be.

He fulfills the desires of those who fear him;
he hears their cry and saves them.

—Psalm 145:19

113) The Knock of Death

It did not take long for us to feel that our feet were under us and we started to function well with the addition of a baby boy in the house. Cassandra took six weeks off and then returned to the studio to get back into dancing, to return to her roles in the repertoire, and to be able and ready when the next tour started. Benjamin was placed into a small pack-and-play in the corner of the studio. He, too, was a trooper in "realizing the expectations placed on him." He knew to take a nap as his mom and dad took ballet technique class and then got nursed during lunch, only to sleep some more during rehearsal. It was months later when, during a "battement fondu" combination, I saw my son in the pack-and-play swaying back and forth to the piano class music, only to pull up, look me in the eye, and with a grin on his face climb over the edge. We knew that the initial season of immo-

bility just ended. Benjamin started touring at the age of three months. The company's tour director worked closely with the individual performance organizers in cities all around the nation to provide a babysitter for the green room of each theater. During the show, we would dance, and Benjamin would be spoiled to death by the lovely ladies who willingly came in to watch him. While traveling, Benjamin would share a bunk with his mom, and I know they both loved the closeness of the space accompanied by the noise and the motion of the traveling bus. When we would arrive at each destination, Cassandra unloaded herself and the baby as I followed slowly and awkwardly carrying her suitcase, my suitcase, her dance bag, my dance bag, Benjamin's diaper bag, the pack-and-play, and two backpacks. I did resemble a well-decorated Christmas tree, and the looks of many clearly indicated their enjoyment watching me struggle as I walked from the bus to the hotel room. Had the iPhones been as popular then as they are now, there would be countless viral videos of this "dad carrying all these bags as his wife waltzed through the lobby with a cute baby boy in her arms"; I am certain of it. Benjamin did well, and his presence brought much laughter and joy into long bus days to the different hosts on the road, to many random people we met along the way, and to his two parents, who treasured every moment as best as they knew how. By the time Benjamin turned one and celebrated his big first birthday, he had already traveled to many states coast to coast, to Europe, and to Asia, where his cuteness and red hair called for countless pictures with the locals who viewed this little Caucasian baby boy as something rare and unique. Benjamin always smiled big, and his little self was absolutely adorable. I would say the same even if I wasn't his dad, I know!

It was a chilly September day in Jackson. That was usually the case only when a rainfall was coming causing the summer temperatures to ease up for a day or two before the humidity kicked back into high gear. I was getting ready for the day as the phone rang.

"Hello," I answered the ring to hear my mom say, "Jiri, good morning." I heard my mom's voice on the other end of the line sounding both tired and sad. "I am calling to let you know that your dad slipped into a coma last night. I know this might be difficult to do, but I think you need to come home to say goodbye if you can." I could tell that my mom tried hard to be strong on the phone. Her world was crumbling, and I needed to be there for her and for my dad as well. "I'll see what I can do, and I will call you back," I said as my mind started to spin to figure out just how I could find a ticket to Prague that day. God provided an amazing price, and before I knew it, I was leaving Jackson on the two o'clock flight home. As I landed in Prague, my brother, Míra, who arrived from Dublin, where he was working as a nurse at the time, was waiting at the international arrival hall. We traveled to Ústí, taking the EuroCity express train and, upon reaching our hometown, went directly to the hospital. Our mom was waiting for us at the door to the Oncology ICU ward. The moment she saw her two sons, the remainder of her strength melted as quickly as ice. Her tears flooded the tiles of the hallway. We said not a word. Our job was to be there and to hold her. "Let's go in," were the first words out of her mouth, and so we did. She took a deep breath before the door to the ICU opened. My mom was fighting a hard fight, and she wanted to be strong for her husband, whom she loved being married to for almost thirty years. My dad was lying there with tubes and machines surrounding his bed. He was thin and pale. His breathing was shallow and weak. Cancer had taken its toll on him. He had fought the disease for three years. Every day, he would rest most of the day as my mom worked to have enough strength to be there for her when she returned. My grandmother who took care of him during these hours was asked to promise that she would not tell Bohunka just how much pain he was in. She never did until he was gone. We visited his unresponsive body for a couple of minutes before my mom started to weep, and I knew we had to take her home. As we left the hospital, I saw her collapse on the sidewalk and, without any hesitation, let all her pain flow out through the massive outpouring of tears. Míra and I picked her frail body up, called a taxi, and drove home. I was thankful to be there. As we walked into the apartment to help her to her bed, I noticed the copy of the Czech Bible on my dad's nightstand. The bookmark was halfway through the book of Mark. I was overwhelmed. Our mom told us that she could not go see Mirek, our dad, anymore, as the state of his body was simply too much for her to bear. We understood completely and decided to take turns in our daily visits to the ICU and in being home with my mom. This was perfect as the visits with my dad were more or less prayer sessions for him and with him. He never responded, but I knew that he could hear me as his lifeless body still had a pulse and a heartbeat. Just a few short days later, as my visit was coming to an end, my dad's rib cage was protruding through the skin. I knew the end was near. I kissed him on his forehead after we prayed for his salvation, and as the ICU unit doors closed behind me, I asked the Lord for me to see dad smile as a sign that he was at peace with Jesus. I walked home from the hospital to have time to be alone, to pray, to think, to ponder how I could be the support my mom needed. As I arrived home, my mom was sitting at the kitchen table cutting photos out of my dad's ID cards and look-ing through photo albums to remember and recall all the good times they enjoyed together. "Can I join you?" I asked as I sat down with-out waiting for her reply. It was good to see her smile holding differ-ent pictures, many of them black-and-white, reminiscing of all the good times spent side by side with my dad. Most of his ID pictures were typical of him, stern faced and very much to the point, as my dad rarely showed or displayed emotions in public. A brown leather jacket was the most common top layer of clothing he selected from his wardrobe no matter the season, current fashion trend, or even the temperature of the day. When pictured, it appeared that removing it would take unnecessary time he did not want to waste, and the result was, therefore, each photo very similar to the next. It was the family pictures that showed more of his personality and of his heart. The very first little booklet I picked up to open and to remove the photo from was a white pocket-size trifold. Muddy smears of fingerprints were obvious on its cover. "Czech Fishermen Association" was the title on the cover surrounding a drawing of a pike fish with a hook piercing its lip. In a moment, I recalled the countless times my dad would leave the house with the gear hoping to bring a fish back, a big one at that. This was his absolute favorite pastime without ques-tion. As I opened the booklet, I saw the only ID photograph of my father with an ear-to-ear grin, smiling with joy flowing from his deep brown eyes. I removed it from the trifold, showed it to my mom, and asked if I could keep this one. "Of course, that is a good one," she replied, smiling herself as she glimpsed over to my side of the table. We had a sweet time that evening as I, Míra, and our mom poured encouragement into one another. Laughter visited our company that evening as well, and for that, we were grateful.

The next day, I opted to walk to the hospital rather than take the public transportation. A little prayer, a lot of thinking, and some simple enjoyment of the city life passing me by on the streets did much good to my heart. I entered the hospital, and as usual, the dis-agreeable feeling of the place overwhelmed me. As I was approaching the ICU sector of the Oncology Department, my father's doctor met me in the hallway. "Good morning, Mr. Voborsky, it is with sadness that I must inform you that your father passed away about an hour ago. He was peaceful and without much immediate pain. You are welcome to still see him. I just wanted you to know." I appreciated the care and tenderness the doctor displayed toward me and my family. The very fact that she did not call my mom to simply tell her over the phone but rather waited for me or Míra to visit to be told in person was a kind thing to do. I took a moment to gather my thoughts, and I knew that seeing him without life was not what I wanted or needed to do. "I will pass, thank you. We appreciate everything you and your team have done to make my father feel as comfortable as possible these past couple of days, as well as throughout the fight of the past three years. We appreciate it more than we can ever verbalize or express. Thank you." I said, looking into the doctor's eyes. She smiled back, saying, "I thought that would be what you or your brother would have decided to do. Here are the few items belonging to your father." She handed me a small bag. "Also," she added, "when I chose to study medicine, and oncology in particular, I knew that there will be many days like these when telling a family member the sad news would simply be inevitable. It was our honor to provide and to do everything we could for your father all throughout the three years. He fought a good and a strong fight. You should be proud!" I did not know what to say as emotions started to stir within me. "Thank you, ma'am," was all I could say. I took the bag and waited for her to walk through the double doors of the ICU. Then I sat on a nearby bench and let the reality settle in. Looking onto the light green tiles on the floor, I was lost in thought. Then

as clear as one can hear the Lord speak, I sensed Him reminding me of the fishing license photograph. I realized that when I requested to see my dad smile as a sign of his salvation, I was thinking in a physical sense, but of all the austere photos of his IDs, randomly choosing the only one where he was smiling was not a coincidence. The Lord honored my request, and I believe He answered my plea and my dad's prayer to be forgiven and saved. It happened on his deathbed, but it happened. That fight was won and that eternal victory, secured through the cross and the empty tomb, received by a man who all his life believed that one needs to be a good, honest, loving person to leave a good legacy and impact on people around. At the eleventh hour, he came to realize that none of it matters if one does not know the saving grace of Jesus Christ. Could it be that my dad is already playing with his grandchildren that even I am yet to meet!

For it is by grace you have been saved, through faith—
and this is not from yourselves, it is the gift of God.
—Ephesians 2:8

114) Unexpected

Being home was both extremely difficult but also a huge blessing. It was a must being there for my mom during the initial days of her widowhood as life was going to be different now. The funeral was a sad reminder of the hopelessness the Czechs and Europeans experience all their lives as death is the ultimate end and the hope of heavenly reunion is nonexistent. A few weeks after I returned back to Jackson, I received a phone call that my uncle, my dad's brother three years his junior, was diagnosed with the same type of cancer. My aunt was devastated as she watched my father battle the disease, and the fear of what was coming her husband's way was overwhelming. It is a must to mention here that, for many generations looking back, there has not been a Voborsky male who lived beyond the age of fifty-two. My grandfather on the Voborsky side of the family lost his life in a mining accident, his father died in a motorcycle crash, and his father lost his life during the war. My father lost his life to cancer, and now his brother was facing the same fate. And, yes, my uncle died three years after the diagnosis. These were strenuous times for my family, who, even in these moments of pain, strongly refused faith, comfort, and peace of God's love.

Meanwhile, Cassandra and I found ourselves pregnant again. Benjamin was a strong two-year-old, and his body was outgrowing his hypotonia, a low-muscle-tone condition that he was born with, and he was progressing well. The excitement in his eyes when he found out that he was going to be a big brother was almost too much to handle. We were excited as well. This new life inside of Cassandra pushed away the memories of our initial struggles with miscarriages, the loss of my dad, and my uncle's illness. We wanted to be ready to receive this new life with joy. As we did not know the gender of Benjamin, yes, we had waited to be surprised; we felt that we needed to know the gender of this new baby. Because of the low-muscle-tone condition of our son, the doctors wanted to keep a close eye on Cassandra, and the baby to come, throughout the course of the preg-

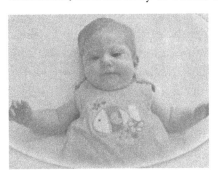

nancy. The very first ultrasound visit showed minor abnormalities, but due to the early stages of the pregnancy, the doctor was not overly alarmed. I, on the other hand, noticed almost immediately the fear that was still quietly residing in my heart waking up and causing a ruckus.

As the pregnancy progressed, we found out that our next baby was going to be a girl. Benjamin was going to have a little sister. All the following ultrasound visits continually confirmed that the initial abnormalities they saw were not going away but actually taking a clear shape. Our little girl, Cosette, was going to be born with club-feet, a condition that is treatable with casting of the legs shortly after birth. We were also informed that often a hidden condition not noticeable during the pregnancy might accompany the clubfeet and should we choose to abort the baby, we were still within the time frame to do so. That was the most upsetting monologue I had ever heard as the nurse simply and mechanically read to Cassandra and to myself these horrific options, giving us a green light for something that we had no right of doing. As God is the sole Creator of each life, shaping it exactly as He sees fit, who are we to decide to end it? Our strong refusal of the option made it clear to the staff of the hospital. Cosette was going to be a beautiful little baby possibly born with a medical condition or even a handicap, but she was going to be ours, and we were determined to do whatever it took to help her grow and be, like her big brother, an overcomer. And surely enough, April 26, 2004, was the day preordained for her to enter the world. Her blue eyes projected peace, and her cheeks were a great temptation for her daddy to want to squeeze and play with. Benjamin was tirelessly requesting to hold his little sister as often as he could. I stood amazed watching the staff of the River Oaks Hospital proceed with the treatment of the clubfeet and create these tiny casts for our baby girl. Just like her brother, Cosette was also born with a low muscle tone, and breastfeeding was simply too difficult for her to do. Cassandra was set to do whatever it took to help Cosette gain the necessary weight, crucial for the overcoming of the hypotonia. Days turned into weeks and eventually months. Another complication knocked on the door of our lives, reflux. Normally, babies outgrow this condition, but when it is met with other obstacles in the early stages of life, the gastroesophageal reflux could become a serious problem. And so it did. As we found a good treatment plan and could see progress in the correction of Cosette's feet, the overall inability to gain weight was difficult to combat. Nearing the completion of her third month of life, it was recommended to us that a feeding tube would be inserted directly to Cosette's stomach to completely relieve the esophagus of any laborious work in hope of bringing the healing, the weight gain, and the strengthening of Cosette's little body. We were burdened by the many obstacles we faced; but we knew that there was simply no other option than to keep walking, one day and one step at a time, looking to Jesus for everything while trusting the medical team of the children's hospital. The day of the surgery came. I was trying to be strong, trying to be there for Cassandra, for Benjamin, and for my daughter. To see our little girl being taken away from her mother's arms and wheeled into the operation hall and disappearing behind the heavy door was excruciating. We had to wait. We were informed of the possible risks and complications, but there was simply no other alternative. The surgery was a success; and Cosette, with her name meaning "victorious," pulled through. I took Benjamin home as Cassandra stayed in the hospital. All this was unfolding as Ballet Magnificat held its annual Summer Dance Intensive, when around three hundred students from all around the globe travel to Jackson to grow as dancers but more importantly to grow in understanding of the real and authentic power of Jesus Christ, manifested in countless different ways in their lives. Hearing about Cosette was going to be a huge testimony of the power of God in her little life that, we prayed, would bring encouragement to their own. A few days following the surgery, Cosette was discharged from the children's hospital. We were given machines, tubes, and pages of instructions as to how to feed her through the tube and how to provide what she would need between the doctor checkups and visits. She was leaving the hospital weak, breathing strenuously. We were told that this is a normal postoperative oxygen level as well as a regular heart activity for a child of her age. We drove home wondering if we knew everything we needed to know. It all seemed overwhelming. We knew that we were not the first set of parents who felt inadequate to handle such a responsibility, but our faith and our prayers were continually focused on the Lord and His assistance. Arriving home, Benjamin was thrilled to have his sister back. All throughout the process, he had been the joy both of us needed. He hugged Cosette, as if letting her know that he loved her greatly. The few days since the implantation of the feeding tube, we even saw a weight gain that she so desperately needed. Everything was going to be all right. Yes, there was a road still to be traveled, but the hardest portion of it was behind us. We placed her into a crib right next to our bed. As every new parent sleeps more or less awake the whole night intently listening to the breathing of the new baby, we were no different. We plugged the tubes as we were instructed to do and slowly allowed the feeding to continue throughout the night as the programmed machine permitted the required amount of formula. The busyness of the past few days overcame us both, as we fell asleep for a couple of early morning hours. Cassandra woke up first, hearing the machine do what it was designed to do. As any mother would, she rose from the bed not to firstly use the bathroom nor to have her cup of coffee but to check up on the baby.

Cosette was sleeping soundly. Cassandra reached into the crib to gently place her fingers onto the cute chubby cheeks, only to feel the coldness of the skin. Her motherly instinct signaled that something was not right. She started to unplug the tubes to pick up our sweet Cosette. It was then when she realized that there was no rising and no falling of the chest. By then I was up. We realized that our little girl was not breathing. Calling 911 help line followed instantly. The calm voice of the dispatcher directed us into administering the cardiopulmonary resuscitation on an infant while she assured us that the emergency response was on its way. We were fighting for our little girl's life. It seemed a long wait. The lady on the other end of the line was continually guiding us in how to proceed even as hopelessness, and fear started to flood our bedroom as if a floodgate of a large reservoir opened for the very first time following a heavy rain and huge amounts of water rapidly filled the valley below. We prayed; we pleaded. We never stopped administering CPR. The ambulance and the local police and fire departments arrived at our house as the paramedics rushed into our room. In a moment, Cosette was being driven to the hospital under a loud noise of the sirens. The police escorted Cassandra and myself as we followed suit. We asked a neighbor to watch Benjamin as we did not want him to go with us. The ride to the hospital was intense. Cassandra clutched my hand as we both prayed prayers that were lacking eloquence but were filled with authentic faith and trust in our faithful and good God. We arrived at the emergency entrance a few minutes after the ambulance. We were escorted to a small private waiting room. The door finally opened. Both of us stood up as we watched the doctor enter in. The facial expression almost did not need any words to communicate what it already indicated, and yet we needed to hear and not guess what the prognosis was. "I am so sorry to tell you that your little girl passed away sometime last night. There was nothing we could do to save her life, and I am very sorry." The world had stopped for us. There was nothing that could have prepared us for this moment. The pain in my heart erupted with destructive power. I feared for Cassandra, and I worried how I myself was going to react and press through this unimaginable moment of sudden and devastating pain. The doctor left the room, and I looked into Cassandra's eyes, flooded with streams of tears. We embraced as our knees gave up strength, and we collapsed to the ground. I held my wife as hard as I could as there were no words and no encouragement I could give. We wept loudly and long. "How could this have happened to us?" The moment seemed so surreal. And yet even there in the midst of all the pain, anger, and confusion, both of us sensed the presence, real, authentic, powerful, and tangible presence of the Lord. His invisible yet powerful arms embraced us—right there on the floor of the small hospital room. The tears continued to flow, but the anger started to melt away. The unwelcome fear was also being crushed and pushed out of the way. We knew that we were going to hurt and ache for a long time to come, perhaps for years; but we also knew that even as painful as this situation was, it was not and we were not hopeless. "To be absent from the body is to be present with the Lord," resonated in our hearts. We knew that our little girl had stepped into the presence of the Lord without casts on her feet and without a feeding tube attached to her side. She was truly free and truly victorious, victorious with Jesus. She was there in the place which we both are looking to one day enter ourselves, a place with no tears, no pain, no worry, no fear—a place where the good and righteous Redeemer prepared a place for Cosette, as He also prepared a place for us. It is only a question of time, but before long, we will all be united again, this time without ever having to have to say goodbye.

The Lord gave and the Lord has taken away;
may the name of the Lord be praised.

—Job 1:21b

115) Isn't He Wonderful!

Cosette's memorial and burial, indeed, took place during the Summer Dance Intensive; and as much as there was a hesitation to expose the students to witness death, we knew that Cosette's short life could make an impact on these young lives in a way we could not even have dreamed of. Cassandra and I felt called to dance at our daughter's funeral as a testimony of our resolve to look up to the One Who holds us in the palm of His mighty hands, rather than to bury our hearts in self-pity and sorrow. We also sensed the call to encourage our family members, our loved ones, our friends through the gift of dance which God had given us with the eternal hope of heaven found in Jesus. And so we danced. Cassandra's brother, Nicholas, shared a powerful message based on the wise words of King Solomon, who knew that it was much more beneficial to enter the house of mourning than it was to enter the house of rejoicing, as the former pricks our hearts to reevaluate our eternal standing where the latter serves more as an invigorating song on the path of life. We were able to say our "goodbye" knowing that, though Cosette's body was being laid into the

ground, her spirit was long gone and completely free in the presence of the Lord. We were surrounded by earthly and heavenly encouragement, humbly resolved to follow the leading of our Father.

And He was ready to pour Himself and His blessings on us anew. Before long, we were pregnant again. Fear in my heart started to bubble up again, and I knew that I can succumb to it and be bound, or I can press into the Prince of Peace, Whose joy is my strength. Easier said than done, I must confess, but life always remains to be a fight, and we can choose how we are going to battle it. We wanted to be surprised and not know the gender of the baby, and as all ultrasounds showed a large belly, I knew that another son was on his way. Then on June 21, 2005, a beautiful and healthy little girl arrived. We named her Maya, after a German cartoon of a little bee whose caretaker was Kassandra. As every life holds its own value and not one life can be exchanged for another, Maya was a tremendous blessing as the memory and the what-would-life-be-like-with-a-girl thoughts and dreams were now going to be lived out through this amazing gift. We found no adequate words to tell the Lord how we felt and how humbled we were to be entrusted with this new addition to our family. The words of an old hymn come to mind. They go like this: "Isn't He wonderful? Wonderful, isn't He? Counsellor, Almighty God, isn't He, isn't He, isn't He?" And, yes, He is all of this and so much more. Maya is a beautiful and talented young lady who fills our house with a continual, often almost too continual, singing of praise and worship to her Savior. We love our daughter!

Your faithfulness continues through all generations.
—Psalm 119:90

116) Österreich

I had no idea. Even in my wildest dreams, I would have not thought that I would one day be a choreographer. As the Lord would have it, that was a part of the "package" of working at Ballet Magnificat. When I was in my early twenties, Kathy, as the artistic director of the company, asked me to do small pieces for the repertoire. My choreographic journey started then. When I was twenty-six, I created my first story ballet, and before long, I was in love. I enjoyed the strenuous process of seeking the Lord for the vision and unique angle for each new work, for the inspiration in finding a powerful and yet appropriate musical score for each ballet. I spent countless hours in the studio early in the morning when no one else was to be found in the building. The need to generate quickly continued to push me as the company toured significantly, and a new repertoire was a must. I desired to create a powerful and clear story in each new piece. It was an incredible gift watching each ballet be "born" as so many creative people of the costume, sets, lighting, and prop departments joined in to make it happen. Like a child on Christmas morning, I looked forward to the day when I could see the audience respond to what they saw and experienced and be ministered to their deepest needs by the Almighty God through the work He allowed me to fashion for His glory. Over the years, there were fifteen story ballets to come in addition to countless projects around the world; and yet, after all this creative power of writing new works, never would I have been prepared for the story I am about to share with you, namely *Austria*.

As we did often, Cassandra, our kiddos, and I were vacationing in Europe. The times spent with their Czech grandmother were sparse, and I wanted them to see and get to know well the place where Daddy grew up. Often when visiting the Czech Republic, we would travel around other parts of Europe as well to broaden our experiences, deepen the "family vacation memories," and allow our children to see life outside of the United States. Cassandra's dad grew up in Austria, or Österreich in the German language, and until this day, many relatives live there. During this particular summer vacation, we connected with family members in the city of Salzburg and planned to spend just a couple of days there, let them see Cassandra again, and meet her husband and children. The *Sound of Music*, as Maria runs down the lush green hills surrounding Salzburg, was playing in our minds as we drove from Ústí toward our southern neighbors. The Czechs and Austrians live in neighborly relations but don't particularly love each other deeply, as some neighbors do. Our history includes chapters of tensions between the two nations, one example being the dual monarchy of the Austro-Hungarian Empire, to which the Czechs were forcefully included. The many years of the Communist regime lurking along the Austrian northern border did not help the Austrians to love the Czechoslovak people and their ideals either. As the Iron Curtain fell in 1989, the two nations had been looking for ways to restart neighborly relations again, and in most cases, this effort produced good fruit.

The rental car was packed with myself, Cassandra, the children, and my mom, Bohunka, whom we always wanted to include in our ventures so she could experience the fun with us. The plan for Austria was just that—to have fun meeting relatives and to enjoy the visit of Salzburg, the birthplace of Wolfgang Amadeus Mozart. The Czech Republic applied for membership in the Eurozone and was on a waiting list to become a member of Schengen at the time, the border free sector of the European Union. As the inclusion was eminent, the borders between the two nations were still in place, and passports were necessary to cross from one country into the other. We pulled up to the small border crossing guard station to enter Austria, just a kilometer after officially leaving the Czech territory. The sunny skies and the beauty of the day did not lend a helping hand in realizing that our vacation plans were about to be radically altered and the visit to Salzburg obliterated. We pulled to the window and politely greeted the officer in German. "*Guten tag! Hier sind unsere Pässe,*" I said as I handed the border guard our passports. I tried to smile at him, but he was not interested in any kind of personal interaction. He opened the passports to examine the infor-mation and to make sure that nei-ther of us was a "spy" working for a foreign government, judging by his facial expression. What nor-mally takes a couple of minutes at the most started to feel like an awkwardly long and unexpected pause. The tension and the tem-perature started to rise in the car and our mood. "What is he look-

ing at?" my mom asked from the backseat. I just gestured with my eyes through the rearview mirror as I did not want to say anything at the moment. An unnecessary conversation at a border crossing is never a good idea. *Slam!* The border guard abruptly closed the win-dow shut and disappeared into the interior of the building with all of our passports in his hands. *Interesting*, was the only thought that flashed through my mind. "What is happening?" Cassandra asked, repeating exactly what Bohunka asked in Czech a few moments ago. "I have no idea, but he took all of our passports with him... strangely... I must say," I said, looking into her beautiful greenish eyes. The mood and the heat started to be uncomfortable as the sum-mer sun was mercilessly shining on us. The doors of the border post opened as two Austrian officers walked out. "*Fahren Sie hier,*" was the command given to us, accompanied by a gesture pointing toward a parking spot off the main road. I pulled the car to the spot and waited for the next request. That came almost immediately as one of the officers leaned into the open window of the car and said, "*Herr*

Voborsky, kommen Sie mit mir," ordering me to go with him into the border post. I looked at Cassandra and my mom, signaling that everything would be fine, as I tried to hide the fact that a certain amount of hesitation started to appear in my heart and through the sweat of my brow. "*Einen moment bitte,"* was the best I could do as I tried to unbuckle and hop out of the car quickly. I followed the officer into the building where another guard was already waiting behind a counter. All our passports were piled up perfectly, all but mine. My passport was held in the officer's hand, interestingly opened to the very last page of the booklet. As I did not know what the problem was, I waited for the next instruction. "*Sprechen Sie Deutsch?"* was the first question, asking whether or not I spoke German. As I was not comfortable in the position I found myself in, I simply responded, "*Nein, Ich spreche Deutsch aber schlecht und wenig,"* I responded, firmly indicating with the tone of my voice that I was not interested in communicating with him or anyone else using German, as my knowledge of it was not sufficient for a situation like this. "Follow me, *bitte,"* said the officer who appeared to be in charge. As I had no idea what the problem was, I did just that. The other officer simply closed the door as if locking the border crossing point completely, only to follow me and his boss. There seemed to be no one else around. I was unable to tell or even hint to Cassandra that a slight problem might be surfacing, but all I knew was to comply. Sandwiched between the two tall blond-hair-and-blue-eyed Austrian border guards wearing deep-green almost-brown uniforms with pistols affixed to brown belts, pants tucked into tall boots, and berets shifted to the right side of their heads, I started to feel uneasy. We walked through a door dividing the entry room from the rest of the facility, only to proceed down the steps into the basement of the station. The bottom of the staircase led to a corridor with three sets of metal doors on either side. Lights automatically illuminated the passage as we entered the narrow and intimidating space. We passed all the doors and finally entered the last set located on the right-hand side. I could feel the close presence of the officer behind me, as that did not assist me in feeling comfortable. We entered a small room. There were no windows. Furbished with a desk and one chair, I knew that I was to stand as one of the officers was to sit down behind the desk while the other was to... My mind went blank. All my previous uneasy feelings started to intensify. The "boss" sat behind the desk, while the other officer rested on the corner of the same, both looking intently in my direction. My passport was tossed onto the surface of the table. "We brought you down here to ask a couple of questions regarding your passport. We see that you have traveled on it extensively around the world, and yet nobody realized that you have forged it!" The little room seemed to sway slightly, at least in my perspective. Did the officer just accuse me of traveling on a fraudulent passport!

"I don't understand... What exactly makes you believe that I forged my passport? That is absurd!" I protested.

"*Hier*," the Austrian pointed to the last page of my travel document. As I looked closely at the page in question, my confusion only increased. There used to be a page in the older version of the Czech passports where parents penciled in their children's information. Instructions in multiple languages, German included, clearly guided how that was to be done as well as the purpose of it. I had penciled in Benjamin's information after he was born. My son has traveled on his own passport ever since he first left the United States at the age of "zero," as that is the law, and I never thought about erasing or further updating this page. I started to explain the purpose of the page, only to be abruptly stopped midsentence.

"*Stille*," German for *silence*, was the next spoken word by the officer behind the desk, who was no longer sitting but standing with his fists resting on the surface. He continued in English, "It is against the law to write anything into an official government document issued to the citizens for domestic and international purposes. You will not be able to use this passport to enter Austria today, and we have to confiscate it from you."

"Excuse me!" was my harsh response. "The passport is the property of the Czech Republic, and no one is authorized to confiscate it. Actually, everyone is requested to assist the bearer of the passport in any way possible. Also, in four days, I am scheduled to fly back to the United States with my family, and I need my passport for that. I am a permanent resident in the US possessing a green card, but I need a passport to travel. You cannot confiscate my passport!" My face was bright red, and my emotions were reaching their limits. I worried that losing my "cool" was inevitable as I understood that any sort of heated argument would only further hinder my circumstance. The officer who sat on the corner of the desk stood up as he saw my frustrations intensify. I knew that should this altercation turn physical, I was sure to lose as any kind of bodily fight would be two against one. The size of the officers alone put me at a disadvantage; that was clear to all of us. But if needed, I would fight hard. My mind was spinning. The officer in charge sat down.

"We can make this end right here and right now," he stated calmly. I was not sure what he was going to say next, but I could not think of a single scenario deemed appropriate outside of them apologizing, giving me my passport back, and letting me go. Somehow, I doubted that to be the case. I was right. "You can pay us a hundred euros each, and we will forget that any of this ever happened. If you don't, we will confiscate your passport. We will have to call in an official Czech-German interpreter and write up a report that will create a five-year record in the database of the European Union. The choice is yours." As the other officer continued to stand uncomfortably close to me, this time, I leaned against the table, and with a quick thought in my head of *Come what may*, I responded, "If I have broken the law, then I deserve to be punished, and I do not see how a payment of any kind would justify my breach of the regulations... sir!" I pushed away from the table as my hands had the urging tendency to close into two fists, expecting a possible physical response of the standing officer. "If that is what you want, have it your way! Step away from the table," he continued as he looked at his colleague, "and step toward the corner." As I did, the second officer prepared a camera to photograph me. If they were bluffing to extort money, they were doing a splendid "Broadway-style performance" job, but if this was real, I was about to be photographed like a criminal. And surely enough, a metal bar was pivoted from the wall and numbers inserted into its edge. "Look directly at me!" was the first command. I complied. "Profile *bitte*," followed...and I complied. The mixture of German and English only made the experience more surreal and uncomfortable. I could not believe this was happening. The officer sitting behind the desk of the small basement room seemed to enjoy the process and my obvious frustration. There was nothing I could do…and he knew it! I was mad and madder still. "Now we will have to check for any potential tattoos and photograph them for the record," he continued.

"I don't have any tattoos," I said firmly.

"Take your shirt off," followed next. My eyes opened widely as my mouth could not produce any response to that command. "Remove your shirt!" the officer repeated himself. I started to unbutton my short-sleeved summer shirt. I was wearing an undershirt and a pair of shorts. The moment I removed it, the standing officer circled around me, examining my tattoo-less arms and neck area. "What do you do for a living…? What is your job?" was the following question.

As all I worried about was what else would be requested of me to take off, I replied swiftly, "I am a professional dancer…ballet dancer." I added that to clarify the statement in case they imagined a different type of "dancing." I was used to all kinds of reactions whenever I shared about what I did for a living, especially residing in Mississippi, where men hunt, play football, go to the gym, and meeting a professional ballet dancer was usually a first for them all. The officers followed suit as a judgmental smirk appeared on their faces.

"Remove your T-shirt," followed. I started to feel uncomfortable as the situation progressed. I took my undershirt off. Another round of circulation around me took place by the assistant officer. "*Nein, kein* tattoo," was the report to the boss, stating the obvious. There were no tattoos to be found. They knew I was not hiding any, but this game was too much fun to stop, I assumed. Surely enough. "Remove your shorts!"

I could not believe it. Panic flooded my mind. *How far would this continue? There is not much more to take off after this, and then what! This is a dream…a nightmare… It must be!* My mind was running in high gear. My shorts dropped to my ankles. "I do not understand this…sir…and I will not remove anything else!" I said as firmly as I knew how. The understanding that I had to do whatever these two requested here in the room without witnesses, without windows, without options was clear to me; but I felt that I needed to articulate my determination and fight for my dignity.

The seated officer behind the desk leaned against the back of his chair; and with his index finger lifted high pointing toward the ceiling, he said, "Rotate *bitte*!" There I was rotating around feeling extremely exposed and frustrated about this situation and the lack of options to resolve it. "*Das ist gut*," was the next statement. I pulled my shorts up in record time. Before anyone could say anything, I was dressed, buttoning my shirt. "Follow us upstairs where we will wait for the interpreter to arrive." We did just that. Over an hour later, a small-framed lady, possibly in her midforties, arrived. Meanwhile, I was permitted to briefly communicate with Cassandra and my family to let them know the situation. They could tell right away that I was extremely frustrated, but there was no time to go into any details. My mom was mad as she saw her grandbabies sit in the heat of the day. There was nothing she could do…but still, her support meant the world.

This lady who was summoned into the border station briefly introduced herself and, between her breaths, indicated that she was a frequent visitor there, often interpreting for cases that would not happen anywhere else outside of "Österreich." Four hours later, I was asked to sign the protocol, and without my passport, I was escorted out of the border crossing station. I settled into the car unable to even begin to convey all that had taken place in the past 240 minutes of sheer ridiculousness. "How am I supposed to enter the Czech Republic without a passport?" was to be my last question aimed at the guard. "We will phone the station letting them know you are coming," the officer replied, seeing the confused looks on my wife's and mother's faces, who knew nothing about the situation and my confiscated passport. Then he added, "I hope you will come back to Austria again!" As I did not think it possible, I got even more upset. "Sir, we have traveled to countries worldwide, and though we enjoy seeing the sites, it is the people of the nations we meet that we love and treasure the most. Understandably, today's experience was not such!" With that, I made a U-turn and started to drive the one kilometer up the road to the Czech side of the border. As we pulled to the customs station, the Czech officer requested the presentation of our passports, to which I responded that mine was confiscated down the road and the Austrians promised to call ahead to inform them of our coming. They never did. He instead called the Austrian side of the border to collect and verify the confusing information I was giving him. As he hung up the phone, he said, "Did they really take your passport?" "Yes, they did just that, sir. I penciled my son's name into the designated page in the back of my passport, and they deemed it fraudulent." My frustration was clear, but I was trying hard to stay calm as none of what transcribed earlier was this gentleman's fault. I was invited to come inside of the border house. He explained to me that the newest passports no longer have the page as each child must have a passport of his own, but to deem it fraudulent was absurd. The passport is the property of the Czech Republic, and to take it by any officer of another nation is illegal. "Sir, I told him all that, and after I refused to pay the bribe they requested, it went downhill in a fast progression, supposedly ending with a five-year 'criminal' record in the European Union." The officer was visibly feeling sorry for what I had been through. "Where do you live?" he asked as he started to enter information into his computer. "Well, I live in the United States with my wife and family, and we are scheduled to leave to go back in four days. I don't know how long it will take to have a new passport issued. This is such a mess... I am so sorry, but I am frustrated by the treatment and the result of being without a passport!" I concluded. "Where are you staying while in the Czech Republic?" he followed. "With my mom, sir. She lives in Ústí nad Labem, where I was born." "Let me call the city hall there and request an expedited issuing of a new passport. They can do it in twenty-four hours," he said while picking up the phone again. Before long, we were driving back north heading toward Prague and, eventually, Ústí. In four days' time, I was on board of a transatlantic flight with a freshly issued temporary passport, valid for three months, sufficient to get me back home, only to exchange it through the Czech embassy for a regular passport.

As many years have gone by since my encounter in Austria, I still wonder what exactly the reason was for the closure of the path and of the plan to visit Salzburg that year. Many times in life, more so than not, we have no answers for the "whys" of life. Whether we understand it or not, we must always—and rather quickly—remind ourselves of the sovereign reign of God over all things, over all circumstances, over all unexpected situations we might find ourselves in. If the Lord needs us to understand, it is nothing to Him to make that happen. And when He doesn't, we must trust that it is best for us not to know. It is funny that until this day, every time I apply for a new Czech passport, there is a request to return the passport that is missing, as that is the Czech law. I always reply that the Austrian Ministry of Interior has it. Or is it collecting dust in a drawer of the now-closed border crossing station in Wullowitz, Österreich? Who knows!

The One enthroned in heaven laughs.
—Psalm 2:4

117) A Call to Shepherding

Cassandra and I sensed the guiding hand of the Lord to transition from full-time touring with the company as our family grew to focus on our two children and to wait and see what God had in store for us when it pertained to Ballet Magnificat. We did not receive the Lord's permission to leave the ballet; nor had any sense of another calling, another field to plow, poetically speaking. The year was 2005. I had been in America for twelve years, and Mississippi had become my home. The five years of marriage to the greatest godly woman did me much good. To watch Cassandra love our children, to pursue Christ every day, to love me patiently and with kindness humbled me daily. I was grateful and happy and satisfied in my Lord and all the blessings He had bestowed upon an unworthy servant such as me. I was prepared to serve Ballet Magnificat whichever way was necessary as I continued to ask the Father to guide Cassandra and me to know the exact way He desired us to serve Him there. I knew that I had a couple of dancing years still to give, but to tour full-time was no longer possible, as I knew that to leave Cassandra on a regular basis was not the direction we were called to go. I did see that modeled by John, who toured for many years while his wife, Karin, stayed behind to hold down the fort of their Jackson home while raising their seven children, working part-time, homeschooling, and supporting her husband, who was called to glorify God with the touring ministry of Ballet Magnificat. They both knew that neither one could do this without the unwavering support of the other; and together, they looked to Jesus for every need, for every provision, for every ounce of strength, for faith, for comfort, for wisdom, and for His leading of their lives. I knew that I was lacking in being called to such a difficult lot, and so it was time to step down from touring full-time and seek new ways of serving my Lord. Cassandra always believed that she would be a stay-at-home mom, who took care of our children, ran the household, and found more private ways of serving the needs of the kingdom of God now that she would be out of the spotlight of the stage. So we waited. I was reminded then, during this season of our lives, how often the Lord only shows us just a couple of steps down the path He laid out before us. His word is a lamp unto our feet. A lamp usually shines in a limited way and manner. It is not a bright powerful light illuminating a large distance. No, it only clarifies the immediate. As we walk these few steps down the path carrying the lamp in our hands, Jesus then illuminates another few steps before us. We knew to stay with the ballet even though the detailed calling and clarity were yet to come. And then the Lord spoke.

Ballet Magnificat was entering a season of growth, enlarging its tent, and sensing the wave of ministry opportunity approaching its shore. The company was busy, and calls for bookings kept coming quicker than we could accommodate. The Trainee Program—which was designed to train and prepare young artists and lovers of Jesus for life of service, both within Ballet Magnificat as well as outside of it— was receiving an increased amount of applications; and its expansion was inevitable. Keith and Kathy, as directors of Ballet Magnificat, knew and understood that the ministry could either answer the challenge of trusting the Lord with stepping into a new chapter or miss out on what God had for it and how He wanted to use the ballet. After a season of prolonged prayer of seeking His will, we knew. It was time to establish a second professional company that would have its own unique repertoire, tour independently of the other company, and, in dividing time and effort, conquer the challenge of answering the need for the incoming booking inquiries. The Trainee Program was to be expanded as well by adding a second level and also initiating the process to be recognized and registered by the government of the United States. This would allow international trainee applicants to receive student visas and study in the program and glean from what God was doing in and through Ballet Magnificat. Kathy knew that she could not give and invest what was required to lead two companies. She was still performing full-time, and her absence would be frequent. Therefore, in June of that year, I was named the artistic director of the new company that God was establishing and laying a foundation for. I was entrusted to lead it artistically and personally oversee the well-being of the dancers while creating a group unified around a common vision, propelled by a shared passion, and inspired by an imparted longing to honor Jesus Christ through excellence, professionalism, and investment in the lives of those met along the way.

As I was excited and frightened all at the same time at the prospect of presented opportunity, I knew that Cassandra was to step into the role of the Trainee Program director, notwithstanding of her presumed role of a stay-at-home-mom. I continued to pray more for her than I did for me; and in every exchange with the Lord, I knew that she was chosen for the post, directly influencing the lives of the trainees. She has taught and mentored over five hundred graduates since then. Many have danced with the companies of Ballet Magnificat. Some have joined other ballet groups. Others have become lifelong missionaries, husbands, wives, parents, nurses, teachers, choreographers, artistic directors... Most of those who graduated from the Trainee Program continually love the Lord and live lives set apart for His glory. As hard and life-consuming as her position is, Cassandra sees the value and the importance it carries as she presses on leading the program and shepherding the hearts under her care. My wife is a hero, and many are the jewels within the crown she will receive on the day when she stands face-to-face with her beloved Redeemer and

King. She cannot wait to lay the crown right back down at His feet in gratitude for Who He is, what He has done, and how He tenderly carried her through the journey of life.

Meanwhile, I accepted the post of the artistic director knowing that Kathy and Keith were to be sources of advice, encouragement, and wisdom along the way. I was thirty years old, and up until then, I was a follower. The transition into a leadership position was daunting, and my imagination of potential mistakes and even disasters along the way was producing countless doubts. Yet I knew that this was my newly found lot to cultivate and plow, trusting the Lord for the harvest to come. Keith knew that naming the company was crucial and important, as it is when parents are in search of a name for their child yet to be born. The Lord spoke again and revealed His will for the two companies to be named Alpha and Omega. The journey had begun. A year later, Omega premiered its first two-act ballet, *Hiding Place*, inspired by the lives of Corrie and Betsie ten Boom, taking place in Dutch Haarlem and the German Ravensbrück concentration camp during the era of World War II. It was an incredible journey of creating this work on the new company and seeing it come to life as the hearts, talents, and hard work of the dancers breathed in what it needed in order for it to profoundly touch audiences with the power of forgiveness woven into its story. Since its California premiere, the *Hiding Place* ballet has been performed all around the world, including special presentations in Auschwitz, Poland; Jerusalem, Israel; Stuttgart, Germany; and the hometown of Corrie ten Boom, Haarlem, the Netherlands.

Two years after premiering *Hiding Place*, the Lord laid upon my heart to create another full-length ballet, *Before His Throne... Boldly*. This production was to be unique in that the vision for it was to usher the audience into the very throne room of God through carefully selected music, by the use of multimedia, through recordings of spoken word and testimonies, live singing, and prayerfully constructed progression of the evening from the very beginning to the very last closing note. The dancers were working hard as the choreography required an unusual amount of stamina and artistry. The rehearsal of a full run-through finally arrived, following months of learning and rehearsing the ballet, completing costumes, and securing French twists. The ballet mistress of Ballet Magnificat—Señora Sol Maisonet, my trusted and dear friend—was invited to watch the ballet. After the rehearsal concluded, the dancers were sweaty and breathing hard. I was proud of them at how far they were willing to go in bringing their all to every rehearsal, including this particular one. Yet something was missing. I looked around the studio, and I noticed Sol shifting awkwardly in her seat. I knew she had something to say. I gave her the freedom to speak openly and frankly, and she did just that!

"I am sorry," she started with her Puerto Rican accent, "I have something to say… What I saw today was…good." She nodded her head in agreement. "But it wasn't good enough. I am not talking about your technique, as Mr. Jiri coached you well." She pointed over to me. "But you must understand this: it is not enough to dance in the outer court. It is not enough to dance in the inner court. It is not even enough to dance in the holy place." She was using the analogy of the Jewish temple that used to stand in Jerusalem, where the presence of God dwelt with His people behind a heavy curtain in the

Most Holy Place. "You must dance in the holy of holies! There the Lord resides in His power and might. There, and only there, the lives of the people can be eternally altered. To do that, you must allow the Spirit to first move in you and then move through you. Keep nothing back, let go, and let God do what only He can do. Then, and only then, will this ballet reach the potential hidden in its power and beauty. I love you all." Sol continued passionately conveying her heart. "But I couldn't disobey the Lord by staying silent." As the dancers stood there listening, the Lord was powerfully moving in their hearts and souls. This was the day when the very heartbeat of Omega changed forever. This correction came, yes, through Sol, but directly from the throne of God. It was the very needed and missing element that transformed the company and granted it the potential to tap mightily, time and again, into the power and strength of the Almighty God and, with anointing and vulnerability before Him, boldly bring each and every audience member all the way—through the temple gates and through the torn veil, into the Holy of Holies, into the very presence of the Great I Am where every life can be changed forever when met by the power and liberty of Jesus Christ.

Over the years, many Omega dancers have come and gone, many new premieres were unveiled, countless tours and performances all around the globe were completed, and yet the greatest gift received through the leading of the company was to see the glory and the fame of Jesus Christ proclaimed in every performance. I have been personally enriched beyond measure by the deep love-filled friendships that were riding strongly on mutual respect and support exchanged and shared among us, knowing that we fought a good fight and finished the race God marked for us, namely to make Him known among the nations and bring Him the glory due His name, during the fifteen years of shepherding and leading the company. As long as I have breath, I will treasure within my heart the privilege of this call on my life to co-labor with these precious people God brought into Omega during its many years of service. Many of the tour directors, road managers, and the artists of the company remain to be dear and close friends long after their last curtain call took place. That alone is a prize unmatched by anything the world is able to offer, unparalleled by any success done with the desire to promote one's self and gain its applause. Thank you, Lord Jesus, for *Woahmega*!

"Ascribe to the Lord the glory due his name; worship the Lord in the splendor of his holiness" (Psalm 29:2).

118) Who Is Me?

The year was 2010, and I just returned from a long European tour with the company. Cassandra stepped well into the role of a "single parent" while I was on tour. She has done just that every year in April and May when I would leave for up to two months to share the hope of Jesus's love around Europe. There were tears in her eyes every time I would leave for the airport as we knew that even though the separation will be hard, long, and painful, we were called to this particular field, to this particular calling. We were willing to offer the comforts of our marriage knowing that this was the very call of God on our lives and our union as a husband and wife. As she cried when I was leaving, I always teared up when I returned and was allowed to embrace her and the children once again. This year was different as Cassandra took Benjamin and Maya up to the Washington, DC, area to visit her parents who now lived in a beautiful Maryland home in the suburb of the city. I returned to Jackson to an empty home. I must admit that the peace and quiet after a long and hectic tour did not bother me one bit. It was me and my own self for a span of four short days. Then came the day to drive to the airport to pick up my family and to enjoy our sweet reunion, once again. Benjamin was eight, and Maya was five years old. They were a perfect pair of energetic children who enjoyed being together as well as doing what every brother and sister tend to do from time to time, mainly to provoke each other and aggravate the parents in the meantime. We love them dearly. I arrived at the airport in time to meet them at the terminal and walk with them to the parked vehicle. I carried the bags and Maya in my arms as she was excited to see her dad and simply would not let go. It was a hot Mississippi day, and the sun was reminding us of its power and strength. Cassandra had the checked bag as, back in the day, flying with one was simply the normal thing to do; Benjamin was pulling his small rolling suitcase; and I carried the backpacks. The kids were telling me of their adventurous experiences in my absence as Cassandra walked smiling but not saying much at all. We found our car, and I gladly placed Maya into her car seat as carrying her and all the backpacks was a challenge under the blazing Mississippi sun. As our bags were sprawling on the ground, I started to place them into the trunk of the car when I heard Cassandra say, "Guess who is pregnant," as she handed me the checked piece of luggage to be loaded. Bending over the open trunk of the car, I replied, "Zinnia?" while carefully placing the suitcase as far into the interior of the trunk as possible. Our sister-in-law and her husband had been praying to conceive and start a family. I was sure that was the correct answer, only to hear Cassandra say, "No, not Zinnia. Try again." Cassandra has three brothers, and I was going through a mental checklist to carefully select the next most probable candidate for the correct response. "I am not sure, but is it May? Are Matt and May expecting again?" Meanwhile, the trunk was full, and all our luggage loaded. Pulling it shut, I stood up to look at Cassandra as drops of sweat rolled down my brow. "No, not May." "Well, I don't know unless Nicholas and Cheryl are expecting again… Hm…is there somebody I am forgetting?" I whispered as I kept thinking of all the possible relatives who could find themselves in the situation of expecting another baby. "It's me," Cassandra said, seeing me running out of options to suggest. "Who is *Mee?*" came out of my mouth as I did not know anyone by that name. "Me," Cassandra continued, "I am pregnant!" "What? How? Us? We are pregnant?" I was shocked. I have heard the phrase of someone being "speechless" many times before. I always wondered if such a thing was even possible. Now I knew that to be true as this was my first time actually experiencing the notion of not being able to utter a single word to describe how I felt. We sat in the car and started to drive. Cassandra kept alternating between looking at me and looking straight ahead out of the car. We had long left the premises of the Jackson International Airport and entered the heavy traffic of Lakeland Drive Boulevard. It was a long fifteen minutes of silence as my mind was continuing in the state of outright shock on the heels of the news. I was thinking of all the difficulties we had to bridge from our past—from the two miscarriages to losing Cosette; and in my mind, I made a deal with the Lord that Benjamin and Maya were the greatest blessings one could ever ask for and let's just leave it at that. We were done having babies; that was a firm conclusion in my mind. No need to talk about it, no need to pray. Our quiver was full, end of the story. And I was wrong. Yes, I had to face my fears again. Yes, I had to submit to the Creator, Who, *unlike* me, was truly in control. And, yes, I had to wrestle with my own pride realizing that walking with the Lord requires obedience and willful submission. But above all, my wife was looking for me to embrace this new gift knitted together inside of her womb by God Himself, and I had to be able to find the strength to do that. Nothing in me wanted to. I prayed silently in my heart in the midst of the crashing waves of confusion and fear. I asked the Lord to help me to be there for Cassandra and to be able to welcome the thought of another child, another blessing, another gift. I needed help, and I needed it fast. By the time we made it to the end of Lakeland Boulevard, slowly approaching a red signal light, I was able to speak. One word and one word only, "*Wow!*" This time, it was not a shocked and angry amazement. This time, my mouth spoke of the wonder of it all. The Lord has blessed us with another creation made beautifully in His image, and He is giving us the gift of another child. As the traffic started to flow, my mouth did the same. Excitement started to flood my heart. "How long have you known that you were pregnant?" I asked first. "I realized it when I was up north, and I did not know how to tell you over the phone when you were in Europe," she replied, smiling and relieved seeing me getting excited about the pregnancy. "That was probably a great call, not telling me over the phone. I appreciate you knowing me that well, my love," I continued, nodding my head. "Well, when is the due date? When can we welcome this new child into the world?" were my next questions. Cassandra just smiled and watched me compute the time frame from before the tour to today. I could not do it… I was struggling. She enjoyed it to the fullest before she suggested late January or early February. I had about seven months to get ready and prepared to embrace this "surprise." And he came early, just a few weeks before the due date. I was at Ballet Magnificat leading our corporate morning devotional when I received the message that Cassandra was going into labor. This was January 25, 2011, when our son, Solomon Jeremiah, came into the world quickly and ahead of schedule. Meeting him for the very first time, the moment he drew his first breath was just as special as when

I met all my other children upon their births. Solomon is a funny, witty, and smart child. But more than any of these great qualities, he belongs to our family; and he is ours to keep, to enjoy, and to cherish.

Looking back, I am embarrassed that there was a moment when I found myself resenting the Lord for allowing us to get pregnant. In a broader sense, I continue to see this tendency frequent on the pages of my life. Often, I react out of my flesh and its understanding and feelings, rather than allowing the Holy Spirit to have a moment to whisper to me and grant me an understanding of His plan and of His doing while He opens my eyes to see events of my life from His *perfect* point of view. I know that I am a work in progress; but I also know that I am a work of art and that my Father, Who is in Heaven, is patient, gracious, loving, faithful, merciful, and tenderhearted and that He has the stamina to finish the great work  He has begun in me. I am a blessed man! Blessed to have been given Cassandra, a wife who loves me faithfully and very patiently, blessed to have been granted the privilege of raising three great children, blessed to know that a day will come when I will be reunited with our daughter Cosette, blessed to know that there are two other children that I am yet to meet! My cup indeed overflows.

As for God, his way is perfect.

—Psalm 18:30

119) Response

It has been a gift to recall and remember the journey as I sit behind the computer and write the pages and chapters of my life story. Even now, as I continue to live, move, and to have my being, I continue to stand amazed that all those years ago, long before I cared to know or even give a single thought to God, He already marked me, marked me to be His. He chose me when I was His enemy. As the arms of my Redeemer were being stretched to be nailed to the rugged cross, my name was running through His mind. The Lord endured the unmatched pain of His death for the joy set before Him. That joy was twofold: firstly, desiring to honor the Father and, secondly, making a way for a sinner like me to be eternally rescued. He allowed me to walk down a path that has been clearly prearranged for me; and on it, there were prepared "hidden" encounters through which my heart of stone began to melt only to, one day, surrender to the love of Christ Jesus. There are ten million Czechs, most of whom do not know the Lord, who live a life leading to eternal loss, separation, punishment, pain, and suffering. But God, in His mercy, captivated me and set me on the narrow road of salvation. This miracle did not hinge on any prospects of what I could do for the Lord, nor was it based on the possibilities of me greatly benefiting His kingdom. No, it was simply because Jesus loved me and loves me still.

As He welcomed me into His royal family, He unveiled a specific calling on my life to serve Him through dancing. I, as all His children are, am an ambassador. I might not work in a building that proudly displays a flag of an earthly nation, but I am a representative of the kingdom of God. I understand that my calling is unique, and frankly even peculiar, but I cannot deny that I have seen the Lord do wondrous things through the performances of Ballet Magnificat here in America and in almost fifty nations of the world—even in my homeland, where people who purchased tickets to a ballet performance did not know that they would be visited by the Lord Himself while sitting in those velvet theater seats and, because of that visitation, their eternal destiny would be forever altered and secured as or if they placed their faith in Jesus Christ.

The Lord has also called me to be a vessel. My Father privileged me to create powerful and moving messages conveyed through the ballets He inspired me to choreograph. Every one of them has been used not only in the lives of the audiences around the world or in the lives of the dancers dancing them; they have been perhaps most impactful in my own life. The hours spent in the empty studio waiting for the step sequences and concepts to be given occasionally turned into unique moments in time when the Lord would simply yet powerfully show up. It was He and I in the room. And there and then, I could taste and experience what it is like to be in the presence of the Holy Majestic God as a prequel to the eternal joy I, and all His children, are promised to forever enjoy. There is a true and lasting freedom. There is joy. There is a prevailing absence of fear. There is peace. During these visits of the Lord, I would dance for my Abba Father with total abandon and, with tearful eyes, loving Him back for all the love He has poured on me while wondering why I would be allowed to know Him like this.

I am not unique nor specially favored. I am just like all the other children of God. We all share the privilege of walking closely with our Father, to be brothers and sisters, to be vessels, to be ambassadors. We can live sold out, or we can miss out on the blessings of running the race and running it well. May we not miss it! The world needs to know the love of Christ; and no matter what our place of calling might be, as most will not be called to pirouette for Jesus or write ballets, may we be bold in proclaiming His truth and living it out. And when our strength and determination waver, let us remind ourselves that He is the well that never runs dry, that this is not our permanent home nor our final destination, that our reward is yet to come, and that we want to be found faithful, like the servant who returned tenfold back for what he was given. May we hear, "Well done, my good and faithful servant. Enter my rest," when we find ourselves standing before the throne of all thrones, the throne of the almighty, perfect, righteous, merciful, and holy Father God.

Not to us, O Lord, not to us, but to your name be the glory, because of your love and faithfulness.

—Psalm 115:1

CONCLUSION

120) And So…

Let us hold unswervingly to the hope we profess, for he
who promised is faithful. And let us consider how we may
spur one another on toward love and good deeds.
—Hebrews 10:23–24

We all are a part of a God-ordained human chain. My professor Evald Rucký heard the gospel when attending a ballet competition in Switzerland. The faithfulness of the messenger changed Evald's life. For years to come, he then shared the message with countless others back home. Because of him and his perseverance, I was able to hear the hopeful message of the gospel offered through the death and the resurrection of Jesus Christ, and now I am a part of the lineage of those who share the hope of the risen Christ with others. I am but a small and yet crucial link of that chain, and so are *you*. I humbly recognize and confess my full acknowledgement and understanding that should anything be imparted through me to anyone's life, it is solely because of God's choosing to do so. Rather than my own character, my own love, my own care, my own strength, my own wisdom given to them, it is the Lord's impartation channeled through my heart and life. All of these and many others have had a far-reaching and deep impact on my life, an impact difficult to capture with mere words. I wanted to conclude my story with just a few notes from some dear and special friends who have deeply influenced my life, as I had the honor to encourage and bless theirs.

Cassandra Voborsky
My wife and my closest friend

When I first met Jiri, I was introduced to a young boy with oversized glasses, suspenders, and a puffy hairstyle. There was a moment after working with him for several years when I "noticed" him as a passionate worshipper. This particular trait of Jiri, expressing a childlike and authentic love for God, was attractive and challenged me to do the same. Time and time again, I would see Jiri put everything aside, whether it was a hard day on tour or an injury that would discourage most people, and he would pour out his heart to the Lord in worship. His sacrifice of praise would point to a God Who is always and supremely worthy of our affection regardless of the circumstances of our day. After twenty years of marriage, I am still motivated and inspired by Jiri's passion to worship our faithful God and by his unapologetic stance in biblical truth. I see this example bear fruit in the shaping of our children and inspiring the next generation of dancing artists.

"Therefore, my dear brothers and sisters, stand firm. Let nothing move you. Always give yourselves fully to the work of the Lord, because you know that your labor in the Lord is not in vain" (1 Corinthians 15:58).

I am humbled to have been entrusted with such a jewel hidden in a quiet, modest, and yet profoundly powerful woman of God, given to me to have and to cherish as my wife. My life would never be of much significance if not for Cassandra's faithful love, support, encouragement, prayers, and patience. Cassandra's passionate love for the Lord and His word has challenged and encouraged me and our children profoundly. She has mentored hundreds of hearts over the years, but little does she know just how much she forever influenced the heart of the man who is privileged to be her husband.

Evald Ruckỳ, ThD
345ᵗʰ Bishop of the Moravian Church
My Czech pastor and ballet professor
My spiritual "Paul"

My name is Evald, and I am the bishop of the Unitas Fratrum Church, in the English-speaking world known as the Moravian Church, a church that in its 560 years of existence counts itself blessed to include giants of faith, men of God such as John Hus and John Amos Comenius. More than thirty years ago, while still under the Communist regime, I became a pastor of a Moravian Church congregation in the city of Liberec. The government was a steady source of persecution and a great prohibitor of our work in the city, but our God prevailed in using this small body to do mighty deeds. I myself did not grow up in a believing family. Prior to moving to Liberec, I studied to be a dancer. Jesus changed my life when I was eighteen years old. I was just beginning my career as a soloist with the National Ballet in Prague, but God had different plans. In 1989, the artistic director of the ballet company, Mr. Pokornỳ, longed to open a dance conservatory here that would be different from the other state ballet schools which solely followed the Vaganova Russian method of dance education. After the Communist regime was overthrown, I was presented with the invitation to join the newly opened academy as a ballet professor. I agreed to join the staff and was assigned to teach the early morning ballet technique classes. This is where I first met a young student, Jiri Voborsky. I started as a teacher, but my heart was burning with the desire to share my hope and faith found in Jesus Christ with the students of my class. Bit by bit, I did just that after every class, offering them the opportunity to ask questions, to explore the unknown sphere of faith, to seek, knock, and prayerfully open the doors of salvation. Only three students were interested, Jiri among them. In 1991, Jiri and his friend Petra, also a student at the conservatory, submitted their lives to Jesus and joined our church where they were baptized in a public pool shortly thereafter. A few years after the Iron Curtain crumbled, I was invited to use my dance expertise in helping, coaching and teaching in Sweden, working as a guest with Kreative Mission and its Eternia Dance Theater, to grow, encourage, and propel the organization. Although I myself was not called to work there full-time, I knew right away that this could be an avenue for Jiri and Petra to combine their newly found faith and their talent and love for the art form of ballet. As a pastor, and now the bishop of the Moravian Church, I am proud to have sent Jiri out as our first post-Communist-era mission-ary who uses his unique talents to share the gospel of the Lord Jesus. From Sweden, the path of the Lord led him to America, and we have remained close and dear friends in spite of the distance and of the long bridge of time. I am proud to see Jiri continually work focused on building the king-dom, and it brings me great joy to watch him mature as he frequently returns to the Czech people with strong ballet performances, where he boldly concludes every evening with a verbal pre-sentation of the gospel. Jiri is not shy to tell the world that it was here in Liberec where he first met his Savior, Who sent him out to the whole world, just as He sent our founding fathers Hus and Comenius to be an instrument and a voice for the glory of God.

Overwhelming gratitude flows out of my heart every time I remember Brother Evald. His boldness for the Lord, his eyes always glued on the prize, and his untiring resolve to keep running the race and fighting the fight had an enormous impact on me and my walk with Jesus. I am grateful that Brother Evald was faithful to the Lord to share the gospel with me so that I could come to understand my desperate need for a Savior. What a legacy he is leaving behind in me and countless other changed lives!

Kathy Thibodeaux
The founder and artistic director of Ballet Magnificat
Award-winning ballet dancer

I will never forget the first time I met Jiri. We had just returned from a long tour. We were all hot and tired, ready to get to our own homes. As we were exiting our bus, we noticed a group of young dancers running out to greet us. Among them was a young man I did not recognize. He had brown hair, wide-rimmed glasses, and a smile that covered his whole face. It was Jiri.

Jiri's plan was to come for a two-week visit... God's plan was different.

That two-week visit turned into twenty-seven years!

Little did I know then how much God would use this young man from the Czech Republic to impact my life and the life of Ballet Magnificat.

I have had the wonderful privilege of seeing Jiri grow from a young teenager into a man of God—full of faith, wisdom, and integrity. I love his passion for the Lord, for his family, for dancing, for choreography, and for sharing the gospel…

Colossians 3:23 says, "Whatever you do, work at it with all your heart, as working for the Lord, not for men."

This is such a beautiful description of Jiri!

He lives this scripture and inspires all of us at Ballet Magnificat to do the same!

I am so amazed how God can use one life that is totally surrendered to Him to impact the lives of so many. I am truly one of those lives, and I will be forever grateful to God for Jiri!

What a wonderful twenty-seven-year (and counting) journey it has been.

Once in a long while a person has the opportunity to cross a path of life with someone special. I received this honor some twenty-seven years ago when I met Kathy. What is profoundly unique about her is Kathy's unwavering faith in Jesus no matter what storms there might be raging around her. Watching her pioneer and carry the vision of building the very first professional Christian ballet company and then sustaining that long-haul run over three decades has inspired me and thousands of other lives worldwide. What an honor it is to consider Kathy one of my dear friends.

Brent Johnston Jr.
President of the Omega Group Advertising Agency

I knew of Jiri Sebastian Voborsky before I actually met him. Jiri and his wife, Cassandra, were performing an awe-inspiring dance at Pinelake, our mutual church home. His professional dance and choreography were an interwoven tapestry of ballet and worship—breathtaking pieces that drew me to the very throne of God. Fast-forward almost twenty years, I now count Jiri as one of my most trusted friends. I have witnessed Jiri teach the book of Revelation in a small-group setting that would make the most studied of theologians proud. I have listened to original piano compositions written by Jiri that should someday appear on the soundtrack of a feature film. I have been witness to many roles of classical and original repertoire Jiri has performed that would rival any performance seen on Broadway or in Times Square. This same man has also taught the word of God in the children's ministry of our church to countless young people for many years.

I am astounded every time I attend a full-length production created by Jiri because of the clarity of the message, the power of the music, and the artistry of the dance. However, the central characteristic in Jiri that inspires me to become a more godly man, husband, father, and disciple is his unwavering commitment to advance the kingdom of God. Simply put, Jiri seeks to lead others to Christ with every fiber in his being, with every gift in his arsenal, and with every opportunity placed before him. As a leader, the mantle that Jiri possesses is resemblant of Moses or King David.

There are many thousands of people across the globe who have been drawn to Christ through the gifting and anointing that God has placed within Jiri as an author, dancer, choreographer, teacher, and creative director. Thousands who have better understood their reason for existence by understanding the Architect of that purpose. And thousands who have been impacted by the Holy Spirit through the creativity, passion, and abandonment Jiri has for the gospel. His willingness to lay his life at the foot of the cross for Jesus's name has inspired others to do the same— and I am ever grateful to be one of those.

The Lord knows just how badly we need other believers in our lives. Brent has been a friend who is steady, wise, caring, compassionate, and on fire for the Lord and His kingdom. It has been a privilege to have known Brent for all these years as the impact he had on me overreached any impact I could ever have had on him. The Lord has sharpened me through this man of God like an iron sharpens iron. I believe this brings God much glory and pleasure.

Samuel Corridoni
Ballet Magnificat Company artist
My "Timothy" and best friend

I met Jiri when I was eighteen years old in January 2012, during Ballet Magnificat's Trainee Program auditions. At most auditions, the auditionee is nothing more than a body with abilities and a number that is pinned to his shirt, but meeting Jiri was very different from the norm. I remember before the auditions started, Jiri walked up to me, shook my hand, and introduced himself, a gesture that no other artistic director made at any of the other auditions I had ever attended. After the addition, he had a few of us boys who were auditioning over to his house to have dinner with his family that night. I remember thinking, *This guy is intimidating, but I hope I can be friends with him one day!*

Little did I know that Jiri would soon become a mentor, a brother, and my closest friend. All this simply began because he made time for me. After moving down south to train with Ballet Mag, Jiri would invite me over to his house once a week; and we would talk about what was happening in our lives, the good, the bad, and the ugly. But we would also study the Bible together. I'll never forget the first time I sat with him at his kitchen table, and we read through Romans 12 and discussed what it means to present our body as a "living sacrifice" unto the Lord. That impacted me deeply, but what impacted me more was the way he modeled what it means not only to be a living sacrifice but also a man of God.

Contrary to what I believed when I was a young boy of eighteen, masculinity can't be measured by the size of one's biceps or the chest hair one can grow. Masculinity is something that is demonstrated by other men, something that boys acquire as they learn from the example set before them. I have seen Jiri in action all these years. I've worked alongside him at Ballet Magnificat, and I am so thankful for the Lord's unique calling on his life as a man of God as well as a dancer and a choreographer. Jiri has demonstrated unwavering faith and confidence in the Lord's power during seasons of drought, as well as humble gratitude unto the Lord during life's seasons of harvest. I've seen him demonstrate what it looks like when life knocks you down and when you allow the Lord to pick you up and set you on your feet again, rather than trying to get back up in your own strength. As Jiri has demonstrated what it looks like to be a man of God, he has pointed me toward Jesus, Who is the perfect example of love and righteousness.

I'm so grateful for Jiri's life and his story. It's amazing to think how different my life would be if Jiri's Czech ballet teacher had never taken the time to share the gospel with him. But because of the Lord's sovereignty and that man's obedience to the Lord, Jiri's life was forever changed, which then in turn forever changed my life as well as countless others who have known Jiri or who have seen one of the many ballets Jiri choreographed over the years. One person's act of obedience can change the lives of generations that will come after. Words can't describe how grateful I am for Jiri's friendship. I am a better man because of him.

I want to start my response to Sam's kind words by saying that I would have never guessed that it would be possible to love another man as much as I love him. The Bible challenges us time and again to love one another in a way that demonstrates God's love to the world. Initially, I used to read these scriptures thinking that I can practice that kind of love only in my marriage and in loving my children. Never would I believe that a friendship with a brother in the Lord can go so deep. Sam and I both recognize the value of the gift the Lord granted us in our friendship, a gift that keeps on giving as the years come and go. We speak freely into each other's lives as we bring a correction, an encouragement, a message from the Lord... I am thankful to have been blessed with such a buddy who is the iron the Lord uses to sharpen me.

Jessica Foxworth
Former professional ballet dancer
Currently living in Central Asia

"What is two years of your life if God has called you to something!" These were some of the first words Jiri spoke to me challenging my new faith. I was in some of his classes during the

Summer Intensive of 2004, and then Jiri and the company just so happened to tour to my home city just two months later. He remembered me and challenged me to audition for the Trainee Program. Little did he know I had already felt like the Father was speaking to me, but I was running in fear as I floundered in my newly surrendered life. Two years later upon being asked to join the Omega Company, I half expected to hear, "What's two years of your life if God has called you to something?" again. But, thankfully, I didn't, as those two years became six amazing, stretching and fruitful ones. Under Jiri's instruction and leadership of Omega, he often challenged our faith both by example and by challenging us to seek God's glorification in our worship and in excellence of our art form as a vessel unto God.

I watched him and Cassandra live lives of complete surrender, from losing their little girl and watching them dance at her funeral in 2004 to spending months apart so that they could both see the advancement of God's kingdom around the world. I watched Jiri spend countless hours with hosts, bus drivers, theater managers, and crews sharing the gospel and his testimony as he also listened to them to share their hearts and hurts. It was in Jiri's home country on tour one year that I first felt called to reach the unreached after meeting someone who had never before heard of the name of Jesus. It was 2014 when Stirling and I (engaged at the time) sat under Jiri and Cassandra as they did our premarital counseling learning from their wisdom and experience. Those conversations complete with espresso and chocolates impacted our family greatly. Little did we know that in the following few years we would be living and working on the other side of the globe, trying to live out our faith in a new place, learning a new language, raising our kids cross-culturally, and walking through the loss of a little girl ourselves.

As I was reflecting recently about the challenges, costs, and joys of living these individual faith journeys that we are on, I realize that Jiri and Cassandra were simply seeking God's face daily and desiring to be faithful to Him day by day. In some seasons that looked like being carried by God, and in others more like leading and serving from strength and fullness. They didn't do it perfectly, and we certainly don't, but the way they lived out their faith and brought others along on the journey is something we are forever grateful for and have tried to implement together in our own marriage and faith journey. We still reference things they've said to us in counseling or in life as we discuss marriage with other young couples, accompanied, of course, by espresso and chocolate. Their lives have certainly impacted us; but it is their faith that has profoundly fueled our lives, ministry, marriage, parenting, and our faith.

Stirling Foxworth
Sod farmer in Central Asia

When I met Jiri for the first time, it was at the headquarters of Ballet Magnificat. I had started pursuing Jessica, and I stopped by the studios with her to meet some of her friends and coworkers. Jiri found me and gave me the biggest hug, followed by asking me all sorts of specific questions based on what he had learned from

Jessica about me. It was so intentional, and he said from the beginning, "You are now a part of my family. I love my family deeply and want to see each member follow God in every way."

When Jessica and I were engaged, we asked Jiri and Casandra to do premarital counseling with us. They spent lots of intentional time with us during our meetings being transparent about their marriage and all they have learned. They asked us deep questions, funny questions, and sometimes uncomfortable questions—but all of them out of love and with a desire to prepare us for a marriage that would glorify God. In that season, they imparted great wisdom and encouragement to us to persevere in the sanctifying work that marriage is, and we are forever grateful for that. As we now interact with those God places in our lives who are newly engaged or married, we share and try to pass on the same love, intentionality, and wisdom Jiri and Cassandra shared with us. We hope one day we'll be able to be as intentional, bold, and loving as we engage with everyone God puts in our path as we have seen Jiri be in ours.

My heart swells with godly pride, if there is such a thing, as I watch the lives of Stirling and Jessica being poured out as an offering before the throne of God and for the benefit of those who would most likely never have been able to hear the name of Jesus. As Jessica and Stirling willingly and obediently follow His call into difficult places of spiritual wilderness, Father God uses them and their marriage to bear fruit—fruit that will last, fruit eternal produced in their own hearts but also in the hearts of countless others. I am grateful to be able to call them both dear friends.

Christina Habib
Former professional ballet dancer
Professional costume designer
Cambridge, United Kingdom

There are those to whom God gives special gifts and abilities beyond average. When coupled with passion, they are a glorious display of God's handiwork!

I was that skinny young dancer who met Jiri by the theater on his first day in Mississippi. Later, we shared many years of touring and remained close friends even after my season at Ballet Magnificat came to an end. His excitement for life and dancing is as tangible as his desire to know God's truth and to walk in it!

Very early on, it was clear that Jiri had a gift for expressing himself through dance and a drive for excellence in his technique and art. That excellence and passion also extends to his personal life, in his pursuit of discipleship, in his faith, in Jiri's pursuit of his wife Cassandra, and his boldness in sharing the gospel around the world.

I often remember some of my most creatively inspiring conversations with him about costumes I would be crafting for his new ballets!

I think about Jiri and Cassandra grieving and dancing at their daughter's funeral, an act of beautiful and real vulnerability but also a declaration that they would trust God no matter what. This has profoundly affected my own journey through life's valleys!

I'm challenged as I see Jiri and Cassandra now investing faithfully in their children as well as in the next generation of dancers, passing on

the passion and excellence while equipping them
to clearly tell the true story of the Gospel!

Yes, Christina was that fair-skinned ballerina who greeted me
when I first arrived in the humid and hot Mississippi. But as time
went on, and the Lord directed our paths, we became "siblings" as she
was a daughter of Tom and Barbara Hudson, the couple who opened
their home to welcome me as their "temporary son." I enjoyed getting to know Christina and her siblings through our close and unique
relationship. Christina's love, faith, and trust in the Lord challenged
me from that point forward, as I could observe her growth in strength
and wisdom. To me, Christina's legacy lies in following Jesus without
looking to the right or to the left. She and her husband, Joseph, are
powerful voices for the glory of our God. I cannot wait to see just
how much God will use them both in years to come.

Carl Macuzzi
Carpenter and builder
Ottawa, Canada

I met Jiri in the summer of 2011, as he toured
with Ballet Magnificat to Ottawa, Canada. After
the first day of interaction with him, I was struck
with a sense that this was a man with a great deal
of wisdom to share about living for and following
the Lord. I must confess I definitely had some
preconceived ideas of what a male ballet dancer
would be like. Jiri blew those ideas completely out
of the water. He struck me as having a physical
strength, along with strength of character. This
was underlined with confidence yet balanced by
a lack of ego. During the week he was in Ottawa,
I had the privilege of interacting with him in
group settings, as well as meeting with him individually for a couple of hours. Considering the
brief time I had known him, he had a significant

impact on me as a young man of twenty-three. Even though we just met, the Lord used Jiri to encourage me, a man in a city and country not his own and a man whom he might not encounter again. As it happened, I had just taken the first step in pursuing the woman who is now my wife, who was one of the company dancers under him. Upon learning of this, Jiri immediately put me in a headlock (mostly good-natured, of course) and threatened my life were I to act in any manner not befitting a man seeking to live for Christ. That also certainly made an impression, haha! Over the next couple of years, as my relationship with the young lady developed, I was able to see Jiri again on several occasions when visiting. After Merry and I were engaged, we had the privilege of going through premarital counseling with Jiri and his wife, Cassandra. This again allowed the opportunity to see the wisdom God has placed in Jiri, and the desire he and his wife have to invest in others, to help strengthen them in their walks with the Lord.

Jiri is one example that God has placed in my life to inspire me to seek to live in a way that honors the Lord and to develop wisdom coupled with humility. That I might be able to speak into the lives of others when the Lord presents the opportunity, and to share from the experiences that God has led me through in life. Jiri also inspires me to encourage and support other couples in honoring God through their marriage, when I am so blessed as to have the opportunity.

It is not even the smallest exaggeration to say that the impact Carl claims I had on him fades in comparison to the impact his young life had on me when we first met. His willingness and boldness to approach me and to speak with me had blessed me and encouraged me profoundly. Little does Carl know that our friendship over the years and miles had a deep impact on me and my life.

Hannah Beaver
Former professional ballet dancer
Cofounder and artistic director of Bright Method Dance

If I could describe Jiri with a phrase, it would be "motivated for more."

My first memory of Jiri is, of course, in ballet class. He was the instructor, and most everyone was terrified of him as he screamed at us while wearing an ultrasweaty blue plaid shirt. I say most everyone was terrified, because I was not. I loved his class! Little did I know that twenty plus years later, I'd have the privilege of sharing in brief how this guy's life has impacted mine, to the glory of God.

As a Christian and a young dancer, it was people like Jiri whom I looked up to. He was on time, was always prepared, and had a high standard of excellence for our art form. His level of energy and dedication challenged me as he showed me by example that the best element we had for the day was worship unto the Lord. In the years we worked together, I observed him bring his best and win, bring his best and lose, but bring his best, nevertheless.

I believe that if we choose to make the most of every opportunity God gives us and if we look for the potential of what could lie ahead because of Him, then our lives will impact others for their good and for God's glory. God has used Jiri's story to impact mine. He is a person in my life that challenged me to pursue things that I sometimes imagined impossible. He *motivated me for more.*

Determination. Dedication. Discipline. These and more are the beaming qualities that I watched sculpt and shape Hannah's life and Hannah's heart. Her love for Jesus directly impacted those around her, me included. There have been many times when a direct propelling challenge to keep following Jesus wholeheartedly has been presented to me by seeing Hannah give her all for Jesus's sake.

Cortne Robinson
Ballet Magnificat assistant artistic director
Professional ballet dancer

I was a teenager when I met Jiri twelve years ago. Since then, he's become a father figure, a trusted confidant, and a friend to me.

I'm one of many who feel their lives have been enriched because of knowing Jiri but, more importantly, because I have experienced the love and grace of Jesus Christ through his life. Jiri is one of the few people I know who has given the Lord his yes. His yes in loving and serving people, his yes in seeing the potential that Christ has placed in an individual, his yes in trusting Christ, his yes in obedience to Christ, and his yes to the sanctification of the Spirit in his life. Because of his yes to Jesus, many lives have been touched. Including my own.

It was the fall of 2016, and I had been struggling with a serious undiagnosed injury for over a year. I was in and out of a boot, visited multiple doctors, and had countless treatments, X-rays, MRIs, injections; and still, I saw no improvement, no healing. I wasn't able to fulfill my job requirements as a dancer in the company that Jiri directed.

I wasn't sure if I would ever dance again or be able to fulfill the purpose for which I felt called—to praise my Savior's name through the gift of dance. When my time of dealing with this injury had come to a climax, Jiri said yes to the leading of the Spirit to pray for me. While praying, he received this word: "Healing comes in the dancing." In that moment, as unlikely as it sounded, I knew it was from the Lord; and if it was from the Lord, then despite my pain, God would fulfill His word and heal me. And that's exactly what happened. God showed Himself as my Jehovah Rapha. He healed me as I stepped out in faith according to the word the Lord gave to Jiri.

There are many things about Jiri's walk with Christ that challenge and encourage me, but what impacts me most is his yes to the Father. It is immeasurable what the Lord can do through each of us, and because of Jiri's example and impact on my life, I want Jesus to always have my yes.

Willingness and submission. These are the first qualities I think of when thinking of Cortne. Endless times, Cortne put aside her own wants, preferences, and even desires to pour into the lives and hearts of those around her. It could be in the middle of a long tour, when everyone was running low on "fuel," and Cortne brought the needed encouragement and uplifting. It could be when she took the time to listen and talk to a hurting student, coworker, or friend. I alone have benefited countless times from Cortne's friendship, wisdom, support, and trust! The Lord used Cortne to spur me and many others on more times than she will ever know. Thank you, Cortne, for loving Jesus like you do.

AN ENCORE

Devotional Encouragements

The Lord has found a unique way to communicate to me through analogies, pictures, and creative ways to help me and others understand His love. Here are some of them. May they be short encouraging devotionals for you as you think about the great love of our God, perhaps, in a new way and light.

1.   The Supermarket Principle

I am sure all of us at some point experienced hunger. Have you ever stepped into a supermarket when hungry? It is a wild ride of senses and aromas causing the hunger in us to escalate and grow. But would being in the grocery store alone satisfy that loud and clear voice within you crying for food? No. Being in the grocery store, with food around you beautifully and bountifully displayed on every shelf, will not in and of itself satisfy your hunger. You must take another step; that is to purchase the food you see. But even the fact of having the food in your possession will not bring the much-needed relief. Only when it is eaten will the food satisfy the hunger you have been experiencing, right? With Jesus Christ, it is exactly the same. It is not enough to be near Him and seeing the bounty Christ offers. You must take action and transition from an observer to a participant. Ultimately, however, it is not until Christ dwells in you when you find yourself satisfied and filled, fulfilled in Him.

2. Close the Umbrella

The Lord speaks to me in pictures. I suppose one of the reasons for that is because I am a dancer, and the process of visualizing concepts has been drilled into me for almost thirty years now. A few months ago, I was spending time with the Lord in prayer. I am still learning to pray "continually" and on an ongoing basis, but this was one of those times when I entered His presence with an expectant heart, waiting to receive directly from the heart of my Abba Father. As I continued to pray and tell Him how truly glorious and amazing He was, all of a sudden, I saw a picture. I was standing in the room with many other people. Their faces were not clearly defined, and perhaps you were one of those standing in that crowd. Then and unexpectedly, the roof of the room lifted up in defiance of the laws of physics. As that occurred, a heavy rain started to pour into the room. As the crowd started to see and feel the rain, some people in it quickly pulled out their umbrellas and opened them to shield themselves from the incoming rain. Others simply opened their arms as wide as they could, and with their heads lifted up, they closed their eyes and let the waters fall on them and completely soak them through. In my heart, I then sensed the following: "The rain represents my blessings and my presence, son. Will you let them fall freely, or will you shield yourself to remain dry, comfortable, but also unchanged?" The message was as clear as day to me. There have been times when I pulled out my umbrella to intentionally or unintentionally shield myself from the blessings and the interventions of God. Not anymore. I pray that I, and perhaps you as well, would be gladly standing in the downpour with our arms wide open, letting the rain fall however and wherever it is guided to do so! Let us close the umbrellas.

3. Hair Analogy

Confession. I like long hair. Not on me, as I struggle to manage the hair I have and do not possess the ability to pull off long hair like others I know. But I love my wife's long hair as there is something dazzling about the light of the day hitting and reflecting beautifully off the long, wavy, strawberry-blond hair as the gentle wind plays with it and allows it to dance and move freely in its flow. Beautiful. Then there is the other side of hair. I am sure all of us have experienced stepping into a shower and seeing one long hair glued to the bottom of the shower or being pressed and becoming one with the wall of the same. Then all of a sudden, the beauty and elegance of the previously described flowing hair becomes the grossest thing known to mankind. Why is that? The answer is quite simple. When the hair is attached to its source, the head, it is thriving and beautiful and purposeful. The moment a disconnect happens, just the opposite is true. The hair is without life, without purpose, and without beauty, and instantly becomes appalling. When we look at our lives, we are just like that. As long as we are rooted in Christ, we are full of life, full of reason, and full of purpose. The moment we disconnect from Him as our source, we become a gross lifeless piece of hair lying on the bottom of a shower, abhorrent to the onlooker. Jesus said it clearly: He is the vine, and we are the branches. He is the head, and we are the hair; and as long as we stay closely connected, His life, wisdom, and power will continue to flow into us and also through us.

4.   Enjoy the Ride

All of us, or most of us, have flown on a jetliner before. It is exhilarating as the metal tube loaded with passengers, luggage, fuel, and its own weight simply takes off. As exciting as that is, try to remember the very first time you got to fly on an airplane. After a while, there is nothing to look at and not much to enjoy, outside of the interior of the plane, that is. Lately, even the fun amenities of flying are vanishing into memory, and the very experience of traveling in style is but a remembrance. And then we are propelled through the air cojourneying with the other travelers to arrive at the designated destination after the allotted time in the air. As we arrive, we cannot tell of the sights we passed, the nature's jewels we traveled over, the rolling hills, or impressive mountains surrounding the path. We cannot testify to any of these, because we simply passed over them, and from the cruising altitude of thirty thousand feet, we could not enjoy them during our passage and journey of "convenience." Now imagine flying in a hot-air balloon or traveling in a blimp. Most of us have not experienced these unique ways of travel, but we have movies that help us understand the concept, *Indiana Jones* for a starter. When one travels in this type of way, the speed of travel is much more lax, much slower paced, at a much lower altitude. The views are there not only to be enjoyed but also to be soaked in, allowing us to be inspired, refreshed, and even refueled along the way. We cannot travel as fast, or even as far in a balloon or in a blimp, but the way of travel is far more memorable than sitting on a jet among hundreds of strangers. The mode of transportation of this kind is truly an experience. The Lord offers us the same kind of a deal. We can choose to hustle. Believe me, I am a "hustler," but in my hurrying, I miss out on the fellowship with the Lord. He is not about the destination as He is about the journey to it. He is a personal God, Who delights in sharing the precious and often fleeting moments with His kids, with those who know Him as their Father. Along the way of life, He offers us experiences, gorgeous, and profound life-changing experiences. Yes, there can be unexpected winds that can affect the path of the hot-air balloon, much more so than of a jetliner; but in those moments, we get to see Him display His power as He calms the storms, stills the waves, and allows us to return to the voyage that steadily, progressively, and, in His timing, reaches the destination. When was the last time you journeyed with the Lord like that? Perhaps it is time to quit hustling and let the real journey, with a sightseeing bonus attached, commence.

5.   Routine Route

I am a creature of habit. I learned at a fairly young age the dangers of slipping into a lack of discipline and laziness. Part of this tendency is being a man, and part of this temptation is being me. To combat this danger zone, I learned to establish checkpoints along the path of life to keep me on track and on target. One of these "checkpoints" is my quiet, or Bible-reading, time. It must happen first thing in the morning before anything else takes place. I cannot fix my cup of aroma-rich Earl Grey hot tea. I cannot go and sit in my favorite reading chair. I must do it in my bed the moment I first open my eyes, or else I get distracted. Crazy, I know. But it works for me. Another routine element of my day is to take the same route to work. I know every pothole. I know every curve. I know every dangerous intersection. I can predict the speed of interstate traffic flow as I catch a glimpse of the travel congestion on it from an overpass. I can get to work in twelve minutes flat. The other day, I was driving to work, and for whatever reason, I took a different route. At first, I found myself distraught over the decision. *What are you doing, Jiri?* my inner voice challenged my reasoning. I was not sure why or for what reason I decided to veer off the familiar and predictable path of the everyday commute. As I was making progress down a road not frequently traveled, I was looking around to notice signs, houses along the path, and new buildings that have sprung up like mushrooms after a good refreshing rain. And then, as I was taking in the new view, the Lord whispered to my heart, *"I know, son, that structure is what you like and need in your daily routine. I know that you see and recognize your danger zones and you combat them with organization and rigid methodology. But when you take a detour, or path less traveled, you notice new things, you are vigilant, and you pay attention. It is not bad to have a routine. It is, however, unhealthy to be mastered by it. Enjoy this unique small diversion from the norm, and open your heart to allow Me to bring unexpected surprises on this journey of unknown and unfamiliar. That way, you will not miss out on my blessings stored for you outside of the predictable routine of everyday life."* The message from the Lord was clear. I trust my Lord fully. I am not abandoning my routine, but I am challenged to open my heart to follow the small still voice of the Holy Spirit that just might lead me on a road unexpected and unique. What about you? Do you ever miss out because you are simply stuck on the routine road? Take and enjoy a detour.

6. Thank You!

Maybe I am like most of you, or maybe I stand alone in the following thought. As I flow through the pages of my life, I imagine myself sitting on a small paddleboat enjoying the scenery surrounding me along the way. And then, often unexpectedly, I find myself surprised by a stream that is quickly leading to small rapids and, at times, to waterfalls of sorts that require a unique set of skills to navigate. Often, I do not possess the expertise to do just that, and I find myself falling over the edge of the rapid flow, falling down with the water. The only thing I can think to do is pray. The prayer reflects the given situation and is raw, lacking poetry, but authentic and real. "Jesus, Lord Jesus, I need Your help…" Have you ever been there? Can you relate? Great! And then the Lord intervenes. Sometimes, I swallow some of the water below. Other times, I find myself overwhelmed with the surge around me, but sooner or later, I surface back up and can draw a deep much-needed breath. Before long, the falls are in the past, and I am back to enjoying the scenery passing me along a peaceful and quiet float. The Lord answered my prayer. He pulled me through. He calmed the storm. He provided what was needed. He supplied what was lacking. He honored my prayer request. I believe that it is of utmost importance to recognize the Savior's intervention and honor Him back with a sincere and heartfelt "Thank you." We do not like it when someone does not recognize us for our effort to lend a helping hand or for being what they needed when they needed it most. Our Lord appreciates and values the recognition as well. Next time, after you have resurfaced from swimming through some rough waters and the Lord has answered your prayers, take some time to thank Him and recognize what He has done for you. It will bless His heart.

7.   Half Full

I can be a pessimist. I know that I am not the only one who finds the darker side of a situation before ever considering the brighter shade of the given moment. Perhaps even the greatest of optimists finds himself straining from his natural ability to always give others the benefit of the doubt while the pessimist simply knows that such benefit does not exist. I have been privileged to work with people who are able to stand strong when pressure of a deadline is breathing down their neck and everything around seems to indicate that it will most likely be missed. They see the glass half full at worst. I, on the other hand, panic and my tendency is to push everyone around me to do the impossible and meet the harsh time line no matter what the cost. My glass is half empty at best. I guess by now you see that I have the innate ability to see the glass half empty and usually with a cracked bottom assuring me that over a short period of time the glass will be bone dry. Can you relate to this at all? Whether you can or not, may the following bring you a new perspective. Not too long ago, and during one of the busiest seasons of the year, I found myself stressing over the many things I had been balancing on my plate struggling to keep them from falling and crashing with an embarrassing splash to the proverbial ground around me. And then the Lord asked me a question, *"Jiri, how is your glass looking right now? Do you see it half full?"* I sensed the burning of the Holy Spirit in my soul; and feeling like a child who got caught with his hand in a cookie jar, after being told that the cookies were off limits for the night, I struggled to find a satisfying answer. As it is usually the case, when the Lord questions us about an issue, we think not of how to answer honestly, but we try to answer "correctly." "Well, Sir," I started, "the glass is actually pretty full… No, no, no"—I tried to correct myself— "it is actually full, indeed." I followed it with a smile as if cementing that answer with a certainty of my heart. The Lord cannot be fooled. Ever! Then He answered, *"Actually, son"*—by now, I know that when the word son is used, I am about to be given a correction from and by my heavenly Father—*"you see the glass less than half full as you focus on your own self, feeling sorry, and treated unjustly. I must speak honestly and openly with you, Jiri."* By now, I usually feel bad that I tried to "stretch the truth" to appease my Lord, as if that was possible, rather than having an honest conversation, a real man of God should be able to have and handle. The Lord continued, *"I am having this conversation not to make you feel badly and sorry but to explain to you a principle that you should long know by now. It is quite simple. With me, the glass is never half full. It is not even completely full, child. With me, your glass always overflows."* I have been treasuring that profound and yet basic theology element close to my heart ever since. There are plenty of days when I struggle to see events around me as a glass half full, which is an upgrade from seeing the glass half empty; but now I know to remind myself that in the Lord's perspective, it is always *overflowing*.

8.   Born with It

How many different ways can we come up with when we are trying to find a new way to convey a message or a principle that we shared a million times before? Parents know exactly what I am talking about. But the following analogy applies to all of us and hopefully will be helpful when you will share it with others. All of us who follow Jesus Christ as our Savior have been commanded to go and make disciples of many nations, to be the beautiful feet that bring the good news, and to be transformed into fishers of men, just like Peter in the Gospels. Sharing the *good news* of the love of Christ is a great "spiritual exercise" to be continually practiced and perfected in ourselves. We need to be ready to do it at a stoplight, when a homeless person approaches us with a stretched-out hand expecting to receive a dollar or two. We need to be prepared to share our faith when challenged by someone who might be practicing another religion and offer them the hope of salvation that is not to be earned but rather a salvation that has been fully and freely provided by the death and the resurrection of the Son of God, on behalf of the ones who spat in His face and ridiculed His meekness and love.

I was about to share the Gospel message with a crowd once, and I was asking the Lord to give me a new way to explain our impoverished state of sin that all mankind found themselves in because of Adam and Eve's act of direct disobedience in the garden of Eden. I wanted to give an illustration to help the listeners to remember my message for a long while past the present evening. Shortly before I walked into the spotlight prepared for me, microphone already in my hand, and while reviewing the scripture passage I knew I was going to use, the following word was dropped into the mailbox of my cognitive, imaginative, and fairly simple mind. "Skin." I love when the Lord does these message exchanges with me. As I stepped into the bright white light, I started with saying, "Psalm 139 teaches us that we were knitted together in our mother's womb. I do not personally know how to knit, but I have watched others knit when sitting on a tour bus for four days straight while bridging the Portland-Jackson span of two-thousand-and-four-hundred-mile route without a major break to finish the West Coast Tour. Knitting takes time. It is intricate. Creating designs and mixing different colored yarns requires vision, expertise, and patience. The Lord knitted us together implementing all of these qualities and many more to make us exactly how He desired and designed us to be. And then on the day when He preordained it to be, we came out of that womb and entered the world to live, to move, and to have our being. As our bodies are a complex entity of organs, tissues, ligaments, fluids, personality traits, physical features, senses, and hidden talents and abilities, there is the one and the largest organ that covers it all, our skin. It is stretchy and at birth extremely smooth to touch. Think of a baby's bottom, for example. It is unique in its color complexion and shade. One thing we cannot do is to step out of that skin. It is ours to have until we breathe our last and are laid to rest in the tomb, waiting for a new body to reunite with its soul and spirit on the day when the Lord comes through the clouds and the dead will rise to meet Him in the air. So exciting! As the skin is the permanent outfit, hopefully loved and taken care of better than the finest luxury piece of clothing we have ever owned, it is a permanent part of who we are. As the skin cannot be removed from us, it reminds us that sin cannot be unfastened either. Not by us, anyhow. It is just as permanent, just as part of our lives from before we ever first saw the light of the world, and unless we clothe ourselves with the mercy of Christ, sin will bind us to eternal separation from Him. As we can cover our skin with fine dresses or suits, we can hide our sin with actions and even pretenses. But as the skin is always underneath the clothing, our sin is always in us, no matter what our façade might indicate. There is nothing we can do about it, and avoiding its consequences is impossible. Unless we receive the free gift of Jesus's love and allow Him to impute His righteousness for our state of hopeless disobedience, we are eternally condemned. But when we do bow our knee before the Messiah, our state of utter despair is in an instant exchanged with Christ's hope of eternal life purchased by His sacrifice and death on the Roman Cross of Calvary, followed by the glorious death-defeating resurrection of the Savior and Redeemer. Take a moment and look at your skin. What do you see? Do you see just an organ that provides the shell for your body? Perhaps from now on you will also be reminded to realize that as you cannot divorce yourself from your skin, you cannot separate yourself from your sin. Not without the divine intervention of your Redeemer."

9. In His Hands

All of us recall and remember the excitement when we see young children start to express themselves with crayons and with large squiggles drawn all over a large piece of paper and to see the parents take the piece of art and place it on the fridge. We were once like these little ones. Then as we matured, some more than others, we traded our shapeless drawings with learned skills to write, to draw images that were recognizable, and for some of us to become painters or even master artists. For different needs, we recognize the benefit of using the appropriate pens, pencils, markers, paintbrushes, and more. Not every one of these tools is useful for every need when writing or drawing. We would not want to use a paintbrush to calculate and solve a math problem, use a pencil to sign an important document, or use a permanent marker to paint a wall of the room or sketch an architectural design. Every writing tool has a specific purpose. But no matter what writing utensil we use, the tool itself is useless unless it is picked up by our hand. The tool is just that, a tool. It is the hand that makes it write, draw, and paint; it is the hand that makes it useful. The hand is connected to the rest of the body of the author, of the one who has decided what utensil to use and how to utilize it the best way. Is this not a great picture of how we are the tools and the Lord is the hand? We cannot do anything on our own. We have to be used by the hand to be useful and able to create anything valuable and beautiful. But what if we are a mechanical pencil that has no lead? What if we are a fountain pen that is inkless?

What if we are a paintbrush that is dry and stiff? We are unable to be of use in any practical way whatsoever. The original design, for which we were created, cannot be fulfilled unless ink is poured in, a lead is inserted, or we are watered and readied to be dipped into a fresh container of paint. If not properly prepared, we have no use for the Writer. But when equipped and picked up by the Artist's hand, we can be used to create something new and beautiful, something that is His creation and not our own. As we allow ourselves to be instruments in the hands of Christ, we need to allow Him to fill us, prepare us, and use us according to His plan. There is no better thing than knowing that we are the clay in the hands of the Master Potter.

10. Faithful, Watchful, Patient

I have been a follower of my Lord for almost thirty years. Over the span of three decades, I have seen the faithfulness of the Lord demonstrated to me and to my family countless times. Many of the received blessings have not even been realized, registered, or acknowledged.

Faithful, patient, watchful, wise, planner, strategist, the one who is near...as this list continues, it seems apparent that I am talking about the Lord. Yes, He is all of these characteristics and many more. But in this list, I am actually talking about Satan. We often disregard the tactics of the enemy or forget that he is willing to be patient, waiting for us to let our guard down to initiate an attack against us. He is faithful to stick close, sit quietly, and whisper discouragement when we feel tired or deliver a strong encouragement when temptation knocks on our door. He desires to be near us, sitting in our very presence, slowly wrapping his arm around our shoulders only to stab us in the back when we least expect it. The enemy hates us. He never plays games. He is never honest. Masterful in disguise, Satan learns by steady observation the best time and the best way to come against us. He desires to destroy and discredit us. Often, we are extremely obliging in giving him a helpful hand as our actions open the doors for him to march right into our circumstances, into our lives, and into our relationships. Inevitably, we give him an opportunity to cause havoc, bring destruction, break and destroy trust between us and people we love, and allow deep heartache. The enemy can convince us of our inability to be used for and in the kingdom of our God. He is ruthless and never plays by the rules. Satan laughs when we trip and fall, when we say something we immediately regret, or when we do something hoping that no one will ever know. He has, and he takes time to launch the greatest attack against us possible, hoping for the greatest wounding attainable. He enjoys spreading the tent of shame and guilt over us, hoping that we will never walk out into the freedom provided by Jesus Christ. And then when we are down, lying in the mud and the mess we made for ourselves, he hopes that we never get up again. He spreads rumors and lies about us but also to us to make us believe in something that might be an imagination in our minds, hearts, and feelings. That is the *faithful* work of Satan.

> *BUT GOD, being so very rich in mercy, because of His great and wonderful love with which He loved us, even when we were spiritually dead and separated from Him because of our sins, He made us alive together with Christ, for by His grace—His undeserved favor and mercy—we have been saved from God's judgment.*
> —Ephesians 2:4–5

If you belong to the victorious Jesus, you are of God, and you belong to Him and have already overcome the agents of the Antichrist, because He who is in you is *greater* than he who is in the world of sinful mankind (1 John 4:4). So, yes, Satan might be faithful, watchful, patient, and wise; but our God powerfully dominates him in every one and all other categories. We need not to fear, yet we need to know that we are in a war fighting an enemy that will never play fairly. The moment we learn this, Satan has lost his grip on us. He has no other choice but to retreat and run. The Holy Spirit, dwelling in the children of God, is much greater than any and every tactic of the enemy. Be watchful, but much more than that, be encouraged, beloved! The victorious Jesus has conquered Satan and forever defeated him on behalf of God's family, His kingdom, and His glory. Our Lord reigns forever, faithfully!

11. The Word of God!

The Bible. I did not have the privilege to ever land an eye on the Holy Bible until I was sixteen years old. My family never owned one, and growing up in a totalitarian regime did not necessarily make it easy to be able to obtain a printed version of the Scriptures. After the fall of Communism, and after I became a Christian, I started to see the Bible in the church circles. It was not until I came to the United States when I started to read it on a regular basis. As I opened the book, I was immediately overwhelmed with the typical struggles of a new Christian—where do I start reading, what if I don't understand it, will I be able to follow its meaning, and will it impact my life? The beginnings were hard, and my reading "plan" consisted of "Let's wait and see where I open it to see what I will read." That did not do much for me, as I took concepts and even passages out of context and the meaning of the Word was lost and meaningless, much of the time. Quickly, I realized that in order to benefit from the message of the Bible, I needed to create a systematic approach to its reading, to its studying, and to its power to speak to my heart and soul. I have been given a few helping pieces of advice to uncover its rich and life-changing power. I want to share them with you:

Firstly, it is crucial to realize that the point of reading the Bible is not to appease our own self by feeling spiritual, disciplined, and accomplished because we read the Bible this day. No, we need to come to a place where we uncover the simple truth: that the whole point of the Word of God is not the Word, but it is the God of the Word. It is not enough to know the Word. We need to get to know its Author, God. The Bible is His love letter to us, written to teach us of who He is, to help us grasp His character, understand His passions, explore His wisdom, discover His plans, embrace His desires, obey His commands, and receive His encouragement. The Bible's purpose is to introduce us daily to the Author, the Almighty and intimate God, Who desires to be in a close communion with His children.

Once I discovered this simple truth, it changed how I approached the Scriptures and how I valued their content.

Secondly, I needed to understand that there is a one overarching story told through the sixty-six books of the Bible. It is an incredible adventure to try to find the thread of this story among the many components of the vastness of the Bible. We also need to remind ourselves that it is God's story much more than it is the story of mankind. He is the benefactor, and we are the beneficiaries.

As I dove into reading passages, often I found myself drifting in my thoughts into other things and staying focused was, well, a bit of a challenge. Please know that the enemy is at work and he understands the "danger" of the power of the living, active Word of God, that will not return void but will accomplish all it has purposed to do. To combat his attempts to distract me, I apply the following method. I would read a scripture and simply shift the focus from one word to the next while reading the verse over and over. Here is an example:

> *He* is the atoning sacrifice for our sins, but also
> for the sins of the whole world.
> He *is* the atoning sacrifice for our sins, but also
> for the sins of the whole world.
> He is *the* atoning sacrifice for our sins, but also
> for the sins of the whole world.
> He is the *atoning* sacrifice for our sins, but also
> for the sins of the whole world.
> He is the atoning *sacrifice* for our sins, but also
> for the sins of the whole world.
> He is the atoning sacrifice *for* our sins, but also
> for the sins of the whole world.
> He is the atoning sacrifice for *our* sins, but also
> for the sins of the whole world.
> He is the atoning sacrifice for our *sins*, but also
> for the sins of the whole world.
> He is the atoning sacrifice for our sins, *but* also
> for the sins of the whole world.

He is the atoning sacrifice for our sins, but *also*
for the sins of the whole world.

He is the atoning sacrifice for our sins, but also
for the sins of the whole world.

He is the atoning sacrifice for our sins, but also
for *the* sins of the whole world.

He is the atoning sacrifice for our sins, but also
for the *sins* of the whole world.

He is the atoning sacrifice for our sins, but also
for the sins *of* the whole world.

He is the atoning sacrifice for our sins, but also
for the sins of *the* whole world.

He is the atoning sacrifice for our sins, but also
for the sins of the *whole* world.

He is the atoning sacrifice for our sins, but also
for the sins of the whole *world*.

As you can see, not only does this simple method cause us to read over the same verse as many times as there are words in the verse, but by shifting emphasis from one word to the next, we notice the power of the message of the verse in a new light, and it speaks to us differently than it did when we just read it once.

Thirdly, and perhaps most importantly, the Word is alive. You might have heard this expression and yet you have no idea what that exactly means. It is simple to explain. Imagine you have two people reading the same passage at the same time. Though the words on the page are the same, and similar conceptual derivations are received, the Lord uses the same passage to speak personally to each reader differently. He speaks into his or her situation profoundly to deliver a customized message that will meet the reader's needs perfectly. Or imagine yourself reading the same passage even a month apart. You might receive a different substance, receive a different personalized word, the first time than you will the second time, even though the words are identically the same. How is that possible? Again, the Lord will use the printed words by highlighting them uniquely to meet you where you are and to whisper to you exactly what you need to hear in order to hear His voice and receive His guidance.

May these simple suggestions be effective in your personal journey of falling in love with the Lord through reading His Word. May you also be disciplined and diligent to read it daily and to continually discover its hidden treasures.

Next time you pick up the Word of God to read it, pray first and invite the Holy Spirit to open your eyes and ears to hear from the Father. Then, with excitement and expectation, dive into the powerful, sharp, divine, brilliant, deep, applicable, anointed, and breathing message of God spoken through His Word.

12. What and Why?

Psalm 33:11 teaches us the following: "But the plans of the Lord stand firm forever, the purposes of His heart through all generations." This is a short and yet profound verse. There are thousands of verses and passages throughout the Holy Bible that are powerful and deeply meaningful for us to understand. There are many exciting treasures ready to be discovered, opened, retrieved, and carried with you, stored forever more in your hearts. What we learn from this verse is the truth that the plans of the Lord stand firm. We also see that His purposes do the same. Our God is a Master Planner. There is nothing that could ever surprise Him, and there is nothing that He did not expect to happen or take place. In this verse, we see that the plans of the Lord are the "what happens" and the purposes of God are the "why it happens." As we place these two discoveries into the "equation" of *Plans + Purposes = Generations*, we see a powerful result. God is the beginning and the end. All generations experience the plans and the purposes of His actions. The "what" combined with the "why" unfold before us the heart of God bleeding and beating for the generations, for each man, each woman and child, and also for the hurting, the sick, the wealthy, the poor, the common, the famous, the popular and the forgotten. The Lord's desires *for us all* to come to know Him, to see His heart, and to know that His plans and purposes are formulated to glorify Him and also designed to bring us to His presence. As you look at the circumstances of your life, your present situation, and the difficult moment you might find yourself in, know and trust God's plans and purposes, His "what" and His "why" designed and carried out with you in mind.

13. Ankle Deep

I grew up in the temperate climate of Central Europe. Four seasons regularly and faithfully change one into the next. Winter days were often beautifully covered with a fresh blanket of newly fallen white snow. Branches of trees, cars, railings, park benches, and more disappeared under the weight of the white ice crystals that accumulated upon them. Winters were cold but full of their unique charm and magic. Then came spring. The beauty of blooming flowers, the fresh aroma of blossoms filling the air enhanced the excitement of all, ready to experience the refreshing newness of life. Birds singing in the trees chirped to let us know that the winter had passed and the rebirth of the world around us had begun. Then came summer. The days were long as the latitude of the Czech nation is located fairly north. Temperatures were warm, and occasional thunderstorms and summer rains brought the much-needed refreshing of the air and to everything that was growing and blooming while washing away the dust collected from the dry days. Lastly, there was autumn. The vivid colors of the leaves, the cold winds, and the bare fields—all these and more were the elements of the fall. Every season had its beauty, and every season had its unique sense, its unique character.

Now I live in Mississippi—a beautiful state located in the southern part of the United States, a state located in the humid, subtropical climate. The four seasons do not really manifest their uniqueness here at all, as hot summers are long; winters are mild; springs are short, often lasting a mere four weeks; and autumns exist only in textbooks, as leaves rarely show up in a display of flashy colors in comparison to their European or northern counterparts. When the heat of the summer hits Mississippi, life seems to be snuffed out of its citizens. The extreme humidity and heat cause everyone to seek the air-conditioned interiors and leave their comfort only when absolutely necessary, and even then only in air-conditioned cars. But once in a while, Mississippians go to enjoy a couple of hours around a pool. As the sunbeams repress the ability to enjoy the outdoors for long, what makes it bearable is the option of taking a plunge in a pool. Rarely would one find a person who would be sitting outside under the direct sun for a long time unless they would be able to dive into the refreshing and soothing body of water. Not to do so would make very little, if any, sense.

Now let us imagine this exact scenario from a spiritual point of view. The heat of life has been endlessly pounding upon you. There has been no relief in sight. And then there is an opportunity given to you by the Lord to plunge into His refreshing presence, to find the needed comfort, restoration, and guidance only He can offer. Would you then only sit on the edge of the pool dipping your feet ankle deep, or would you, without hesitation, submerge fully into the living waters of the Lord? As simple as this illustration is, sadly in reality, we often just dip in. We try to find our own way to safety, our own path to relief, our own solution for the given problem. We approach the Lord and try to negotiate His involvement that would be submissive to our conditions. We are as if dipping our feet and ankles into a pool not interested to take and utilize the full advantage of what it can offer. The Lord never agrees to our stipulations. He always offers us His solution, His way, His provision. It is up to us then to decide whether we will dive in fully and let Him lead or whether we will simply sit on the edge of the spiritual pool and, with only our ankles dipped in, continue to fight in our own way, with our own limited understanding, with our finite vision unable to see the full picture. May we be quick and wise to always dive fully into the provision of the Lord and, like on a hot summer day, find in Him the much-needed relief of a cooled and refreshing pool.

14. Danger of a Single Degree

I am not the greatest runner. As a matter of fact, I hate running. As a dancer, I can "hop and twirl" on a stage for two hours straight without major difficulty most of the time, but if asked to run from where I am to the other side of the room or the other end of the house, I find myself quickly out of breath and fatigued. Growing up, it was a mandatory requirement for all elementary and middle school students to do cross-country runs through the woods surrounding my hometown. Growing up behind the Iron Curtain, we were taught from an early age of the dangers posed by the imperial countries of the West and of the need to be ready should an imminent and unexpected attack against our nation and its values take place. Thus, these runs were done in gas masks affixed to a long hose to which a container of oxygen, I assume, was attached. Then we were veiled in plastic from head to toe, given a map and a compass, and sent to the woods to hopefully not die and, in expected time, to find our way to freedom and security on the other side of the forest. I suppose that these drills killed in me any potential love for running, but that is another matter altogether.

I love maps and the aid they provide in finding a way in an unfamiliar territory. In the woods, the best tool for navigation is the little metal compass. Back in the day, compasses were simple. They contained no technology that could potentially backfire. The God-ordained magnetic field of the planet always and faithfully drew the small pin inside the compass to point to the north. Once that was established, I knew how to adjust the direction of my running accordingly to arrive at the desired destination. Then, and if followed perfectly, the compass directed me to the finish line. But if I were to veer off the course even a single degree, initially everything looked and seemed to be on track; but with each passing kilometer, as we Europeans measure distance, the initial small mistake starts to cause a great problem. I would eventually find myself to be lost.

The Holy Spirit, Who dwells inside of every Christian follower and disciple of Jesus Christ, serves to be a compass in our hearts and souls to guide us to the finish line perfectly. If along the way, we disconnect from following Him closely, we will find ourselves lost and missing out on being firmly established in running the course and the race the Lord has prepared for us to run. May we check the "Compass" daily and be quick to realign ourselves with His clear instructions and directions. That way, we will be most useful to serve the King of kings on the journey called life.

15. Look Closely

I am not a big nature fan. I grew up in a city. I enjoy the hustle of it. The busyness of it gets me going. One of my favorite elements of traveling to different countries is to take a moment to sit in a café in a foreign city and watch the locals go about their business. I get a sense of the spiritual climate of the visited nation and of its people. But this analogy actually has nothing to do with a city and much to do with nature—the woods, to be specific. As a walk through the woods brings a refreshing to most, it has the opposite effect on me. As I would approach a densely lush forest, I would often see it as if it was a wall of trees. They might be settled on a hill, they might be sprawling around a lake, or they might be surrounding a field. My tendency is to enjoy the woods from afar. From a distance, the forest and the woods are one unit.

It is not until closely approached when the individual trees are noticed. The image of the woods is one from a distance and another from up close. But even then, the impact of the woods is not fully realized until one enters in. Then the shade the trees provide, the aroma of the forest, and the unique sounds heard there that the city does not have are fully realized, enjoyed, and personally impactful. Treasures of freshly grown mushrooms, berries, animals to be hunted if one is into that kind of thing, small brooks of refreshing water filled with small fish, or even a meadow to sit and enjoy a picnic on are discovered only when one ventures inside of the forest.

The Lord is exactly the same way. We can view God as a distant entity, see Him as God Who is mighty and powerful but best left at a distance. Or we can approach Him and start to see the unique qualities that are a part of His character, His qualities that were not seen from a distance. He is merciful, loving, holy... But the best way to experience God is to enter into a close and intimate relationship with Him. Then, and only then, do we get to experience the refreshing He provides to His children. We see the treasures He offers that were completely hidden when viewed from a distance. We find the rest we so desperately need when sitting in a meadow of His peace and having a picnic with the Father. As I am learning to enjoy the beauty of the woods and find the value of strolling through the paths of the forest, I am seeing the benefits this provides when translated into my spiritual life.

Take time to approach the Lord up close, and find the special refreshing brook of His presence. The Father wants to have a picnic with you.

16. Gain a Perspective

The Holy Land. Ever since I married my wife, who loves everything related to the Holy Land, I grew in my desire to visit Israel and experience firsthand the very place that is the epicenter of history, the birthplace of Jesus Christ, a key component of the future, and on and on and on. Ballet Magnificat was invited to tour Israel in 2008, and my opportunity to go had finally presented itself. Israel was everything and much more than what I hoped for and even imagined it to be. The very highlight of every trip to Israel is always a visit to Jerusalem. There is much to see, much to experience, and much to explore. And so we did. A few days into our stay in this ancient capital of Israel, we (my wife Cassandra and I) discovered a way to sneak up onto the rooftops of the Old City. It was as if entering a whole new adventure. The rooftops of Jerusalem are a world in and of itself. The perspective of the town is brand-new and completely unique from the experience of the "regular" way of being acquainted with this magnificent city. We enjoyed this unique experience to its fullest—returned there many more times during our stay, as well as told others in the company about a new way to see Jerusalem. We thought we knew the city, we thought we saw the city, and we thought we enjoyed the city as much as one can do until we found this unique and very much unorthodox angle of the awe-inspiring city of David.

Isn't this a way we so often view and relate to the Lord? We think we know Him, we are familiar with Him, and we have enjoyed Him as much as He can be enjoyed. Simply put, we have grown bored in the relationship with the living God. Our view of the mighty God has lost its shine and excitement. That should never be. But unless we take time to put aside our preconceived ideas of the Lord, we might miss out on all the wonders He wants us to explore of Himself and of our relationship with Him. Therefore, let us pray and ask Him to show us even just a glimpse of Himself in a new way and light. Jesus can never be overexplored. There is going to be a never-ending, forever-expanding opportunity to find newness of Christ and of His character. We just need to take time to see Him in a new and fresh light.

17. Freshly Cut

I have never been graced by patience. I am a man who enjoys quick results, immediate outcomes, and swift turnarounds. I admire those who can enjoy the process as much as the product. I focus on the result while the actual enjoyment of the process is being learned. I was mowing my yard recently. It is right up my alley to step out into the Mississippi heat and spend two hours in the hot sun to turn my yard into a masterpiece of neatly cut grass and laser-sharpened edges. As I was pushing my mower up and down the corner lot of our home, my mind was focused on the Lord as I wanted to utilize the 120 minutes in conversing with Him. Occasional interruptions by a passing neighbor or a tree root getting stuck in the blade of my mower are to be expected. But when all is said and done, I enjoy—and I mean *enjoy*—looking at the yard and seeing the immediate result and product of my labor. This day was no different; and with the mower back in its place in the garage, I took the short walk around the property to, firstly, inspect if everything was up to my standard of perfectionism and, secondly, to soak in the beauty of the nicely sculpted yard. As I admired the job well done, the Lord spoke to me: *"Jiri, as you marvel at your completed work, imagine with me for a moment how I feel when I look at you. Two hours ago, this yard was a hot mess. It took your sweat, it took some tools, it took your dedication, and it took your determination, but look at the outcome. It's beautiful. Do you know that the same is true about you? You were a mess. It took Jesus's sweat and even blood. It took the Roman tools of hammer, nails, and a rugged Cross. It took Christ's dedication to Me and His determination for you. But look at the outcome. You are beautiful! Now I enjoy looking at you, son, as all this effort of the begotten Son of God created a masterpiece out of a 'yard' full of weeds, unwanted branches, dried-up leaves, and ugly and uneven messy grass."* I stood there speechless. I rarely consider myself worthy, much less beautiful, and I am not quick in recalling the value God deems me to have and possess. I see the "weeds," the sins, of my life, and I tend to disqualify myself to be a masterpiece. Again, the Lord, Who knows our every thought, reminded me, *"You need to remember that you continually require to be edged and regularly sculpted and realigned, as your fleshly tendencies reappear time and again. But as you never give up on your lawn knowing that it will need to be mowed again and again, it is the 'Gardener's' joy and pleasure to continually reshape you into the child of the living God that is continually beautified for His Majesty's purposes and enjoyment."* I was thankful for this simple yet profound reminder of just how uniquely God views and values His beloved children. As it is a joy for me to labor for my yard to look beautiful, it is the same for the Lord to do so in me and in you. Hallelujah!

18. Never to Be Repeated

Have you ever made or created anything? I have. I must admit that not everything my hands have made is a work of art. Most things actually are simple ordinary creations that others could do much better than I. Once in a while, I am able to succeed in making something that I find valuable and worthy to call my creation. I am not Michelangelo, Picasso, Marius Petipa, or Shakespeare; but whether it is a powerful ballet that reaches deeply into the hearts of the audience members, whether it is an intricate paper castle model constructed over a period of many sleepless nights, whether it is a nicely painted room in our house, or whether it is a loaf of a delicious freshly baked sourdough bread, these are creations that I am proud of and that are special to me. I find myself delighting in these. When I spent time on creating something and I invested time, energy, and even some monetary value into its creation, the product will be, and should be, valuable to me. At times, it might be of value to others, but, regardless, it will have a value in "my books." I would hate, and perhaps even find myself discouraged, if others would overlook my creation or, even worse, if they would belittle it or disrespect it. But what if someone were to take my piece of art, my creation, and then destroy it, throw it away, or waste it? That would be devastating. My feelings would be hurt, and my willingness to continually create more new works of art could be affected and discouraged. Let us then consider the creation of our God and how we take it for granted at times, waste it at times, disregard it at times. I am not talking about the beautiful planet earth and the Lord's creation around us. I am not even talking about human life that is carefully knitted together one creation at a time. I am talking about God's creation of *each new day*. God puts time and effort in making each day unique and beautiful. Powerful sunrise that washes over a coastline, gorgeous night skyline that features the bright stars with the beauty of the full moon hanging peacefully over us, the power of the autumn wind that sweeps the colorful leaves, the sunset, springtime rain, afternoon sun, morning at the beach, and on and on. But what about the plans of God for that day? What about the purposes of the Lord for us, each of us, to live to our fullest and utilize those 86,400 seconds to bring Him all the glory He deserves. Sadly, often we view a particular day as "ordinary" or "same old, same old," and we waste that unique creation by simply focusing on what we desire to do or not to do during those precious twenty-four hours that will never be repeated again, that will never present the opportunity to be lived once more. I am not saying that to rest is wrong. To rest is a command of the Lord as He Himself rested after creating the world. But we must be careful that we do not overlook God's creation of each new day, disregard its value, waste the given time, because we see it as a "just another day." And what if it were our last? Would we live it differently? Let us live our days in view of appreciating the efforts and the purposes the Lord Himself placed into creating each new day, each new twenty-four hours, each new 1,440 minutes, each new 86,400 seconds. Let us approach them as moments that are offered to be lived just once.

19. Frequency

I am one of those who can enjoy a long drive. Touring for the past twenty seven years has taught me to enjoy the passing scenery, to invest in meaningful conversations and fellowship with the co-travelers, to spend time with the Lord, and to do what I enjoy doing whenever an opportune time is given, simply rest. Whenever we take a road trip as a family, we pack our seven-passenger van, pile in, and hit the road. My daughter often requests a Christian station K-love to be the radio station played on the van's radio. Most of the time, that wish is not granted as I enjoy catching up on conservative news and perspective aired on stations such as the American Family Radio, stations that I do not have time to listen to during the regular day-to-day busy life. On our out of town trips, no matter what the selected station might be, once we leave town and travel down the road, eventually the strong signal of the given frequency gets interrupted or mixed by another station as the signals might not be as strong in the given stretch of the interstate, usually surrounded by woods or vast pasture lands of sorts. Has that ever happened to you? All of a sudden, neither station can be heard, neither can be enjoyed, and neither has any value other than annoying noise. Eventually, we turn the radio off and choose to play a podcast or music from our handheld devices or simply have a conversation with one another. Just recently, this very unfortunate occurrence of losing the signal took place while taking a family trip out of town to visit friends. As the station that we were intently listening to started to mix and be interrupted by other waves and frequencies, the Lord reminded me to think about this same element occurring in my spiritual life. There are times when my spiritual frequency is tuned up and receives an uninterrupted reception from the Lord. The communication channels are opened and cleared, and the information between the throne of God and the heart of Jiri flows well to be received and obeyed. But then there are times when distractions and noise of other voices, opinions, my own will, and even my own spiritual laziness cause an interruption of the frequency of the Lord. These other noises do not necessarily provide any substantial information. Most of the time, they are just a noise, but they do distract me from hearing the voice of God, and when successful, they even cause me to turn my spiritual radio off. As the Lord pointed this simple truth to me, I was surprised to realize just how often I allow this to take place in my life. I prayed to the Lord that I would be able to tune in and remain on the "divine" frequency without major interruptions and empty noise as I continue to travel on the path of life. How strong is your "Voice of God" frequency reception?

20. Knowing versus Knowing About

Touring globally for the past thirty years allowed me the privilege of meeting many interesting people along the way. Some would consider themselves ordinary, some would assess themselves important, some were influential in the realm of theology, some in the realm of science, some were presidents, and others were ambassadors. Some are powerhouses in the recording music industry as their records and concerts, based on their steady and faithful personal relationship with the Lord, point thousands to Jesus through every lyric, every album, and every performance they produce and deliver. So many I met on the path of life brought me great encouragement, blessing, and fellowship. Some were to be enjoyed for a brief period of time; others have become dear and close friends for a lifetime.

One fine memory, when it comes to meeting interesting people, was the invitation received to meet His Royal Highness Prince Alexander II, the crown prince of Yugoslavia, and his wife, Princess Katherine. The company was invited for an afternoon tea at the royal palace in Belgrade during our European tour. It was a special afternoon enjoyed in the presence of my dearest coworkers while enjoying chocolates, sipping tea, and, *yes*, meeting royalty. As exciting as it was to meet someone who has blue blood flowing through their veins, I have to be honest in admitting that I had never heard of Prince Alexander. I didn't even know that Yugoslavia was a kingdom. Crown Prince Alexander is directly related to the British royal family and personally knows Her Majesty Queen Elizabeth II. If I were to ask you if you know who Queen Elizabeth is, most, if not all, of you would say yes. But if I followed that question asking you whether or not Queen Elizabeth knows you and who *you* are, most, if not all, of you would say no, me included. I could boast in saying that I know Prince Alexander, who personally knows the queen of England, but that statement alone would not change the true fact that the queen does not know who I am, even though I have met her godson.

Let us then apply the same principle in the realm of spiritual life. There are many people around the world who have heard of the name of Jesus Christ. Millions of those do not believe that He is the Son of God, the Savior of the world, the promised Messiah. But they know His name, nonetheless. Then there are millions who would also quickly answer yes when asked if they know Jesus Christ, believing that their answer is authentic, heartfelt, genuine, and true. But the real question needing to be asked is whether or not the Lord Jesus Christ knows them and whether He knows them personally. It is not enough to know about Her Majesty, nor it is enough to know a member of her family, for us to say that we know the queen. What is crucial is the fact of whether or not the queen knows us. There might be absolutely nothing we can do to ever meet Her Majesty; and most likely, she will never know us personally, know us by our name, or know and get to enjoy our personality traits.

Praise be to God that with Him, the King of all kings, the opposite is true. He knows us all, and all of us are welcomed to approach His presence. Yes, there is only one way to do so, by faith in the completed work of Christ, but the way and the invitation to come and enter boldly have been personalized and delivered when the arms of Christ were forced open on the cross of Calvary. If you have never met Him and do not know Him personally, today could be the day when this fact changes forever. Come to Jesus and be eternally embraced, adopted, and known by receiving the great gift of salvation as you accept the pardon He purchased on your behalf and for your benefit on the rugged cross of Golgotha.

REFERENCES

Scriptures taken from the *Holy Bible, New International Version.* Copyright © 1973, 1978, 1984 by International Bible Society. Used by permission of Zondervan Publishing House. All rights reserved.

The NIV and *New International Version* trademarks are registered in the United States Patent and Trademark Office by International Bible Society. Use of either trademark requires the permission of International Bible Society.

Jiri's Grand Jeté Photo by Tomasz Iwanski

Saldovo Divadlo Interier by saldovo-divadlo.cz

Amazon Indian Photo by NTM

Poem "Strach" (Fear) written by Eva Picková

"It Is Well With My Soul" lyrics written by Horatio Spafford

"Isn't He" lyrics written by John Wimber

Book cover designed by Anna Hays, COO; and Brent Johnson, President of Omega Group

ABOUT THE AUTHOR

Jiri Sebastian Voborsky is a Czech-born dancer. He is an honors graduate of a state ballet school and a former ballet company member of the F. X. Šalda State Theater in the Czech Republic. His performance experience also includes touring with Eternia Dance Theater in Sweden. Jiri came to the United States in 1993 at the age of eighteen. As a first soloist, Jiri danced with Ballet Magnificat, a professional Christian ballet company headquartered in Jackson, Mississippi, where he now serves as the creative director and the resident choreographer. Jiri was privileged to perform in communities across the United States as well as in cities such as Paris, London, Moscow, Berlin, Brussels, Jerusalem, Toronto, Yerevan, Singapore, Tegucigalpa, Kiev, Amsterdam, and countless others. As a choreographer, Jiri created over a dozen full-length productions that had been performed in nearly fifty nations all around the world. As a guest teacher, Jiri conducted classes for professional companies such as the State Opera Ballet in Prague, the National Ballet of Kosovo, Macedonian National Ballet in Skopje, Cape Town City Ballet in South Africa, and others. He served as an adjunct professor at the Dance Department of Belhaven University. Since April of 2000, Jiri is blessed to have been married to the love of his life, Cassandra. Together, they are proud parents of three children—Benjamin, Maya, and Solomon. Growing up under the Czechoslovak Communist regime, Jiri is grateful to his Savior and Redeemer, the Lord Jesus Christ, to have been rescued from atheism and adopted into the family of God. Jiri desires to live a life that honors and spotlights Christ in every aspect of his life.